CLIMATE CHANGE AND THE SYMBOL DEFICIT IN THE CHRISTIAN TRADITION

T&T Clark Explorations in Theology, Gender and Ecology

Series editors
Hilda Koster
Arnfríður Guðmundsdóttir

CLIMATE CHANGE AND THE SYMBOL DEFICIT IN THE CHRISTIAN TRADITION

Expanding Gendered Sources

Jan-Olav Henriksen

LONDON • NEW YORK • OXFORD • NEW DELHI • SYDNEY

T&T CLARK

Bloomsbury Publishing Plc

50 Bedford Square, London, WC1B 3DP, UK
1385 Broadway, New York, NY 10018, USA
29 Earlsfort Terrace, Dublin 2, Ireland

BLOOMSBURY, T&T CLARK and the T&T Clark logo are trademarks of
Bloomsbury Publishing Plc

First published in Great Britain 2022
Paperback edition published 2023

Copyright © Jan-Olav Henriksen, 2022

Jan-Olav Henriksen has asserted his right under the Copyright, Designs and Patents Act, 1988, to be identified as Author of this work.

Cover image: Iceberg melting in Disko Bay in Greenland © Paul Souders/Getty

All rights reserved. No part of this publication may be reproduced or transmitted in any form or by any means, electronic or mechanical, including photocopying, recording, or any information storage or retrieval system, without prior permission in writing from the publishers.

Bloomsbury Publishing Plc does not have any control over, or responsibility for, any third-party websites referred to or in this book. All internet addresses given in this book were correct at the time of going to press. The author and publisher regret any inconvenience caused if addresses have changed or sites have ceased to exist, but can accept no responsibility for any such changes.

A catalogue record for this book is available from the British Library.

Library of Congress Cataloging-in-Publication Data
Names: Henriksen, Jan-Olav, author.
Title: Climate change and the symbol deficit in the Christian tradition: expanding gendered sources / Jan-Olav Henriksen.
Description: London; New York: T&T Clark, 2022. | Series: T&T Clark explorations in theology, gender and ecology | Includes bibliographical references and index. |
Identifiers: LCCN 2021035321 (print) | LCCN 2021035322 (ebook) | ISBN 9780567704962 (hardback) | ISBN 9780567705013 (paperback) | ISBN 9780567704979 (pdf) | ISBN 9780567705006 (epub)
Subjects: LCSH: Climatic changes–Religious aspects–Christianity. | Human ecology–Religious aspects–Christianity. | Ecotheology. | Signs and symbols–Religious aspects–Christianity. | Symbolism.
Classification: LCC BT695.5 .H463 2022 (print) | LCC BT695.5 (ebook) | DDC 261.8/8–dc23
LC record available at https://lccn.loc.gov/2021035321
LC ebook record available at https://lccn.loc.gov/2021035322

ISBN: HB: 978-0-5677-0496-2
PB: 978-0-5677-0501-3
ePDF: 978-0-5677-0497-9
ePUB: 978-0-5677-0500-6

Series: T&T Clark Explorations in Theology, Gender and Ecology

Typeset by Deanta Global Publishing Services, Chennai, India

To find out more about our authors and books visit www.bloomsbury.com and sign up for our newsletters.

Is there a more sacred state than that of pregnancy? To do everything in the silent conviction that it will benefit the one who emerges within us in one way or another? ... Our only influence is indirect: blessing and protecting it.
– Friedrich Wilhelm Nietzsche (The Dawn of Day, 552)

CONTENTS

Preface — xi

Introduction
THE DEFICIT THESIS AND THE TASK IT PRESENTS — 1

Part I
CONTEXTS FOR THE SYMBOL DEFICIT

Chapter 1
FROM ACTS OF GOD TO THE ANTHROPOCENE — 11

Chapter 2
CULPRITS FOR THE PREDICAMENT — 16
    Lynn White revisited — 16
    Nature as modernity's other: Adorno and Horkheimer — 18

Chapter 3
CONSUMER IDOLATRY — 27
    System of idolatry: Abuse of God's gifts — 29
    Captured in the consumer society — 31
    Calling out heresy — 33

Chapter 4
RELIGION IN DENIAL — 38

Chapter 5
TO EMPOWER THOSE WHO SUFFER AND GIVE VOICE TO THOSE WHO LACK A VOICE — 44
    An encompassing vision — 44
    Gendered injustices — 47
    Doctrinal challenges — 49

Conclusion, Part I
LESSONS FROM THE CONTEXT — 53

Part II
CONDITIONS FOR SYMBOLIC PRACTICES

Chapter 6
SYMBOLS AS MEDIATING PRACTICE — 59
- Introduction: Symbols, practices and semiotics — 59
- Tillich on symbols — 61
- From Tillich to pragmatism: Neville — 62
- Symbols and experience — 65
- Symbolic practices are practices of orientation, transformation and engagement — 67
- Symbols mediate, constitute and engage embodied human experience — 70
- Perspectives from evolutionary theory — 71
- To live by metaphors — 73
- Formative psychological elements for symbolically mediated relationships — 78

Chapter 7
CONDITIONS FOR AGENCY: A CRITIQUE OF MODERNITY'S DETACHED SUBJECT — 83
- An expanded view of agency and freedom conditions — 83
- Overcoming anthropocentric conditions for agency: From Habermas to Vetlesen — 88
- Preliminary concluding reflections — 96

Chapter 8
SYMBOLS FOR ENHANCING MORAL MOTIVATION AND AVOIDING DEFECTION — 98
- The stick: Supernatural punishment as moral motivation? — 99
- A better way, but no carrot: On emulation of goodness — 101
- Linda Zagzebski: Goodness as admirable — 105
- On the virtue of ecological care — 109
- Virtues as relational and articulations of self-interpretation — 110
- Virtues and climate crisis: Michael Northcott — 114
- The virtue of ecological care and other virtues — 117

Chapter 9
AN INDUCTIVE, EXPERIENTIALLY ORIENTED THEOLOGY — 121
- Theology and experience — 125
- A pragmatist theology — 127

Part III
SYMBOLS FOR PRACTICES

Chapter 10
GOD AS CREATOR: A CRITICAL SYMBOL? — 133
- God of life or God of death? — 133

Creation: Interconnectedness deep down entails responsibility	138
Responsible stewardship?	142
Responsibility for more than human nature: From Levinas via Latour to Vetlesen	146

Chapter 11
FROM ANTHROPOS TO ALL OF CREATION — 151

The experiential basis for a metaphor that mediates actions	151
Hans Jonas: Responsibility for future generations	151
Hannah Arendt on natality	154
Creation's future under your heart: Elaborating the fundamental metaphor	158
Virtues of motherhood for all of creation	163
Ecological virtues in the context of exemplarist moral theory	166
A foundation in Christian narrative elements	168

Chapter 12
SYMBOLIC DEFICITS IN APOCALYPTICISM: TOWARDS A PRESENTIST ESCHATOLOGY — 171

Catherine Keller's warnings	171
Further criticism: Hermann Timm	174
Eschatology reconfigured to address the present: Hope and healing (Barbara Rossing)	175

Chapter 13
SIN — 179

Uses of sin 1: To defer and deflect political action and environmental concern	181
Uses of sin 2: An entry point for self-criticism and repentance	182
Uses of sin 3: Sinful actions in specific contexts	185
Narcissism: A metaphor for a sinful relationship between humans and nature	188
Sin as interpretative category: Summary of findings	191
Symbols for the ecological consequences of sin, and their implications for practice	192
Lost in the desert	192
Judged by our actions	193
The ecological hell: Created by humans	195

Chapter 14
CARING RELATIONSHIPS: FUNDAMENTAL MOTIFS REVISITED — 199

Introduction: That which is closest to us: The caring body	200
The born and embodied God of Cosmos: Deep incarnation	204
The world as God's body?	208
Creation as gift? On gift and responsibility	212
Nature as sacred?	219

Chapter 15
SACRIFICE, HOPE AND GRACE — 222
    The sacrifice of Jesus as informative? — 223
    Sacrifice as life-condition: Sarah Coakley — 227
    Motherhood and sacrifice — 233
    Hope and grace reconsidered — 235
    Overcoming ambiguities of orientational symbols:
        Exodus and Paradise — 243

Conclusion — 250

Bibliography — 253
Names Index — 263
Subjects Index — 265

PREFACE

Most of this book was developed and drafted during the Covid-19 crisis 2020-1. The pandemic is still present as it comes to a conclusion. For scholars like me, this has been a strange time – no conferences, no travelling, teaching digitally, no commuting. The pandemic offered more quiet time to think through things without interruption. Still, listening to those who hope that the pace will increase for the economy can pick up again so that everything can recover to 'business as usual' has made me more than worried: What does a return to business-as-usual mean? That the world will return and continue the deadly path towards more ecological destruction and an increase in carbon emissions? Or can we find a better, more sustainable path in the foreseeable future?

Furthermore, as I finished the polishing of the manuscript over Christmas 2020 before submitting it to my editors, climate change consequences came close: in another county in my diocese, 70 kilometres away from my home, heavy rain caused a landslide in which ten people lost their lives and many more their homes. Such events manifest dramatically and tragically what is usually not so apparent to us in terms of what climate change entails for many people around the globe.

During the months drafting the book, the *World Wildlife Fund* reported that since 1970 the decrease in the Earth's species is 68 per cent – more than two-thirds of all known living beings have disappeared after my birth (1961). Other reports suggest that one-fifth of the world's countries face ecological collapse in the foreseeable future – including some highly developed European countries. Hence, changes are not far from any of us, although not always visible and possible to experience directly, as the Christmas catastrophe mentioned earlier. However, if we consider all these factors, a return to business as usual appears as futile, ignorant and impossible.

This book will not change the situation, but it may provide some motivation for people who think about why things must change and change soon. This change entails more than thinking – it implies a change in everyday practices, priorities and concerns. Moreover, change over time is necessary – to stop the present ecological catastrophe (albeit unseen for most of us) means a persistent change in practices and effort for the rest of our lifetime – and for the generations to come. The Christian tradition's resources may help motivate this – for those who still identify with it or can find it meaningful as a resource for relating to the world we share.

I am indebted to many people during this book's writing, and not everyone can be named here. The number of writings in the context of ecological theology has grown immensely since I first started working on these matters in the mid-1980s. It is simply impossible to pay tribute to all that work in a volume like the present.

Hence, references to others' work cannot offer anything other than a limited perspective on all the work presently done by scholars on these matters.

I want to thank the editors of the series, Arnfridur Gudmundsdottir and Hilda P. Koster, for their encouragement and support and their willingness to include the book in the *T&T Clark Explorations in Theology, Gender and Ecology* series. Thank you also to three anonymous reviewers and to Odin Lysaker, who read a draft and offered constructive suggestions for improvement. Colleagues and friends Niels Henrik Gregersen and Arne Johan Vetlesen deserve a special thanks for discussion, input and encouragement. With them, I have had decade-long discussions about some of the topics on the following pages. Traces of their work can be detected there. Andri Snær Magnason gave permission to quote from his *Letter to the Future* at the end of the closing chapter. Whatever the reader might find missing or mistaken is my responsibility.

Ås, South of Oslo, 11 May 2021
Jan-Olav Henriksen

INTRODUCTION

THE DEFICIT THESIS AND THE TASK IT PRESENTS

- I was a boy, perhaps ten years old. I came across a magazine. On the front page, in colours, a picture of a mountain of waste, garbage. I had never seen anything like this landfill. To me, it was scary, appalling, disgusting, ugly. I still remember vividly the feeling that picture created in my gut. It was the world as I did not want it to be. The picture has been with me ever since.
- I was a student of philosophy. The topic: Karl Marx and Marxism. The lecturer presented Marx' notion of work and how the exploitation of natural resources that it necessarily leads to represented no problem to him. I asked a question about how to deal with ecological side-effects and was told Marxism saw it possible to overcome these by other types of work through which humans continue to realize themselves. I was not convinced.
- Before we entered a discussion at a TV panel, deep ecology philosopher Arne Næss remarked to me: 'I envy you believers, who can perceive the universe as something else than cold, dark, and irrelevant to us humans.' He was aware that believers had another way of experiencing the world than he had. However, in what ways it mattered for what we *do* is not clear to me.
- I was on sabbatical in Princeton, New Jersey, end of October 2012. The night of Hurricane Sandy. No human action could prevent or control her. We sat in darkness during the night, listening to something like a loud train passing through over the roof of our house. The day after, it was silence and destruction and debris everywhere. No long-term plans or initiatives to prevent such things from happening again existed. A few years later, the next American president leaves the Paris Agreement and places the United States outside the community of those who want to make a common effort to deal with the present catastrophe.

We all have stories like those above that shape our perception of the problems that presently face humanity. They represent experiences we bring with us and the context within which we interpret our faith and its resources for living. Theology at its best orients us when we experience something, and sometimes it suggests possibilities for transformation as well. Thus, it does something to us and to our experience, or, to put it otherwise, we do something with our experience when we employ theology to interpret it. Theology is not an opportunity to ignore or reject experience but a way to deal with it. This world, and what we experience in it, is the place and context where we meet the reality of God – not somewhere else.[1] This point also applies to the experiences referred to earlier.

However, how can theology help us address the profoundly complicated topic of climate change – which is, in fact, a cluster of problems? Increasing temperatures, soil degradation, deforestation, desertification, loss of species and many other problems are connected to it. The life-giving ability of our planet is at risk.[2] Can theology help at all, to orient us in this situation and to point in directions of transformation? Not without reservation.

The main thesis behind the discussions in this book is that Christian theology suffers from a symbol deficit. Although intense work is done presently to develop theological work that addresses climate change in an adequate manner and aims at overcoming some of this deficit,[3] the focus seems to be more on modes of understanding and interpretation than on *symbols that can engender consistent action for transformation over time*. It is these symbols I will focus on in this book. The tradition's symbols must be revised, adjusted, reinterpreted, specified and developed further to be relevant and applicable to the problems humanity presently faces.

Accordingly, the connection between symbols and practices shapes the concern behind this book. Practices can become symbols, or they can engender symbols. On the other hand, symbols can motivate practices. Hence, they are interdependent. To overcome the deficits in practice- and action-engendering symbols, theological work needs to rethink and reappropriate the tradition critically and develop new

---

1. Cf. Sallie McFague, *Models of God: Theology for an Ecological Nuclear Age* (London: SCM, 1987), closing.
2. Cf. Katharine Hayhoe, 'Foreword', in *Ecotheology: A Christian Conversation*, ed. Kiara A. Jorgenson and Alan G. Padgett (Grand Rapids, MI: William B. Eerdmans Publishing Company, 2020), xv. Cf. also her description of the interconnectedness of the problems, ibid., xvi:

    > Climate change is not more important than biodiversity loss, pollution, or deforestation. Rather, the reason we care about it is because it multiplies all of these other threats. From planetary boundaries that affect all living things to our entirely human challenges of poverty, hunger, disease, lack of access to basic health care and employment opportunities – climate change makes all of these worse.

3. The list is long. For documentation, see the list of literature in the comprehensive volume E. M. Conradie and Hilda P. Koster, *T&T Clark Handbook of Christian Theology and Climate Change*, T&T Clark Handbooks Series (London: T&T Clark, 2019)., and in Michael S. Northcott, *Systematic Theology and Climate Change: Ecumenical Perspectives* (London; New York: Routledge, Taylor & Francis Group, 2014). See also Cynthia D. Moe-Lobeda, *Resisting Structural Evil: Love as Ecological and Economic Vocation* (Minneapolis, MN: Fortress Press, 2013). Of special interest is also the work of Sallie McFague, whose contributions to this field would require a study of its own.

symbols of this kind that can be connected to central elements in the tradition.⁴ Because the Christian tradition has its origin in a time radically different from ours, ecologically, this deficit should not be surprising. However, the change since then calls for reconsidering its pragmatic contexts. Its contemporary relevance depends on such work.

This task calls for interdisciplinary work, which is the reason why the following pages also engage with philosophical contributions that are relevant to the topic, as well as some material from other disciplines.⁵ Theology is not an isolated discipline but needs to be informed by other disciplines, which can provide knowledge that theology needs to be guided in its interpretation and orientation of believers.⁶ Nevertheless, even when such a task is completed, the problem is not solved: climate change will be with us for the foreseeable future and increasingly impact our lives. Moreover, we should not be under the delusion that religion and theology will present the primary solution to the problem at hand – at best, it can be a small but vital part of motivating people to take action. Thus, the only thing we can hope for is that a renewed consideration of possible symbols rooted in the Christian tradition may engender an enduring commitment for change – and contribute to the obstruction of the ongoing processes of climate change.⁷

---

4. This concern is not least motivated by the recent investigations that suggest a lack of engagement for ecological concerns from a variety of Christian communities. I address this research in the following chapter.

5. As Anne Primavesi writes, 'Christianity cannot simply be dismissed as incapable of revision without losing rich resources to help us face the challenge of climate change. Instead it can and must be re-envisioned in the light of present understandings of its history and of earth's history.' Anne Primavesi, *Gaia and Climate Change: A Theology of Gift Events* (London; New York: Routledge, 2009), 12.

6. Thus, I agree with Sallie McFague, when she writes that 'as theologians, we should aim for coherence or compatibility between the scientific view and the interpretation of our basic doctrines. That is the bottom line: a theology that avoids this task and settles for an outmoded view is irresponsible and will eventually be seen as incredible'. Sallie McFague, *The Body of God: An Ecological Theology* (London: SCM, 1993), 76. A similar principle for theological work runs through the work of Wolfhart Pannenberg. See Wolfhart Pannenberg and Niels Henrik Gregersen, *The Historicity of Nature: Essays on Science and Theology* (West Conshohocken, Pennsylvania: Templeton Foundation Press, 2008), passim.

7. My formulation of this challenge also entails a warning against an approach to climate change that sees it as a mere symptom of humanity's *spiritual* predicament. As one reviewer of recent contributions notes, 'Climate change is a unique problem that upends previous visions of the theology.' Accordingly, he warns that climate change must be seen as something else than 'as a signifier for our crisis of meaning and the failures of humanity. . . . By making climate change merely an emblem for a larger concern, the distinctive features that the problem presents are masked for theological reflection, making it a stranger and an enigma to contemporary religious thought'. Forrest Clingerman, 'Theologies of the Climate', *Religious Studies Review* 42, no. 2 (2016): 76.

Religion is rooted in practices aimed at and shaping orientation, transformation and reflection.[8] All of these practices are mediated through symbols. Practices are the context in which symbols find use, and they determine their meaning.[9] We have a rich array of theological and other resources for understanding ourselves and what is happening in the world. These resources can orient us. The symbols are also at work in how we reflect and offer reasons for what we do. However, the symbol deficit claimed earlier is especially apparent when it comes to symbols that can mediate *transformative* practices and processes that represent alternatives to 'business as usual' and the continuation of all the different things humans do today that promote climate change. Hence, the task is to reason about symbols for transformation that motivate, engender and sustain the struggle against the acceleration of climate change and ecological degradation and destruction.

Symbols are important because they guide us, orient us and sometimes transform us. They impact how we orient ourselves in our environment, what we direct our attention towards and how we relate to others and transform the world in which we live. They shape cognitive and emotional responses. It is not the symbols in themselves but how we can employ them for these purposes that occupy me in this book. From a Christian point of view, the context and impact of climate change entail that we need to rethink more than the human relationship with God or God's relationship with God's creation. We need to reconsider and critically rethink the

---

8. This is, in short, my fundamental understanding of religion, and one I will not elaborate much on in the following, although it is the premise on which it is developed. For further on this theoretical backdrop, see Jan-Olav Henriksen, *Christianity as Distinct Practices: A Complicated Relationship* (London: Bloomsbury, 2019); *Religion as Orientation and Transformation: A Maximalist Theory*, Religion in Philosophy and Theology (Tübingen: Mohr Siebeck, 2017). The relevance of this approach is spelled out clearly in the following statement: '[R]eligions may be able to encourage a response to climate change via their influence on believers' or cosmologies. These narratives provide meaning and purpose, and explain the individual's and group's place in the world, thereby creating the context for ethical deliberation. Such narratives also establish what is sacred, which in turn is often set aside to be preserved, respected and protected. Considerable research shows that religions shape adherents' perceptions of and behavior toward the natural environment, so the idea that this influence extends to climate change seems plausible. . . . [R]eligions have the potential to provide connectivity (e.g., in the form of social capital) that fosters the achievement of collective goals Church affiliation is one of the most common forms of association, reaching more people in some countries (including the United States) than political affiliation or other voluntary associations.' Robin Globus Veldman, Andrew Szasz and Randolph Haluza-DeLay, 'Social Science, Religions, and Climate Change', in *How the World's Religions Are Responding to Climate Change: Social Scientific Investigations*, ed. Robin Globus Veldman, Andrew Szasz and Randolph Haluza-DeLay (London: Routledge, 2016), 5.

9. Accordingly, to see symbols as polyvalent is only possible insofar as one ignores their contexts of use. The symbols' context limits their fundamental semiotic indeterminacy.

imaginative frameworks for how humans see their role in relation to the rest of creation and *as part of it*. Nancy Pineda-Madrid states this task well when she writes, 'If the interconnectedness of all human beings and all nonhuman creatures takes center stage, then might such a focus give rise to an understanding that promotes greater ecological justice?'[10] Moreover, she argues that 'without the wider scope that this new framework conveys through its focus on creatureliness, the possibility of our knowing and loving God is lessened'.[11] Against this backdrop, the task is to produce habits of action that are informed by our best account of truth:

> The forging of a new imaginative framework is for the purpose of reorienting how we act in the world through reimagining ourselves in relation to God and the cosmos. Ideally, such thinking encourages a truer way of living in the natural world and a truer way of relating to God. These two, humans' relationship to the natural world and to God, are utterly integral to one another, thus inseparable.[12]

To critically examine and reinterpret the Christian tradition thus entails that not only written sources are relevant. So is the lived experience of faith communities.[13] Pineda-Madrid's work is one example of the theological work already done with this in mind. However, as indicated, this book aims not only to develop symbol and imaginaries but, as she also put it, to see how some of these can produce habits of action. I share this aim.

In the following parts of the book, I will in the first part analyse some of the contextual elements we need to be aware of to show that what I identify as the deficit in symbols are related to deep patterns and trajectories shaped by human agency and its conditions in culture, society and economy. The next part will provide theoretical elements that we need to consider when we look for relevant symbols that can provide informed habits for action. Then, in the third part of the book, I will discuss different candidates for the type of symbols I am looking for to show what resources are possible when we work to overcome the aforementioned symbol deficit. The selection of such symbols will nevertheless be restricted because the Christian tradition is so rich in potential symbols that it can be developed for the purpose at hand.

---

10. Nancy Pineda-Madrid, '¡Somos Criaturas De Dios! Seeing and Beholding the Garden of God', in Kim and Koster (eds), *Planetary Solidarity*, 310.

11. Ibid.

12. Ibid.

13. Cf. the following reason for addressing lived experience: 'Many inadequate interpretations of the tradition take place because lived experience – human and otherwise – sometimes has not been considered normative in the construction of theology, allowing abstract doctrinal claims to assert a logic detached from the concrete reality of actual existence.' Joyce Ann Mercer, 'Environmental Activism in the Philippines: A Practical Theological Perspective', in *Planetary Solidarity: Global Women's Voices on Christian Doctrine and Climate Justice*, ed. Grace Ji-Sun Kim and Hilda P. Koster (Minneapolis: Fortress Press, 2017), 290.

The different parts and chapters can be read separately if the reader is interested in the specific topics discussed there. However, the book's overall arguments are only accessible in detail if they are read in conjunction with each other. The first two parts present different 'building blocks' on which the third part builds. Whereas the first part identifies a selection of contextual conditions that seem important to be aware of and have in mind in the following discussion, this selection is not meant to be comprehensive or exhaustive. It nevertheless identifies elements that a theological discussion of the symbol deficit will benefit from when addressing this deficit. It is also only against the backdrop of this context that it makes sense to speak about how symbols work and how they condition moral agency – which is the task of Part II. Part III, which discusses different symbols, their deficits and potential, finds its underpinning in the previous parts.

The task ahead is not restricted to one of the theological disciplines. It entails systematic-theological work and work with some of the philosophical insights that inform and guide theological work in general. It also requires that we think about the contributions of theology within a broader scholarly and scientific context – a point that will be especially relevant when we discuss the theoretical conditions for understanding symbols that can engender agency in Part II of the book.

No book is without limitations, and this one is no exception. Firstly, I do not discuss all the symbols that could have been relevant to take up. There are symbolic elements in the tradition that I pass over without discussing, such as flood,[14] kenosis, asceticism, more extensive discussions of models of God, death and resurrection, sacraments involving nature, as well as others.[15] However, I had to balance the choice of topics with more constructive systematic proposals. Hence, the work has no intention of being exhaustive, and work remains.

Secondly, my emphasis on practice and experience invites making proposals for concrete practices or analysing concrete experiences. That is not the task in this book, and one argument for not taking it up is that practices and experiences are always rooted in contextual conditions and need to find their form and shape there. However, finding motivation for enduring practices in the Christian tradition can encourage believers to develop dynamic practices that serve the crucial aim of saving the planet from future devastation. The lack of proposals for concrete practices should not be read as a suggestion that they do not matter.

Finally, during the last decades, many have taken up the task of addressing climate change from a theological perspective. I have not been able to address all

---

14. For a creative and important interpretation of the flood in relation to contemporary (lack of) responses, see S. W. Herman, 'On Primal Fear and Confidence: Reinterpreting the Myth of the Flood as the Climate Changes', *Word & World* 29, no. 1 (2009).

15. Several of these elements are addressed in Sallie McFague, *Blessed Are the Consumers: Climate Change and the Practice of Restraint* (Minneapolis, Minnesota: Fortress Press, 2013). The following pages may provide a further theoretical framework for what she writes there about kenosis and about saints.

of these valuable contributions here. The choice of materials is based on what I found to be the most constructive contributions to the overall argument, which is accumulative and proceeds by discussing contributions and topics that I consider important if theology should have a say in how we are to understand the future of the planet and its fate.

Part I

CONTEXTS FOR THE SYMBOL DEFICIT

This part aims to identify features that constitute, contribute to and testify to the deficit of symbols that a theological response to climate change needs to have in mind. The point is not to develop a complete picture of all relevant elements but to gesture towards a selection of features that can help interpret why this deficit exists and the challenges we need to be aware of when trying to overcome it.

Firstly, it addresses the radical change of the conditions for human agency in the Anthropocene before addressing the challenge against theology from Lynn White Jr – a challenge that will provide an important backdrop for a more careful and empirically based consideration later on. As a counterexample to White, who blames (versions of) Western religion, the work of Adorno and Horkheimer seems to suggest another version of the root causes of ecological problems, situated in modernity's approach to nature, and with no reference to religion. Their contribution is significant because they also consider gendered aspects to some extent.

Moving on from genealogical approaches, a sketch of elements in Western consumerism provides an experiential backdrop that also displays the predicaments of the contemporary situation. The understanding of this context is then expanded with an analysis of an empirical contribution of religious responses to and denials of climate change. These denialists then cause us to consider more in detail the symbol deficit insofar as it represents doctrinal challenges and important lessons to consider from the point of view of context. Together, these chapters constitute a contextual horizon and contain elements to which I will point in the latter parts of the book, as well.

Chapter 1

FROM ACTS OF GOD TO THE ANTHROPOCENE

Acts of God: events in nature outside human prediction and control. The notion signalizes a division of labour or differences regarding imagined agency. Acts of God are different from and need to be assessed in another way than acts performed by humans. The acts of God suggest a hiatus between nature and history, between that which passively befalls humans and that of which humans are the cause. Hence, the very notion suggests a way of considering the world that can ease the burden of human responsibility: as long as we can speak of 'acts of God' in nature, we are not responsible. Pious as it sounds, this notion has severe consequences nevertheless, if we employ it in the present global situation:

The notion 'act of God' separates nature and history, divine and human agency, control and contingency, responsibility, and lack of culpability. Although sounding like a theological or religious term, it is used predominantly in a legal context. There, an act of God is defined as 'a natural catastrophe which no one can prevent such as an earthquake, a tidal wave, a volcanic eruption, a hurricane or a tornado. An act of God is generally considered an act attributable to nature without human interference'.[1] Such acts have legal significance because 'acts of God' provide a legal excuse for delay or failure to fulfil an obligation. But sometimes it is not clear who is responsible, or if anyone is responsible at all. In a legal context, disputes arise 'as to whether a violent storm or other disaster was an act of God (and therefore exempt from a claim) or a foreseeable natural event'.[2] Hurricanes Katrina (2005) and Sandy (2012) were examples that point to the interaction of human agency (or failure of it) and natural causes, thereby also making it less evident if these events were acts of God.[3]

The neat separations suggested by the notion of 'act of God' do not work any longer, and the notion itself appears obsolete. In light of the systemic and interrelated changes in the eco-systems that are presently most apparent in climate change, it is, to speak with Sallie McFague,

---

1. https://definitions.uslegal.com/a/act-of-god/ (accessed 28 June 2020).
2. Ibid.
3. For a study of the relevance of human agency to the consequences of Katrina, see Jeffrey Stout, *Blessed Are the Organized: Grassroots Democracy in America* (Princeton, New Jersey: Princeton University Press, 2010).

elitist and self-indulgent to dwell on natural evil as if it were, as the insurance writers put it, 'an act of God,' perpetrated by natural (or supernatural) forces outside our control, when systemic evils of massive proportions, which daily destroy huge numbers of human bodies as well as other bodies, lie within our power – the power of the privileged – to alleviate.[4]

I will return to the potential wisdom in speaking about 'acts of God' later. Prior to that, however, we need to acknowledge that the planetary situation that once made it possible to operate with the distinctions suggested earlier no longer exists. We have moved from acts of God to the Anthropocene.

The notion of *Anthropocene* is relatively new, first presented by Paul Crutzen in 2000.[5] He points to the geologic-scale changes humans have caused, such as how their activity has transformed between a third and a half of the planet's land surface. Moreover, most of the world's major rivers have been dammed or diverted, and fisheries removed more than a third of the primary production of the ocean's coastal waters. Moreover, humans use more than half of the world's readily accessible freshwater runoff.[6] Although scientists discuss the dating of this epoch, it is not controversial to assert that 'humans are not passive observers of Earth's functioning: To a large extent the future of the only place where life is known to exist is being determined by the actions of humans'.[7]

However, in their considerations on the Anthropocene, Lewis and Maslin suggest that 'the power that humans wield is unlike any other force of nature because it is reflexive and therefore can be used, withdrawn or modified'.[8] Thus, they point to the human potential to act responsibly, which is a feature that will underly most of the considerations in this book. Moreover, the far-reaching changes that human actions cause to 'the life-supporting infrastructure of Earth . . . may well have increasing philosophical, social, economic and political implications over the coming decades', they argue.[9] This comprehensive understanding of different perspectives and implications must be kept in mind as an essential backdrop for the following analyses in this book, as it entails that one cannot single out one element or factor as more significant than others. The Anthropocene is characterized by the fact that 'the human imprint on the global environment has now become so large and active that it rivals some of the great forces of Nature in its impact on the

---

4. McFague, *The Body of God: An Ecological Theology*, 178.

5. Crutzen presented the notion in a conference in Mexico in January 2000, and published further elaborations on it in Paul J. Crutzen, 'Geology of Mankind', *Nature* 415, no. 6867 (2002). See also Crutzen P. J., 'The "Anthropocene"', in *Earth System Science in the Anthropocene*, ed. Krafft T. and E. Ehlers (Berlin, Heidelberg: Springer, 2006), 1.

6. Crutzen, 'Geology of Mankind', 23.

7. S. L. Lewis and M. A. Maslin, 'Defining the Anthropocene', *Nature* 519, no. 7542 (2015): 178.

8. Ibid.

9. Ibid.

functioning of the Earth system'.[10] Hence, speaking of the Anthropocene points to human power over the fate of the planet. However, we cannot fully control or hamper the developments, control the consequences of our actions or foresee in detail all that will happen.

Accordingly, to speak of the Anthropocene as a new epoch in world history (or the history of nature) in which human activities impact all of nature is not sufficient to grasp the severity of what is at stake here: The Anthropocene is not a neutral term, as it points to the catastrophic effects and consequences that human action has on the biosphere, climate and species and to the deterioration of essential elements like water, air and soil, to name just a few. Accordingly, we should not back away from describing the present era as *catastrophic*: we are not only facing particular problems or challenges but a tremendous change in living conditions for all living beings on this planet. This change has devastating consequences both in the short term and in the long term. Philosopher Arne Johan Vetlesen does not hesitate to label this as *Catastrophism*, because this notion 'captures the first thing to say about it, never to be lost from sight. It is, fundamentally, an unprecedented geological event, one lacking not only in predecessors but in valid comparisons and analogues as well, leaving us at a loss as to where to turn for lessons about how to understand it and – somehow – cope with it'.[11] Vetlesen further points to how the Earth System that is the new object of the Anthropocene has ontological significance because nature 'as impacted and altered, as unpredictably and erratically changing owing to our practices' thereby is also 'profoundly impacting and altering us, human society, in a dialectic intertwinement of unprecedented vehemence'.[12]

Like Vetlesen, I want to point to the importance of practice for facing the situation – we cannot make it merely a matter of understanding. However, a change in understanding is also needed. However, whereas Vetlesen turns to a secular version of panpsychism, I want to investigate how there are, in fact, potential elements in the Christian tradition that can mediate action and practices that allow us to face the situation given with the Anthropocene. Of course, we cannot accomplish this unless we acknowledge that this tradition contains elements that are controversial at best and have had some devastating ecological consequences at worst.[13] Hence, a reappropriation that leads to the development of practice-mediating symbols needs careful consideration of potential symbols and

---

10. Christophe Bonneuil and Jean-Baptiste Fressoz, *The Shock of the Anthropocene: The Earth, History, and Us* (London: Verso, 2017), 4. The book documents the different aspects of the Anthropocene in more detail than what I can do here.

11. Arne Johan Vetlesen, *Cosmologies of the Anthropocene: Panpsychism, Animism, and the Limits of Posthumanism*, Morality, Society, and Culture (New York: Routledge, 2019), 6.

12. Ibid.

13. Cf. the discussion of Lynn White in the following chapter.

experiences with the environment.¹⁴ Such development needs to take into account insights and critical lessons learned about the separation of humans from nature, and the realization about how there are other agents in nature than humans, who exist in their own right and whose interests we need to acknowledge for their own sake, and not only for the sake of our own survival. The fundamental tenet here is to understand humans as part of – and therefore participating in – the web of nature – with our capacity for making history. We do not exist separate from nature, but history and nature are weaved together in the totality that theology calls creation.¹⁵

We cannot speak about creation without reference to God. However, it is not possible to think of God as an 'interventionist' – which is the image suggested when one speaks of 'acts of God' in contrast to human action. The main thing about thinking of God as a creator is not in terms of identifiable, otherwise inexplicable acts, but in terms of continually creating new chances for flourishing, love, care, compassion, interaction, relationality and diversity. Thus, God's main act is one of *gifting*. This is the only wisdom when we speak of 'acts of God' – it means that God, as the creator, provides the planet with the conditions for flourishing life in all its various forms.¹⁶

Moreover, to speak of God as creator entails speaking of interdependence between creator and creation. God is dependent on humans for the full realization of the qualities just mentioned, just as much as humans are dependent on God's continuous gifting activity as a creator when it comes to the possibility of realizing them.¹⁷ To be dependent on God as creator cannot be separated from being dependent on creation. The interrelation this dependency suggests prevents us

---

14. I remain critical of using the notion 'environment', to the extent that it can be read as something surrounding, and not part of, human life. Hence, my emphasis on interrelatedness and participation is an attempt to suggest that it should not be read in such a way. But sometimes it makes sense to use it. Whenever possible, I use the notion ecological, instead.

15. I have developed the basic elements for such an understanding and its relevance for the ecological crisis in my doctoral dissertation thirty years ago, but not with reference to the present situation of the Anthropocene. See the following for theological presuppositions, of which some will also be discussed in the following chapters: Jan-Olav Henriksen, *Mennesket Som Natur: En Systematisk-Teologisk Analyse Av Forholdet Mellom Antropologi Og Naturforståelse I Wolfhart Pannenbergs Teologi* (Oslo: Det teologiske Menighetsfakultet, 1989) and Pannenberg and Gregersen, *The Historicity of Nature: Essays on Science and Theology*.

16. I develop these strands of thought further in Part III.

17. Further on the relationship between divine and human agency, see Christoph Schwöbel, 'Divine Agency and Providence', *Modern Theology* 3, no. 3 (1987); Jan-Olav Henriksen, 'God Revealed through Human Agency – Divine Agency and Embodied Practices of Faith, Hope, and Love', *Neue Zeitschrift für systematische Theologie und Religionsphilosophie* 58, no. 4 (2016).

from thinking about God, nature and humans as separate from each other: nature and humanity co-exist as creation *within* the divine source that enables them to be and become.[18]

Thus, theological imaginaries that aim at dealing with the Anthropocene situation will need to counter the notion of separate 'acts of God' that are set apart from our responsibilities. The optic that this notion entails about the world cannot articulate the problems at hand, and it also rests on an understanding of the world which – at least in part – may be seen as reflecting the causes for the present situation. History and nature are bound together, and humans cannot suspend their responsibilities for the present situation by employing conceptual distinctions that separate realms that are connected at the deepest level: it is the evolution of nature that is the root of our capacity for agency and to pretend otherwise is not helpful.

These short lines of reflection also suggest that we cannot place any responsibility for the present situation on God, thus allowing ourselves to ignore our role in creating it. How we take care of or steward the gifts of God as listed earlier is of utmost importance. That is one of the lasting implications of the optic created by the Anthropocene. On the other hand, theology needs to insist on the fact that there is more to life and flourishing that can be determined by human agency – and this is the reason why it needs to maintain the notion that creation is the gift that is the presupposition of all value and all agency. We depend on something larger than ourselves.

* * *

In this chapter, I have developed a contrast between two different approaches to the situation in which we find ourselves. Whereas the notion of 'acts of God' suggests that there are events in nature that are outside of human control and which belong to another sphere than events impacted by human action, the notion 'Anthropocene' suggests that the former notion is obsolete and covers up the impact of human action on the current catastrophic development on the planet Earth. Both notions illustrate their power in shaping our perceptions of what is happening. But neither of them can, by themselves, generate or inspire actions or symbols that engender responding practices that constructively deal with the severity of the situation. In the following chapters, we will trace further features that mirror similar deficits, thereby substantiating the need to develop an optic rooted in symbols that can mediate adequate and informed practices.

---

18. Hence, the adequate model for understanding the relationship between humans, nature and God is *panentheism*. To exist as creation means living and being within God without being identified with God. Perhaps the best symbol for expressing this is one that will occupy us from another angle later. We exist within God as a child in the womb of her mother – intimately connected to, but still distinct from, the one on which we depend with all our capacities.

Chapter 2

CULPRITS FOR THE PREDICAMENT

Lynn White revisited

Among the many elements in historian Lynn White Jr's seminal essay on the historical roots of our ecological crisis is his pointing to how humans have ways changed their ecological context by their advances in technology, ways of habiting, growing food and so on. However, he claims that 'Our ecologic crisis is the product of an emerging, entirely novel, democratic culture', which has merged technology and science into a hitherto unforeseen unity.[1] What made his essay so influential, though, is its argument for the religious roots of the ecological crisis.

Basically, White argues that a change in religious cosmologies paved the way for a change in humans' relationship with nature: Whereas farming before the seventh century was done in a way that made it possible to support a family, developments in technology in medieval times made it possible to plow and produce far more than the family needed.

> Thus, distribution of land was based no longer on the needs of a family but, rather, on the capacity of a power machine to till the earth. Man's relation to the soil was profoundly changed. Formerly man had been part of nature; now he was the exploiter of nature. Nowhere else in the world did farmers develop any analogous agricultural implement.[2]

The change means that humans now coerce the world around them, and humans and nature become separated – with the human as master over nature.[3]

White identifies the religious backdrop to this development in Christianity's idea of time as non-repetitive and linear, and creation as gradually progressing, with humans at the top, dominating all other creation. According to White, 'God

---

1. For a discussion of White's contribution and impact, see Elspeth Whitney, 'Lynn White Jr's "The Historical Roots of Our Ecologic Crisis" after 50 Years', *History Compass* 13, no. 8 (2015); and Willis Jenkins, 'After Lynn White: Religious Ethics and Environmental Problems', *The Journal of Religious Ethics* 37, no. 2 (2009).

2. Whitney, 'Lynn White Jr's "The Historical Roots of Our Ecologic Crisis" after 50 Years', 5.

3. Ibid.

planned all of this explicitly for man's benefit and rule: no item in the physical creation had any purpose save to serve man's purposes. And, although man's body is made of clay, he is not simply part of nature: he is made in God's image.'[4] Consequently, Christianity is, according to White 'the most anthropocentric religion the world has seen'.[5]

In White's further retelling of the story, he mostly overlooks that humans in the Genesis story are made of clay and therefore part of nature. His emphasis is on a version of Western theology that underscores how humans transcend nature and that 'it is God's will that man exploits nature for his proper ends'.[6] Hence, a dualism between humans and nature is affirmed. Furthermore: 'By destroying pagan animism, Christianity made it possible to exploit nature in a mood of indifference to the feelings of natural objects'.[7]

White is well aware that Christian traditions are diverse and that the broader context shaped by Christian culture also has impacted the development he criticizes. However, his almost-idealist understanding of Christianity's impact comes clearly to the fore when he writes about how 'science and technology have grown out of Christian attitudes toward man's relation to nature which are almost universally held not only by Christians and neo-Christians but also by those who fondly regard themselves as post-Christians'.[8] His awareness of the traditions' diversity nevertheless allows him to suggest a solution: He points to Francis of Assisi and his 'belief in the virtue of humility – not merely for the individual but for man as a species'.[9] The reason for pointing to Francis as a model is that

> Francis tried to depose man from his monarchy over creation and set up a democracy of all God's creatures. With him, the ant is no longer simply a homily for the lazy, flames a sign of the thrust of the soul toward union with God; now they are Brother Ant and Sister Fire, praising the Creator in their own ways as Brother Man does in his.[10]

White's use of Francis as a model here is relevant in this context because it points forward to an element that will be developed in the next part of the book. I will argue that models for emulation are more appropriate for developing moral virtues than notions shaped by negative concepts and imaginaries. Nevertheless, we need to consider White's view of history in a critical light: When he sees religion as the ideological culprit for how our present science and technology could develop and views them as 'so tinctured with orthodox Christian arrogance toward nature that no solution for our ecologic crisis can be expected from them alone', he can conclude, famously, that 'the roots of our trouble are so largely religious, the

---

4. Ibid., 5–6.
5. Ibid., 6.
6. Ibid.
7. Ibid.
8. Ibid., 7–8.
9. Ibid., 8.
10. Ibid.

remedy must also be essentially religious, whether we call it that or not'.[11] In other words, we need to develop another type of theology that allows us to understand nature differently and as something else than a mere object of exploitation if we are to overcome the predicament of the ecological crisis.

However, White's approach calls for several comments: First of all, it seems to operate with religion as a more or less independent variable that provides the chances for adverse technological and scientific developments. He traces the problems back to religion as a single factor *explanans*. This view underplays how religion is always mediated in a cultural, social and technological context that determines what is used and not of the tradition's symbols and imaginaries. Moreover, this fact becomes visible in how White himself speaks out of an American context – and generalizes this context to a large extent (although he also points to elements in Eastern Christianity and in Francis that are different). More importantly, White's approach is unable to see theology as emerging out of (religious) practices and as the main tool for explaining or justifying these practices – and not for developing them. That theology also has been essential in critiquing certain scientific and technological practices is not within his argument's scope.[12]

White's proposal is further insufficient insofar as it only points to attitudes and different types of understanding nature and not to the symbols that mediate concrete practices. Another deficit in his suggestion for an alternative is the lack of recognition of the need for collective and critical action that expresses itself through practices that can and must be maintained collectively over time. It is not to be expected that religious traditions rooted in another world than the Anthropocene will be able to do that. Hence, although his pointing to Francis as a model ecological saint is a positive suggestion, it is far from sufficient given the present state of affairs.

Nature as modernity's other: Adorno and Horkheimer

We can contrast Lynn White Jr's 'idealist' approach by engaging another famous and critical study: Adorno and Horkheimer's *Dialectic of Enlightenment* and the surrounding writings that substantiate its central thesis. This contrast presents itself because Adorno and Horkheimer focus so extensively on the practices and the material conditions for thinking. They understand modern rationality as intimately linked to dominion over nature. Moreover, they also link the dominion

---

11. Ibid.

12. Ueli Hasler argues that theology adapts to more than it generates the development of science and technology, and that to view it as White does entails that the role of social and economic factors for the development is underrated, whereas the role of religious attitudes is overrated. See Ueli Hasler, *Beherrschte Natur: Die Anpassung Der Theologie an Die Bürgerliche Naturauffassung Im 19. Jahrhundert (Schleiermacher, Ritschl, Hermann)*, Basler Und Berner Studien Zur Historischen Und Systematischen Theologie (Bern: P. Lang, 1982).

over nature to the oppression of women and minorities, as well as to the capitalist society. In their analysis, modernity's understanding of human rationality and practical reason is not considered as the result of a specific theological or religious imaginary, but as the result of how the Enlightenment develops its understanding of rationality in a dialectic that sees nature, that is, nature in its different forms, as the *other* of reason:

> As soon as man discards his awareness that he himself is nature, all the aims for which he keeps himself alive – social progress, the intensification of all his material and spiritual powers, even consciousness itself – are nullified, and the enthronement of the means as an end, which under late capitalism is tantamount to open insanity, is already perceptible in the prehistory of subjectivity. Man's domination over himself, which grounds his selfhood, is almost always the destruction of the subject in whose service it is undertaken; for the substance which is dominated, suppressed, and dissolved by virtue of self-preservation is none other than that very life as functions of which the achievements of self-preservation find their sole definition and determination: it is, in fact, what is to be preserved.[13]

Accordingly, Adorno's and Horkheimer's work circles around modernity's fatal denial of humans as (part of) nature.[14] To what extent this is a secular corollary to the theological position that White criticizes is open for discussion. That may, in fact, be the case. However, Adorno and Horkheimer are able to 'update' the medieval conception of nature by analysing how it appears within the confinements of modern rationality. As Eric Nelson shows in his thorough analysis of their work: 'A primary thesis of Dialectic of Enlightenment is the mutuality of the human domination of nature and the domination of humans by each other.'[15] Moreover, 'enlightenment rationality undermines its own emancipatory promise in becoming increasingly complicit with domination.'[16]

Contrary to White's interpretation of religion as the cause of dominion, Adorno and Horkheimer see Enlightenment's rejection of myth as part of what constitutes dominion over nature. In this dominion, myth (and thereby implicitly religion and theology) plays the role of that *Other* from which rationality has to distance itself. However, myth nevertheless returns and plays a role in 'bureaucratic steering, instrumental calculation, and the manufactured spontaneity of consumerism and

---

13. Theodor W. Adorno and Max Horkheimer, *Dialectic of Enlightenment*, Verso Classics (London: Verso, 1997), 54f.

14. I refer to the human here as 'herself' to contrast the very male-gendered language of Horkheimer and Adorno, which I have not adjusted in the present text.

15. Eric S. Nelson, 'Revisiting the Dialectic of Environment: Nature as Ideology and Ethics in Adorno and the Frankfurt School', *Telos* 155 (2011): 110.

16. Ibid.

affected freedom of the culture industry'.[17] As Knut Wenzel has stated, the modern subject thereby establishes itself by means of *consumption*.

Consumption is the means by which one can forget one's nature and its inherent vulnerability. In a profound analysis of modernity that reflects the insights of Adorno and Horkheimer, Wenzel writes:

> The history of emancipation, inscribed in the heart of modernity, bears a traumatized memory of violence that has accumulated the complete complex of survival from the beginning of humanity. The impetus to survive already bears in its core a will to total command: total knowledge, total control, total power, total productivity, total consumption. The history of humankind's survival – which in fact is a dialectical history of loss and survival – recalls the human subject as vulnerable rather than vital. The human subject is the one that could get lost, and knows it.[18]

Wenzel roots the need for emancipation, so strongly underscored in the Enlightenment, in the human condition itself: it entails the struggle for survival and freedom. However, if unhinged, this struggle will lead to total control, productivity and consumption, thereby covering up the awareness of vulnerability, at least to the extent that it succeeds. In modernity, the impetus towards transcendence manifests itself in ever new modes of consumption. Progress becomes manifest in consumption abilities. What is valuable is that which can be subjected to transformation and change. Consumption thus is a means for manifesting transcendence as the overcoming of the present state. And freedom entails the ability not only to change according to will but to consume according to individual, self-set goals.

Nature testifies to vulnerability as long as we can approach and understand it as something other than potential for consumption. The one who is aware of the loss of species or the degradation of soil can recognize these features as a testimony to nature's vulnerable condition. However, if the focus is exclusively on consumption, it allows for ignoring one's vulnerability and overlooking the impact that patterns of production and consumption have on the environment's quality. Thus, a culture of consumption entails oblivion about our intimate dependence on nature's qualities – which are essential not only for us but also for its continued development and flourishing.

In societies where there is sufficient access to essential means for living and living well, vulnerability is easily forgotten. But this is not so in all global contexts.[19]

---

17. Ibid., with reference to Adorno, *Minima Moralia*, 140.

18. Knut Wenzel, 'The Other Language: Religion in Modernity', in *Dynamics of Difference: Christianity and Alterity: A Festschrift for Werner G. Jeanrond*, ed. James Matarazzo and Ulrich Schmiedel (London: Bloomsbury, 2015), 158. I will return to what this notion of consumption means for the ideology of the consumer society in the next section.

19. See in the following text the section on who is afflicted.

Moreover, for Adorno and Horkheimer, 'humanity's earthly dominion, or the transparency and controllability of nature for reified reason, is a defining tendency of the enlightenment from the beginning'.[20] Hence, their analysis differs from White's. For them, 'enlightenment legitimates interhuman domination because it never interrogates the human domination of nature'.[21]

The lack of critically questioning the human dominion over and relationship with nature has recently been criticized by several authors investigating the conditions for enlightenment rationality and the agency it underpins. Unlike Kant, the realization of the mutuality of natural history and human history we find in Adorno and Horkheimer entails that it is impossible to separate them. When Kant and recent communicative ethics 'uphold human dignity by questionably isolating it from animality and materiality, a number of implications follow for diagnosing and responding to the intensifying environmental crises of our time', claims Eric Nelson.[22]

Hence, Adorno and Horkheimer's analysis of the separation of humankind and nature follows a pattern distinctively different from the one suggested by Lynn White Jr. Kant's understanding of human dignity, which intended to shield humans from mere instrumental exploitation, was dependent on him separating practical from theoretical reason, that is, the ethical from the natural world. Nelson sees this as a move that 'encourages the instrumentalization of nature (i.e., the reduction of its meaning to means) and accordingly of human beings as sensuous material and as animal beings. The unity of pure and practical reason is the mastery of nature. Animals and sensuous humanity are condensed into causally calculable nature, while rational humanity is exempted from nature'.[23]

Thus, Kantian ethics, which has important and valuable elements in emphasizing universal binding norms, nevertheless fails to circumscribe the constitutive elements for a moral subject that can face the catastrophic situation resulting from nature being approached simply as a means for exploitation and consumption. Nature is defined as being in opposition to the constitutive elements of morality. Adorno writes:

> Ethical dignity in Kant is a demarcation of differences. It is directed against animals. Implicitly it excludes humans from nature, so that its humanity threatens incessantly to revert to the inhuman. It leaves no room for pity. Nothing is more abhorrent to the Kantian than a reminder of the resemblance of

---

20. Nelson, 'Revisiting the Dialectic of Environment: Nature as Ideology and Ethics in Adorno and the Frankfurt School', 111.
21. Ibid.
22. Ibid.
23. Ibid., 108. This analysis also points to the futile and problematic presuppositions behind visions about *geoengineering* in order to counter climate change. For a critical discussion of these suppositions from a theological point of view, see Forrest Clingerman, 'Geoengineering, Theology, and the Meaning of Being Human', *Zygon* 49, no. 1 (2014).

human beings to animals. This taboo is always at work when the idealist berates the materialist. Animals play for the idealist system virtually the same role as the Jews for fascism. To revile human animality – that is genuine idealism. To deny the possibility of salvation for animals absolutely and at any price is the inviolable boundary of its metaphysics.[24]

Inspired by Adorno and Horkheimer, Nelson suggests that we need to overcome the problems in Kant's conception (mirrored in the last generation of the Frankfurt school) by 'dissolving the transcendental duality between intelligible normativity and corporeality [. . .] by exploring the natural and human worlds as historically intertwined and mutually constituting'.[25] Thereby, he is consonant with the critique directed against Habermas that Vetlesen articulates when he speaks of 'the nature deficit in critical theory'.[26] The Kantian conception systematically excluded nature, animals and ecological concerns from morality's constitutive conditions.

The severe consequences of this framing of the conditions for moral agency mean that we conceive the biopolitical contradictions of present capitalist consumerist society inadequately. When what constitutes practical rationality by definition excludes nature, it means that

> the Kantian-Habermasian strategy of theoretically and practically domesticating and excluding the abject and subaltern – i.e., that which and those who cannot come to 'rational discourse' – is consequently problematic. By not recognizing the animal in the human and the ethical in the animal, so to speak, the partition of the human and the non-human devalues those forms of life that lack and/or resist this separation. In not listening and responding to animals, environments, and the materiality of the world, which correlates with not being able to address and be addressed by them, numerous human forms of life and suffering are silenced.[27]

---

24. Adorno, *History and Freedom*, trans. Rodney Livingstone (Stanford, CA: Stanford University Press, 2007), 209–10. Here after Nelson, ibid., 108.

25. Nelson, 'Revisiting the Dialectic of Environment: Nature as Ideology and Ethics in Adorno and the Frankfurt School', 112.

26. Arne Johan Vetlesen, *The Denial of Nature: Environmental Philosophy in the Era of Global Capitalism*, Ontological Explorations (London: Routledge, 2015), Chapter 2.

27. Nelson, 'Revisiting the Dialectic of Environment: Nature as Ideology and Ethics in Adorno and the Frankfurt School', 114. The exclusion of suffering from experience of nature in modernity is also addressed in an interesting analysis by Alison Stone, where she argues that Adorno's *Negative Dialectics* and *Aesthetic Theory* show how constellations and artworks generate an alternative form of re-enchantment to the one overcome by modern concepts of rationality. This re-enchantment is critical of modernity and its domination of nature and finds natural beings to be mysteriously meaningful because they embody histories of immeasurable suffering. Consequently, this experience engenders guilt and antipathy to

Adorno's and Horkheimer's analysis points to how this conception of humanity as establishing its rationality by control over nature also have consequences for human dominion over other humans, including women. This point is important not only because women are among those who are first affected by the catastrophes of climate change but also because it places women and their (embodied) experiences (as well as any other embodied experience) outside the scope of moral rationality. Thus, a vital source for moral agency is eliminated – a point that I will try to correct in Part III of this book. As Andrew Hewitt comments, 'Horkheimer and Adorno are aware of the exclusion of women as a condition of possibility of the philosophical discourse within and against which they work.'[28] Hewitt goes on, however, to argue that it is not enough 'simply to problematize this exclusion, power is about inclusion. It is necessary to ask how women are included – or rather, how are they constituted within an all-inclusive discourse'.[29] This can be read as a comment to Enlightenment's undermining of its own emancipatory power for some members of the human species and other species.

Hewitt's point is well taken – and it relates not to women only, but to all that is considered the other of disembodied rational thought. The dialectics of Enlightenment exclusion of nature from conditions of rationality thus opens up the profound problem of how it is possible to include that which is ignored, overlooked and fundamental for the continued existence of life in all its various forms on the planet. As long as the subjectivity and moral standing of that which is considered other than disembodied human rationality is denied, it will entail that dominion by means of this rationality is the only possible way to act rationally. It is not surprising that feminists have been at the forefront of contradicting this mode of thinking. They point to how rationality must include embodied knowledge and knowledge that includes concrete, embodied experience. Hence, the inclusion of men's and women's embodied experience, as well as sensual experiences of nature in its concreteness, requires a reconfiguration of how to think about substantial and inclusive conditions for moral agency.

---

human domination over nature. See Stone Alison, 'Adorno and the Disenchantment of Nature', *Philosophy & Social Criticism* 32, no. 2 (2006): especially 248–9.

28. Andrew Hewitt, 'A Feminine Dialectic of Enlightenment? Horkheimer and Adorno Revisited', *New German Critique* 56 (1992): 147.

29. Ibid. Hewitt's analysis of Adorno and Horkheimer is not uncritical, as he sees their work as one in which

> 'women are included ... – somewhat paradoxically – precisely by their exclusion. Women are instrumentalized as the representatives of the possibility of exclusion understood as an *escape* from the all-inclusive system of power. In other words, the initial – and damning – exclusion of women from the philosophical project is reworked as a potential exemption from the totality both of power as ontologized domination and of reason as a system of closure' (147).

This challenge can also be directed against the position we find in Habermas.[30] Nelson concludes his reading of Adorno and Horkheimer by pointing to how their understanding of how the domination of humans by one another and domination over nature are intimately related is not a problem that can 'be solved exclusively in its own terms, purely "humanistically" or "communicatively" by separating human beings from natural and material relations. Instead, issues of human justice and injustice cannot be removed from critical reflection on and engagement with both "external" and "internal" nature'.[31] Catherine Keller formulates this pointedly in a contribution that addresses the racial bias in climate change: 'Being human right now will mean embracing the mattering of black lives along with the living matter of our planet. A growing mass of us must be – may already be – learning to hold the intersections, the planetary connections, in consciousness, the knowing-together that fosters a broad enough coalition, and therefore a deep enough transformation.'[32]

A final comment before we conclude this section: 'Nature' is a concept that may contribute to cover up and hide what is at stake. Nature is not one object or even something we can understand adequately as objects. It is an abstract notion that covers concrete experiences of processes and relations. Nature entails interrelation and interdependence. This point is not clear in Adorno and Horkheimer's critical analysis. Hence, the concept 'nature' might contribute to the opposite of what it should, in my view: It should not make something into an object, or cover up the complex interrelations in terms of influence, sensation, mediation, process, interaction and so on:

> The multiplicity of phenomena associated with the category of the natural – or with the animal . . . – does not appear in one homogeneous and invariable manner. The natural reveals itself in myriad different and incommensurable guises, some terrifying and fateful, others liberatory and redemptive for the fragile historically and organically embodied subject joined through its biological life with the life of the world. Nature appears under the oppressive guise of fate and destiny, assigning bodies to abjection and death via physical characteristics associated with race, gender, and class. Nature can be ideologically

---

30. I treat elements in Habermas more extensively later, in the discussion of conditions for human agency. For a general introduction and overview with reference to the topic in general, see Paul Rutherford, 'The Problem of Nature in Contemporary Social Theory' (Australian National University, 2000), 35–58.

31. Nelson, 'Revisiting the Dialectic of Environment: Nature as Ideology and Ethics in Adorno and the Frankfurt School', 126. 'It is this possibility of a different relationship with nature that informs the direction of *Dialectic of Enlightenment*, since human domination draws nature into its equation via the bodily and material basis of human life.' Ibid.

32. Catherine Keller, '"I Can't Breathe": The Whole Earth Echoes the Cry for Justice', *ABC Net*, https://www.abc.net.au/religion/catherine-keller-i-cant-breathe-the-cry-for-justice/12332954.

manipulated in perpetuating injustice and inequality, it can become visible in scientific inquiry, it can function as an uncritical refuge from an alienated and artificial civilization, or it can be voiced through traces of the non-identical and redemptive. Since such traces are mediated even in their appearance of immediacy and spontaneity, they can themselves be fixated and fetishized in the betrayal of the utopian, messianic, and new in the idolatrous instant of their adulation.[33]

As the quote shows, nature as 'the other' needs to be specified. It can be the placeholder for a variety of concerns and conceptions. We could perhaps say that the theological dictum *deus semper major* has a corollary in the expression *natura semper major*, hence indicating that nature – whatever it is, no matter how it is to be understood, transcends us just as much as we are part of it. Hence, we can recognize it as the *Other that is different from but still plays an important role in our understanding of ourselves and the world.*[34]

Martin Buber talks of Nature as a Thou, an image of the Creator, thus an 'other' to us. To deal with questions of nature and world view is futile if we do not also try to get access to this experiential dimension. It is a condition for experiencing that nature has a value in itself –not only for the sake of something else, and that it thus can resemble God. Here is also a recognition of otherness – that which is not there for us, our purposes, for our sake, and which opens us up to a larger context than the one determined by our agency.

* * *

The analyses in this chapter have tried to develop how the contrast between humans and nature is closely tied to understandings and conceptions that make it hard to understand humans as part of nature and to include embodied experience and (sensual) experience of nature as morally relevant. Thus, modernity's conception of human rationality and ethics bolsters anthropocentrism. I have pointed to elements in Adorno and Horkheimer that lay bare the profound difficulties that face us when thinking about moral agency on distinctively modern terms. Apart from White's suggestion for using St Francis as a model for action, not much constructive has come out of this chapter. Instead, we have seen how profoundly

33. Nelson, 'Revisiting the Dialectic of Environment: Nature as Ideology and Ethics in Adorno and the Frankfurt School', 124–5.

34. Langdon Gilkey is among those who have pointed out that modern science contributes to this elusiveness of nature – it is becoming increasingly difficult to comprehend. 'It has seemed impossible any longer precisely to specify the nature of nature. The referents of our microcosmic theories are no longer available to us, either phenomenally or conceptually. The more we know of the fundamental structure of nature, the clearer it is that nature itself has become a mystery.' Cf. Langdon Gilkey, *Nature, Reality, and the Sacred: The Nexus of Science and Religion* (Minneapolis: Fortress Press, 1993), 163.

intricate it is to develop a positive account of nature based on the dominant positions in contemporary ethical theory. Morality itself is thus complicit in what creates the contemporary predicament: In Enlightenment rationality, the legitimate moral subject is the one that is able to repress the embodied conditions for its existence. Non-human nature and humans as embodied subjects are devoid of moral subjectivity as well as the capacity for being a moral object. The problematic consequence of this is that those who base their moral concerns on embodied conditions or experiences appear as immoral – since these conditions are defined as irrelevant or as compromising proper moral agency. Hence, the modern model for the ideal moral subject can ignore or bracket nature from consideration.

Chapter 3

CONSUMER IDOLATRY

The purpose of this chapter is twofold. Firstly, it will continue the previous chapters' aim to describe the cultural, social, political, economic and ecological conditions that make it necessary to seek new symbols and practices or reconsider and reinterpret old ones. Furthermore, similar to what we saw in the last chapter, it will point to how specific religious imagery may hinder us in seeing what is at stake in the context we find ourselves. Hence, it will analyse the theological depths inherent in Western consumer societies.[1]

Let me start by reporting two different experiences.

In 1990, I was asked by the Norwegian Lutheran bishop's conference to chair a task force on the consumer society. The work resulted in a report that got some attention – the English version was published under the title *The Consumer Society as an Ethical Challenge*.[2] However, despite the public attention the report got, it did not lead to any changes. It made me even more sceptical as to what academics can contribute to social and political change than I was beforehand. This experience is one reason why I have increasingly stressed that religion must be seen as a practice and not merely as a collection of beliefs if it is to have any significance or impact on humans' lives. At the end of writing the report, I pondered how to state what was needed, as the task force concluded that we remain captives of the consumer society. I considered writing: we must rebel against this society. However, this sounded too radical to some, and the conclusion ended on a somewhat softer note. Now it says: we need to break up from this society. Although I regret this change today and would have preferred my initial phrasing, I do not think it would have mattered. No change has occurred in the thirty years that have passed since then.

How visible this lack of change is: In the spring of 2020, during the first phase of the Covid-19 pandemic, the US government, more or less in denial about what science could tell them about the consequences of the outbreak, started sending

---

1. A far more challenging and in-depth analysis of the entanglements of, and problematic conditions for, Western consumer society that the sketch I offer here can be found in Moe-Lobeda, *Resisting Structural Evil: Love as Ecological and Economic Vocation*.

2. Jan-Olav Henriksen and Bispemøtet, *The Consumer Society as an Ethical Challenge: Report for the Norwegian Bishop's Conference 1992*, 2nd ed. (Oslo: Church of Norway Information Service, 1995).

checks with money to American citizens to speed up the economy. Consumption was considered the rescue for a crippled economy. Some even said that the sacrifice of some individuals for the sake of saving the economy was needed. Note the use of religious language here: the practice of consumption had to be saved by the sacrifice of humans. The economy thus becomes god, that is, the all-determining reality to which everyone must submit.[3] This god demands sacrifice. At the same time, due to the pandemic, reports came in on the radical drop in CO_2 emissions caused by it. However, those who got their hopes up from these reports were soon disappointed: the low patterns of emissions would have to remain for an extended period to contribute substantially to improvement. Commentators said emissions would pick up again as soon as the economy restarted after the pandemic. Hence, we continue to remain trapped in the same system, downward spiraling towards more emissions, more consumption of fossil fuels, more degradation and loss of species and more injustice – fuelled not only by oil and other non-renewable resources but also by a system for which most people see no obvious or attractive replacement.

In many places in the world today – in West, East and South – there is an ongoing process of what Davis Harvey calls 'accumulation by dispossession'.[4] This process expresses a dimension in the neoliberal economic dynamics that has a significant and devastating ecological impact. The notion 'accumulation by dispossession' refers to markets' ability to continue growing even in the absence of the reproduction of capital through privatization of assets and redistribution of its benefits from the public to private sectors. Dispossession means

> a transfer of public assets (such as natural resources, geographical spaces considered to be public or held by a benevolent state for the public use, and so on) into private ownership. It dispossesses the public of a given asset (for example, ancestral lands) and commodifies it, while also resulting in the concentration of capital in the hands of private owners.[5]

Hence, land, water, soil and plants, all are in the hands of the few.

This dispossession contradicts the fundamental understanding that God has given the natural world to all living beings to share. Instead of understanding and practices grounded in the notion of a world we share and have in common, dispossession processes promote practices that enhance privatization and the narrow-sighted ideology of consumerist ignorance. As I will demonstrate in the remaining part of this chapter, the consumer ideology and practice systematically

---

3. For a critical analysis of present-day economics and suggestions for response informed by elements in Christian theology, see Kathryn Tanner, *Christianity and the New Spirit of Capitalism* (New Haven: Yale University Press, 2019).

4. David Harvey, 'The "New" Imperialism: Accumulation by Dispossession', in *The New Imperial Challenge*, ed. Colin Leys and Leo Panitch (London: Merlin, 2004). In my description of Harvey, I follow the points developed in Mercer, 'Environmental Activism in the Philippines: A Practical Theological Perspective', 298.

5. 'Environmental Activism in the Philippines: A Practical Theological Perspective', 298.

impede perception and acknowledgement of the interrelatedness of all living beings on the planet and their mutual dependence, which also includes the absurdity in claiming that some of them 'belong' only to some groups of others. Moreover, consumerism as an ideology 'means the ability to compartmentalize and separate one's actions as they affect the self from the consequences of one's actions as they affect others, both human and nonhuman'.[6] Thus, consumerism and dispossession processes are profound adversaries of a theology that can counter climate change – and religiously speaking, they encourage what can be considered nothing less than idolatry.

System of idolatry: Abuse of God's gifts

Social scientists often see consumerism as an 'identity-forming, meaning-making activity that rivals religious practice in its importance for humans' sense of self and community'.[7] Hence, it is about more than the satisfaction of individual materialistic needs. Fredrik Portin claims that 'it entails a formative practice that shapes the individual's orientation in life and his or her fundamental outlook in life'.[8] Consequently, the 'individual's religious aspirations are formed according to his or her desire to consume'.[9]

Accordingly, the consumer society is a system of idolatry. Consider what this claim entails: it means that the very system that we live in moves us away from the true God, the one whom we should worship because this God is the God of love, care, compassion and justice. Instead, the god of the consumer society is an idol. This idol is disguised as the one who can offer us meaning, orientation, well-being and happiness. It promises to fulfil our desires. To consume is the means for obtaining the goods it promises. However, to take part in the practices of worship connected to this idol does not provide better chances for love, care and compassion but enhances and perpetuates injustice and death. It is the opposite of what should be the result of worshipping a true god.[10]

---

6. Ibid., 303.
7. Laura M. Hartman, 'Consumption', in *Routledge Handbook of Religion and Ecology*, ed. Willis Jenkins, Mary Evelyn Tucker and John Grim (London: Routledge, 2017), 316. Here quoted from Fredrik Portin, 'Consumerism as a Moral Attitude: Defining Consumerism through the Works of Pope Francis, Cornel West, and William T. Cavanaugh', *Studia theologica* 74, no. 1 (2020): 5.
8. 'Consumerism as a Moral Attitude: Defining Consumerism through the Works of Pope Francis, Cornel West, and William T. Cavanaugh', 5.
9. Ibid.
10. The reference to death here is not rhetorical: the evening before this section was drafted it was reported that 120 persons were killed in a landslide caused by heavy rain in Myanmar. They were working in the jade mines. The rain was the effect of climate change,

Although the concept 'idolatry' is theological, pointing towards false gods, its use is not related exclusively to a theological context. To describe the consumer society as a manifestation of idolatry can point to experiential features in all humans' conditions – and not only to religious ones. In his explanation of the first article of faith, Martin Luther writes about what a god is – from what I would call a pragmatic, experiential point of view:

> What is to have a god? What is God? Answer: A god is that to which we look for all good and in which we find refuge in every time of need. To have a god is nothing else than to trust and believe him with our whole heart. As I have often said, the trust and faith of the heart alone make both God and an idol. If your faith and trust are right, then your God is the true God. On the other hand, if your trust is false and wrong, then you have not the true God. For these two belong together, faith and God. That to which your heart clings and entrusts itself is, I say, really your God.[11]

From this quote, it becomes evident that how a human being orients herself in the world by means of the trust inherent in faith is the decisive element in defining her god. It points to that in which one trusts as that which makes a difference in a person's life. Only in this way can belief in God make a difference: by guiding and orienting one's trust. Thus, to speak about God is to speak about the instance from which one governs one's own life. Hence, it all hangs on believing in a true God, that is, a God who deserves to be called God and who *can* be God.[12]

The consumer society is not such a god. It offers false security, as it covers up the consequences related to its own foundation: the experience of happiness that the consumer gets from being able to purchase his or her goods covers up the expenses that others have to pay. These expenses are never present on display, in promotion or advertising. The sense of security that the power of consumption buys, the feeling of power and entitlement, are built on the insecurity and exploitation of those who work in the clothing factories, the mines, the gas stations and the farms in two-third of the world's countries. The consumer society that creates a feeling of safety and security is nevertheless the most imminent and present danger to the future life for many species on this planet – including humans. It is an idol that demands sacrifice by many and in many forms.

The consumer society is based on the unjust use of God's gifts to all of humanity. These gifts for all are exchanged to possession for the privileged few. We receive these gifts in common from God to be shared by all, and a true gift might disrupt

---

and the deceased's presence in the mines was caused by the demand for gems in affluent societies.

11. M. Luther, *Large Catechism*, I, 1.

12. I have developed these points further in Jan-Olav Henriksen, 'God in Martin Luther' (Oxford University Press, 2016). I return to a more extensive discussion of Luther's text in Chapter 10.

and challenge the consumer economy by presenting something unconditional, surprising and undeserved. To pretend that the fundamental gifts from God are deserved entails that we compromise their gift character, and it bolsters the feeling of entitlement and privilege – with the exclusion of others as a consequence.

There is a possible reference in this last point back to what we developed in the section about nature in Adorno and Horkheimer's *Dialectic of Enlightenment*. That we cannot integrate the gifts of God under our control is an important insight when it comes to the conditions for human agency and its limitations. There are elements and relationships in the world that must be received and appreciated as a gift instead of being categorized as a commodity for control and exploitation. Receiving with a grateful attitude excludes a sense of entitlement, and it means that one can consider other receivers than oneself for these gifts and ask: How is this gift best received and put to use to be a source of goodness for all involved?

Moreover, from a theological point of view, consumer idolatry bases human security on what the human herself can establish as merit: I live here because I deserve it, because I am entitled to it or because my efforts have made it possible. Thus, the world I live in is a world that fits and serves *me* well. Thus, we face here a modern, Western version of self-righteousness, in which human effort and privilege sustain the worship of the society in which one can maintain this self-delusion. This idol is the diametral opposite to the only God who deserves to be God, that is, the one who is trustworthy as being able to provide a safe and reliable basis for human life in community; *the gifting God*.

Captured in the consumer society

I live in one of the most affluent societies in the world. It is one of the safest countries on the planet. Taxation is high in Norway, but it is worth it: we have qualities that people living in other countries envy: good and inexpensive healthcare, a good educational system with free access to universities and social security that safeguards people affected by unemployment or illness. But the main concern in the annual negotiations on wages is focused on an increase in consumption power, even though most, but not all, have more than they need, and the population's life quality is not likely to increase in ways that are correlated with the increase in wages.

Although it may sound attractive, the level of consumption in Norway – and in the West in general – cannot continue in the way it does. The affluent lifestyle in Norway is based on the production of fossil fuels. In Western countries in general, the consumption levels and the concomitant carbon emissions are, together with China's and India's, the primary source for global warming. To imagine that the rest of the world should be developing a similar level of affluence is both ignorant and impossible: it would mean an ecological disaster of unforeseen proportions. Thus, the injustice is not only in terms of equal power of consumption of access to goods. It expresses itself in how it is impossible, from a systematic point of view, to imagine that we in the West should or would be willing to give up the securities of our lifestyle. On the other hand, we cannot allow or encourage others to develop to a similar level of consumption as we have.

To get across the message that the affluence in the West relies on a fundament of injustice is not easy. It is never easy for people to give up the privileges that they have once obtained. Nevertheless, my country's social safety is built on elements of injustice and production with negative ecological impact. The injustice is hidden from the sight of most of us: we do not see those who will never become able to live as we do. They are the invisible victims of our lifestyle, those who must sacrifice their workforce and their commodities for us to be able to maintain our way of living. They must buy our oil – which we prefer to sell at the highest price possible to secure our future. It does not seem likely for us to move away from an oil-based economy as long as we have no alternative: We remain captured as long as we want to maintain the qualities of our society.

Although the Christian tradition contains criticism against wealth and greed, not much of it is present in the contemporary consumer society. One observer, Gary Gardner, writes under the heading *silence about false gods*: 'It is difficult to find religious initiatives that promote simpler living or that help congregants challenge the consumerist orientation of most modern economies. (Indeed, an extreme counterexample, the "gospel of prosperity," encourages Christians to see great wealth and consumption as signs of God's favor.) Simplicity and anti-consumerism are largely limited to teachings that get little sustained attention.'[13] Gardner follows up these reflections with some apt comments about the risk of not being silent about worshipping the false gods of consumerism: it may be perceived as bringing politics into religion – as we will see in the next chapter is the tacit case in some of the Evangelical responses to climate change. To counter a culture of consumption that is, for example, associated with the freedom inherent in 'the American way of life' could alienate some believers. However, it would also suggest that the priorities of believers have to be other than those set by the increased ability for consumption: Gardner argues that 'one of the greatest modern threats to religions and to spiritual health [is] the insidious message that the purpose of human life is to consume, and that consumption is the path to happiness. Tackling these heresies could nudge many faiths back to their spiritual and scriptural roots – their true source of power and legitimacy – and arguably could attract more followers over the long run.'[14]

However, to develop a culture and a society different from that of a consumer society will entail that one can perceive the world from another perspective: it is about developing as self-in-relation-to-others who live under other conditions and are less able to consume, or who suffer from the injustices that the consumer society and its priorities mean for herself and her society. This self is the neighbour who makes me responsible by her very presence. Consequently, the first thing we

---

13. Gary Gardner, 'Engaging Religions to Shape Worldviews', in *State of the World 2010* (Island Press, 2010), 26.

14. Ibid., 26–7.

need to do is acknowledge that she exists and that she suffers. Consumer society aims at hiding suffering. It does not recognize or depict the vulnerabilities of the human condition. It enhances our desire for that which others possess (mimetic desire) and thrives on our addiction to consumption. It can only be replaced if we develop societies where people relinquish their attachment to finite things as if they were infinite.[15]

Calling out heresy

As will be apparent throughout this book, I am concerned with religious symbols insofar as they have consequences for practices that are related to climate change. Some of these symbols are parts of doctrinal clusters. These clusters contribute to shaping doctrines that, in turn, legitimize practices of religious communities. I would argue that it makes sense to address doctrines as heretical if they lead to ecological devastation, global warming and the concomitant decreased chances for a flourishing planet. If we assess them from the point of view of their consequences, religious doctrines are not mere manifestations of different points of view but linked to and may support practices that lead to life or death. Hence, to call out heresies is not a thing of the past but is something we still need to do for the sake of future generations.

In this section, I will discuss such heresy briefly to make this point and illustrate its importance. The doctrine in question is at the centre of the so-called prosperity gospel. This 'gospel' claims that Christians will receive a particular blessing when they join the Christian community, and this blessing is not merely spiritual. It also entails an increase in wealth – which is why it has been given this name. Material wealth is seen as a gift from God and a sign of God's care and blessing. Part of the message is that God wants believers to enjoy material wealth.

If it were a phenomenon at the margins, not much reason would exist for addressing it. However, this doctrine is increasingly more widespread, especially in poorer parts of the world. It finds fertile soil in the contexts of big cities with an increase in destitute populations and people searching for belonging, identity and community in a new context far away from their rural origin. The churches built on this gospel also offer chances for social mobility.[16]

---

15. Cf. Jay B. McDaniel, 'The Passion of Christ: Grace Both Red and Green', in *Cross Examinations: Readings on the Meaning of the Cross*, ed. Marit Trelstad (Minneapolis, MN: Fortress Press, 2006), 204.

16. For an analysis of prosperity gospel as a global social phenomenon, see Sven Thore Kloster et al., *Global Kristendom: En Samtidshistorie* (Oslo: Universitetsforl., 2018), 35–8, 270–4; K. Attanasi and A. Yong, *Pentecostalism and Prosperity: The Socio-Economics of the Global Charismatic Movement*, 1st ed. (New York: Palgrave Macmillan, 2012). For a theological critique that focuses primarily on this gospels American proponent, and which identifies main features that may apply to other contexts as well, see Peter Mundey, 'The

It has been argued that this gospel 'constructs a vision of happy living that blends well with our consumerist self-indulgent culture and offers a narrative of hope grounded in the discourses of religious and bourgeois American middle-class sensibilities'.[17] Health and wealth are the main signs of one's faithfulness. The more faithful one is, the larger is the consumption capacity. The faithful are also encouraged to 'demonstrate their high levels of faith through extravagant spending on luxury cars, clothes, and private planes'.[18] Consumption and religion thus become linked together, because 'ever-increasing discretionary consumption is essential to fulfilling God's vision for one's life'.[19] Hence, consumer culture becomes the unquestioned plausibility structure within which faith can play itself out as validated. 'Denying oneself consumer luxuries is thus tantamount to denying God's blessings and rejecting the abundant life Jesus came to earth to give Christians.'[20]

In this religious context, mimetic desire also seems to play a role similar to the one we find in consumer culture in general. Believers should appear blessed and prosperous because they can create envy among other persons, who would then want to share similar blessings.[21] 'Enjoying the luxuries of consumerism is a way of showing off God's power to provide abundantly.'[22]

Admittedly, there are versions of the prosperity gospel that do not promote unfettered consumerism. These suggest that believers should share their God-given blessings, 'that God blesses them with their needs, not necessarily their wants, and that God's blessings are often immaterial in nature'.[23] However, in the end, giving is simply a practice one should engage in to receive more, and 'those who faithfully obey God's command to tithe will be richly rewarded, receiving back more money than they gave in the first place, which will ultimately increase, not decrease, their purchasing power'.[24]

From the above, admittedly short analysis, it becomes clear that this is an individualist approach to Christianity. It focuses on the individual's life and practices that identify consumerism as a prominent sign of blessing. Hence, it substitutes material qualities over more personal ones. Moreover, it is a gospel in which the existing limits to the use of natural resources are absent.

Prosperity Gospel and the Spirit of Consumerism According to Joel Osteen', *PNEUMA* 39, no. 3 (2017). In the following, I draw on Mundey's work, without going into the details of his analysis.

17. Lee and Sinitiere, here quoted from Mundey, 'The Prosperity Gospel and the Spirit of Consumerism According to Joel Osteen', 320, note 5.
18. Ibid., 321.
19. Ibid.
20. Ibid., 326.
21. Ibid. The point about mimetic desire is mine.
22. Ibid., 330.
23. Cf. Ibid., 321–2.
24. Ibid., 334.

If your private jet is a sign of God's blessing, it means that God blesses your contributions to global warming. If you are given the opportunity to consume, you may well do it at the expense of those who have less than you, those who are underpaid so you can live comfortably. In this gospel, the future means less than the fulfilment of your wishes in the present. Furthermore, in the future perspective, the other, who is less wealthy than you are, is outside of the picture of what matters. He or she does not represent an important point of orientation for your life.

The Christian Gospel is based on God's will for the future and the community, not for fulfilling the individual's desires in the present. It is a gospel that entails hope for the other and her flourishing and engenders practices of care and commitment, even when it means letting go of personal wealth, or restraint in consumption. During the ages, restraint in consumption and relative poverty has been among the practices that Christian groups have been engaged in to benefit those less fortunate than themselves. These are practices that fall totally outside the prosperity gospel's scope, not only because they are other-oriented but because they do not see material wealth as a sign of God's blessings.

In short, I argue that the prosperity gospel is false and only serves to bolster a consumerist culture that leads to death for the planet. It ignores those who suffer, it has nothing to say about its implications for global warming and the decrease in species, and its future and long-term perspectives seem absent. It turns God into an idol that encourages consumption and the believer into an obedient slave of capitalist consumer culture, with no resources for asking critical questions.

There is no lack of Christian responses to the moral failures of consumerism. Some of these responses can contribute further to the analysis of the heresy I discuss here. In an analysis of some of these responses, Fredrik Portin[25] argues for a definition of consumerism that understands it as a fundamental attitude towards the good. Accordingly, 'Consumerism is a moral attitude that trivializes the good and enables indifference towards suffering. Furthermore [. . .] I would argue that consumerism is the result of the prioritization of personal preference, and is a moral attitude that affects every person across the economic, social, political, and cultural spectrum.'[26]

Portin bases his definition on the analysis of Pope Francis in *Laudato Sí*, according to whom 'Western societies encourage individuals to think and behave as if they have the sovereign right to control their own destinies and pursue their own desires. Thus, anything that does not conform to the individual's personal preferences is relativized'.[27] He continues with a quote that suggests the close

---

25. For the following, see Portin, 'Consumerism as a Moral Attitude: Defining Consumerism through the Works of Pope Francis, Cornel West, and William T. Cavanaugh'.
26. Ibid., 18.
27. Ibid., 7.

connection between social injustice and the suffering of the poor, on the one hand, and ecological destruction, on the other hand:

> '[We] have to realize that a true ecological approach always becomes a social approach; it must integrate questions of justice in debates on the environment, so as to hear both the cry of the earth and the cry of the poor'. He [Francis] stresses that it is primarily the poor who are forced to suffer because of climate change (and other natural disasters) in the form of drought, extreme weather conditions, floods, pollution of drinking water, and so forth. However, even though the poor are the ones that are the most affected by climate change, the attempts to minimize its consequences have rarely benefitted them: 'Frequently, we find beautiful and carefully manicured green spaces in so-called "safer" areas of cities, but not in the more hidden areas where the disposable of society live'. The height of contempt for the poor, according to Francis, is when the well-to-do argue that the poor are the problem in dealing with climate change – when they, for example, argue that the most significant challenge for mitigating climate change is uncontrolled population growth.[28]

If we apply Francis's perspective here, as referred by Portin, to the heresy of the prosperity gospel, it becomes evident that consumerism presupposes more than the desire to consume – sometimes with religious legitimation. It represents an attitude that trivializes suffering. When Francis argues that consumerism is a form of moral deficiency, it entails that unhinged consumption cannot continue if it entails the suffering of the world or the poor. However, the consumerist culture of comfort promotes a lack of sensitivity to the cries of other people and even leads to 'the globalization of indifference', Portin writes, referring to the Pope.[29]

Furthermore, the prosperity gospel restricts the venues where people can learn to embrace nonmarket virtues that enable resistance to suffering and provide strength for their struggle for justice. Portin argues, with reference to Cornel West, that consumerism thereby becomes a fundamental expression of the lack of commitment to a new vision of a just society. Consumption culture contributes to the eclipse of utopian energies in the West and the conditions for the possibility of prophetic vision and progressive practice. It manifests moral bankruptcy: 'This disgraceful numbing of the senses, dulling of the mind, and confining of life to an

---

28. Ibid., 7–8. The quotes in the quote are from Pope Francis, *Laudato Si': On Care for Our Common Home* (Frederick, Maryland: The Word Among Us Press, 2015).

29. Portin, 'Consumerism as a Moral Attitude: Defining Consumerism through the Works of Pope Francis, Cornel West, and William T. Cavanaugh', 9.

eternal present – with a lack of connection to the past and no vision for a different future – is an insidious form of soul murder.'[30]

Hence, it is crucial to confront the heresy of the prosperity gospel's and its promotion of consumerism because it is not only about life and death, and the death of the moral soul of Westerners, but also about the suffering and death of those who live on the underside of the consumer society.[31]

---

30. Ibid., 13. The quote is from Cornel West, *Democracy Matters: Winning the Fight against Imperialism* (New York: The Penguin Press, 2004), 176.

31. Given the critique I have offered here, it is worth noting that observers do not see much of effects of theological warnings like these, and hence, they need to be vocalized more consistently and thoroughly in preaching and teaching:

> Despite the logic for engagement, religious intervention on this issue is sporadic and rhetorical rather than sustained and programmatic. It is difficult to find religious initiatives that promote simpler living or that help congregants challenge the consumerist orientation of most modern economies. (Indeed, an extreme counterexample, the 'gospel of prosperity,' encourages Christians to see great wealth and consumption as signs of God's favor.) Simplicity and anti-consumerism are largely limited to teachings that get little sustained attention, such as Pope Benedict's July 2009 encyclical, *Charity in Truth*, a strong statement on the inequities engendered by capitalism and the harm inflicted on both people and the planet. Or simplicity is practiced by those who have taken religious vows, whose commitment to this lifestyle – while often respected by other people – is rarely put forth as a model for followers.

Gary Gardner, 'Engaging Religions to Shape Worldviews', in *2010 State of the World: Transforming Cultures: From Consumerism to Sustainability*, ed. Erik Assadourian, Linda Starke, and Lisa Mastny (New York; London: W. W. Norton & Company, 2010), 26.

Chapter 4

RELIGION IN DENIAL

Religions are not independent variables. Their symbolic resources are appropriated and utilized in different contexts, and these contexts contribute to the actual performances of religious traditions. If the symbolic resources are utilized within a context with a restricted vision for other concerns than the immediate, it will impact how religious believers address climate change. Heather Eaton provides a succinct comment on the nation-centric or short-sighted approach to climate change. The following can stand as a critical comment to the analysis in this chapter:

> The denial of climate change science, the protectionist stances, the economic fears, and the ongoing gridlock around responses are directly related to the social and economic organization of nation states. Climate change action requires, at least, a functioning image of a global human community. Some resist this image because it can erase differences among, as well as the structured inequities within and between cultures. Moreover [. . .], it is evident that ecological planetary systems do not dovetail, in any manner, with political configurations. To see the planet as a composite of nation states, or as a global human community, impedes an ecological planetary awareness. Thus, responding to climate change is forcing new political alignments and new ecological perceptions of planetary realities.[1]

The planetary awareness Eaton writes about here, which requires a radical change in perception of what is necessary to counter climate change, is missing among those who either are climate change deniers or have a limited perception of what is needed. Instead of further developing this point on a theoretical level, this chapter will analyse how religious imagery that impedes change is employed in actual life. Robin G. Veldman's empirical study of evangelical Christians and their opposition

---

1. Heather Eaton, 'An Earth-Centric Theological Framing for Planetary Solidarity', in *Planetary Solidarity: Global Women's Voices on Christian Doctrine and Climate Justice*, ed. Grace Ji-Sun Kim and Hilda P. Koster (Minneapolis: Fortress, 2017), 21.

to climate change will serve as the primary source for the points I will develop in this chapter.²

Polls show that white evangelical Christians are the most sceptical religious group in the United States concerning climate change.³ This fact immediately presents us with the question if there is something in the practices and imaginaries of this group that can help us understand why it is so. An answer to this question may, in turn, help us understand something about how religious symbols play a role in addressing climate change – or not.

One of the advantages of Veldman's empirical study is her focus on evangelicals as a group different from the US group designated as the 'religious right'. Evangelicals are 'Protestants who affirm a belief that lives need to be transformed through a "born-again" experience and a life-long process of following Jesus' and who believe they are called to demonstrate the gospel in missionary action and social reform actions. They see the Bible as the ultimate authority and Jesus's death on the cross as making humanity's redemption possible.⁴ Veldman looks into the laity as well as some of the leaders of this group, which comprises republicans, democrats and independents. Hence, from a political point of view, Evangelicals are not a monolithic group. The group has also shaped the *Evangelical Environment Network* that aims at addressing climate change. Hence, the object of her study makes a good case for looking into the extent to which the greening of evangelicalism is actually taking place and under what conditions.⁵

Among the imaginaries that Veldman investigates is the often-reported notion by environmentalists that evangelicals do not care about ecological destruction because they believe we live at the end of times and Jesus will return soon. As a consequence, critics portray evangelical Christians as not caring about the environment. This assumption had not been empirically investigated until

---

2. Robin Globus Veldman, *The Gospel of Climate Skepticism: Why Evangelical Christians Oppose Action on Climate Change* (Oakland, California: University of California Press, 2019).

3. Ibid., 2. For an interesting analysis of how issues related to ecological concerns are high on the agenda of neither evangelicals nor progressive Christians in the United States, see Daniel Bernard Zaleha, *A Tale of Two Christianities: The Religiopolitical Clash over Climate Change within America's Dominant Religion* (2018). Similar conclusions are supported by David M. Konisky, 'The Greening of Christianity? A Study of Environmental Attitudes over Time', *Environmental Politics* 27, no. 2 (2018).

4. Veldman, *The Gospel of Climate Skepticism: Why Evangelical Christians Oppose Action on Climate Change*, 3.

5. For more statistics and nuances with regard to Evangelicals in relation to other religious groups in the United States, see Mark Chaves, *American Religion: Contemporary Trends*, 2nd edition (Princeton, NJ: Princeton University Press, 2017).

Veldman did her study, and she names it *the end-time apathy hypothesis*.⁶ It is notable that she finds limited warrants for this hypothesis.⁷

Veldman's investigation is significant because it engages the flip side of my concern in this book: examining the empirical basis for religious imagery's effects may tell us to what extent it serves to impede or hamper engagement for the environment, or shape such engagement in ways that are inadequate or misconceived. She finds a correlation between religious views and climate scepticism, but it does not seem to be linked exclusively to specific ideas about eschatology.⁸

The result of Veldman's negative findings with regard to the end-time apathy hypothesis led her to another imaginary, as she found other results more illuminating: Responses to talk about climate change were mostly framed within a context that juxtaposed faith and secular society – in which the latter included elements from science:

> The end-time apathy hypothesis was not the best way of conceptualizing the relationship between my informants' faith and their environmental attitudes. A small number of the evangelicals I met were so convinced the end is near that they cared little about environmental decline, viewing it as one of many indicators that history was drawing to a close. But a larger, more politically engaged contingent was convinced that the climate was not changing at all – or, if it was changing, that humans were not the cause and/or that the changes would not be catastrophic. For these individuals, climate change was not evidence that the end times were beginning, but instead a hoax – a competing eschatology

---

6. Veldman, *The Gospel of Climate Skepticism: Why Evangelical Christians Oppose Action on Climate Change*, 7. Veldman refers to a version of this hypothesis (although formulated as a claim more than as a conjecture) on p. 27, from environmentalist Roderick Nash: 'Christians expected that the earth would not be around for long. A vengeful God would destroy it, and all unredeemed nature, with floods or drought or fire. Obviously this eschatology was a poor basis from which to argue for environmental ethics in any guise. Why take care of what you expected to be obliterated.' Although I share with Nash the conviction that symbols and narratives are important, it is hard to avoid seeing his picture here as somewhat home-made and sweeping. Which Christians are he talking about, and in what context? Discussions about religion and environmentalism is not well served by such context-less claims. Moreover, the construction here seems to ignore substantial claims to the opposite in the biblical narrative – God's promise to Noah after the flood is an apparent example. Moreover, it is interesting that Nash is not alone among the not-so-religious in promoting anecdotal ideas about such religious imaginaries as the origin of climate scepticism, cf. Ibid., 39f.

7. Ibid., 26ff. Among the important contribution of her work is how Veldman is able to trace the origin of this idea more to environmentalists than to actual believers.

8. Cf. ibid., 42f. See the following text for further details.

concocted by secularists who sought to scare people into turning to government instead of God.⁹

We can draw several implications from this analysis that are important for the present project. First of all, it means that climate change is actually neglected or seen as unimportant by the evangelicals Veldman studied, despite the concerns expressed in the organization referred to earlier. Moreover, this neglect or rejection is not due to merely religious imaginaries about something not present in experience. It builds on and reinforces actual experiences of how actual life as a believer can be in a society that one experiences as secular and in which religion is in decline. The 'embattled' mentality that Veldman identifies reinforces the experience of a divided world where those who care about climate change and ecology stand opposite those who believe in God. Climate scepticism seems to be built into a much larger framework that has to do with politics, 'social conservativism, attitudes toward collective action, community norms and media consumption habits.'¹⁰ This division is also mirrored in how the church is depicted as existing in a sphere distinct from the larger society.¹¹

Against this backdrop, other, religious and imaginaries also come into play. The idea that humans can change Earth's climate was rejected by many of Veldman's informants, who referred to the notion of an omnipotent God 'in control'.¹² Any idea about climate change would challenge this notion.

In addition to investigating lay Evangelicals, Veldman also looks into the Christian Right and its communication outlets. Leaders in the Christian Right has been urging people to dismiss climate change through the evangelical mass media. Religious imaginaries and not arguments based on scientific knowledge were used to dismiss climate change and promote climate scepticism.¹³ However, Veldman is careful in pointing out that traditionalist evangelicals are climate sceptics not only for, or even primarily due to, religious reasons. She argues that the leaders in the Christian Right who promoted climate scepticism did two things:

> First, they supported and amplified the efforts of secular climate change sceptics, ensuring that their message reached evangelical audiences. Second, many of their communications explicitly framed climate change as a religious issue, and in so doing helped transform climate skepticism and denial from a political opinion into an aspect of evangelical identity. This transformation had

---

9. Ibid., 8. Cf. ibid., 101, on climate change as a competing eschatology.
10. Ibid., 8–9.
11. Ibid., 89. The embattled mentality is also, according to Veldman, what frames scepticism about evolution. 'It was the embattled mentality, not distrust of science, that was the common thread connecting opposition to evolution with opposition to global warming.' Ibid., 109.
12. Cf. ibid., 97f.
13. Ibid., 11.

serious repercussions. Most critically, the mocking, disdainful, and suspicious tone that leaders and pundits in the Christian Right adopted when speaking about climate change sent a clear signal to evangelical audiences not only that skepticism was the more reasonable position, but more subtly that it was the more socially acceptable position. The result was that anyone considering expressing a different opinion knew that they risked being challenged or viewed with suspicion themselves. When climate advocates became enemies and climate advocacy became suspect, the greening of evangelicalism, which had been a growing chorus, fell to a whisper.[14]

Hence, it is possible to read Veldman's analysis as a story about how climate skepticism was employed within a religious-political framework aimed at overcoming the evangelicals' sense of marginalization in American culture. To confront those advocating action against climate change became part of Evangelical identity. Leaders and pundits in the Christian Right cultivated a particular vision of evangelical identity as normative and convinced evangelical audiences during the 2000s that certain environmental attitudes that included skepticism were the natural expression of this identity.[15]

Veldman historicizes climate skepticism with religious backing by placing it in a specific context. She illustrates how religious imaginaries and conceptions are variables that work within a larger framework of cultural and political conditions. Thus, she, as well, moves beyond the Lynn White thesis:

> Against the tendency to view Christians' environmental attitudes as the product of ahistorical religious doctrines, I underline that it was not inevitable that so many evangelicals would come to regard climate skepticism as a matter of faith. This view was cultivated by specific individuals operating in unique historical and political circumstances in order to achieve specific ends. I hasten to add that this is not merely a cynical view of religion and religious actors, but one that invites a dynamic conception of how religions are related to environmental attitudes and behavior. Not by nature, but by convention. And what is conventional can be changed.[16]

Context matters: not images, symbols or texts as such, but practices informed by and expressing them are of importance for shaping and directing people's attitudes and concerns. Veldman's work suggests that

> it is not that certain scriptural passages have a universal effect, but that evangelicals' experience in American culture has encouraged particular practices of scriptural interpretation. In the case of climate change, skepticism was not simply what happened when evangelicals considered the issue in light of

---

14. Ibid., 11–12.
15. Cf. ibid., 13
16. Veldman, *The Gospel of Climate Skepticism: Why Evangelical Christians Oppose Action on Climate Change*, 13.

scripture, but in part the result of certain evangelical leaders and pundits having an interest in portraying skepticism as the scriptural view.[17]

In terms of practical action, Veldman's study identifies the absence of interest and absence of concern regarding climate issues among the people she studies.[18] Other things matter more. Like many other Americans, the evangelicals lack the environmental skills or literacy that allow them to perceive the biosphere and the magnitude of changes there.[19] To the extent that they practice anything that comes close to caring about climate and ecology, it is within a framework where other things matter more and where science and politics are excluded from attention. She calls this 'practical environmentalism', which is mostly concerned with the local and immediate situation. It is based on the idea 'that human treatment of the natural world should be governed by common sense, in keeping with local mores, apolitical, enacted at the individual level, locally scaled, and proudly anthropocentric'.[20] This attitude entails seeing certain practices as wrong, but it is not based on any anxiousness or urgency about ecological issues.

In sum, other things matter more. The practical environmentalism Veldman identifies does not preclude her informants for holding other topics as a top priority:

> Worrying about the environment or focusing on environmental problems as problems in and of themselves would indicate a lack of faith in God, and a subversion of the true purpose of life on earth: to seek redemption from sin and thereby attain salvation. In this context, 'doing what you can do' – not being wasteful or purposefully harming the environment – was their ideal.[21]

From this analysis, we can infer that the problem is not only the employment of religious concerns as the main priority but also the individualism and spiritualization that it entails. When religious concerns are individualized, it precludes what is necessary to develop in terms of common and consistent practical actions to deal with the situation. Insofar as it is part of modern Western religion, religious individualism appears as a problem for dealing religiously with the situation. When religious concerns lead to spiritualization, the actual empirical conditions, in terms of suffering, causes and effects, as well as a responsible agency, are downplayed and thereby risk being ignored or counted as less significant.

---

17. Ibid., 216.
18. Ibid., 48ff.
19. Ibid., 49.
20. Ibid., 48.
21. Ibid., 48. Cf. also 62 f., where the religious framework spiritualizes the situation to such an extent that the main concern is about the souls of those who suffer, and not about the suffering itself.

Chapter 5

TO EMPOWER THOSE WHO SUFFER AND GIVE VOICE TO THOSE WHO LACK A VOICE

An encompassing vision

There is no view from nowhere and no God's-eye view accessible to humans. This is among the lessons we need to repeat when discussing the possibilities of developing a theology for action when we face climate change. From it follows the need to listen to other voices than those in our proximity and especially to those already affected by climate change and ecological degradation in ways hidden to those of us who live in affluent, consumerist societies. It also entails that we need to be aware of the danger of developing empty abstractions that hides from the concrete realities of those affected by climate change and injustice from our sight. Only in this way can we get some grasp on the totality of what is at stake.

The life in the biosphere of which we are part is differentiated and dynamic, 'yet deeply integrated. Earth sciences support the concept that the Earth's processes are entangled, intermingled, and mutually dependent: a self-regulating organism'.[1] The deep integration means that life conditions on this planet, be it organic or inorganic, interact dynamically and cannot be understood as discrete processes. Hence, an anthropocentric outlook is misleading for guiding our practices, despite its prevalent position in many cultures worldwide.

We cannot neglect the important task of overcoming anthropocentrism in religion and as a fundamental way of approaching and dealing with nature. I want to emphasize the practice dimension implied in it. Philosopher A.J. Vetlesen has pointed to anthropocentrism as 'not merely, or even primarily, descriptive. It is normative in postulating that human beings are superior to all other beings and forms of life on Earth, thus meriting a moral standing denied everything nonhuman'.[2] Accordingly, he sees anthropocentrism as a practice – acted upon by individuals and collectives alike, and manifest in most institutions around the

---

1. Cf. Eaton, 'An Earth-Centric Theological Framing for Planetary Solidarity' in Kim and Koster, *Planetary Solidarity*, 20.

2. Vetlesen, *Cosmologies of the Anthropocene: Panpsychism, Animism, and the Limits of Posthumanism*, 2.

globe. Addressing the neglect of other-than-human interests inherent in this fact, he writes the following in a quote that deserves full length, and which also should be informing the entanglements of religion (which he does not mention):

> Whether it be the institutions of economy, of politics, of education, of health or of law, they are either exclusively or primarily preoccupied with human agents and their perceived interests and needs. That this is so, and ought to remain so, serves as the pivotal 'reality principle' on which the socialization of every new generation is premised: in the course of childhood the anthropocentric point of view is internalized so as to become second nature – always presupposed in relating to other-than-humans as well as fellow humans, never seriously questioned by adults taken seriously by others. Internalized from early childhood is a sense of being profoundly different from all other living beings, promoting an ethos of entitlement in treating all such beings as mere means for human ends, as so many 'resources' whose alleged indifference to what we do to (against) them conveniently justifies our own, institutionally as well as individually. Owing to its seminal role in guiding all our practices, anthropocentrism is one of the most deep-seated and pervasive features of modern culture and of ourselves as products and reproducers of that culture.[3]

This quote poses severe questions to the fundamental formative elements of Western culture and, as mentioned, also to how human beings are socialized and internalize their second nature as 'standing over against' nature. To imagine oneself thus has promoted the devastating consequences which today manifest themselves in climate change driven by carbon-based consumer culture.

As suggested earlier in the chapter on consumerism,

> the devastating effects of climate change are unfathomable, however, to many who live in the wealthy Western world, who are shielded from the most brutal aspects of its reality. Women and children, the poorest and the most vulnerable people in the world, are the ones who bear the brunt of and are most especially affected by the consequences of climate change.[4]

However, the deeply integrated situation just mentioned suggests that not only women and children are suffering, but also non-human organic living beings, including species that live under the threat of extinction. Moreover, although it is hard to say that landscapes and rivers suffer, the loss of ecological qualities that they represent is a real loss, not only to those dependent on them but to the inherent value in what evolution has brought forth during millions of years of interrelated evolvement of landscape, species, climate, water and air. Hence, not only humans lacking a voice need to find ways to become empowered; also those who do not have a voice must be included in *planet solidarity*:

---

3. Ibid.
4. Kim and Koster, 'Introduction: Global Women's Voices on Christian Doctrine and Climate Justice', in *Planetary Solidarity*, 1.

The planet is entering a new period of extinction with scientists warning that species all over the world are 'essentially the walking dead'. Most of the demise and disappearance of animals is silent. They simply die off from habitat loss, pollution, or food shortages. In other instances, they are pushed off their land for human development or killed for food, skins, tusks, horns, or trophy hunting. Climate change impacts on animals are difficult to measure. [. . .]. Although there are multiple causes, overall it is anthropogenic activities and pressures causing this extinction – again, a planetary phenomenon. The suffering and loss of animals is, at times, seen to be an extraneous concern for those focused on social injustices. It is a cause carried by the affluent, ecotourists, animal rights activists, or those not in dire need of food, land, or capital. This is fundamentally shortsighted for ecological and ethical reasons.[5]

This concern entails an encompassing vision of interrelatedness that precludes an anthropocentric approach to climate change that only addresses it to the extent that it is traceable in human experience. An adequate understanding and its concomitant practices require that 'we broaden and deepen our solidarity to include the nonhuman world and the planetary systems and processes on which all life depends'.[6] For theology, it entails that it cannot be 'humanity' versus the rest of creation. What theology must address is human practices as they impact all of creation, including conditions for the life of humans that we do not usually meet and species that we usually do not experience.

Not everyone may be affected by not being able to see tigers anymore. But those of us who have seen them know that they are beautiful, and we can sense the loss

---

5. Eaton, 'An Earth-Centric Theological Framing for Planetary Solidarity', in *Planetary Solidarity*, 25. Cf also the following:

> To deliberate evolution can induce a revolution of awareness of the meaning of human embeddedness in planetary processes. All our attributes and sensibilities have evolved from planetary processes. This changes all our customary reference points. Evolution provides us with a planetary timeline, of histories that do not involve us, of our kinship with other animals, and of our radical dependency on innumerable organisms for basic survival. Evolution bends the mind, expands the horizon, and reverses the reference points. The planet is not our context, and we are not the key reference point. Although Earth is our home, it is not as an occupant or as a global citizen. This is a significant conceptual shortcoming in promoting the image of the Earth as our home without any ecological or evolutionary literacy. Earth is our source, origin, and basis for everything that makes and keeps us alive. Evolution beckons us to become scientifically literate and to situate ourselves in larger planetary processes.

Ibid., 23.

6. Kim and Koster, 'Introduction: Global Women's Voices on Christian Doctrine and Climate Justice', in *Planetary Solidarity*, 7.

or even the grief when they become extinct. One of the challenges facing climate change is to encourage people to develop practices that can engender sentiments of ecological grief, as such emotional competencies may become a resource that motivates practices of care for all of the planet. However, all of us may be affected if bees disappear: they are vital for diversified food production, and their disappearance may cause a lot of harm to ecological contexts, including some in which humans are not a vital part.

Moreover, although all life on the planet will be increasingly affected by climate change in one way or another, it is essential not to use metaphors that cover up the differences between different groups and nations. The injustices caused by the wealthy nations against the Earth, which also promote an ideology of consumerism and individualism, need to be countered by practices of resistance informed by solidarity with others. Instead of perpetuating the totalitarian idolatry that places economic growth that benefits the few above everything else, 'It is otherness in togetherness, not in isolation or competition' that is required in an age of anthropogenic climate change.[7]

Gendered injustices

In Chapter 2 on culprits, I pointed to how Adorno and Horkheimer made a connection between the exploitation of nature and the exploitation and othering of humans. There are many vivid examples of how this happens. Hilda Koster points to one when she describes the exploitation of women that takes place in the shadow of the fracking industry in the Dakotas. Her analysis also shows how such practices are legitimized by ideologies that cover up what is happening and simply reframes exploitation in terms of what is positively achieved:

> Societies typically use powerful ideology to prevent public outcry about the cost of war. In the case of warfare, the violence done to concrete human bodies and the Earth is covered up and presented as a good – for instance, the good of 'keeping America safe.' When it comes to the fracking and sex-trafficking industry, the violence done to women's bodies and the Earth is kept hidden by the neoliberal belief in economic growth as an unquestionable good, the promise of energy independence, and a gender ideology that views prostitutes as 'fallen women' and prostitution as a victim-less crime.[8]

Koster's analysis is important as it points to how different reasoning lines are used for different elements in the total picture. On the one hand, fracking is legitimized by pointing to how it makes the United States less dependent on foreign oil.

---

7. Ibid., 7.
8. Hilda P. Koster, 'Trafficked Lands: Sexual Violence, Oil, and Structural Evil in the Dakotas.', in *Planetary Solidarity*, 165.

Hence, the practice of fracking is an attempt to reduce the vulnerability that stems from being dependent on global partners. The attempt to increase energy independence allows for oil consumption in high numbers to go unquestioned, and likewise its concomitant consumerist lifestyle. Moreover, fracking's ecological impact and devastation are downplayed by pointing to the 'gains' of independence. Thus, ecological costs are disconnected from the lifestyle it continues to promote and from the actual concrete lives of those women who are exploited in these industrial areas. For them, another line of reasoning is employed: one that depicts them in terms of moral degradation. Consequently, the interconnectedness that constitutes the full picture remains absent from view.

Koster thereby shows the consequences of 'missing the full picture' and disconnecting the different elements at play in the fracking practices. I argue that to speak of ecological injustice, as she does, means that one must connect the dots between these different elements and see that injustice is related to humans and the land that is destroyed in this case.

Furthermore, the gendered dimension inherent in climate change contributes to our understanding of the whole picture necessary to contemplate and should not be seen as an attempt to promote sophisticated anthropocentrism in which injustices are only affecting humans. Against this backdrop, Kim and Koster are right, in my view, when they point to climate justice in the context of global warming as 'not just an environmental matter but also a moral, political, sociological, and religious concern.' It cannot be ignored that 'climate change will have the most adverse effects on the livelihood and health of people with the least political and economic power.'[9]

Hence, although climate change affects everyone, it affects some more than others. To put it differently, it is more apparent to the woman who has to collect cow droppings for fuel after another flooding in Bangladesh than to the woman who goes shopping in one of the airport malls in central Europe. Despite these differences, 'women make up the majority of the world's poor and tend to be more dependent on natural resources for their livelihoods and survival, they are at a higher risk. In the exploited world, poor women are often the primary caregivers of their families and hence play an important role in securing household water, food, and fuel.'[10]

Despite their central role in making families' livelihood possible, women's means for social and political influence and power is not at the same level as men. The fact that women lack independence and decision-making power means that they cannot adequately influence community strategies as to how to adapt to changing weather patterns in ways that support their rights and priorities. Their lack of power significantly constrains their ability to adapt to climate change.[11] In many

---

9. Kim and Koster, 'Introduction: Global Women's Voices on Christian Doctrine and Climate Justice', 2.
10. Ibid., 3.
11. Ibid., 3.

contexts, this lack of power is underscored by a patriarchal ideology supported by religious imagery. When men are in power, women become dependent on their priorities, and women's experiences become secondary and less significant. Hence, one of the tasks that theology must take up is how women's experiences can be prioritized when it comes to developing symbols that can mediate adequate and consistent action for the future of the planet. As we shall see in Part III of this book, prominent practices then present themselves.

Part of the reformation of theology needed to cope with climate change is to challenge some of the consequences emerging from a male-coloured image of God: 'Deep down, and with few exceptions, most Christian women, poor and rich, continue to imagine God as a male authority that helps and protects them. In most cases, it is a projection contrary to the reality that they experience with the men around them.'[12] This imagery keeps women captive in a situation from which they cannot escape if they only interpret their situation from the resources it represents. 'They receive and project an image of God that sustains them and understands their difficulties without realizing that often the key problem lies in everyday relationships, in the materiality of everyday life. Something close to a contradiction is outlined in this experience.'[13] The basic orientations in their religious culture prevent them from being subject of transformation. Instead, it 'leads them to believe in an entity capable of supporting and helping them but whose historical image is male'.[14] Because of the male origin of this religious imagery, it projects – 'albeit with varying nuances – male behavior toward women'.[15] Thus, the male image of a good and just God regulates women's wishes and initiatives: 'The God of religious and social officialdom continues to command and demand compliance, with obligations sometimes maladjusted to the current reality. In general, this God confirms the might of those who dominate the Earth with their exacerbated will-to-power and their portrayal that God is the same for everybody.'[16] Thus, it is called for a radical transformation of religious imagery and doctrine.

Doctrinal challenges

To speak of a deficit in the Christian tradition of symbols that can mediate consistent action to counter some of the causes and consequences of the climate crisis does not mean that no such symbols exist presently, and no such practices are available. Instead, it means that we need to seek out and reappropriate such

---

12. Ivone Gebara, 'Women's Suffering, Climate Injustice, God, and Pope Francis' Theology: Some Insights from Brazil', in *Planetary Solidarity: Global Women's Voices on Christian Doctrine and Climate Justice*, ed. Kim and Koster, 71.
13. Ibid., 72.
14. Ibid.
15. Ibid.
16. Ibid., 71–2.

symbols either by finding them in traditional sources or by developing new ones related to this tradition. Thus, theology contributes both to interpreting the experiences we face and to opening up to new, hope-engendering practices. Whereas it has traditionally been among the tasks of feminist theology to explore 'how Christian faith grounds and shapes women's experiences of hope, justice, and grace, as well as instigates and enforces women's experiences of oppression, sin and evil',[17] this task cannot any longer exclusively be one that feminist theology takes up. As indicated earlier, women's experiences must play a prominent role as the interpretative source and context of climate change theology and practice, given their crucial role as those affected by the change. We need to shape theological, practice-engendering symbols that are not anthropocentric, androcentric, heterosexist, racist, Eurocentric or essentialist. It is necessary to develop a theology that involves sentiment and experience and confront traditional anti-body spirituality. Both women and men are not 'other' than nature and set apart from it but are created – and therefore part of the creation that is will either find ways to live *with* or not live well at all. To repeat symbols and past versions of doctrine is not enough. We need to imagine alternatives creatively and, in doing so, rework 'interpretations of doctrines that have reinforced colonialism, patriarchy, climate change, racism, and other injustices'.[18]

I have argued elsewhere that Christian doctrines cannot be separated from the everyday practices in which we partake and that they, largely, may be seen as special ways of attributing religious significance to such everyday practices. Moreover, practices for living and living well by manifesting the qualities needed for life take priority over doctrinal interpretations of the practices themselves. What follows from this view is that doctrines relate to, interpret and render significance to what we do, as they allow us to see our practices from a specific point of view.[19] Accordingly, I agree with Serene Jones, who sees doctrines as much more than propositional statements or static rules; instead, they serve as 'imaginative lenses through which to view the world. The purpose of engaging doctrine, then, is to

---

17. Kim and Koster, 'Introduction: Global Women's Voices on Christian Doctrine and Climate Justice', 5.

18. Ibid., 5. The fact that climate change is not a mere ecological catastrophe but also entails persistent injustices in terms of gender and race cannot be overlooked. It is, however, not possible to deal with all of these connections in the present context. Developments over the year this book has been written (2020) reminds us that concerns about global warming is no excuse for caring less about racism and gender inequality. For comprehensive elaborations on these matters, see, *inter alia*, Cynthia D. Moe-Lobeda, 'Climate Change as Climate Debt: Forging a Just Future', *Journal of the Society of Christian Ethics* 36, no. 1 (2016).

19. For further on this point, Henriksen, *Christianity as Distinct Practices: A Complicated Relationship*. The theoretical basis for this understanding of practices is developed in *Religion as Orientation and Transformation: A Maximalist Theory*.

open up fresh possibilities for life together—with one another and with the Earth'.[20] Theology needs to examine its past formulation of doctrines and scrutinize the practices they have contributed to consolidating and legitimizing. Only then is it possible to 'critically participate in and transform public life so as to forge solidarity with marginalized groups and thereby better embrace and begin to enhance this life together'.[21]

Practices bolstered by theology may be of different kinds. Rosemary Carbine distinguishes between rhetorical, symbolic and prophetic practices. *Rhetorical practices*, according to her, 'include a variety of aesthetic genres that give voice to and urge solidarity with marginalized peoples often denied political subjectivity and agency. These practices educate about institutionalized injustices, contest the contours of commonly held constitutive values of US and geopolitical life that feed these injustices, and pave an alternative path for empathy and solidarity'.[22]

Carbine describes *symbolic practices* as those that 'reflect on the sociopolitical significance and implications of central religious symbols in order to construct a transcendent normative moral framework of shared rights and responsibilities in public life'.[23] Such practices confront the tendencies to 'sacralize a theocratic nation-state, justify a certain sociopolitical order, or demand confessional conformity to a Christian theological imaginary'.[24] They 'draw on or extend Christianity's organizing symbols, especially God-talk, in order to craft a shared political space of moral discourse and practice about the meaning of human being and the mutual obligations of human beings to one another and to the world'.[25] Thus, 'they reinterpret a religious symbol system to redirect our sociopolitical moral imaginary toward justice'.[26]

Finally, prophetic practices 'challenge injustices in public life and simultaneously engage in practices that both imagine and perform more just future alternative possibilities. These practices mediate the present and future reality or point the way toward a more just common life by dramatizing injustice and attempting to partly actualize an alternative possibility to that injustice through different forms of collective action'.[27]

---

20. Kim and Koster, 'Introduction: Global Women's Voices on Christian Doctrine and Climate Justice', 5, who quote Serene Jones, *Feminist Theory and Christian Theology: Cartographies of Grace*, Guides to Theological Inquiry (Minneapolis: Fortress Press, 2000), 16.

21. *Rosemary P. Carbine*, 'Imagining and Incarnating an Integral Ecology: A Critical Ecofeminist Public Theology', in *Planetary Solidarity: Global Women's Voices on Christian Doctrine and Climate Justice*, ed. Kim and Koster, 50.

22. Ibid.
23. Ibid.
24. Ibid.
25. Ibid.
26. Ibid.
27. Ibid.

Together, these practices embody different forms of public participation. They build on an alternative and shared sense of the common good, in which no voice should be excluded. They contribute to 'a constructive theology of world making or "envisioning and enacting worlds – that is critiquing and deconstructing oppressive worlds, on the one hand, and noticing, constructing, or creating more liberative alternate worlds, on the other"'.[28]

Two features in Carbine's presentation are especially important to notice. The first feature is that it refuses to separate theology from politics. Thus, it confronts those who will say that climate change is a political and not a religious topic and, thus, keep it outside the scope of what can be considered relevant or a priority for believers. To criticize the present injustices is necessary also from a theological point of view. However, this also opens up to the second, important feature that emerges from her understanding of theological practices: these practices need to mediate between the present and the future and to suggest different, innovative ways of living together as a planetary community.[29] As she sees it, some work still needs to be done in terms of developing these practices because the imagery presented so far can only address the current situation in a limited way.[30] Accordingly, her analysis provides a warrant for the task to be accomplished in this book's following parts.

---

28. Ibid., 51. The quote in the quote is from Laurel C. et al. Schneider, *Awake to the Moment: An Introduction to Theology*, (Louisville, KY: Westminster John Knox Press, 2016), 108.

29. Carbine, 'Imagining and Incarnating an Integral Ecology: A Critical Ecofeminist Public Theology', 50–1.

30. Cf ibid., 51. Cf. how she comments on Pope Francis' Encyclia: 'On my reading, the Vatican's most recent venture into global eco-public theology through the encyclical Laudato Si' does not fulfill the twofold purpose of feminist hermeneutics – namely, to criticize Christian traditions that continue to prescribe patriarchy/kyriarchy and to constructively engage with Christian traditions so as to foreground and foster women's innovative and salient contributions. Pope Francis's God-talk as an absolute dominating father retains a patriarchal/ kyriarchal theology of power, which consequently creates a theological lacuna that leads him to tackle gender justice insufficiently as well as contradicts the promising eco-pneumatology that enlivens the encyclical's integral ecology. Moreover, Francis's ecological theology of the Spirit completely disregards and therefore invisibilizes longtime salutary feminist theological work in this field.' Ibid., 65.

CONCLUSION, PART I

LESSONS FROM THE CONTEXT

In the analyses in this part, I have demonstrated several important features to keep in mind as we move towards the development of action-engendering symbols. In this conclusion, I will reflect more on how they are interconnected and suggest why they all are gesturing towards an explanation of the symbol deficit and what we need to do to overcome it.

The introduction of the notion *Anthropocene* suggests that all life on planet Earth is now affected by human agency. Although it entails elements that are clearly not caused by human activities such as tsunamis and other natural catastrophes, their effects are impacted by human organization, action and features like tourism and how humans develop their habitats. Ignorance of old wisdom about where it is safe to stay or to build sometimes also produces devastating effects on humans and other species, the landscapes and the living conditions for plants.

In light of this knowledge, it is not adequate to say that events are simply 'acts of God' – meaning that their effects are outside of human control. Instead, it opens up a perspective that suggests that humans have to consider that all of their actions and interactions with the environment have consequences – some foreseen, some possible to foresee and some that we do not know about but about what we should seek to know more.

From a theological point of view, the recognition that we now live in the Anthropocene leads to two, quite different, insights. Firstly, it means that we need to have a far more profound understanding of human agency, its conditions and what it entails for the whole of creation and our role in it. We cannot separate ourselves as 'standing over against nature'. Instead, our interdependence and intertwinement with nature mean that nature is us and that we are nature. Although traditional symbols suggest this fact (We are dust, made of clay etc.), none of the existing images and imaginaries is directly informing how we need to see ourselves as interacting with the rest of creation. Thus, as Donna Haraway writes, 'we need stories (and theories) that are just big enough to gather up the complexities and keep the edges open and greedy for surprising new and old connections.'[1]

---

1. Donna Haraway, 'Anthropocene, Capitalocene, Plantationocene, Chthulucene: Making Kin', *Environmental Humanities* 6, no. 1 (2015): 160.

Moreover, our existence on Anthropocene conditions means that we cannot ascribe to God some events as God's acts, outside our control or concern. The climate change denials that are bolstered by religious imaginaries are therefore not only inadequate. They are promoting and enhancing the conflict between religion and science, as well as contributing to not addressing climate change as a political problem. The latter point is a specific challenge since recognizing and confronting climate change from a religious perspective as a political problem entails that one, at some level, has to mix religion and politics. It also means that one, at some stage, will have to take up the task of confronting the consumer society and its ideology. It does not belong to the freedom of humans to develop societies as they please by ignoring the effect on the lives of others and the environment. Consumerist freedom and the life sought for in many other post-industrial societies that want to emulate consumer society's model leads to death – and this death is the consequences of human actions and not some unforeseen 'act of God'.

Both notions like 'act of God', 'God is in control' and the caricatures of Christian theology that Lynn White presents suggest that religious symbols, narratives and notions may have some impact on human action. Some of them limit the scope of human agency or deprive humans of understanding how they are involved in climate change and are responsible for it. However, it is crucial to underscore that such symbolic elements are not independent variables. They exist and are utilized in the context of practices. Therefore, I side with those who see White's critique of Christianity as essentialist and ahistorical. We can develop this critique of White even more if we try to understand how Christianity employs symbols. We need to see this employment against the backdrop of, and relating to, the complicated relationship between three interrelated elements:[2] (a) the individual, which relies on, (b) the community to which the individual belongs, which would not exist apart from, (c) the religious tradition that constitutes the community and provides practices through which it lives and articulates itself.

The analysis of climate change denial testifies to how symbols are employed in relation to specific contextual circumstances. Because a religious tradition is always contextually embedded, it cannot be understood apart from its historical conditions and how they impact the individual, the community and the interpretation of the tradition. Christianity as a religion is a cluster of practices for orientation, transformation and legitimatization, and it mediates itself in and through the interplay between these practices. Therefore, the mediation between these three interrelated elements is due to different practices conditioned by social, historical and other contextual features in which the relation between them is expressed. Practices reside in contexts. Christians navigate between contextual concerns, community, tradition and individual conditions for appropriation.

At present, no symbols exist in the Christian tradition that is constituted by the awareness of climate change or the situation of the Anthropocene. As mentioned,

---

2. The following line of reasoning is based on Henriksen, *Christianity as Distinct Practices: A Complicated Relationship*, 91–3.

the symbols that exist have emerged from another historical context, and to the extent that they can prove relevant, illuminating and providing cause for action, they will have to be reconstituted on the basis of the present predicament. Thus, a radical reconsideration of the symbolic resources of the tradition is necessary – a point that I have suggested in relation to notions of God, of humans as participants in creation as well as idolatry. As we shall see, part of this task entails taking women's experiences and situation into consideration as constitutive. We cannot consider these experiences a mere supplement to a pre-existing, more or less disembodied theology.

Theology cannot be developed without taking the actual experiences of those who already suffer from climate change into consideration. Theology's task is to interpret these experiences and open up to new experiences, based on the sources it has access to in the Bible, the tradition and the actual experiences of all afflicted. In the section referencing women's experiences, it became apparent that feminist theology provides important resources to the task at hand. Without falling into the trap of essentializing women, the experiences they report to and address suggest that we need another understanding of the self than the one who sees theology's subject as the detached, disembodied person who is not influenced by sentiment. As Adorno and Horkheimer pointed to, because they have been considered 'the other' of the rational self of modernity, women have been defined as less moral subjects because of the traits they have in common with all of humanity: feeling, interrelatedness, embodiment, involvement and dependence on nature and on others. Today, we need to include these traits when we discuss what is required for moral subjects and moral agency that addresses the climate crisis. These traits are also closer to what actually marks all features of human life: that we are involved in practices of participation and community that lead to experiences of empathy, suffering, joy, thriving and flourishing, and a sense of meaning. These elements of human experience are not present for a disembodied rational subject who sees the ideal as being detached from concrete practices and circumstances.

This last point is especially challenging because it relies on a critical analysis of one of the dominant contributions in recent moral philosophy, discussed in relation to Kant and Habermas. We need to develop another understanding of the capacities that the moral subject requires. Fortunately, we shall see in Part II that there exist alternatives that are closer to the actual experiences and competencies of most humans – and that the development of another moral subject that is embodied and able to take sentiment into moral consideration can provide us with a better model for emulation – and thereby development – of moral agency.

Here we are at a crucial point for the following work. Although the notion of the Anthropocene suggests that everything that now happens on planet Earth is influenced by human agency; human agency does not determine everything or is the only condition for what happens. Humans live on the conditions of their participation in nature and the environment. They do not produce all that is. Their existence is a given, as are the conditions for it. To articulate this point in a framework of a theology of creation without positioning humans in a situation of pure passivity is one of the challenges we face. This theology must develop an understanding of human beings as responsible and active while simultaneously maintaining that we are dependent on the living system that conditions our existence.

Terra Schwerin-Rowe's argument against the use of the word 'interaction' for describing what takes place between humans and the environment is worth contemplating here. She holds that this concept is insufficient for bringing forth the actual entanglement of all that is. Accordingly, she suggests instead speaking of 'intra-action' because this notion is adequate for recognizing how all that exists on the planet are intertwined and part of each other, physically, biologically and socially.[3] When they intra-act, all parties involved will change. One important consequence of this approach is that the concept of an individual as an autonomous being is impossible.[4] Moreover, instead of contemplating connecting or reconnecting with the world around us, the existing and insoluble connection becomes the starting point of agency. Against this backdrop, any recognition of responsibility for others or for the ecological condition entails that we also are responsible for ourselves, and vice versa, because of our intra-action and entanglement.[5] Thus, the ontology of intra-action entails an essential remedy against the prevailing elements of individualism in ethics, in contemporary Western theology and in consumerist societies.

---

3. Cf. Terra Schwerin Rowe, *Toward a Better Worldliness: Ecology, Economy, and the Protestant Tradition* (Minneapolis, Minnesota: Fortress Press, 2017), 114. Rowe builds her use of the term 'intra-action' on the work of Karen Barad. See Karen Barad, 'What Flashes Up: Theological-Political-Scientific Fragments', in *Entangled Worlds: Religion, Science, and New Materialism*, ed. Catherine Keller and May-Jane Rubenstein (New York: University of Fordham Press, 2017).

4. Cf. Rowe, *Toward a Better Worldliness: Ecology, Economy, and the Protestant Tradition*, 115.

5. Ibid., 116.

Part II

CONDITIONS FOR SYMBOLIC PRACTICES

Religions may not change the world or save us from the climate crisis. Nevertheless, they can play a role in overcoming some of the predicaments facing us because they continue to be a vital motivating factor in many peoples' lives. Religions mediate the relationship between humans and the rest of the world through a wide variety of action-motivating symbols. These symbols are based on practices of orientation, transformation and reflection, and without them humankind would lack significant resources for self-interpretation. The symbols, narratives and imaginaries of religions interact with our personal experiences and help us in dealing with the challenges we face.

This part of the book will present and discuss some of the theoretical conditions for understanding religious symbols as a means for mediating practices that can counter the climate crisis. Accordingly, the material I discuss is not only of theoretical interest. The analysis of it focuses on its relevance for practices. However, through the discussions in this part of the book, I develop a specific understanding of symbols as conditions for human agency and for theology as rooted in and expressed in practices.

As indicated, the relationship between symbols and human practices are of special interest in this part. The aim is to develop a sufficiently comprehensive approach to symbols that can help us see how they need to be employed in the present situation. The main aim here is not to present every relevant aspect in detail but to highlight the fundamental elements that can help us understand symbols as engaging and engaged by practice. Here we can draw on pragmatism, evolutionary theory and psychology. The main thesis that follows is that symbols mediate, constitute and engage embodied human experience. Against this backdrop, it follows that the notion of humans as separate individuals that can stand detached from reality and nature is profoundly mistaken and does not represent an adequate understanding of the contemporary conditions for the required human agency. Hence, we need to develop an approach to human moral agency that can take into account an evolutionary perspective that links humans with nature and simultaneously is sufficiently nuanced to see morality as more than a mere rational capacity. Accordingly, the fundamental conditions for moral agency are then developed into an analysis of virtue ethics that will be important for the argument in the remainder of the book. The focus on moral practice developed in this part ends with some fundamental considerations about the contribution of a pragmatist theology in the face of the climate crisis.

Chapter 6

SYMBOLS AS MEDIATING PRACTICE

Introduction: Symbols, practices and semiotics

In a dense comment on how our dealings with nature are shaped by societal and cultural conditions, Eric Nelson writes:

> The sensuous physicality of things does not consist of an extra-linguistic substrate, as language is central to how the object is addressed and is not external to it. Even as communication and rationalization do not exhaust nature, humans do not intuit or access nature 'in itself' or 'as such,' unmediated by their own historically situated activities and constructs. Since nothing seems more natural than attempts to master nature, this includes the ideologies of nature – consisting of what conceptually and practically counts as natural – that perpetuate human subordination and ecological devastation.[1]

Nelson's remarks here entail that even though we need to recognize that nature has value independent of us, how we experience it is not independent of the way we develop our understandings and interpretations of it. 'Nature' is always interwoven in practices of interpretation that manifest different ideological approaches to it. To be aware of these may help us see what is at stake behind the practices and conditions we saw in the previous chapter. All symbols are connected to human practices. The practices they are connected to, mediate and engender allow us to understand symbols' meaning. Hence, with a twist on a Wittgensteinean phrase, we can say that the meaning of a symbol is in its use. However, what is a symbol? In order to specify this topic further, we need to distinguish symbols from other types of signs.

In his semiotics, C. S. Peirce distinguishes between three different types of signs: index, symbol and icon. Indexes are pointers to something else and related to their objects by some direct connection (like traffic signs). Icons represent something else that we assume that they have a likeness to. They relate to their objects by

---

1. Nelson, 'Revisiting the Dialectic of Environment: Nature as Ideology and Ethics in Adorno and the Frankfurt School', 115.

some kind of resemblance – portraits being the obvious example). Symbols do not directly connect to what they signify – but the connection is determined by how we have made decisions about their meaning.[2] It is this latter type of sign – the symbol – that will occupy us in what follows.

According to the aforementioned, symbols are many different things. Words are symbols insofar as we use them to speak about something – their meaning is in the use we have designated for them. Nevertheless, words are not the only symbols: in the church, the colours symbolize different parts of the liturgical year. When an eagle is carved out at the pulpit in some churches, it is nothing obvious that tells us that it signifies John the Evangelist, but this symbol is established with a firm meaning in many churches. Much religious life relies on and depends on symbols in this sense: Wine and bread could not be a sacrament unless there was some kind of symbolic dimension in which the meaning of the practice had some kind of established meaning that the community shared and maintained by performing the sacramental practice. The symbolic dimension of the Eucharist depends on how wine and bread are involved in a specific practice.

Symbols both mediate and determine how we see the world. However, our mode of vision is tied up with our mode of being. We need to underscore this point because it helps us understand why people in different parts of the world, who live under different circumstances and conditions and with various types of access to the experiences that provide them with the interpretative context for their symbolic worlds, see the world differently. Our perception of the world is not determined by theoretical choices and notions but by the very practices in which we are involved and which determine our use of symbols. Larry Rasmussen writes:

> If our mode of being changes, if circumstances change and the life we live is altered, our way of seeing will likely change as well. We are historical creatures whose life-worlds and institutions shape our mental maps. While symbolic consciousness always organizes our perception, and limits it, it is mutable. While it always strives for meaningful totalities, they are partial, inherently biased, and temporal. Nonetheless we crave absolute categories and love to canonize our perception and judgments.[3]

Accordingly, we do not see the world as it is – we see the world from our perspective, based on who we are and what we do. 'Creatures of symbolic consciousness have no unmediated apprehension of nature, their own nature included. Our notions of nature, not raw nature, shape our response.'[4]

---

2. For an accessible presentation of Peirce's theory of signs, see Andrew Robinson, *Traces of the Trinity: Signs, Sacraments and Sharing God's Life*, (Cambridge: James Clarke Co., 2014), 6–11.

3. Larry L. Rasmussen, *Earth-Honoring Faith: Religious Ethics in a New Key* (New York: Oxford University Press, 2013), 30.

4. Ibid., 76.

I underscore the relationship between symbols and practice here because the topic in the following is how *we can understand specific practices as symbols*. Moreover, the understanding of symbols presented earlier also suggests that a practice must be understood by a community as holding a specific meaning to display and maintain symbolic significance. We cannot neglect the communal dimension in symbolic practices that bear theological significance. However, the communal dimension is not only inherent in the religious employment of symbols. The relation between a symbol and its object is conventional and governed by rules shared by all who employ (and therefore understand) it.

Before I proceed with some further reflections on symbols, we need to make a note related to the fact that words are symbols, as indicated earlier. This means that symbols are related to the everyday of all humans. Many symbols also engage different dimensions of nature. Symbols are everywhere, and we live our lives in ways that constantly interpret them. When I look at my watch, it is to interpret how it symbolizes what time it is. When I hear the train signalling, I know it approaches the station. When someone knocks on my door, I know it means that a student or a colleague wants to see me. Hence, the figures on the watch, or the different sounds, constitute part of everyday life and help me understand what I should do. There is a semiotic element in all of reality, and it is intimately linked to our practices and our agency.

Tillich on symbols

Paul Tillich understands the words 'sign' and 'symbol' in a way that seems to contradict Peirce. He writes:

> while the sign bears no necessary relation to that to which it points, the symbol participates in the reality of that for which it stands. The sign can be changed arbitrarily according to the demands of expediency, but the symbol grows and dies according to the correlation between that which is symbolized and the persons who receive it as a symbol. Therefore, the religious symbol, the symbol which points to the divine, can be a true symbol only if it participates in the power of the divine to which it points.[5]

In this quote, we can ignore the first part about how the sign bears no necessary relation to that which it points. This is how Peirce defines a symbol. What is important here is Tillich's further understanding of a symbol. He pinpoints how the life or death of a symbol depends on its use by those who receive it as such. Here, he points to a feature that will occupy us in the following: we can see our symbolic practices as pointing towards and participating in the reality of God.

---

5. Paul Tillich, *Systematic Theology (Volume 1)* (London: SCM Press, 1978), 239.

To understand our practices in this way, we need to see how our practices can be identified and understood as manifesting God's reality as it comes to expression in faith, hope and love. In other words, our practices need to be possible to identify as manifesting a reality where goodness, compassion, hope for the future and love for all of creation is present. As Tillich points to, our relationship with the divine power is not tangential or arbitrary but based on our participation in the divine reality. We would not be had it not been for God. God conditions our very being and we participate in God. Accordingly, our agency as finite beings can point beyond ourselves towards the God who is the ground of being and the source of a future of goodness for all of creation. Not all of our actions do that, but there may be actions that do. Hence, the task is to identify these and find actions or practices that are based on and engender faith, hope and love for all of creation and motivate for consistent and sustained actions that can counter climate change.

Against this backdrop, we can also constructively interpret what Tillich says about the life or the death of a symbol. A symbol will die if it is unable to express (any longer) our relationship with the divine reality. 'The judgment that a religious symbol *is* true is identical with the judgment that the revelation of which it is the adequate expression is true.'[6] Hence, Christian symbolic practice is only true if it expresses love, care or compassion in the same way that God has revealed Godself as loving, compassionate and caring. The criteria for assessing symbolic practices rooted in Christian faith are given with their relation to this revelation. We shall later see how this point suggests that even everyday practices may bear witness to and express an internal relationship with the reality that this revelation discloses.

From Tillich to pragmatism: Neville

In his extensive work on religious symbols, Robert C. Neville takes his point of departure in how Tillich used the notion of a broken symbol to indicate a symbol that can engage us, whereas we are also aware of its limitations.[7] Broken symbols relate us to what they symbolize but are different from their referent. Therefore, they cannot be understood as a substitute for the reality to which they relate us.[8] What makes Tillich's theory so apt in our (and Neville's) context is his understanding that *religious symbols symbolize the infinite but are themselves finite*.[9] Moreover, Neville is informed and builds on Peirce's pragmatic understanding of signs.

---

6. Ibid., 240.

7. Robert C. Neville, *The Truth of Broken Symbols*, Suny Series in Religious Studies (Albany: State University of New York Press, 1996).

8. For an extensive analysis of Tillich's own theory of symbols, which addresses fully also the elements in the distinction between finitude and the infinite, see Lewis S. Ford, 'The Three Strands of Tillich's Theory of Religious Symbols', *The Journal of Religion* 46 (1966): 104–30.

9. Neville, *The Truth of Broken Symbols*, x., where he refers to Tillich, ST 1, esp. 239–40.

A pragmatic approach does not entail that religious symbols are mere instruments for symbolizing some feeling or intention other than the symbol itself. Instead, they are *guiding principles for behaviour* that we may, on occasion, criticize based on the kind of behaviour they engender.[10] On the other hand, though, they may have value due to their ability to mediate personal and communal transformation. However, this is not possible to understand solely from the point of view of a mere instrumentalist approach to their meaning.

Finding sustainable practices that carry symbolic value and engender enduring motivation for countering the climate crisis thus finds a theoretical context: a practice or an action that serves as a religious symbol might guide other actions. Such practices and symbols can be identified as *positive* insofar as they guide constructive human behaviour and practices that improve ecological conditions. Such symbols can, in turn, engender practices that are based on the emulation of other practices – a point that I will return to in subsequent chapters. Negative symbols, on the other hand, are symbols that identify behaviour that affects the climate and ecology negatively. They aim at precluding humans from destructive actions and practices.

Important for our purposes in this regard are two things: (a) Neville, following Peirce, holds that symbols guide behaviour that engages us in/with the world and are then in some way always referential. (b) As this behaviour is one in which we are already relating to 'the exterior', symbols are not mere instruments for handling and mastering the world but are actually shaping us and the world simultaneously. Thus, Neville sees symbols in relation to practices that rely on agents' interpretation and not from the point of view of what they are 'in themselves'. Accordingly, any analysis of religious symbols implies a threefold task. The first is to analyse *what* religious symbols refer to and *how* they refer to it. The second is to analyse the meaning of these signs by placing them within semiotic systems that allow us to trace their coded connections with other signs. The third mode of analysis focuses on the contexts where religious symbols appear in actual interpretations; the analysis of the context in which they are put to use, so to say; and *how* they are put to use.[11]

These three levels of analysis entail that we analyse religious symbols with regard to meaning, reference and interpretation to come to grips with their pragmatic function. Neville points to further topics that need to be addressed and which expand the implications of this pragmatic approach even further. One (fourth) topic is *engagement*: 'Religious symbols, under a given interpretation, either do or do not engage the interpreters with that to which they refer. If they do, the symbol is a living one. If they do not, the symbol is dead. A religious symbol might have the capacity to refer to a real object; but if it is not properly interpreted, the symbol will be dead.'[12] Moreover, symbols also have to be assessed from their

10. Ibid., xiii f.
11. Ibid., xviii.
12. Ibid., 20.

possible *truth* (fifth topic) and from the *consequences* (sixth topic) they may have beyond their actual interpretation.[13] However, the point about the engagement is of particular relevance here because it allows us to think about a possible internal relation between the symbolic practice and the divine reality.

Neville sees all registrations of the divine as symbolic. The recognition of the fundamentally symbolic character of our interaction with the divine means that the symbols in question are not there at our will only, arbitrarily, and interchangeable. How one relates to the symbols themselves has to do with how one relates to what is symbolized. In a dense sentence, he summarizes the implications of this for religious piety: 'Piety before the sacred then means the disciplined development of symbols and their interpretation that registers the divine within the interpreters without distorting the sacred in the respects interpreted, and then living in light of these registering interpretations without running counter to the divine, participating where relevant in the initiatives that flow from the interpreted divine nature.'[14] Hence, symbols always mediate between the religious object and the interpreter. It is only through symbols that one can refer to a religious object. 'Only through symbols can there be a content (even emptiness) ascribed to the objects. Only through symbols can the object be interpreted so as to relate to the life of the interpreter and interpreting community.'[15]

The communal dimension in the use of symbols, which I have already pointed to, here seems to correspond well with the fact that we can find the origins of intersubjectivity in language and the relation with the other. Neville's understanding of symbols implies that we are opened up to others by symbols, but also that others open us up to symbols and their possible resources for interpreting diverse dimensions of life. Hence, symbols take on a mediating character between the finite (of me) and the infinite (of the Other) in a dialectical manner.

Religious symbols always reference something *in some respect*. Identification of the interpretive respect is necessary for understanding how the symbols, with their constellations of meaning refer to their objects. Symbolic meaning abstracted from the respect of reference is misleading, Neville holds.[16] The *primary reference* of all religious symbols he understands as follows: 'All religious symbols have a primary reference directly or indirectly (as determined in the respect of interpretation) to boundary conditions contrasting the finite and infinite.'[17] This thesis is the justification for the extensive engagement with his theory, as it places the understanding of religious symbols at the very heart of religious commitment and implies that we cannot understand either the finite/infinite contrast or the function of religious symbols if we look away from their mutual relation.

---

13. Ibid., 20.
14. Ibid., 30 f.
15. Ibid., 31.
16. Ibid., 46.
17. Ibid., 47. My italics.

Symbols and experience

If symbols are to have any motivating force, they need to interpret what we can consider valuable, important, and vital to our and others' flourishing, and make this available to the human experience. Therefore, the relationship between symbols and experience is of the utmost importance. Symbols are more than cognitive – they may encapsulate and mediate both emotional and moral experiences as well. Thus, writes Neville,

> experience is much richer than sensation. Things that appear in experience include one's emotions and those of one's neighbors; institutions and their effects, for instance political, educational, and familial; ideas, traditions, cultural projects; obligations in morals, politics, arts, descriptions, theories – anything at all that can be experienced as real can appear in experience, shaped by the form of appearance. Many if not most of the things that appear are shaped themselves by human signs, including images as well as interpretations and theories.[18]

Against this backdrop, the importance of religious symbols reveals itself: what we experience as important in the world is significant because it is not only part of the world, but these symbols *shape the world* as such. Neville sees them as *paradigmatic orienting appearances*, and they have symbolic value for defining what may be the world's ultimate contours. Hence, he also calls them *world-construction elements*.[19] In its basic function as world-making, imagination based on symbols is religious *because it is world constructing*. Here the relevance and importance of seeing the contribution of religious symbols (as based on the finite/infinite distinction) to imagination comes to the fore: Imagination cannot frame its experiential elements without the orienting importance of certain appearing images that function as boundary conditions for worldliness. Thus, '*Religion is the name of the cultural enterprise that shepherds the symbols of the boundary conditions.*'[20]

The sources of such symbols of boundary conditions may be diverse and need in no way be religious – they may also come from art and science. However, such symbols *function* as religious if they frame the dimensions or boundaries of experiential worldliness.[21] Neville here points to an essential element in what may count as a viable religious symbol. It is precisely by their ability to address our finitude, and nevertheless place us in a world that is not only occupied with ourselves or what is immediately given in the preconceptions of it, that religious symbols serve their purpose concerning the basic features of human life. By pointing toward these boundaries, they help us experience our finitude and thematize what may be possible (and impossible) modes of self-transcendence, as

---

18. Ibid., 52.
19. Ibid., 54.
20. Ibid., 55. My italics.
21. Ibid., 55.

well as the relevance of the world which is not us. Their relevance for actions that have an ecological impact is, therefore, apparent. A finite human needs religious symbols to make sense of how she is situated as finite in a world that offers the conditions for her life and her participation in a broader context than the one established by her agency.

The ability to formulate symbolic expressions of the world's boundary conditions is crucial for how humans can experience their situation. Symbols, therefore, both orient and contribute to modifications and transformation. As long as religion can articulate meaning that in some way helps people engage with these fundamental elements of life, it may be a vital resource for engagement with and participation in the world, with others, and with the development and growth of one's self-in-relation.

Neville's defines religious symbols as 'those religiously functioning images that so shape the worldliness of the world that they also indexically point beyond it', and, thus, he does not separate the religious realm from the secular realm. Instead, he sees the everyday elements as those which, given communally established conventions, can serve as symbols for that which is beyond the reach of human agency and need to be recognized. 'As shaping the basic dimensions of the world – its temporal and spatial structures, its values and importances, and the place of the human in all this – religiously functioning images refer to what makes the difference between cosmos and the transcendent.'[22]

The word that makes the difference here is – exactly – *difference*. If religion is about what makes the difference between the world as it appears to me and the infinite that transcends my immediately given world, *religion is about how the infinite presents itself within the framework of finitude, in its difference to it*. Neville summarizes his position in a way that sheds light on my concerns in the following quote:

> The interpretation of religious objects that has been offered here is that they are finite things that have some world-constructing importance, either in a cosmological sense or a sense having to do with the ground, meaning and goal of human life. Because of this importance, the real object is not the finite thing as such but the finite thing in contrast with the infinite, with its supra-finite context, with the situation that would obtain if the finite thing did not exist or have its world-constructing importance. In short, the contrast has to do with the importance of the finite thing for the contingent existence of the world, in some respect, or the world of human meaningfulness.[23]

Hence, when we see specific human practices as symbolic expressions that serve to construct our emotional and cognitive experience of the world in a certain way, these are religious to the extent that they manifest what we see as the ground,

22. Ibid., 65.
23. Ibid., 71.

meaning, and goal of human life. It is by interpreting the symbolic character of practices in this way that human life becomes meaningful.

Symbolic practices are practices of orientation, transformation and engagement

Symbols and how we practice them shape the way we experience the world. The most obvious example of this is how language helps us to experience and order our situation. Language, understood as symbols, mediate our cognitive appropriation of a situation. Ritual practices such as baptism constitute our understanding of how God acts with the baptized child. Looking at the thermometer gives an indication of what I need to wear.

On the other hand, symbolic practices also shape us and our self-experiences. This point will be developed further in a later chapter where the relevance of virtues is the main topic. Here I just want to point to how symbols shape both the world and ourselves. We do something with the world when we employ symbols and engage in symbolic actions, but these actions also do something to us and with us.

This *pragmatic* understanding of symbols and symbolic practices entails that they have shaping effects on us and our relationship with the world. Hence, it matters what we do and what rituals and practices we take part in. it matters to ourselves and the world to which we relate.

One important consequence of this understanding of symbols and symbolic practices is that the relation to the world by means of symbols cannot be understood as neutral. Pragmatism overcomes the separation of facts and values because it sees our practices as guided by concerns that are shaped by how we understand a situation – and this situation is always someone's and about something – it is, as we saw earlier in Neville, an understanding of the world in some respect. This point is relevant with regard to addressing the climate crisis because the way we understand it will shape different types of action that are dependent upon the way we decide to understand it. It leads to different responses if we see it as a threat to the future that can be avoided or as an already-growing catastrophe that requires all the Earth's inhabitants' immediate and comprehensive action.

Because we cannot live in the world without interpreting it,[24] practice is primary in human life. We can distinguish practices analytically as follows: practices orient us, they transform us and they engage us. 'Us' must here not be understood in an abstract, detached or individualist way. We always exist in a given situation, confronted with certain tasks, challenges or concerns. Against this backdrop, we can see religious symbols as resources by which we respond to fundamental human life experiences. I follow Ulf Zackariasson in seeing religious traditions as offering *paradigmatic responses* to existentially significant situations

---

24. This point is central to pragmatists, but it is shared by Heidegger, as well.

through narratives, myths, symbols, sermons, ritual and so on.[25] What counts as existentially important may differ due to context and depends on various variables. However, contrary to those I referred to in Part I of the book, who see the climate crisis as something that can be left to God and which is not challenging Western consumption patterns, it is essential to see that this crisis calls for engagement by religious symbols that shape our adequate response(s) to it. The climate crisis is existentially important, and so also from a religious point of view because it involves matters of life and death, justice and destruction, loss and community, illness, and hunger. Such elements cannot be described in value-neutral terms because they affect fundamental conditions for life and flourishing for all life on the planet, and not only for humans. Thus, religious symbols and symbolic practices mediate agency that may engage us in, orient us and transform the catastrophic situation at hand. Or, in Zackariasson's words: 'Religious agency can then be seen as our way of bringing the responses transmitted to us [by tradition, J.-O.H] to bear on situations in which we find ourselves through the development of habits of *thought, action, and judgment*.'[26] The three elements he lists belong together, and we cannot separate or focus on only one of them without losing a full grasp on the severity of the situation.

From a pragmatic point of view, as humans, we have the task of integrating our various views of ourselves and the world and 'find a meaningful orientation in life. Finding a meaningful orientation is not . . . a matter of finding a set of doctrines to live by, although it certainly includes having views; it is much more a matter of developing a *sensibility*.'[27] An orientation not based on how we are connected with the environment and depends on the ecology of which we are part falls short of the task required. Therefore, religious symbols are insufficient if they only address humans' place in the world without making explicit our interdependence and intra-dependence with the non-human life and the other ecological conditions for life. Only against this backdrop is it possible to develop, shape and be shaped by religious symbols that contribute to transformation in the right direction and find transformative practices that counter the harmful and destructive developments in the present.

The emphasis on symbolic practices as producing orientation, transformation and engagement is not anti-intellectual because these need to be related continuously to practices of reflection and probing of consequences. However, as should be clear from the aforementioned, religious symbols that address the present climate crisis must avoid three pitfalls: (A) It must avoid suggesting a

---

25. See Ulf Zackariasson, 'Religious Agency as Vehicle and Source of Critique', in *The Reformation of Philosophy*, ed. Marius Timmann Mjaaland (Tübingen: Mohr Siebeck, 2020), 216. The notion *paradigmatic responses* is from Douglas James Davies, *Emotion, Identity, and Religion: Hope, Reciprocity, and Otherness* (Oxford: Oxford University Press, 2011).

26. Zackariasson, 'Religious Agency as Vehicle and Source of Critique', 216. My italics.

27. Putnam, here quoted after Richard J. Bernstein, *The Pragmatic Turn* (Cambridge; Malden, MA: Polity, 2010), 153.

generic 'God's eye view'-approach that does not start with the problems at hand (as, e.g. when one speaks theologically and abstractly about the climate crisis as the consequence of human sin – period). (B) It must avoid a 'spectator approach' to the world and the environment. Instead, it needs to underscore the inter- and interrelatedness, dependence, relationality and vulnerability of everything that is alive. (C) It must avoid a fact-value-distinction that makes the paradigmatic objectifying and control-oriented 'scientific' approach to the climate crisis one in which sensibility to all dimensions of the crisis is downplayed. We must avoid neglecting how the scientific approach itself is based on specific concerns and values. Our engagement must be based on rich experience and consider all relevant elements.

I want to emphasize the point about rich experience and its significance for the workings of our symbols by pointing to how the modern lifeworld has, in fact, contributed to the loss of chances to access these experiences due to urbanization and technology. A.J. Vetlesen describes what is taking place and the critical consequences of it:

> [T]he entire experiential domain of cross-species relations, with all their manifestations of otherness, of difference and variation, fades into oblivion, so that encounters and interaction with *others* are limited almost exclusively to human as opposed to, and to the detriment of, nonhuman others. The result is a tremendous loss of experiential diversity, inseparable from the twin-losses of cultural and biological diversity. In this situation, the supposedly unique human capacity of narration [. . .] is eclipsed by another, one perhaps both more definitively uniquely human and easier than ever before to fall prey to: the capacity for denial, as in refusing the truth about the conditions of life upheld in cross-species relations.[28]

Hence, the experiential context of symbols proves to be of utmost significance for how they work. Symbols are more than cognitive vehicles. They manifest our relationship with the world and shape it, as well.[29] This point is, of course, relevant with respect to the climate crisis: if 'nature' as a concept is one by which we separate ourselves from the environment and distinguish nature from culture, humans from 'the rest of life' or so on, to start with the concept nature may not be able to lead our engagement in the right direction. However, a theological notion such as 'creation' can encompass the intra-action and interconnectedness, the embeddedness of humans in the environment, and the interrelation between nature and culture, by addressing all these features as related to and depending

---

28. Vetlesen, *Cosmologies of the Anthropocene: Panpsychism, Animism, and the Limits of Posthumanism*, 170.
29. Consequently, the theory about symbols presented here meets the challenge of Marx' in his Theses on Feuerbach, which also emphasizes the importance of practice. See https://www.marxists.org/archive/marx-/works/1845/theses/theses.htm

on God's creativity. The reason for pointing to this here is motivated by Tillich's idea about symbols as participation above. As participating in practices that open up to chances for life, love and hope in future generations, we are not only dealing with nature, but we are participating in God's continuous work of allowing creation to flourish. Shaped by imagination, sensibility and awareness of interdependence, symbolic practices that enable humans to participate in God's creation contribute to a deeper and broader practice-based understanding than the practices that understand the climate crisis mainly from the point of view of instrumental reason. What we do then not only implies that salvation is the overcoming of wrongness, but a participation in the reality of salvation that is enabled by our passivity and activity as a response to God's gifts and primordial activity.

Symbols mediate, constitute and engage embodied human experience

As argued, symbols shape our experience, and they can open up to new and different experiences of the world. They condition our agency, and they result from our interpretative activity – as we need to interpret symbols as something to have them serve their function.

Symbols relate us to different realms of human life, and they may serve the purpose of allowing reality to be richer and more nuanced than it would be without them. Obviously, this is the case when we consider the different realms of experience to which symbols are related. As humans, we participate in the *natural* realm, where biological and physical conditions of life are present and influence us, independent of our cognition and decisions. Moreover, we partake in the *social* realm, where communication and interaction through language and symbols are crucial for shaping a common world in which we depend on cognitive understanding and the skills needed for it. Each of us also has an *inner* realm of experience, which consists of our personal experiences, emotions, desires, memories, traumas and hopes – the psychological elements that partly shape us and our experiences of others, and partly are something we can work on in order to reshape our experience of the world, ourselves, and of others. Finally, we have a spiritual or mystical realm that consists of experiences beyond our cognitive grasp, which occurs as disturbing, surprising, puzzling, suggesting that there is more to life than what can be determined by human agency.[30]

My point here is simply to suggest that the recognition that all these realms interact and shape our experience of the world is of utmost importance for understanding the role of symbols – and why we need to address the symbol deficit in the Christian tradition when it comes to dealing with the climate crisis. We can

---

30. I have developed the hermeneutical relevance of these different realms of experience somewhat further in Jan-Olav Henriksen, *Life, Love, and Hope: God and Human Experience* (Grand Rapids, MI: William B. Eerdmans Publishing Company, 2014), 35ff.

illustrate this by considering what happens if we reduce our understanding of the world to only one of these realms. If we restrict our understanding of the world to what happens in the natural world, we lose sight of how the present situation is caused not only by causations in the natural realm but by human actions and priorities that are in no means 'natural' or necessary. The Anthropocene, therefore, calls for a more comprehensive understanding of the interaction than one simply expressed in, for example, the interpretation of the natural sciences. We also need an understanding of what shapes human societies and why they prioritize what they do. On the other hand, if we understand the climate crisis only from the point of view of human sinfulness, we lose sight of how societal priorities, specific understandings of nature and stewardship of nature (cf. Lynn White, above) determine human action. Hence, a reduction to either a mere scientific or a mere spiritual/theological interpretation of the situation will not suffice.

In the previous part, I have suggested some of the elements in the natural and the theological realm that may contribute to the crisis (nature as other, or left as an object for a sovereign God to deal with). In the following, I will develop some of the conditions in the inner realm and the biological realm that we also need to be aware of, and may employ, on our quest for more adequate, constructive symbolic practices that can counter the climate crisis.

Perspectives from evolutionary theory

In his seminal book *The Symbolic Species*, Terrence Deacon writes:

> Though we share the same earth with millions of kinds of living creatures, we also live in a world that no other species has access to. We inhabit a world full of abstractions, impossibilities, and paradoxes. We alone brood about what didn't happen, and spend a large part of each day musing about the way things could have been if events had transpired differently. And we alone ponder what it will be like not to be.[31]

Our ability to do what Deacon describes here depends on our capacity for using symbols. Symbols shape our way of life and the ways we experience the world, and the experiential realms described earlier. For Deacon, language is an outward expression of the mode of thought that comes to the fore in symbolic expression, and the capacity of this type of expression allows us to live in a virtual world. It is a specific human capacity that no other species have. Symbolic thought, writes Deacon, does not come as built innately into humans but develops when we are internalizing the symbolic process that underlies language. Humans are the only species that have acquired the capacity for symbolic thinking, and therefore we

---

31. Terrence William Deacon, *The Symbolic Species: The Co-Evolution of Language and the Brain*, 1st edition (New York: W.W. Norton, 1997), 21f.

are also the only species that can think about the world as we do.[32] Our symbolic abilities help us to recode experiences – a point of main interest in my context here, when I stress that experience can be understood and interpreted in diverse ways. They also guide the formation of skills and habits[33], which are features important for human cooperation, for the development of ritual, and in turn, for morality.

One important inference follows: we are not determined simply by our biological or historical past. Instead, we may enter different symbolic universes that allow for specific types of experience that may be life-changing. Symbols can change lives. This point also applies to religious symbols. The ways we use language represent not only objects and immediate situations but relationships and events, as well as abstractions. Deacon points to how our mode of using language 'offers a means for generating an essentially infinite variety of novel representations, and an unprecedented inferential engine for predicting events, organizing memories, and planning behaviors.'[34]

Accordingly, the role of religion in human life cannot be identified with a specific doctrine, world view, or just a way of interpreting things that happen. Religion should rather be understood as a mode of being in the world, mediated and shaped by different types of symbolic activity. This symbolic activity comes to the fore in narratives, practices, concepts, symbols, different ways of organizing social groups and so on. Therefore, we cannot understand religion without having a grasp on what is specific for human beings in terms of employing symbols, and we would not have religion had it not been for this latter capacity. Following Deacon, it further means that language in the course of evolution has become its own prime mover and that the evolution of language has triggered the evolution of the human brain – which, in turn, has led to the evolution of even greater language complexity.[35]

Deacon holds that because symbols enable us to live in a world that is not merely constituted by our immediate experiences, we can have experiences that no other species have. We live in 'a world of rules of conduct, beliefs about our stories, and hopes and fear about imagined futures.'[36] Furthermore, 'This world is governed by principles different from any that have selected for neural circuit design in the past eons of evolution.'[37] We are also able to assume that there are purposes behind what other people do to us. And, because we expect to find purpose, we

---

32. Ibid., 22. For an appropriation of Deacon's work within the context of a Peircean-shaped systematic theology and theological anthropology, cf. Andrew Robinson, *God and the World of Signs: Trinity, Evolution, and the Metaphysical Semiotics of C. S. Peirce*, Philosophical Studies in Science and Religion (Leiden; Boston: Brill, 2010), especially 147ff.

33. Deacon, *The Symbolic Species: The Co-Evolution of Language and the Brain*, 423.
34. Ibid., 22.
35. Ibid., 44.
36. Ibid., 423.
37. Ibid.

can ascribe purpose to events that as such do not have any observable purpose. In its fundamental religious mode, this feature leads to seeing all that happens 'as signs and symbols of an all-knowing consciousness at work' – or, as Deacon also says, the entire universe has become a symbol.[38] When the entire world becomes a symbol, we are at the root of religion.

To live by metaphors

In this section, I will develop an understanding of metaphors in light of the basic capacity to develop and employ symbols as described earlier. Metaphors are a subgroup of symbols. Although the following analysis focuses on metaphors as part of language, my concern is different: I want to explore *the extent to which we can see actions and practices as metaphorical expressions of that which is not immediately obvious in them, namely their relevance for the future flourishing of the planet.*

Fundamental features of metaphors relevant for understanding them in the context of the present book are articulated in Paul Ricoeur's seminal *The Rule of Metaphor*.[39] In his view, which I will only touch upon briefly here, metaphors not only revive our perception of the world. They have the capacity to make us aware of our ability for seeing the world anew. Thus, metaphors produce meaning and enable the discovery of a different understanding of the world. Hence, in some respect, a metaphor mediates the experiences of the world in which the subject takes part, as Neville intimated was generally the case with symbols. Moreover, metaphors typically say more than one thing simultaneously; they are the product of sentences, not the result of substituting one word for another. Thus, they belong in a context and a narrative. They allow for the possibility of a redescription of reality, and among these are, of course, religious ones.

In their work on how metaphors rely on human experience and permeate our understanding of the world and our language, Lakoff and Johnson find that 'metaphor is pervasive in everyday life, not just in language but in thought and action'.[40] Accordingly, they argue that 'Our ordinary conceptual system, in terms of which we both think and act, is fundamentally metaphorical in nature'.[41]

In certain respects, what Lakoff and Johnson say about metaphors also applies to symbols. Whereas symbols allow for something to have a meaning in terms of representing something that is not immediately present but which we nevertheless can partake in by employing the symbol, a metaphor is constituted by how one

---

38. Ibid., 435.

39. Paul Ricoeur et al., *The Rule of Metaphor: Multi-Disciplinary Studies of the Creation of Meaning in Language* (London: Routledge & Kegan Paul, 1978).

40. George Lakoff and Mark Johnson, *Metaphors We Live By* (Chicago: University of Chicago Press, 2003), 3.

41. Ibid.

applies one feature to another in a non-literal way. My concern here is about the extent to which we can understand specific human actions and practices metaphorically, that is, as guided and inspired by features and practices that they usually are not connected with. To understand that what I do as a consumer is leading me 'on the road to hell' is one example. Another example would be understanding myself and my actions 'as pregnant with the future conditions for the flourishing of planetary life'. To understand myself metaphorically in this way may open me up to practices and actions that express concern for the future of life in a time of ecological collapse.

Metaphors and symbols are, as said, constituted by how they refer to something else in some respect. They establish a connection between two different elements, of which at least one is related to our experience. Metaphors are also related to and based on experience – often experiences of the immediate kind and with embodied character. 'The essence of metaphor is understanding and experiencing one kind of thing in terms of another.'[42] Thus, both symbols and metaphors reveal the meanings the world holds for us. What they help us detect is related to all realms of human experience, not just our cognitive abilities:

> The concepts that govern our thought are not just matters of the intellect. They also govern our everyday functioning, down to the most mundane details. Our concepts structure what we perceive, how we get around in the world, and how we relate to other people. Our conceptual system thus plays a central role in defining our everyday realities. If we are right in suggesting that our conceptual system is largely metaphorical, then the way we think, what we experience, and what we do every day is very much a matter of metaphor.[43]

We can illustrate this rootedness in embodied experience by way of two of the main concepts I use in the overall argument of this book. I speak of symbolic practices as practices of orientation and as practices of transformation. Orientation means to place oneself in a specific place and in a certain position with reference to some objects and relations. The term 'Orient' derives from the Latin *oriens* meaning 'east' and, hence, names 'the proper direction', which meant turning towards the east or where the sun rises (*oriens* stems from *orior* which means 'to rise'). Thus, traditionally when I orient myself, I turn towards the east. But when I engage in practices of orientation, it means that I situate myself and my actions towards that which shapes my orientation: in this case, the climate crisis and my concern about its consequences for life on earth.[44] Similarly, with regard to transformation:

---

42. Ibid., 5.
43. Ibid., 3.
44. Cf. ibid.: 'Just as the basic experiences of human spatial orientations give rise to orientational metaphors, so our experiences with physical objects (especially our own bodies) provide the basis for an extraordinarily wide variety of ontological metaphors, that is, ways of viewing events, activities, ideas, etc., as entities and substances.'

transformation means, literally, a change in shape. But it is not a change in shape we speak about when we speak about transformative practices, but changes in our mode of being or in the situation that is present with the climate crisis, its conditions and its consequences.

The experiential and embodied basis of metaphors is a crucial element in the overall argument of this book. From a metaphorical point of view, when I claim that we can consider our actions as being pregnant with the future, it refers to an experience that only pregnant women have first-hand. But as a metaphorical symbol, this claim can provide us with another means for understanding our role, action and practices concerning the future. Due to our skills in using metaphors and our communicative abilities, we can figure out what it means for the way we carry our bodies, perform our agency, consider the life with which we are intimately connected and so on. Thus, our actions may also take on some symbolic meaning if we understand them based on this metaphor. For, we not only bear the future under our hearts metaphorically but also relate to and participate in this future no matter how we act.

As Lakoff and Johnson regularly remind us, our bodies are important starting points for our metaphorically based conceptual structuring of the world and our experience. They are the very place or space from which all experience is construed. It has a profound consequence because it means that

> what we call 'direct physical experience' is never merely a matter of having a body of a certain sort; rather, every experience takes place within a vast background of cultural presuppositions. It can be misleading, therefore, to speak of direct physical experience as though there were some core of immediate experience we then 'interpret' in terms of our conceptual system. Cultural assumptions, values, and attitudes are not a conceptual overlay which we may or may not place upon experience as we choose. It would be more correct to say that all experience is cultural through and through, that our experience our world in such a way that our culture is already present in the very experience itself.[45]

Hence, we can identify substantial arguments for problematizing the assumption that humans can have an objective and detached relationship with reality. Because all language is shot through with metaphors, it highlights and makes certain aspects of our experience coherent. In fact, sometimes a 'given metaphor may be the only way to highlight and coherently organize exactly those aspects of our experience.'[46] Moreover, as they may create realities for us (especially social realities), metaphors also guide future action. 'This will, in turn, reinforce the power of the metaphor to make experience coherent.'[47] Lakoff and Johnson conclude their rejection of objectivism as follows:

---

45. Lakoff and Johnson, *Metaphors We Live By*, 57.
46. Ibid., 156.
47. Ibid.

> What objectivism misses is the fact that understanding, and therefore truth, is necessarily relative to our cultural conceptual systems and that it cannot be framed in any absolute or neutral conceptual system. Objectivism also misses the fact that human conceptual systems are metaphorical in nature and involve an imaginative understanding of one kind of thing in terms of another. What subjectivism specifically misses is that our understanding, even our most imaginative understanding, is given in terms of a conceptual system that is grounded in successful functioning in our physical and cultural environments. It also misses the fact that metaphorical understanding involves metaphorical entailment, which is an imaginative form of rationality.[48]

As we saw in our analysis of Neville's understanding of symbols, symbols always point to something *in some respect*. This is also the case with metaphors. Lakoff and Johnson write on this topic:

> New metaphors, like conventional metaphors, can have the power to define reality. They do this through a coherent network of entailments that highlight some features of reality and hide others. The acceptance of the metaphor forces us to focus only on those aspects of our experience that it highlights, leads us to view the entailments of the metaphor as being true. Such 'truths' may be true, of course, only relative to the reality defined by the metaphor.[49]

Metaphors are thus intimately linked to human action and their relevance, or truth cannot be assessed apart from how they lead to appropriate action. 'In most cases, what is at issue is not the truth or falsity of a metaphor but the perceptions and inferences that follow from it and the actions that are sanctioned by it.'[50] Thus, all realms of human life and experience are defined in terms of metaphors, and we 'proceed to act on the basis of the metaphors. We draw inferences, set make commitments, and execute plans, all on the basis of how we in part structure our experience, consciously and unconsciously, by means of metaphor.'[51] Moreover, it means that 'truth is relative to our conceptual system, which is grounded in, and constantly tested by, our experiences and those of other members of our culture in our daily interactions with other people and with our physical and cultural environments'.[52]

From what I have presented so far, Lakoff and Johnson seem to come close to a pragmatist understanding of metaphor: they underscore its significance for adequate action. This approach also informs their understanding of the truth of a statement (made by metaphor). It is true, 'in a given situation when

---

48. Ibid., 194.
49. Ibid., 157f.
50. Ibid., 158.
51. Ibid.
52. Ibid., 193.

our understanding of the statement fits our understanding of the situation closely enough for our purposes.'[53] Thus, they argue for a position that they call 'experientialist', which shares central concerns with a pragmatist view.

Metaphors unite reason and imagination: 'Reason, at the very least, involves categorization, entailment and inference. Imagination, in one of its many aspects, involves seeing one kind of thing in terms of another kind of thing – what we have called metaphorical thought.'[54] Accordingly, ordinary rationality is imaginative by its very nature. The products of imagination are partially rational in nature and cannot be rejected as irrational but should rather be seen as expanding our potential for experiencing reality. 'Metaphor is one of our most important tools for trying to comprehend partially what cannot be comprehended totally: our feelings, aesthetic experiences, moral practices, and spiritual awareness. These endeavors of the imagination are not devoid of rationality; since they use metaphor, they employ an imaginative rationality.'[55]

The embodied, experiencing, gendered subject thus shapes symbols and orders the world with the help of metaphors. Although Lakoff and Johnson do not address the gendered aspect specifically, I want to point to the fact that what I have suggested earlier as a crucial metaphor draws on experience that is gendered: only women can be pregnant. However, from a metaphorically based self-understanding and practice, all humans can consider themselves pregnant with the future. Because attitudes toward the environment are shaped and embedded in the social world and the practices that constitute it, they cannot be understood apart from the broader narratives and resources shared by a community as a whole. In this context, women's experiences can be of crucial relevance.

Metaphors shape orientation. This point is underscored by cognitive sociologist Eviatar Zerubavel, whom Robin G. Veldman refers to in her work. He argues that the process of learning what to notice and what to ignore in the world around us is fundamentally social, read in the light of how women's experience with pregnancy can inform how we relate to and partake in the environment, his words take on a profound meaning:

> We learn what is relevant and irrelevant from those around us, and we internalize these choices so thoroughly that relevance seems to be intrinsic to the phenomenal world, rather than what it really is: a result (largely) of choices that we are taught to make [. . . S]uch choices are learned through participation in different 'thought communities' – groups such as churches, professions, political movements, or generations – that shape our habits of attention and concern. Thought communities teach us to see the world through a particular lens, one that highlights certain features as salient while de-emphasizing others as unimportant background information. These communities have wide-ranging

---

53. Ibid., 179.
54. Ibid., 193.
55. Ibid.

power when it comes to our social lives, for they teach us to 'assign to objects the same meaning that they have for others around us, to both ignore and remember the same things that they do'.[56]

Veldman uses these insights to argue that the thought communities that establish our mental horizons and determine which issues are worth noticing, 'also establish our moral horizons, determining which issues are worthy of moral reflection'.[57] Women's experiences cannot be ignored when churches represent thought communities that define the specter of relevant actions for the future. Because symbols are always shared and shape how we see the world and act in it, women's experiences are of utmost importance.

Formative psychological elements for symbolically mediated relationships

The fact that we are always entangled with the rest of the world also manifests itself psychologically in ways that may highlight gendered conditions for our relationship with nature. Nancy Chodorow addresses the difference between male and female psychological development that shed light on gendered differences in the development of relational patterns. I argue that they shape how both male and female agents relate to nature and not only to significant others. In a traditional mother–child relationship, the mother is the primary caregiver, and, thus, a girl that grows up remains connected to her primary object. On the other hand, a boy must mobilize himself to break the identification with the mother, and this break usually has an aggressive component. 'Femininity is thus characterized by empathic connection and caring, whereas masculinity is defined by a defensive need for distance and denial of connection. Aggression against women becomes the core of masculine self-definition.'[58]

Considering what these different patterns might entail for a relationship with and interaction with nature: whereas females can transition their bonds to those they are dependent upon in how they relate to and connect to nature in terms of experienced connection and care, males will develop their identity by denying dependence (sometimes even aggressively). Care and connection are not at the top of their list. Chodorow's analysis suggests that human relationships with nature as our origin and fundamental condition take on different shapes due to gender

---

56. Here from Veldman, *The Gospel of Climate Skepticism: Why Evangelical Christians Oppose Action on Climate Change*, 115–16. The work she refers to is Eviatar Zerubavel, *Social Mindscapes: An Invitation to Cognitive Sociology* (Cambridge, MA: Harvard University Press, 1997).

57. Veldman, *The Gospel of Climate Skepticism: Why Evangelical Christians Oppose Action on Climate Change*, 116.

58. James William Jones, *Religion and Psychology in Transition: Psychoanalysis, Feminism, and Theology* (New Haven, CT: Yale University Press, 1996), 10.

differences. Hence, our inner, psychological world determines how we relate to and experience nature. She writes:

> Through their early relationship with their mother, women develop a sense of self continuous with others. . . . The basic feminine self is a self connected with the world. . . . Men develop by contrast a self based more on denial of relation and connection on a more fixed and firmly split and repressed inner self-object world: the basic masculine sense of self is separate.[59]

The denial of connection and the defensive need for distance are, according to Chodorow, sublimated in the masculine search for knowledge as it comes to expression in Western natural science, in parts of the social sciences, and in empirical philosophy. 'This a-relational masculinity, based on the need to dominate and deny women, has become institutionalized in notions of scientific objectivity and technical rationality.'[60]

Building on Chodorow and others, James W. Jones claims that it is not coincidental that Newtonian science, anomic individualism and an atomistic and uncaring vision of nature characterize the modern age.[61] Hence, he contributes to my argument earlier about how the different realms of human experience interact with each other and depend on their symbolic expressions regarding what they can express. The interpenetration between scientific, philosophical, and gender discourse thus allows for a critical approach to traditional notions of objectivity that sees it as intertwined with notions of masculinity – as we have seen that Adorno and Horkheimer also do.

There is, however, more to this than a basis for criticism of (male) ideals of objectivity. The ideal of objectivity is connected to a reductionist approach to reality and to ordering it that is based on dichotomies. Jones argues that both these features are deeply related to gendered conditions. He quotes from Keller and Flax:

> The same sexual division of emotional and intellectual labor that frames the maturation of male and female infants into adult men and women also, and simultaneously, divides the epistemological practices and bodies of knowledge we call science from those we call not-science. Modern science is constituted around a set of exclusionary oppositions in which what is named feminine is excluded and what is excluded – be it feeling, subjectivity, or nature – is named female.[62]

---

59. Nancy Chodorow, *Feminism and Psychoanalytic Theory* (New Haven, CT: Yale University Press, 1989), 184. Here quoted after Jones, *Religion and Psychology in Transition: Psychoanalysis, Feminism, and Theology*, 10.

60. Chodorow, *Feminism and Psychoanalytic Theory*, 184.

61. Jones, *Religion and Psychology in Transition: Psychoanalysis, Feminism, and Theology*, 125.

62. Evelyn Fox Keller and Jane Flax, 'Missing Relations in Psychoanalysis: A Feminist Critique of Traditional and Contemporary Accounts of Analytic Theory and Practice',

We see here the psychological backdrop to what Adorno and Horkheimer described in *Dialectic of Enlightenment*. Hence, the idea of objectivity, being the notion that we can describe nature and reality independent of who we are as psychological subjects, seems to be dealt a severe blow. The search for knowledge, which 'depends on dichotomous reasoning – objective versus subjective, outer versus inner, reason versus emotion', reflects a 'masculine' dynamic of separation that is not shared by all of humanity. To privilege the masculine perspective entails the silencing of essential elements related to care and connection. This silencing also affects the fundamental way women relate to that on which all life depends: beings and ecologies outside dominance and control.

In his discussion of the male and female patterns of psychological development, James Jones points to how the aforementioned account may itself contribute to further dichotomizing and thus be part of the problem. However, one needs not, without further specification, see femininity linked with connection and masculinity linked with separation. The patterns of development are conditioned by the culture in which these identities are formed. Both genders begin life as selves-in-relation, and it is not the case that females must remain dependent, whereas all men become independent. Jones argues that *culture* shapes their development in different directions, respectively as passive or independent: 'What Chodorow and Keller see as essential developmental patterns are, rather, the result of patriarchal culture. The aggressively reductive sciences of modernity may well be the expression of masculine development, but only masculine development as shaped by patriarchal society.'[63] He suggests a more constructive approach that draws on the development of the sensitivity and sensibility suggested in the previous chapter when he writes:

> [A]ggression is often directed at nature (and other human beings) in the form of domination. Perhaps the undermining of the myth of absolute objectivity in contemporary philosophy of science and its replacement by a less traditionally masculine and more mutual metaphor of interaction and interconnection, if introjected into the psyches of scientists and therefore into the deep structure of science itself, might result in a less aggressive and dominance-oriented science.[64]

Gender-sensitive approaches to psychological development reveal that the culturally conditioned symbols by which humans develop, orient themselves

---

in *Hermeneutics and Psychological Theory: Interpretative Perspectives on Personality, Psychotherapy and Psychopathology*, ed. S. B. Messer, L. A. Sass and R. L. Woolfolk (New Brunswick: Rutgers University Press, 1988), 337. It is tempting to remark here that the pragmatist insistence on pluralism and its concomitant rejection of binary dichotomies counter both the features mentioned here.

63. Jones, *Religion and Psychology in Transition: Psychoanalysis, Feminism, and Theology*, 126.

64. Ibid., 127.

and transform their relationships with others and the environment contribute to the upholding of a given, patriarchal society. This symbolic world builds on and depends on reductionistic science. Hence, these symbols continue to express 'the desires of the unconscious, not only in terms of motivation but also in its content and practice, and also reveals that these desires may reflect the different developmental trajectories of boys and girls'.[65] However, against the backdrop of his critical analysis, Jones argues in favour of finding alternative approaches than those modernity has idealized: the 'combination of investigation by detached observation, a motivation to dominate and control nature, and an impersonal model of the universe, all of which serve as sublimations of the need for distance and separation. Men (and women) find such reductionistic methods and images compelling to the extent that their character is fashioned around the same unconscious drive for distance'.[66]

At present, however, we need symbols that can engender relationships other than those of control and separation. Symbols that shape and express participation, inter- and intra-connection are called for. From the point of view of cultural analysis of the inner realm of experience in modern individuals, however, this presents a challenge for Jones. According to him, 'The obsession of the modern age becomes control. And technology has given us the means to act out that obsession'.[67] He continues:

> Psychologically there appears to be a connection between the cultural values of control and detachment and a fear of subjective experience, especially emotional experience. Existing outside the perimeters of reason and often threatening to break down our carefully wrought walls of control, affect appears dangerous, chaotic, or threatening. Often its existence is simply denied.[68]

By giving preference to a symbolic representation of the world based on the physical or natural realm only, which does not allow any interference with emotions or subjective, sensual experience, the relationship with nature is substantially impoverished.

It is easy to illustrate Jones's point here. Some afternoons, after work, I walk in the woods next to our house. It gives me a sensual and embodied experience of silence, rest, emotional calm, participation and connection with the surrounding environment of which I am part. I often meet people who smile and greet me in a way they would not do if we met in the street. These walks in the woods are important elements in my experience of nature and its role in my life. So is sitting by the seaside in the summer evenings. However, such experiences are entirely subjective and not something I can willfully create – instead, I enter into them and

---

65. Ibid.
66. Ibid.
67. Ibid.
68. Ibid., 128.

allow myself to receive them. Contrary to this are the experiences of what Jones, building on Bollas, calls the 'normotic personality'. This personality type

> rejects any intrusions of subjectivity and seeks to become entirely objective, to see himself or herself as an object in a world of objects. The normotic personality collects facts and 'takes refuge in material objects'. . . . They may describe themselves in quasi-mechanical terms, in a discourse purged of subjectivity.[69]

The normotic personality is encouraged by cultural symbols that favour objectivity. But, as anyone might see, this is a person with low capacities for relationships and self-experience. For Jones, whom I use here in order to see the relevance of adequate symbols for guiding good practices towards nature, this personality type is the psychological counterpart to the relationship with nature that we need to find symbolic practices to overcome and develop alternatives to. He writes:

> This refusal of subjectivity in the name of total objectification is readily expressed by a reductionistic science that seeks to collapse the kaleidoscope of human experience into a mechanical system. Here again modern culture reinforces the refusal of subjectivity by propounding theories that reduce subjective experience to mechanical activity and by broadcasting models of the mind as a computer or electrochemical machine. I am not arguing against the usefulness of such metaphors . . . but, rather, asking what psychodynamic forces drive such models and make them attractive. A reductionistic theory which says that consciousness is unreal correlates comfortably with that form of self-experience which, paradoxically, seeks to deny self-experience.[70]

Accordingly, this chapter ends with the following conclusion: The symbols that can help us mediate a relationship with nature require and presuppose that we consider what can be learned from embodied experiences (especially, gendered experiences). Moreover, they require a context of psychological maturation that allows for broad access to experiences of nature in all its concrete and various manifestations. We never experience nature in the abstract. Hence, the embodied and emotional components in symbolic practices should not be underestimated when it comes to developing symbolic practices that can endure and continue to motivate change.

69. Ibid.
70. Ibid., 128–9.

Chapter 7

CONDITIONS FOR AGENCY

A CRITIQUE OF MODERNITY'S DETACHED SUBJECT

This book is not a study of ethics or moral philosophy. That fact notwithstanding, it is nevertheless necessary to address some issues discussed regularly within the context of those disciplines. The topics discussed in this and the next chapter emerge directly or indirectly against the backdrop of previous chapters in this part of the book and in Part I. The following chapters focus on human agency as conditioned by epistemological and morally relevant conditions.

As long as Christian thinking, preaching and theology align with modern ideas about the human being and its concomitant notions about human autonomy and individualism, it will remain impotent when it comes to establishing good and paradigmatic practice for combating climate change. Theology, therefore, finds itself in a precarious situation. On the one hand, it does not want to advocate that Christians retreat to pre-modern practices based on obedience to heteronomous commands imposed without consent or understanding. On the other hand, theology will not want Christians, and others who want to combat the crisis in which we find ourselves, to uncritically adapt to the modern ideal that portrays humans as independent and self-sufficient. The latter ideal is connected closely to ideas about human beings as separated from nature and as being in control over our fundamental life conditions.

This precarious situation for theology should not lead to an impasse about how we understand the conditions for moral agency on contemporary terms. A reconstruction of the conditions for moral agency needs to consider the fundamentally relational character of human life and how we are dependent on and intertwined with nature. We need to overcome ideals about detachment, distance and a mode of rationality that allow us to ignore our emotional responses and sentiments in the face of environmental loss and destruction, species extinction and the rapid changes in habitats for living beings, humans included.

An expanded view of agency and freedom conditions

In the previous chapter, we saw that it is possible to identify a psychological and cultural backdrop for the modern view of rationality as a means to control the marginalized human and the more-than-human world, and as disconnected from emotions or embodied relationships. From a philosophical angle, Charles Taylor has been arguing that the very shape of modern natural science works in tandem with these ideas. His extensive critique of a naturalist approach underscores how this reductionist approach to reality impacts how humans relate to their agency conditions and to nature. He argues that behind 'the understandable prestige of the natural science model, stands an attachment to a certain picture of the agent. This picture is deeply attractive to moderns, both flattering and inspiring. It shows us as capable of achieving a kind of disengagement from our world by objectifying it'.[1] The disengagement has consequences in two directions: On the one hand, it leads to a specific understanding of the human self, and on the other hand it leads to a specific way of viewing nature. Let us start by looking at the latter:

When modern humans objectify nature to control it, the source of all concerns can be found within the human sphere, understood as isolated from that of the environment. It is human purposes and ends that matter – and nature thus becomes 'a neutral environment, within which we can effect the purposes which we determine out of ourselves.'[2]

The challenge is to reshape the concerns that humans have for ecological topics and expand the concerns behind human agency so that not merely isolated human interests are taken into account. It cannot be done simply by adopting a neutral and distanced position. It requires the development and training of sensibilities that overcome human self-perceptions shaped by the ideals of disengagement. As our understanding of what counts as human nature and the environment are closely linked, an alternative must build on seeing ourselves as part of nature and intertwined with it. This approach can provide a venue for developing symbolic practices that contribute to combating climate change. Thus, we can join with Taylor in criticizing the modern ideal of disengagement that defines the modern notion of freedom as 'the ability to act on one's own, without outside interference or subordination to outside authority'.[3] This world view promotes a form of agency that builds on a notion of freedom similar to the one we saw in our earlier reference to Kant – for whom nature must be excluded from the conditions of human agency in order to secure 'true' freedom.

Instead of subscribing to this reductive and impoverished view of human agency, Taylor analyses it as a far more complex phenomenon. Its conditions are dynamic and diverse and relate to all the realms of experience that have been addressed previously. It is shaped by our desires, motives, goals and aspirations. Moreover, it is also shaped by our life history, our memories and our 'social mindscapes'.[4]

1. Charles Taylor, *Human Agency and Language* (Cambridge, UK; New York: Cambridge University Press, 1985), 4.
2. Ibid.
3. Ibid., 5.
4. Cf. the reference to Zerubavel, *Social Mindscapes: An Invitation to Cognitive Sociology*, in Chapter Six.

The latter notion is especially valuable because it points to how the mental space in which we orient ourselves is composed of all these elements, with some more dominating than others. Moreover, the human ability to *evaluate* our desires is a feature that separates humans from other species, and it is, I argue, crucial for understanding human agency when it comes to the climate crisis. It enables us to view our short-term desires in light of our long-term goals – and distinguish between first- and second-order desires.[5] Accordingly, one of our tasks as moral agents is to establish the foundation for such evaluations. The ability to realize that long-term goals may be contrary to our immediate desires is one of the skills required for human agency that adequately addresses the climate crisis.

Concomitantly, the ability to evaluate our desires is linked to self-evaluation – and such evaluation cannot be developed unless we also have developed a self-understanding that entails what matters and what not. Taylor points to how our self-understandings contribute to what kind of meaning things have for us.[6] Thus, the constitution of self-understanding and its resources for self-evaluation provide us with fundamental means for orientation. The resources that shape our identity also orient our lives and sometimes call us to engage in transformation processes. Taylor writes:

> Much of our motivation, our desires, aspirations, evaluation – is not simply given. We give it a formulation in words or images. Indeed, by the fact that we are linguistic animals, our desires and aspirations cannot but be articulated in one way or another. Thus we are not simply moved by psychic forces comparable to such forces as gravity or electromagnetism, which we can see as given in a straightforward way, but rather by psychic 'forces' which are articulated or interpreted in a certain way. These articulations are not simply descriptions, if we mean by this characterizations of a fully independent object, that is, an object that is altered neither in what it is, nor in the degree or manner of its evidence to us by the description.[7]

Because our self-interpretations are partly constitutive of our experience, how we understand ourselves will impact how we view and relate to nature, and, hence, it motivates and shapes our practices. An altered description of our self-interpretation can be inseparable from a change in this motivation. Accordingly, how we understand, relate to and practice our relationship with nature is never given in a mere naturalist fashion that ignores the self's understanding. It means that 'certain modes of experience are not possible without certain self-descriptions. Because of this constitutive relation, our descriptions of our motivations, and our attempts to

---

5. Taylor, *Human Agency and Language*, 15.
6. Cf. ibid., 22.
7. Ibid., 36.

formulate what we hold important, are not simple descriptions in that their objects are not fully independent'.[8]

Taylor argues for an interpretivist approach in which a wide variety of conditions shape our experiences, evaluations and relationships. Moreover, he points to how the elements that shape our identity contribute to how we understand freedom: our freedom is not given with independence, but with the extent to which we can realize that which we consider being valuable. Christian theology has usually understood human freedom as fully realized in love – that is, in a relationship. Without love, there is no freedom. Freedom cannot be realized without a relationship, evaluation about what matters and emotion. The absence of relationships does not constitute freedom; it is realized by participating in that which allows life to flourish. Hence, relationships, and not the individual's isolated capacity for agency, are fundamental for realizing freedom.

One would not consider a mother who is pregnant with a child unfree. Assuming that her pregnancy is voluntary, her relationship with the unborn child is part of how she allows the world to realize new possibilities.[9] She realizes her freedom in this relationship. This example casts another light on how we need an understanding of nature as the other to which we are intrinsically related if we are to realize our freedom. The realization of our freedom is dependent on our relationship with nature and our ability to recognize it as an *Other on whom I depend* and from which I cannot separate myself because we are internally involved with each other.

Although we cannot reduce nature to what we think of it, it is, in our actual experience, determined by our conditions, evaluations, and conceptions. Nature and culture cannot be separated. Eric Nelson underscores this when he writes:

> The natural and biological context of human life is socially-historically configured, and as the material basis of human life and activity that is inevitably more than an image or model, material nature is irreducible to any one social system. It is accessed through language, history, and the sciences while being irreducibly non-identical with its appropriation, interpretation, and explanation through them. If nature was purely a social or ideological construct, it would disappear in its domination by 'spirit,' or the coercive integrating totality of the existing order and the calculations of instrumental rationality, such that a crisis of the environment could not even appear.[10]

Nature presents us with resistance and with elements that cannot be reduced to components determined by our agency. This 'resistance' is part of how we

---

8. Ibid., 37.

9. I will develop this example further in Part III, when I discuss the relevance of Hannah Arendt's notion of natality for our relationship with nature.

10. Nelson, 'Revisiting the Dialectic of Environment: Nature as Ideology and Ethics in Adorno and the Frankfurt School', 124.

understand and experience it, but it also entails that we need to shape our self-understanding accordingly. To take nature into consideration and recognize it as an independent instance on its own account requires another notion of action than we find in Kant and his followers' emphasis on autonomy. Autonomy cannot mean overcoming or separating oneself from any non-human determinative factors. It may still mean that humans, informed by whatever knowledge they have access to, can decide what to do based on the conditions they have themselves appropriated for their action. My point here is that although much of the Enlightenment critique of unquestioned *tradition* as a basis for human practices were justified, this critique also had devastating consequences in its focus on the autonomous and independent individual. It meant the reduction – and even elimination – of conditions that humans need to consider if they are to act with responsibility for future generations and the totality of species on the planet.

Knut Wenzel has suggested another approach to freedom that would fit both humans and nature. It takes into account the need for relating to nature in ways that recognize both its relevance and its standing apart from human interests and concerns. He suggests that it is a mistake to 'found the idea of freedom in agency, capability, or self-consciousness – not in any concept of a sovereign self – but in unavailability'.[11] The German word that Wenzel translated with unavailability – *Unverfügbarkeit* – resonates with words like 'inaccessibility' and 'unattainability'. Hence, it suggests that something is impossible to acquire, manipulate or appropriate. The self is free to the extent that it is unavailable. Wenzel suggests that this entails 'a core momentum of absence, of tranquility constitutive to human subjectivity, a point of indefiniteness or indeterminability, of essential inconceivability'.[12]

Although Wenzel admits that his notion of freedom defined as in the quote here is vague, it has two main advantages nevertheless. Firstly, it resists a definition of the human being that reduces it to a function of natural causes. Human freedom is not determined by our ability to act as a response to causes and reasons alone but also by the fact that we are more than these responses. There also is a transcendental dimension behind our agency that engenders the experience of freedom. Moreover, and secondly, his notion of freedom is able to incorporate an understanding of nature as free to the extent that it is not reduced to a function of human interests. Nature has its own standing and value also apart from the concerns and interests of humans. Although Wenzel does not explicitly conceptualize this notion of freedom with regard to nature, he points to how this notion enables another self-experience, writing: 'Self-experience is joined by an openness to reality as such as well as by the experiential presence of the possibility conditions of one's existence as basal accompaniments of each particular experience. Freedom, conceptualized

---

11. Knut Wenzel, *Negativistic Affirmation – Doing Theology in a Secular World* (University of Oslo Guest Lecture, 2019).

12. Ibid.

in this way, resists any embedment into a comprehensive narration of progress.'[13] In the next section, I will develop this trajectory further.

Overcoming anthropocentric conditions for agency: From Habermas to Vetlesen

Against the backdrop of the aforementioned notion of nature as independent but nevertheless shaped by our concepts and interests in how we experience it, we can enter more deeply into an analysis of how nature and human agency are related. An obvious point of departure is linked to the discussion of Jürgen Habermas's philosophy.

Jürgen Habermas's work on knowledge and human interest elaborates the implicit or unacknowledged interests in different types of knowledge. For him, it is empirical technical knowledge that constitutes the human relationship with nature. It aims at possible control over objectified processes of nature, in accordance with what we have seen previously. Critics claim that this type of knowledge is central to his inability to address the climate crisis issues adequately.[14]

Furthermore, Habermas identifies knowledge related to human practices as hermeneutical knowledge oriented at mutual understanding and communicative action at the social level of reality.[15] This latter type of knowledge he can call *practical*, as it is related to human *Lebenspraxis*.[16] It is based on symbolic interaction, whereas the former is technical and objectifying. However, the two are linked, as 'Knowledge-constitutive interests mediate the natural history of the human species with the logic of its self-formative process. [. . .] But they cannot be employed to reduce this logic to any sort of natural basis'.[17] Hence, it is possible to detect an element in his thinking that aligns with how different capacities are involved in the realization of the specific human mode of living in the world. Like Taylor, he will resist attempts to reduce human agency to natural conditions only. This point is foregrounded strongly in the following quote:

> I term *interests* the basic orientations rooted in specific fundamental conditions of the possible reproduction and self-constitution of the human species, namely *work* and *interaction*. Hence these basic orientations do not aim at the gratification of immediate empirical needs but at the solution of system problems

13. Ibid.
14. 'For Habermas, our relation to nature, insofar as nature is taken as an object of cognition, can only be one of *instrumental* control'. J. Whitebook, 'The Problem of Nature in Habermas', *Telos* 1979, no. 40 (1979): 55.
15. Cf. Jürgen Habermas, *Knowledge and Human Interests*, 2nd edition (London: Heinemann, 1978).
16. Ibid., 194.
17. Ibid., 196.

in general. [. . .] Knowledge-constitutive interests can be defined exclusively as a function of the objectively constituted problems of the preservation of life that has been solved by the cultural form of existence as such. [. . .] [T]he knowledge-constitutive interest rooted in the conditions of the existence of work and interaction cannot be comprehended in the biological frame of reference of reproduction and the preservation of the species.[18]

As becomes apparent in this quote, the *social level of reality* is at the centre of Habermas's thought – and there are, admittedly, good reasons for it. However, this prioritizing of the intra-human sphere as the determinative sphere for human action has its cost. It leaves non-human nature out of the picture. The cost is increased further when Habermas identifies another knowledge-constitutive interest, namely the *emancipatory* interest. This type of interest is constitutive for the act of reflection that changes a life and reorients human action or society.[19] It is this type of reflection that can disclose that 'What may appear as naked survival is always in its roots a historical phenomenon. For it is subject to the criterion of what a society intends for itself as a good life.'[20] Accordingly, Habermas holds that knowledge equally serves as an instrument for and transcends mere self-preservation.

Habermas is willing to acknowledge how the struggle for self-preservation is part of human life. However, he nevertheless emphasizes that humans' historical and social life-form makes it essential to stress the communicative and emancipatory interests as the most relevant for human self-understanding and moral motivation. This prioritizing is echoed in how he sees moral motivation as based on intra-human communication. There are no resources for developing a sensibility for nature as something else than objectified and as a natural resource for commodification and exploitation in his thinking. As Whitebook writes, 'While providing a superior theoretical grounding for critical theory, Habermas's transcendentalism necessarily precludes any reconciliation with nature.'[21] This point is addressed in many critics, and recently in Arne Johan Vetlesen's critique of Habermas, to which we now turn.

Vetlesen's critique of Habermas's position in *The Denial of Nature* (2015)[22] claims that Habermas is unable to address or conceptualize nature as 'a natural other' that should affect our reasoning. Nature is always addressed as an object for a technical interest only. According to Vetlesen, Habermas's theoretical approach (and the inherent practices it entails) displays poverty on different levels, be it epistemically, evaluatively and conceptually, because 'within its framework, the 'other' is always

18. Ibid., 196.
19. Cf. Ibid., 212.
20. Ibid., 313.
21. Whitebook, 'The Problem of Nature in Habermas', 41.
22. Vetlesen, *The Denial of Nature: Environmental Philosophy in the Era of Global Capitalism*.

a social other, never a natural other, always another human person, not a tree or a bird or a river'.[23] Vetlesen, like Adorno and Horkheimer, sees the entanglement of nature and society as underdeveloped in Habermas's thinking. The fact that we cannot anymore relate to nature in ways that are recognized as valid for orientation insofar as these express our sensibilities for nature's effect on us to be immediate, intuitive or personal, Vetlesen sees as part of the cultural de-learning that takes place within a Western approach to engagement with nature. '[T]he technical cognitive interest continues to set the context and define the framework for scientific knowledge',[24] and Habermas understands this as the only appropriate stance to nature.[25] Thereby, he underestimates the relational and interdependent dimension in human interaction with and engagement with nature.[26] As a warrant for the one-sidedness of Habermas's position, Vetlesen quotes from *Theorie des kommunikativen Handelns*:

> While we can indeed adopt a performative attitude to external nature, enter into communicative relations with it, have aesthetic experience and feelings analogous to morality with respect to it, there is for *this* domain of reality only one *theoretically fruitful* attitude, namely the objectivating attitude of the natural-scientific, experimenting observer[27]

On his part, Vetlesen underscores the relational aspect. In doing so, he allows a broader, more experiential and multilayered approach to nature to be foregrounded. Vetlesen backs this alternative up by arguing that

> The more intensely one is involved in the relationships – in a multi-sensuous, performative attitude, as distinct from an objectivating and detached one – the more precise, nuanced and rich becomes the knowledge – knowledge not only about trees in general or birds in general but eminently *in situ* knowledge to be accessed and attained *here* and *now*, since *about* that particular tree or bird, living here, not on its own but as part of that particular habitat, landscape, ecosystem.[28]

Vetlesen's critique implies that Habermas's limited understanding of the constitutive elements in a human sensibility for nature precludes him from identifying the roots of the cultural devastation in the Western world, as this comes to expression in the ecological crisis.[29] In short, Habermas's position is too anthropocentric and is 'Championing the epistemic superiority of abstraction over

---

23. Ibid., 75.
24. Ibid., 77.
25. Ibid.
26. Ibid., 77, cf. 78.
27. Ibid., 77. The reference is to Habermas's *Theorie des kommunikativen Handelns* (1982), 243f.
28. Ibid., 79.
29. Cf. Ibid., 87.

first-hand experience'.³⁰ The alternative is to advance a different self-perception and perception of the world that engenders another motivation for moral agency. Thus, Vetlesen argues for a more substantial recognition of the interdependence and relation between human beings and nature. He also argues for a sensibility regarding nature's impact or effect on our being in the world that more radically places humans within the framework or nature as valuable in itself, not only for us as we stand over against it. Hence, he is in full consonance with the position I have suggested so far.

One way of developing a new and stronger sensibility for nature that can help us become more aware of all elements related to the climate crisis is to see *the world as our extended body, and concomitantly, to treat the natural world as we would take care of and treat our own body in order to let it flourish.*³¹ It will allow for a new sensibility for nature deeply connected to our mode of embodied being-in-the-world *as both social and natural beings*. Furthermore, this would enable a stronger emphasis on the common efforts necessary to overcome this crisis that affects all dimensions of reality, not only the social and political dimensions.

It is as *embodied* beings that humans engage in practices of orientation and transformation throughout life. In terms of *orientation*, we need to develop a sensitivity to who we are and what befalls us at an embodied level as well as at a cognitive one: we must consider access to pure water and clean air, to temperature and dangers in the environment, because such elements directly influence our life conditions– and thinking. Furthermore, when we engage in transformation practices, these are related to what we may consider necessary to improve such conditions. The reflective practices for orientation and transformation that cares for the embodied human as internally related to the rest of nature build on knowledge, experience and sensibilities about the natural world. These practices produce wisdom about the capacities we have for agency and for what we can do and not do and go beyond what can be expressed in the terms provided by (natural) science.

Ethical reflection is part of the wisdom necessary. It is contextually based reflection about the relational and interdependent human being that aims to identify wise ways of acting – and can never be about mere empirical facts or generic and/or universal principles for human agency. Aristotle's notion of wisdom may be a point here: in his *Nichomachean Ethics*, he points to how the wise man is the one who can deliberate what is good and expedient for the good life in general, and not only for this or that particular aspect. He also points to the difference between knowledge and practical wisdom. Nevertheless, we need to go beyond Aristotle, or rather, to relate his definition to our current situation. Thus, when Aristotle says that 'Practical wisdom, then, must be a reasoned and true

---

30. Ibid., 93.
31. This is a point I have developed further in several earlier contributions, for example in Jan-Olav Henriksen, 'Body, Nature and Norm', *Irish Theological Quarterly* 55, no. 4 (1989).

state of capacity to act with regard to human goods',[32] we now know that human goods are not separated from what is good for the totality of the ecosystem we call Earth. This point can be elaborated further by a point that Whitebook identifies in Habermas. Whitebook writes:

> Returning to Habermas, if the entire realm of human cognition can be exhaustively subdivided, as he claims, in terms of the three knowledge-constitutive interests- instrumental, communicative, and emancipatory – then our question becomes: where are the biological sciences to be located within his scheme? We know that Habermas emphatically denies the possibility of conceptualizing nature – presumably including living nature – under the categories of communicative rationality: 'Nature does not conform to the categories under which the subject can conform to the understanding of another subject on the basis of reciprocal recognition under the categories that are binding on both of them.' If the only two possible alternatives available in this case are communicative and instrumental rationality, and if the domain of communicative rationality is exclusively reserved for speaking subjects, then it follows that the biological sciences must be assigned to the domain of instrumental rationality. Our only possible cognitive relation to other living beings in this scheme is one transcendentally oriented to technical domination.[33]

At this point, an approach that recognizes in principle that the human being is an animal, and that the animalistic nature of humanity (its biological constitution) may be affected by its environment presents itself as a correction to the Habermasian approach, precisely because it allows for such influence. Although not all of nature is able to communicate through language, a new sensibility for nature and nature's condition can contribute to shaping humanity's understanding of itself and the environment. Under such conditions, the active elements that shape human agency may develop beyond what can be articulated in communicative action among humans alone. It may entail a relation with nature in ways parallel to and in accordance with how humans relate to their own embodied character and the conditions for this embodiment.

Finally, to understand how humans with a natural dimension are affected by the climate crisis points towards an understanding of the individual and the *social* self as porous, hence vulnerable, and therefore with capabilities for developing stronger sensibilities for nature in general. The aforementioned suggests a human mode of being in the world that is more porous and not so strongly buffered against (sensual) influences from nature as has been the ideal of the modern, secular Western person.[34] A self-perception that acknowledges this porosity will have

---

32. *Nichomachean Ethics* VI, 5, 1140b.

33. Whitebook, 'The Problem of Nature in Habermas', 59. The quote in the quote is from Habermas, *Knowledge and Human Interests*, 33.

34. Cf. Charles Taylor, 'Buffered and Porous Selves', *The Immanent Frame*, 2008.

not easily allow short-term economic interests to be prioritized ahead of long-term interests for the best environmental conditions for all of the embodied and vulnerable nature, humankind included. A self-perception where one sees nature as the extended body of humans and humans as intertwined with and conditioned by nature implies a stronger recognition of how nature influences concrete human beings' health. It also entails a stronger affirmation of how the human agency may impact vulnerable living species other than humans, but for which humans are responsible.

In an extensive analysis of Vetlesen's contribution, Odin Lysaker[35] has pointed to further elements that are worth pondering in the present context because they allow us to see more of the conditions that shape and give content to human agency and practices, whereas simultaneously also connecting humans intimately with the rest of nature.

Vetlesen points to how human susceptibility allows us to see that not only humans have moral standing. We can be affected in a 'very wide sense' – and not only by humans.[36] This also has consequences for how we consider our *moral agency*. Vetlesen holds that

> although an animal, for example, cannot be a moral agent in the sense here defined, an *animal* can be, and often is, directly affected by – and on that account can be, and often is an addressee of – an action of ours. Hence, beings that are not moral agents may still be moral addressees; the former is not required for the latter. An animal can be harmed, can be hurt, can suffer, and it can for that very reason be an object of unjust and immoral conduct. I therefore grant moral status to animals, to nonhuman beings, on account of their capacity for suffering, which I see as a sufficient condition for moral status.[37]

Lysaker underscores how Vetlesen defines non-human beings as moral addressees due to their capacity to indirectly become 'affected' by and hence 'suffering' from humans' actions.[38] Hence, the precondition of possible affectedness is sufficient to broaden moral concern that guides human agency. This approach allows for a non-anthropocentric version of preconditions for agency. Vetlesen writes:

---

35. See Odin Lysaker, 'Ecological Love: Reflections on Morality's Existential Preconditions', in *Between Closeness and Evil: A Festschrift for Arne Johan Vetlesen*, ed. Odin Lysaker (Oslo: Scandinavian Academic Press, 2020). I owe much of the following presentation to Lysaker's work.

36. Cf. Arne Johan Vetlesen, *Perception, Empathy, and Judgement: An Inquiry into the Preconditions of Moral Performance* (University Park, PA: Pennsylvania State University Press, 1994), 3, 5.

37. Ibid., 169.

38. Lysaker, 'Ecological Love: Reflections on Morality's Existential Preconditions', 72.

> [a] *cross-species* empathy (. . .) needs (. . .) to be more precisely linked with the impact of what I call *the 'negatives'* of contemporary culture, namely *limits* of various sorts and *dependency, vulnerability*, and *death* in particular [. . .][C]ontemporary culture tends to present the givens of human existence as wholly unwelcome, as conditions to be fought against and actively resisted, in what amounts to a cultural revolt against their impact, collectively as well as individually. The acceptance of limits that is at the heart of emotional maturity is flatly contradicted, and clinically frustrated, by the pride of place given in an 'individualized society' (. . .) to autonomy over other-directed concern, control over exposure to suffering and death, independence over vulnerability and loss.[39]

Lysaker furthermore points to the dynamic between vulnerability and dependency, which Vetlesen views as preconditions for moral agency, and elaborates on how these can be expanded to cover more than intra-human relationships. At this point, we can consider the Earth and human mothers to be in similar situations:

> The 'mother' of all holding environments, providing a sense of safety, of being looked after, held and protected, of being loved and accepted even though one is capable of experiencing and even acting upon feelings of hatred and rage, envy and jealousy, is the Earth, containing all the particular and local mothers. (. . .) [T]he harm inflicted on the Earth exhibits the same structure and dynamics as that inflicted by the human infant at his or her mother. Being dependent, having to face the vulnerability at the hands of the one – co-human or non-human (nature) – upon whom one is dependent for one's wellbeing and survival, has never been easy, never easily accepted. Our existence is borne – held – not only by inter-human (social) relationships and bonds, not only by our internal but also by our (for lack of a better word) external environment. In this sense, 'an ecologically healthy relatedness to our nonhuman environment is essential to the development and maintenance of our sense of being human.'[40]

One need not be a moral agent to be a moral subject, Vetlesen holds.[41] As a consequence of this position, he can develop a more detailed description of the moral status or value of the non-human nature than what we have seen that Habermas is willing to:

> All living beings have an indisputable and objective interest in going on doing so, and thus, in each individual case, they embody a stance of non-indifference, non-neutrality, with respect to the difference between life and death, being and

---

39. Vetlesen, *The Denial of Nature: Environmental Philosophy in the Era of Global Capitalism*, 11.
40. Ibid., 13.
41. Ibid., 106f.

not-being: the former is better than, is superior to, the latter. It is so as a matter of fact, and this fact is the objective fact of value: that life, that being is the valued state. The fact of this value is not imposed from without, is not the product of projection or attribution from some external source or point of view. Instead, it resides in the dimension of being – *in re* – as one of its essential properties.[42]

It is the fact that matters of life and death, being and non-being, cannot be regarded merely from the point of view of human interests that makes Vetlesen's position stand out as a clear alternative to an anthropocentric and reductionist view. The recognition of value in other living beings calls for a moral response and for developing the capacity for responsiveness. Hence, Vetlesen comes close to elements in virtue ethics when he speaks of protection-intending respect as 'the appropriate response to the value of the various entities the unfolding world consists of. Value as met upon in outer reality issues a demand on us as human agents to act so as to observe what the protection of that value requires, value being often a precarious quality, a quality whose safeguarding the entity in question may not itself be capable of securing.'[43] He underscores that the binding moral call here stems from '*the world my care responds to* – the world to which *care is the appropriate response*', and not from human consciousness of reasoning.[44] Thus, the fact that we respond to the world entails an element of passivity that is prior to our moral agency, as this response is determined by our ability to become affected, our susceptibility. Humans are not the source of value – we have grown out of and are the result of a valuable environment that consists of 'nonhuman entities, not only in animals but in trees and plants, entities each of which pursues, in their species-specific manner, a good of their own'.[45]

Vetlesen also makes a point that will be taken up later in the discussion about the world as a gift, present prior to human agency. Our 'sheer power in being able to undercut, endanger, and perhaps eventually all-out destroy value in the world that we are part of does not mean that we are the creators – origin, source – of the value destroyed. We destroy what is given independently of us, what has historically evolved prior to us, a quality whose true character is that of a gift we should treat with gratitude and awe, since as a species we owe our existence to the flourishing of a host of other species and life forms.'[46] These words from the philosopher could just as well have been articulated by a theologian who shares his concerns.

---

42. Vetlesen, *Cosmologies of the Anthropocene: Panpsychism, Animism, and the Limits of Posthumanism*, 51f.
43. Ibid., 52.
44. Ibid.
45. Ibid.
46. Ibid.

Preliminary concluding reflections

The reflections in this chapter lead to the following concluding points:

1. As responsible agents, the only way to deal with the climate crisis is to acknowledge that our agency has led to this crisis, and it is our *common* agency that will be instrumental for us to overcome it. Individual efforts, no matter how radical, will not do it. To claim that humans did not cause the climate crisis is to hand it over to fate, neglect the impact of human agency on the environment and concomitantly neglect the impact of humanity on basic and natural human life conditions. The latter is a position that is similar to how one in earlier times saw political institutions as unchanging instruments created and sanctioned by a deity. This position legitimized status quo and precluded a critical attitude towards the present condition as well as hindered processes that could lead to change and more just conditions. The parallel to what climate crisis deniers do now is striking.
2. To acknowledge that climate crisis has to do with the very concrete living conditions for present and future generations of humans, as well as for the quality of the ecosystems around the globe, implies that all actions taken are not only actions related to the environment and to nature – it is related to how our own nature and our own bodies will be in present and future. The relational approach that implies recognition of the interdependence of humanity and nature means that we cannot defer the situation to others and ignore our own responsibility for ourselves and future generations. Moreover, we cannot isolate the future state of our own embodied existence from the living environment and the non-living beings that have enabled this existence.
3. To orient ourselves and our agency appropriately in the face of the climate crisis means that we must go beyond an Aristotelian way of thinking about nature and the world as a set stage of unchanging beings and elements with a fixed set of qualities: The world is in change no matter what we do or not, but it is due to our agency in what way we can influence its positive transformation towards goals that are more in accordance with sustainable development.[47] There is, however, no guarantee that our agency will be able to realize such a positive transformation – but to do nothing with the elements that cause the climate crisis is a guarantee for collapse.
4. A new sensibility towards nature requires, as well, that we need to engage with nature in ways that go beyond those described as technical, communicative or emancipatory interests (Habermas). A prudential approach to the climate crisis requires a systematic and comprehensive

---

47. Cf. Agustín Fuentes, 'Becoming Human in the Anthropocene', in *Religion in the Anthropocene*, ed. Celia Deane-Drummond, Sigurd Bergmann, and Markus Vogt (Eugene, OR: Cascade, 2017).

basis of different types of knowledge and sensibilities, including contextual knowledge, in order to deal with the situation. It is more than likely that different actions and practices will be needed in different places, situations and circumstances. Ethical reasoning oriented towards orientation and transformation in the context of the climate crisis cannot be done merely based on universal moral principles but needs to be informed by a prudential attitude that includes sensibilities that go beyond the communicative aspect of engaging with the world.

The four traditional sources for theology – scripture, tradition, experience and other bodies of human knowledge – need further specification if the deficits of theology for developing symbolic practices can be overcome. Not generic 'experience' of the wealthy Western population should orient the transformative moves necessary, but the 'standpoints of people who are on the losing side of the global economy and more specifically, people whose lives are damaged or threatened by ours'. Moreover, '"Experience" no longer will refer primarily to my experience or the experience of people "like me". To learn from experience entails learning from the experiences of people who suffer because of the systems that provide us our material excess and who are proposing alternatives'.[48] In addition to the four traditional sources of knowledge necessary for moral agency, a fifth source has been proposed: other-than-human voices of the Earth. The warrant for this proposal is obvious. We should seek 'moral wisdom from the underside of power and privilege. Earth's waters, soil, air, fauna, foliage, and biosphere have joined that underside. Human creatures are invited to learn, from the other-than-human parts of creation that now groan under our weight, wisdom for living in sync with Earth's well-being'.[49]

---

48. Moe-Lobeda, *Resisting Structural Evil: Love as Ecological and Economic Vocation*, 241f.
49. Ibid., 241.

Chapter 8

SYMBOLS FOR ENHANCING MORAL MOTIVATION AND AVOIDING DEFECTION

I have argued for an integrated approach that takes all realms of human experience into account when it comes to how we establish and understand our relationships with nature. One of the consequences of this approach is that when we consider the conditions for our agency, we need to see that ideals and aims can build on, and take into account, the fact that we have evolved from natural conditions. To operate on aims and ideals that ignore this fact is not commendable. Enduring moral issues need to align with the basic tenets of nature. This point has theological implications as well. It means that morality informed by the Christian tradition should not be developed *contra naturam*.

Against this backdrop, this chapter will continue to present conditions for human agency. However, it will move beyond self-understanding and towards elements that allow for a more expansive space for moral motivation. This approach will lead to reflections on virtue ethics as a context for moral practices that can counter climate change.

Action can be motivated by different means. The actions required for countering the climate changes may be motivated by the dangers they pose to continued human flourishing or to the existence of life on the planet in general. We can identify such motivations as negative: they represent the 'stick' in the famous picture of how to make the donkey move. They describe the actions we need to avoid if we want to hinder pain, danger or catastrophe. On the other hand, the carrot is the metaphor for the positive gains that may result from specific actions. Actions motivated by a carrot are based on our positive desire for goodness and flourishing and can, therefore, serve as part of long-standing practices that build society, community and sound ecologies.[1] Both positive and negative motivations

---

1. In this chapter, as in the rest of the book, I hesitate to use the notion of 'environment' as it contributes to the anthropocentric notion of humans and nature as distinguishable. We partake in the environment – it is not external to us but interwoven with us and our lifestyle – for good and bad.

require that we establish them by symbolic means – what previously was called positive or negative symbols.[2]

However, this chapter aims to move beyond the stick-and-carrot structure of motivating moral agency, because the stick-and-carrot motivation structure asks, 'What's in it for me?' Hence, it fosters a subject-centred, even individualist approach to moral agency. The approach is insufficient and inadequate, as it overlooks the necessary considerations for future generations and the need for human cooperation in the present. It concentrates on the costs or gains for the present subject and measures all agency and cooperation in light of its outcome for individuals.

Models for understanding human cooperation based on religious symbols that appeal to the 'stick' model exist in recent scholarship. It is possible to develop traditional religious imagery along lines that suggest that God will punish or reward us according to how well we can deal with the challenges of climate change. It is possible to integrate such imagery into an evolutionary theory about how human cooperation. This chapter will discuss some of the main challenges that stem from such accounts and suggest an alternative. The outcome of this discussion is that we can identify good alternatives to the 'stick' model that may rest on positive symbolic elements. The alternative is not only countering the stick model but also serves as a better foundation for a sustained and positive moral agency – and can contribute more than the occasional 'carrot.'

The stick: Supernatural punishment as moral motivation?

What can motivate humans to act morally on long-term conditions that express solidarity and commitment to justice is a problem that still presents itself in modern thinking. It also entails profound challenges about the role of religion for moral motivation.[3] Why should humans act morally? In the following, to act morally is primarily understood as acting on other terms than self-interest only – it means taking into consideration commitments, concerns and relationships that can go beyond the either-or of stick-carrot reasoning.

From the perspective of faith and religion, it is obvious that moral motivation is usually related to personal belief in God or the orientation of one's life made possible by religious narratives, teaching and rituals that shape one's identity. One cannot detach one's moral motivation totally from the commitments they shape. However, as we shall see, these commitments can be shaped very differently, even when we speak about what belief in God entails for moral agency.

---

2. Cf. above, p. 63.

3. For a recent comprehensive discussion on the role of religion as a provider of motivation for actions of solidarity, see Jürgen Habermas, *Auch Eine Geschichte Der Philosophie Band 1: Die Okzidentale Konstellation Von Glauben Und Wissen Band 2: Vernünftige Freiheit. Spuren Des Diskurses Über Glauben Und Wissen* (Frankfurt: Suhrkamp, 2019).

Religion is identity-shaping and among the most powerful motivating forces in human culture.[4] From an evolutionary point of view, its role in fostering cooperative alliances among members of the same religious community is of particular relevance. The flip side of this is that it can also contribute to hostile attitudes towards out-group persons. Scholars agree that 'living in cooperative groups brings significant adaptive benefits both to the individuals in the group as well as to the group as a whole'. Moreover, in 'social collaboration between individuals, cooperation generates the twin benefits of increased size and specialization of function which allows groups to interact with their local environment in ways that permit them to extract greater benefits, to better resist challenges, and to do both with greater efficiency'.[5]

In light of the climate crisis, which calls for extensive human cooperation, it is noteworthy how *defection* remains a possible problem for cooperation. Some choose to opt out, as President Trump did when he pulled the United States out of the Paris Agreement. From an evolutionary point of view, this is the 'free-rider' position, which aims at harvesting benefits without making the same efforts that others do. Evolution scientists Schloss and Murray describe this challenge as follows:

> If all members of the group cooperate, contributing their resources to serve the common good, the group as a whole reaps maximal benefit. However, each member of the group has incentives to cheat others, reaping greater individual benefits for themselves while helping others minimally or perhaps even causing them harm. In a situation where such defection is a tempting strategy, the fragile economy of cooperation threatens to erode rapidly, splintering former cooperators into cheating opportunists, ultimately surrendering the benefits of cooperation. Interacting group members thus face a deep and vexing problem: how to achieve and sustain cooperation in the face of incentives to defect?[6]

---

4. This point is recognized by many who discuss the role of religion in the context of the Anthropocene, for example, inter alia, Heinrich Bedford-Strohm:

> The role of religions in global civil society in the age of the Anthropocene is especially important for another reason. Religions reach not only the minds of people but also their hearts and, even more, their souls. Since ecological reorientation fundamentally includes (besides political and economic structural changes) a change in lifestyle patterns, the success of the intended transformation is dependent on the input of institutions that reach people at the deep levels of their existence.

See Heinrich Bedford-Strohm, 'Foreword', in *Religion in the Anthropocene*, ed. Celia Deane-Drummond, Sigurd Bergmann, and Markus Vogt (Eugene, OR: Cascade Books, 2017), xiii.

5. Jeffrey P. Schloss and Michael J. Murray, 'Evolutionary Accounts of Belief in Supernatural Punishment: A Critical Review', *Religion, Brain & Behavior* 1, no. 1 (2011): 46.

6. Ibid., 47.

Although Schloss and Murray write from an evolutionary point of view, it is hard not to read the quote with the contemporary political situation in mind. Climate change deniers are cheaters: they hope to get away with doing nothing, although it is imperative that everyone contribute to counter the crisis. However, in the present context, it is ideas of punishment for defection that is the topic. Although there is, due to secularization, presently not much to expect in terms of motivating forces when it comes to the notion of a punishing God, this notion has nevertheless been suggested as one of the strong and effective elements behind the evolution of human cooperation. The effectiveness of the notion would, ideally, 'involve minimal or no cost, along with no possibility of corruption and no chance of failure to detect defection'.[7] Its implementation 'would involve belief in moralizing gods or some other form of supernatural sanctioning'.[8]

Without going into detail here, the point is that 'supernatural beings or cosmic forces can take the burden of punishing off of group members by imposing sanctions and rewards via their presumed control of natural or supernatural processes'.[9] Therefore, we can find elements in religious traditions that serve to enhance cooperation by employing notions of a punishing God, purgatory, hell and karma.[10]

I argue, however, that the notion of punishment, which entails negative sanctions for defective actions (i.e., what one does not do, and should have done), is not a well-suited foundation for morally informed practices when facing climate change. We need to find a different symbol that is not dependent upon negative motivations and which does not entail a division between self and others, those within and without. This notion creates aggression and provides no attraction towards goodness for its own sake. Furthermore, such a negative symbol fosters egotism: it is concerned with what we should try to avoid (punishment) and not the positive aims that all might benefit from realizing when we cooperate with others.

A better way, but no carrot: On emulation of goodness

The notion of a punishing God as the religious image for providing moral motivation has been addressed as insufficient and having limited validity.[11] Recently, Lenfesty and Morgan have added to this discussion. Based on insights into the evolution of prestige psychology in humans, they identify alternative means by which religions can shape human behaviour. 'Prestige psychology means

---

7. Ibid., 48.
8. Ibid.
9. Ibid.
10. Cf. ibid., 49. I will discuss some of these imaginaries in the next part.
11. See, e.g. the contribution in Jeffrey P. Schloss and Michael J. Murray, 'How Might Evolution Lead to Hell?', *Religion, Brain & Behavior* 1, no. 1 (2011).

that humans are predisposed to show deference toward individuals that display the key markers of prestige: generosity and benevolence, as well as being deferred to by other individuals. This applies to deities and supernatural agents, as well as flesh-and-blood individuals: a divine being that displays these traits can tap into human prestige psychology and prompt deference and imitation.'[12]

Lenfesty and Morgan argue, in a way that supports the aforementioned suggestion, that 'while fear of punishment may inhibit some anti-social behaviors like cheating, it is unlikely to motivate other prosocial behaviors, like helping'.[13] The warrant for their argument is not phenomenological or philosophical, however, but the empirical fact that 'human physiology has evolved separate neurological systems with differential behavioral correlates either for (1) processing fear and responding to threats or (2) facilitating social interactions in environments which are deemed safe'.[14] Whereas the first approach is punitive and closely resembles the notion of a punishing god, Lenfesty and Morgan argue in favour of the second model, which provides an empirical backdrop for a virtue ethics approach to moral practices in the face of the climate crisis. This approach implies that model agents present and represent attitudes and actions that appear as prestigious, attractive and desirable to emulate by others.[15] We will develop this approach in later sections and chapters.

Furthermore, Lenfesty and Morgan present a hypothesis about human prosociality (costly practices and behaviours such as helping, sharing, caring). It entails that 'benevolent supernatural agents and their human representatives may be as effective at promoting prosociality as fearsome gods'.[16] Contrary to the dominance system presented earlier, which builds on ideas about genetic fitness and survival, they see human prosociality as 'due to the evolution of prestige psychology in response to our constructed cultural environments'.[17] They advance this hypothesis as an explicit alternative to the punishing god hypothesis as the only way to explain human cooperation and the avoidance of defection.

---

12. Hillary L. Lenfesty and Thomas J. H. Morgan, 'By Reverence, Not Fear: Prestige, Religion, and Autonomic Regulation in the Evolution of Cooperation', *Frontiers in Psychology* 10 (2019): 10.

13. Ibid., 1.

14. Ibid.

15. This point is developed more extensively in the context of an exemplarist moral philosophy, to which I return later in the text. See, for the importance of emulation Linda Trinkaus Zagzebski, *Exemplarist Moral Theory* (New York: Oxford University Press, 2019), Chapter 5 (128ff). Lenfesty and Morgan do not refer to Zagzebski, but it there are several and obvious possible connections between them – of which some are also highly relevant for the present book.

16. Lenfesty and Morgan, 'By Reverence, Not Fear: Prestige, Religion, and Autonomic Regulation in the Evolution of Cooperation', 2.

17. Ibid.

The contrast between the two approaches is obvious: Whereas notions of dominance lead to aversion, fear and shame, 'prestige hierarchies are characterized by physical proximity and eye-contact, as well as emotions like admiration and respect for leaders'.[18] Moreover, such relationships also enable the flow of cultural information and learning:

> [C]oupled with prestige biased social learning, it opens up a means for prestigious figures, including deities, to support the spread of prosocial behaviors. Thus, in addition to theories that emphasize religious fear as a motivating factor in the evolution of prosocial religions, we suggest that reverence – which includes awe and respect for, deference to, admiration of, and a desire to please a deity or supernatural agent – is likely just as important. In support of this, we identify cases of religions that appear to be defined predominantly by prestige dynamics, and not fear of supernatural punishment.[19]

Hence, the direction in prestige hierarchies goes towards favourable actions instead of using threats and coercion to avoid specific actions. Whereas systems of dominance are linked to emotions like shame, fear and fear-based respect, in prestige systems, positive emotions are characterized by qualitatively different emotions. 'A prestigious individual is someone who is esteemed for their skill, knowledge, or success in locally valued domains.'[20] Individuals who are less prestigious desire to be near prestigious individuals and 'feel admiration, awe, and respect – reverence – for the prestigious figure. Prestigious figures are well-liked compared to dominant individuals who are not liked'.[21] Thus, 'prestigious figures gain influence simply by being good at something and valued by others for it; moreover, prestigious individuals show generosity and benevolence toward low-status individuals'.[22]

Among the benefits of establishing conditions for agency based on prestige systems is that it is not necessary to operate with a supernatural, invisible, all-powerful being to motivate positive action. Prestigious persons who motivate emulation of behaviour can be ordinary, and they are possible to experience first-hand. I want to stress this point for two reasons: firstly, it places the site of moral motivation within the realm of ordinary human experience, and secondly, it enhances human cooperation on a positive basis. Prestigious persons do not necessarily need to be leaders, though they certainly can be, to motivate others. However, when they are leaders, prestigious persons 'don't command deference by

---

18. Ibid.
19. Ibid.
20. Ibid., 3.
21. Ibid.
22. Ibid.

force, and [...]followers don't show deference simply to reduce the threat from the leader; rather, followers willingly defer to the leader'.[23]

Because the main component of prestige is attracting and influencing followers, this feature can take on religious components. As Lenfesty and Morgan point out, 'gods and supernatural agents are also revered, admired, adored, respected, and loved. In short, gods and supernatural agents are prestigious as well as dominant'.[24] However, the prestige system taps into the level of human psychology 'which is biased toward imitating prestigious individuals to promote cooperation without the need for threatening punishment'.[25]

This explanation overcomes the problem that fear is a weak motivator for pro-social behaviour. In human prestige psychology, we can identify the origin of the 'active desire to be like prestigious individuals at all times, and not just in their presence'.[26] Thus, this explanation is more than a supplement to supernatural punishment theories. However, Lenfesty and Morgan do not see these as mutually exclusive options. Instead, it allows for understanding how 'different groups within the same religion may emphasize and focus on either the fearful or benevolent aspects of a given deity'.[27] They substantiate their hypothesis by providing an overview of historical cases in which prestigious gods and revered figures act as teachers and guides (as opposed to domineering aggressors), and disperse their knowledge and skills to followers who are inclined to imitate their ways.[28] Concerning social practices within religious communities, they conclude:

> We expect that when cultural narratives of benevolent and prestigious supernatural agents are reinforced through collective rituals such as singing, prayer, reading of texts, and listening to sermons, this can create safe environments where positive emotions and behaviors – like the desire to be like a help [to] others – can, as a result of calm autonomic states, thrive.[29]

Although based in evolutionary psychology, the benefit of Lenfesty and Morgan's approach is that it can be linked easily to moral theory and become integrated into a culture of specific human values that goes beyond fitness or individual interest. This point is possible to develop further by analysing the contribution of philosopher Linda Zagzebski.

---

23. Ibid.
24. Ibid., 7.
25. Ibid.
26. Ibid., 8.
27. Ibid.
28. Ibid., 8f.
29. Ibid., 10.

Linda Zagzebski: Goodness as admirable

Prestigious persons serve as exemplars for behaviours that others desire to emulate. Linda Zagzebski[30] suggests that such exemplars play a significant role in moral development. She understands morality as rooted in practice and not primarily in reasoning. We do not typically 'first articulate an exhaustive definition of a moral property such as courage, and then go on to look for cases where that property is instantiated'.[31] Instead, we start with identifying or observing exemplary cases of courageous behaviour or of courageous persons. We identify these exemplars not by way of rational arguments, but rather by way of *admiration*, which is a matter of affection. Only after we have been affectively attracted do we begin to discuss in earnest what exemplary people have in common, what we can learn from them, and so on.[32]

One attractive feature of this approach is that it is explicit about the value-laden character of philosophical reflection. In reflection, as everywhere else, we must start from where we stand and acknowledge the influence that a given position has on us. To identify something as courageous, for instance, is to acknowledge the value in the courageous practice, even when that courage is exercised in the pursuit of causes that we do not support.[33] Thus, the critique launched previously against a neutral and detached approach to topics in which nature and the environment are involved as objects of our concern is supported by this position.

Zagzebski's approach implies that narratives about admirable (or prestigious) persons are useful in moral education and improvement. Such narratives engage our motives in a different way than abstract theories do. They tell us about which persons to admire or emulate and contribute to shaping our vision of a good life. Narratives thus motivate moral behaviour in a concrete manner, not based on theory. They also make possible a discourse about moral attitudes, concerns and values across cultures, and such discourse can be 'sensitive to the beliefs of individual communities, including faith communities', she claims.[34]

A strength in Zagzebski's approach is that it can combine ethical reasoning with empirical and experiential elements in moral education and combine ethics with empirical research in psychology and neuroscience. Thus, she, as well, points to how morality may be linked to fundamental elements in humans' natural conditions and not work in opposition to it.[35] Moreover, her point of departure

---

30. The texts of Zagzebski used in the following are Linda Zagzebski, 'Admiration and the Admirable', *Supplement to the Proceedings of The Aristotelian Society* 89, no. 1 (2015) and 'Moral Exemplars in Theory and Practice', *Theory and Research in Education* 11, no. 2 (2013).
31. Cf. 'Moral Exemplars in Theory and Practice', 193.
32. Ibid.
33. Zackariasson, 'Religious Agency as Vehicle and Source of Critique', 210.
34. Zagzebski, 'Moral Exemplars in Theory and Practice', 193.
35. Ibid., 194.

in practice means that she has an affinity to a pragmatist approach to ethics, in which it is not the abstract individual who is a moral agent, but concrete persons in concrete situations. Hence, she objects to a moral theory that leaves out the identities of persons.[36] She summarizes her position thus:

> [M]oral theory aims primarily at explaining and justifying moral beliefs and practices, and only secondarily at telling us what to do in any given situation. There are many elements in our moral practices that pre-exist theory and which we seek to understand. These include reactive emotions such as admiration, praise, blame, remorse, indignation, and horror; practices of punishment; rules such as the Golden Rule or the Ten Commandments; and values such as freedom, fulfillment, and social cohesiveness. Some of these elements are reflected in narratives that are cherished by a community and passed down from generation to generation. Of course, there are many other elements of our moral practices that pre-exist theory. My point is that a moral theory is about something that already exists.[37]

Zagzebski argues that there should be a connection between the moral reasons offered by moral theory and what actually motivates us. But as mentioned, the starting point is not theory but a situation in which we find ourselves motivated to moral improvement because we admire someone else's practice. Her theoretical position is not foundationalist in a conceptual sense but is rooted in – or founded upon – specific experiences. It begins with the 'direct reference to exemplars of moral goodness, picked out by the emotion of admiration'.[38]

Accordingly, the content of basic moral concepts is anchored in exemplars of moral goodness. Moreover, the identification of good persons is not dependent on theoretical knowledge about goodness. Zagzebski claims that 'it is not necessary that anybody knows what makes a good person good in order to successfully refer to good persons, any more than it was necessary that anybody knew what makes water "water" to successfully refer to water before the advent of molecular theory'.[39] Instead, 'people can succeed in referring to good persons as long as they, or some people in their community, can pick out exemplars'.[40] The identification of persons we admire as moral exemplars is embedded in our moral practices and articulated in various narratives. Such narratives are part of the 'pre-theoretical aspects of our moral practices that theory must explain'.[41]

Moral learning starts with imitation. 'Exemplars are those persons who are most imitable, and they are most imitable because they are most admirable.' As already

36. Ibid., 195.
37. Ibid.
38. Ibid., 198.
39. Ibid., 199.
40. Ibid.
41. Ibid., 199f.

indicated, they are identified by the emotion of admiration, and 'that emotion is subject to education through the example of the emotional reactions of other persons'.[42] Narratives that are part of a common tradition shape these reactions.[43] Our experience of what makes a person good is, therefore, linked to our actual experiences of good persons. However, narratives can also suggest which persons stand out as exemplars in one respect because they offer detailed observations. The emphasis on the role of narrative for detecting admirable features also entails that it is not necessarily so that all good persons have something in common:[44]

> There is not a single essence of good personhood, but there is a set of interesting, yet different ways in which a person can be good. It is also possible that the set of exemplars gradually changes over time. After a moral revolution such as the revolution in attitudes towards persons of different races or ethnic backgrounds, some, but by no means all, features of the persons we recognize as exemplars changed. I am suggesting that these are all testable hypotheses.[45]

To identify a person as good means that this person is admirable in some respect. Accordingly, he or she is also *imitable* in that respect. 'The feeling of admiration is a kind of attraction that carries the impetus to imitate with it.'[46] However, there are many reasons why we do not or cannot imitate those we admire. But that does not exclude that we can admire them. The impetus to imitate them nevertheless constitutes moral motivation.

Thus, Zagzebski develops a position that can be seen as a version of virtue ethics: A virtue is, namely, 'a trait we admire in an admirable person. It is a trait that makes the person paradigmatically good in a certain respect'.[47] It is not a virtue because of its desirability, but because of its admirability.[48] She continues with a comprehensive analysis of the different components involved here:

> So a virtue is a trait we admire in that person and in persons like that. A good state of affairs is a state of affairs at which persons like that aim. A good life is a life desired by persons like that. A right act is an act a person like that would take to be favored by the balance of reasons.[49]

As suggested, Zagzebski aims for a theory that can provide a framework for cross-cultural dialogue on morality. Insofar as we can identify virtues in persons who

---

42. Ibid., 200.
43. Ibid.
44. Ibid., 200f.
45. Ibid., 201.
46. Ibid.
47. Ibid., 202.
48. Ibid., 206.
49. Ibid., 202.

are identifiable by admiration that is educated by narratives, we can 'identify both cross-cultural similarities and cross-cultural differences in moral beliefs by linking the traits a group of people call virtuous, the acts they call right, and the lives they think are most worth living to the people they admire as exemplars'.[50] It is not impossible to understand why the exemplars of a different culture or religious community are admirable. But cross-cultural exchange on moral virtues has the advantage that people outside one community can notice features that are missing in that of others. The articulation of such lacunas or differences can be important because they open up to cross-cultural critique and discussion about what it is commendable to admire and why.[51]

The role of moral education is also significant because we may, at times, admire the wrong things. Hence, to be morally educated means that the emotion of admiration needs to be informed and adjusted by moral standards shared by the community in a specific context. When there is a lack of fit between our emotion and its object, this point is obvious. Nevertheless, admiration is not a mere cognitive feature but includes a distinctive feeling, and perhaps physical responses, as well as common behavioural responses, Zagzebski claims.[52] She refers to research that calls admiration an 'other-praising emotion' arising from witnessing of others,[53] and more specifically, admiration for virtue as 'associated with the feelings of being uplifted or elevated by witnessing or reading about something admirable'.[54] It is 'a positive emotion, not only because its object appears good in a distinctive way, but because it feels good to have it.'[55] Moreover, when in 'a state of admiration the object appears admirable, and if the agent trusts the emotion upon reflection, she will use it as the ground for a judgment of admirability'.[56]

When we admire Greta Thunberg, Frans of Asissi or the mother who cares for her unborn child, the admiration is based on how we identify their virtue in some respect by relating to them as exemplars. We would not have been able to do this if their example only had instilled fear in us. However, as concrete persons, we can identify their virtues and qualities in relevant respects. Three different elements emerge from this analysis:

a) It is concrete persons in concrete situations that display virtue – virtue is not an abstract phenomenon.
b) We can identify virtue only by seeing these exemplars as related to us in a way that makes us want to imitate their virtues in our context, to the extent

---

50. Ibid., 204.
51. Ibid.
52. Zagzebski, 'Admiration and the Admirable', 207.
53. Ibid., 208.
54. Ibid., 209.
55. Ibid.
56. Ibid.

that they are relevant for it. As exemplars, they present us with a model of virtuous behaviour. However, they need not be virtuous in every respect.
c) Virtues are expressed in practices.

Against this analysis's backdrop, it is possible to see how a mother caring for her unborn child can serve as an admirable person we identify as virtuous in her capacity for caring for the future. But she can also be seen as a metaphorical symbol for another type of virtuous behaviour, because her care for the child with whom she is internally connected also has parallels to the practices involved in caring for the future life on the planet. Thus, she can serve as one exemplar of virtuous behaviour and represent an enduring practice that other persons can emulate in other contexts. The mother is not only a model, but she is also a symbol of responsible behaviour. We can identify her actions as having metaphorical bearings on a wide variety of human behaviour towards the environment. Moreover, to focus on the caring mother means that we, when trying to develop a symbolic model for persistent action, find our point of departure in practices and situations that already exist. It can give us a basis for considering the whats, the whys and the hows of our actions towards the future of the planet. Hence, the task is not necessarily to invent something totally new that is not based on already-existing practices and agency. It is to recognize that already-existing caring practices may be expanded based on model modes of relating to the future that we find in those who carry this future under their hearts. This is recognized and expressed clearly in Willis Jenkins' work. He writes, with reference to Anna Peterson:

> Everyday acts of caring for children can give rise to a broader ethic of care for all the relationships that sustain us. If cultivated as a moral and political practice ... caring for children can make parents respect and protect the sustaining relations that mother us all. . . . Parenting decenters us, orients us to the bodily needs of others, and makes us recognize the fundamental dependency and relational character of human personhood. It might also make parents and caregivers identify with life-nurturing aspects of earth.[57]

Assuming that Peterson and Jenkins are right, we already have accessible practices that can inform our care for the future of the planet.

On the virtue of ecological care

So far, we have considered the role of symbols in connecting us to and engaging us with ourselves, nature and God. Symbols help us manoeuvre reality and interpret it. They orient us and contribute to our notions of what needs transformation.

---

57. Willis Jenkins, *The Future of Ethics - Sustainability, Social Justice, and Religious Creativity* (2013), 197.

Thus, symbols shape the experiences we have in our 'social mindscapes'. Symbols may have positive or problematic effects on how we relate to and order nature and our relationship with it – depending on how they are employed. We have seen that symbols constitute conditions for human agency in ways that interact with our psychological dispositions. We cannot be self-interpreting animals without involving our psyche. Moreover, we cannot be self-interpreting animals unless we also relate to and interpret that which is not us.

Different psychological conditions shape and are shaped by our self-interpretations. The relational web in which symbols are engaged may cause fear or admiration for prestigious achievements. Against the backdrop of all we have developed so far in this part, virtue ethics suggests itself as a resource for understanding conditions for agency. Virtues are about conditions for an excellent and admirable agency. By considering virtues as part of the personal conditions for agency, we identify a crucial element involved in developing symbolic resources for practices that counter the climate crisis. Whereas virtue ethics is not the only answer to the question about an adequate moral theory for countering the climate crisis, I do argue that it is a necessary element of such a theory in that it links so closely the personal dispositions and self-interpretation with different practices and symbolic resources that mediate them.

Virtues as relational and articulations of self-interpretation

In an article on virtue ethics, Hurstgrove and Pettigrove make some observations that support the move from the previous chapters towards an analysis of elements in virtue ethics. They hold that the 'best available science today (including evolutionary theory and psychology) supports rather than undermines the ancient Greek assumption that we are social animals, like elephants and wolves and unlike polar bears'.[58] A consequence of this observation is that they see no need for a 'rationalizing explanation in terms of anything like a social contract . . . to explain why we choose to live together, subjugating our egoistic desires in order to secure the advantages of co-operation. Like other social animals, our natural impulses are not solely directed towards our own pleasures and preservation, but include altruistic and cooperative ones'.[59]

These points are essential not only as a correction to notions of a social contract-based notion of morality and sociality. They ground morality in the inherent other-directed and relational character of human life. Against this backdrop, it becomes comprehensible that moral virtues – and virtues of excellence in general 'are at least partially constitutive of human flourishing'. They also counter the

---

58. Rosalind Hursthouse and Glen Pettigrove, 'Virtue Ethics', in *The Stanford Encyclopedia of Philosophy*, ed. Edward N. Zalta (Stanford 2018).

59. Ibid.

objection that virtue ethics is, in some sense, egoistic.[60] Human flourishing cannot be sufficiently understood if our intimate inter- and intra-relationship with nature, as mediated through virtuous action, is not taken into account as a vital condition. Accordingly, the following explorative consideration of virtues provides a contrast to the basis for a scientific ideal that sees the detached and neutral observer as the default position for making decisions about what to do. In that respect, virtue ethics, as advocated by Zagzebski and others, entails important corrections to this ideal.

Traditionally, virtue is understood as an excellent trait of character.[61] It is an enduring disposition for action that expresses itself in practices. To act in a virtuous way requires a mindset that considers specific reasons for action and allows these to shape action. This mindset, I argue, is socially construed, but in the case of virtues that are needed for countering climate change, it is not only the social world of other humans and their values that must be taken into consideration. The virtues required must be developed primarily on the basis of the recognition of how humans and other parts of nature are intra- and interconnected. This allows for acknowledging that emotional and aesthetic sensitivities contribute to shaping the experience of humans living in a community with other living beings and the environment.

The position for which I argue here entails that moral considerations expand beyond the inter-human sphere. A person who is virtuous concerning the climate crisis needs to have the good and well-being of all of nature in view and cannot detach herself from experiences of change, suffering, devastation and destruction that take place or the emotional impact they have on her. She has to consider the natural, biological, social, cultural and spiritual effects of her actions permanently. Insights into these effects guide her actions, and she allows them to count as valid and essential for her agency. They are not contingent or occasional to her agency but fundamental for it.

The Christian tradition has advanced fundamental virtues with traits that we can build into what I would – for the lack of a better name – call *the virtue of care for ecology*. However, no virtue, no action and no symbolic resources in the Christian tradition have been developed with such care in mind as a fundamental attitude or virtuous disposition. There is nevertheless, as I argue throughout, a fundamental human experience we can identify as the basis for a metaphor for practices oriented by this virtue: the experience of being pregnant with a future child. What that means in detail, I develop in more detail in the next part of the book.

To be engaged with and committed to countering climate change requires that one develops theoretical understanding, empirical insight, reasons, sentiments

---

60. Ibid.

61. The following section is based on the main elements in Hursthouse and Glen Pettigrove, ibid. However, the considerations I make about how different elements in virtue theory are related to taking up responsibility for the climate crisis are mine.

and choices that reflect and support a profound understanding of the crisis. The virtue of ecological care will reflect in a person's choice of practices, actions, what she does and does not do, her work priorities, her choice of colleagues and friends, and how she raises her children. Moreover, she will disapprove of those who do not care about the present crisis and articulate a lack of understanding of its seriousness or simply deny its existence. Hence, a virtue is a multitrack disposition.

At this point, it is essential to underscore that possessing a virtue is a matter of degree. In the context of the climate crisis, this is both an obvious fact which we need to remind ourselves and others of, to not de-motivate the development of the virtue of ecological care. We sometimes cannot avoid using a fossil-fuel car or use an airplane to go to a conference. But we can try to restrict such behaviour as much as possible and work for sustainable alternatives. It is the orientation towards developing more consistent and encompassing alternatives that show our willingness to become better or more virtuous. In contrast, the absence of such orientations displays our lack of willingness to transform ourselves and the present situation. We also need to acknowledge that to be virtuous concerning countering the climate crisis does not necessarily entail what we are virtuous in every other respect.

One of the tasks of developing the relevant virtue(s) is to bring one's emotions in accordance with one's rational recognition of the reasons for action. This challenge motivates virtue theorists to distinguish between full or perfect virtue, under which conditions the virtuous person does not have to fight against contrary desires, and the continent person who needs to control a desire or temptation to do otherwise. This distinction is especially relevant concerning the present situation, in which many people in the Western world are bombarded with options for action that will have adverse effects on climate and the environment. Combined with the aforementioned recognition of virtue as a matter of degree, it entails that it is necessary to see the development of the virtue of ecological care as one that requires a continuous process of personal, social and economic transformation because change will not be brought about only by individuals developing their virtuous character. A mere individual approach to virtue ethics is insufficient insofar as '[e]ven people morally shaped by narrative and habit to practice the ecological virtues (...) are limited in capacity for earthkeeping if those virtues are not joined by a commitment to recognize and counter social structures that breed ecological destruction'.[62]

---

62. Cynthia D. Moe-Lobeda, 'Response to Steven Bouma-Prediger', in *Ecotheology: A Christian Conversation*, ed. Kiara A. Jorgenson and Alan G. Padgett (Grand Rapids, MI: William B. Eerdmans Publishing Company, 2020), 158. Moe-Lobeda points to how the structural perspective needs to be added to the one represented by virtue ethics, because there are 'social structure factors that (1) limit the impact of individual virtue, (2) limit the formation of individual virtue, and (3) act as moral players in other ways. Said differently, virtue ethics alone does not adequately address the power of societies (and other metasocial structures) as moral actors. Nor does virtue ethics account adequately for structural sin'. Ibid., 157.

When we develop these considerations about the virtue of ecological care, it is especially important to keep in mind that it cannot be only about a person's dispositions for action, but also has to involve the consequences of her actions and her life for a wider environment. To focus exclusively on what constitutes virtue in a person will, in the context of the environmental crisis, fall short of taking into consideration the interrelation between persons and their environment in the social and natural world alike. When 'a virtuous person is a morally good, excellent or admirable person who acts and feels as she should',[63] this assessment cannot be made unqualified because we need to take the actions and their consequences into account.

This point then leads us to the role of knowledge in the context of virtues. I previously mentioned that virtue is a multitrack disposition. A person who is virtuous in the face of climate change cannot be so unless she has sufficient knowledge about what this change entails. She will also have the disposition to gain more insight into it, to act adequately better. However, knowledge also works on the part of the person who identifies another as virtuous. She will not only need this knowledge to understand that she is a person who holds the virtue of ecological care. Moreover, this knowledge constitutes the foundation for why she finds her morally good, excellent or admirable. Linda Zagzebski holds that the ability to recognize the admirable requires knowledge, and such knowledge is necessary for moral learning.[64]

When consumers ignore warnings about the effects of carbon emissions, or when Christian groups say that climate change is a hoax made by secular scientists and politicians, they thereby effectively block the way to recognizing the virtue of ecological care in others and the chance for developing it in themselves. In this respect, their practices of consumption, worship or (not) acquiring of knowledge work against developing the necessary virtues. To counter such tendencies, they need to be informed and shaped by knowledge and practices that display the admirable and morally good in being oriented by taking care of the environment. As long as such knowledge and practices are not present to them or mediated in their context as part of their social mindscape, their ability to become virtuous is severely impeded. Not only are models of virtuous actions lacking, so is the knowledge necessary for its identification. Moral learning about climate change and the necessary virtues remains outside the scope of attention.

Virtue requires willingness both to do good and to acquire the knowledge that enables us to identify what it is. The process of acquiring knowledge is permanent. This is a challenge for those whose attitude and context are shaped by the idea

---

63. Hursthouse and Pettigrove, 'Virtue Ethics'.

64. These brief comments on knowledge can lead to a critical analysis of how the educational systems work in different parts of the world with regard to providing students and pupils sufficient knowledge about what is at stake with the planet, and the concomitant need for urgent action. That, however, is not the primary topic here. See, nevertheless, Arne Johan Vetlesen and Rasmus Willig, *Hva Skal Vi Svare Våre Barn?* (Oslo: Dreyer, 2018).

that all we need to know about human action is given with God's revelation in the Bible. I will take up that notion in the subsequent next chapter on the challenges to theology, but here it is necessary to point to how this idea of having sufficient knowledge works to not only block the access to relevant and necessary scientific knowledge but also possibly exclude believers from the community that can have any positive effect on the climate challenges. In terms of virtue ethics, they prevent themselves from the ability to act wisely. To do so requires practical wisdom. Such wisdom has several features worth considering here.

One needs experience to develop practical wisdom. The ability to learn from experience and develop the capacity to identify and differentiate between what is essential and what is not in a situation is crucial for practices of orientation and transformation – both are needed for dealing with the crisis. The Christian tradition has usually recognized this element. 'Classical and Christian virtue ethics is a process of education of intention and sentiment so that individuals choose the right action in particular situations because their training in the virtues has disposed them toward the right and the good.'[65] Hence, there exists in the Christian tradition a recognition of the importance of knowledge to develop virtues. However, this recognition is lacking among religious groups that ignore science and experience and encapsulate themselves in an attitude that deems questions about the environment as irrelevant for their lives and their faith.

Virtues and climate crisis: Michael Northcott

In his analysis of the role of virtues in the context of climate change, Michael Northcott emphasizes how a virtuous person is always embedded in a context from which she cannot distance herself. The relationship with the context is part of what constitutes the virtuous self. The connection between context and self makes it necessary to report on these virtues in a narrative, as Zagzebski also pointed out. 'Belief in the specificity of certain moral excellences or virtues — such as courage, justice, patience, and temperance — and their role in guiding individuals and groups through harms and dangers gives historical depth and narrative unity to the self,' he claims. Moreover, '[t]he virtues in the Aristotelian and Christian traditions have a narrative, relational, and ideological shape which enables a fit between the actions of an individual and the common good of the community. They, therefore, facilitate the realization of the goods for which persons are made.'[66] With regard to the topic of this book, the connection between individual virtuous action and the common good is of specific interest:

---

65. Michael S. Northcott, *A Political Theology of Climate Change* (Grand Rapids, MI: William B. Eerdmans Publishing Company, 2013), 253.

66. Ibid.

The emphasis of the virtues tradition on fulfilment, happiness, or well-being, and on the ultimate end of human being as the perfection of the soul, gives to this moral tradition a distinctive shape. This shape is lacking in modern moral philosophy, which tends to reduce morality either to inner states or sentiments which are not clearly connected with history, biology, the social, and the spiritual or to rules which force individuals to behave in ways they would often not prefer.[67]

Northcott builds on Alastair MacIntyre's account of virtues, in which ethics is a communitarian project. Moreover, it is also 'an education *senti-mentale*, which trains individuals in the performance of practices in which those things which are truly admirable, excellent, good, and beautiful are honoured'.[68] Again, we see how relationships with others and emotions are relevant and not to be ignored.[69] According to MacIntyre, the life of the virtues are socially sustained in a community committed to a common enterprise. The community is involved in two kinds of evaluative practice. It will 'praise as excellences those qualities of mind and character which would contribute to the realisation of their common good or goods'.[70] On the other hand, it has to 'identify certain types of action as the doing or the production of harm of such an order that they destroy the bonds of community and so make the completion of the project impossible'.[71]

Northcott considers three crucial claims that are relevant for an informed and knowledge-based approach to climate change. The first claim is that

> human moral experience is embodied in a way that modern moral philosophy does not allow, and that this embodiment is particularly manifest in relations of dependence and nurture that humans, like other animals, experience at birth, in childhood, and, often, in the last months or years of life; the experience of dependence unsettles the narrow modern liberal conception of the individual moral reasoner choosing her own goods and deciding autonomously on paths of action to realise them.[72]

The second claim entails that 'the nurturing and group behaviours of other animals reveal that practical reasoning and the virtues do exist, albeit in rudimentary form, in other than human biological communities and have therefore a biological

---

67. Ibid.
68. Ibid.
69. Ibid.
70. Ibid., 254. Northcott here refers to Alasdair C. MacIntyre, *After Virtue: A Study in Moral Theory*, 2nd edition (London: Duckworth, 1985).
71. Northcott, *A Political Theology of Climate Change*, 254. Northcott here refers to MacIntyre, *After Virtue: A Study in Moral Theory*.
72. Northcott, *A Political Theology of Climate Change*, 260. A fuller account is given in 'Do Dolphins Carry the Cross? Biological Moral Realism and Theological Ethics', *New Blackfriars* 84, no. 994 (2003).

reality which exceeds the cultural and historical contexts in which virtue theory was developed'.[73]

I want to pause by this second claim for two reasons: the first is inspired by Arne Johan Vetlesen's insistence that non-human nature has a profound moral standing that humans need to consider. In a post-cartesian approach to nature, this realization falls outside the scope of relevant factors, but it needs to be included and sustained as important for future action. Furthermore, the second reason for pausing with this insight is the one to which Northcott also points: the necessity of human education in this context: 'Because of the uniquely volitional and personal character [of humans, we], have a greater capacity than other animals to fail to achieve their good, they therefore stand in need of more education and ritual legitimation of the moral life than do other animals'.[74]

The third relevant claim underscores the close connection with the two former, and with topics already touched upon earlier: Northcott points to how the experience of dependence leads to a revision of the account of virtue: '[E]xperience of dependence is truer to the human condition and the biological condition than the experience of autonomy'.[75]

I have already briefly suggested that the fundamental human experience of being pregnant points to the fundamentally relational character of existence. Our (inter-)dependence at the biological as well as the cultural level is manifest in this phenomenon. When Northcott insists on morality as based on the biological feature of dependence, he supports the intuition on which the overall argument of this book is based: These fundamental relationships can provide us with model practices for dealing with the present crisis. To present knowledge as sufficient, or to reject the relevance of any sentiment that emerges from this fact, is to stop short of what is necessary for developing the necessary virtues.

At this point, Northcott also takes up a topic touched upon earlier in relation to the psychological conditions for relational maturity. He points to 'good parenting as a foundation and context for the development of morally sensitive individuals capable of expressing the virtues'.[76] To this, he adds moral psychologist Darcia Narvaez' complementary perspective. It points to three ethical 'orientations' that are crucial for developing a well-balanced ethical orientation: security, engagement and imagination. These are explained as follows:

> Security concerns individual survival needs. Engagement is the capacity to empathise with others and to engage with their projects as well as one's own. Imagination refers to higher moral and aesthetic functions, including deliberative reasoning, cultural activities such as play, and artistic and intellectual endeavours. [. . .] In particular, there is a close relationship between physical

---

73. *A Political Theology of Climate Change*, 260.
74. Ibid.
75. Ibid.
76. Ibid.

touch of infants and young children and their later ability to empathise with and care for others.[77]

I want to highlight two features in this quote that connect to previous lines of reasoning: firstly, that imagination is of crucial importance for the ability to develop alternative states, situations and actions. It entails a capacity to do more than to observe 'neutral facts' – imagination is necessary for us to understand the situation and experiences of others. It opens us up to the broader contexts of the reality in which we participate. Furthermore, the experience of physical touch as an entry to the development of empathy suggests that sensory experiences are crucial for the ability to feel and not only cognitively understand what kind of impact our actions and those of others may have on the environment and other living beings. The primary site for such experiences we find in the mother–infant relationship. Hence, 'embodied experience of dependence on others, both human and wild, is key to the formation of individuals who can express empathy and care to others, human and wild'.[78] Dependence, the foundational importance of physical attachment and love in the nurture of children are therefore closely connected, as we can also see in the New Testament, according to Northcott.[79]

The relevance of the Christian tradition's concern for the weak and the vulnerable and the concomitant 'moral priority of the weak' comes to the fore in this move. Northcott claims that the Christian narrative and ethics entail a way of reading the human moral drama through history. According to him, the 'priority of love over justice, of nonviolence over violence, of care over power is validated both by Christian history and by modern moral psychology'.[80] Hence, the question now becomes, what does this mean for the aforementioned multitrack disposition of virtues? Can the traditional virtues in the Christian tradition be re-shaped to include and maintain a fundamental concern for the good of the planet, not only for an anthropocentric approach to the human community and its conditions for flourishing?

The virtue of ecological care and other virtues

As indicated earlier, developing virtues require sound relationships, sensitivity, and the use of intellectual and emotional resources. Moreover, one learns virtues by observing those who practise them. Virtues do not exist outside of practices. Hence, model practices and model practitioners are crucial.

Traditionally, the four cardinal virtues, that is, the virtues on which all others depend, are prudence, justice, fortitude and temperance. Together with the

77. Ibid., 261.
78. Ibid.
79. Ibid.
80. Ibid., 262.

three theological virtues, faith, hope and love, these virtues constitute the main virtues in the Christian tradition. To what extent may the cardinal virtues allow us to counter the lack of positive symbolic practices (as expressing virtues) in the Christian tradition for countering the climate crisis?

I have already tacitly presented the virtue of prudence, regarding what is needed to act wisely: the combination of the search for knowledge and acquiring sufficient experience. 'Prudence is the virtue that disposes practical reason to discern our true good in every circumstance and to choose the right means of achieving it.'[81] Prudence is crucial because it guides the other virtues. It also guides the judgment of conscience.

If we consider prudence as the foundation for the virtue of ecological care, it means that prior to any climate action one needs to have a comprehensive grasp on the conditions for action, on the array of possible actions and on their consequences vis-à-vis the future of the planet as a whole. This comprehensive grasp entails that we must focus attention on elements that go beyond (but also include) the flourishing and well-being of humans. Thus, we can define prudential action that articulates wisdom as the opposite of attitudes and actions that ignore the concerns for this totality. Present prudence must include non-human nature.

The second cardinal moral virtue, justice, 'consists in the constant and firm will to give their due to God and neighbor'.[82] This virtue entails firm respect for each person's rights and the will to establish in human relationships the harmony that promotes equity concerning persons and to the common good.[83] Concerning the climate crisis, the question of justice is crucial on several levels, traditionally ignored in the classical definitions of this virtue. On the human level, the question of justice places all humans on the same level. Then, it becomes clear that the access to, and consumption of, goods are not equally distributed. Injustice permeates the world, and inequality is apparent in terms of race, gender, geography, class and so on. Moreover, we also know that if all were to consume at the level of Western societies, the Earth would be radically less sustainable than what it already is. Hence, justice is a crucial virtue for transforming the situation already at the level of humanity. However, at the level of ecosystems, one can also ask if humans pay sufficient respect to other species' needs and rights to live and live well. The notion of eco-justice includes equitable practice towards other living beings as well. It is necessary for securing ecological sustainability and protection. Again, we see the need for the expansion of the traditional scope of concern inherent in the virtues. This is well expressed in the following quote by American eco-theologians:

---

81. See 'The Cathecism of the Catholic Church: Chapter One: The Dignity of the Human Person. Article 7: The Virtues', https://www.vatican.va/archive/ccc_css/archive/catechism/p3s1c1a7.htm. 1806.
82. Cf. Ibid., 1807.
83. Ibid.

Justice – creating right relationships, both social and ecological, to ensure for all members of the Earth community the conditions required for their flourishing. Among human members, justice demands meeting the essential material needs and conditions for human dignity and social participation. In our global context, economic deprivation and ecological degradation are linked in a vicious circle. We are compelled, therefore, to seek eco-justice, the integration of social justice and ecological integrity. The quest for eco-justice also implies the development of a set of human environmental rights, since one of the essential conditions of human well-being is ecological integrity.[84]

Concomitant with this notion of eco-justice is the notion of *bioresponsibility*. It means that justice has to include all other life-forms as created and loved by God, and as expressions of God's presence, wisdom and glory. Accordingly, it is not humans who determine the value of other living beings, and they should not be treated as mere means for the gratification of human wants and needs. Other living beings 'deserve a "fair share" of Earth's bounty – a share that allows a biodiversity of life to thrive along with human communities'.[85]

The virtue of fortitude 'is the moral virtue that ensures firmness in difficulties and constancy in the pursuit of the good. It strengthens the resolve to resist temptations and to overcome obstacles in the moral life'.[86] This is probably the only virtue that is not in need of any substantial adjustment – but it is surely one that is required for practising the virtue of ecological care – and eco-justice. Concomitant with this is also the virtue of integrity – to practise the virtues without compromise or flaw and live up to one's prudential insights.

Perhaps *temperance* is the moral virtue that is lost in the modern consumer society and in contemporary struggles for power, wealth, recognition and status. According to the Catholic Catechism, this virtue 'moderates the attraction of pleasures and provides balance in the use of created goods. It ensures the will's mastery over instincts and keeps desires within the limits of what is honorable. The temperate person directs the sensitive appetites toward what is good and maintains a healthy discretion'.[87] Hence, this virtue still seems relevant to integrate into the virtue of ecological care.

What about the three theological virtues: faith, hope and love? I will return to these in detail in Part III because they are relevant for elaborating the symbols and practices I will discuss. Here, it is sufficient to point to how faith entails trust in a God who cares for all, and this faith can serve as a correction to the human desire to consume and acquire wealth. To trust in God and to love God's creation is,

---

84. Larry Rasmussen and Paul Santmire et al., *God's Earth Is Sacred: Essays on Eco-Justice*, (National Council of Churches Eco-Justice Program, 2011).
85. Ibid.
86. 'The Catechism of the Catholic Church: Chapter One: The Dignity of the Human Person. Article 7: The Virtues'. 1808.
87. Ibid., 1808.

therefore, also the reason why we can have hope for the future: faith, hope and love are all entangled in the human commitment to the future of God's creation. Sin, as the opposite of faith, hope and love, is that which closes us off from that future.

Faith in God means nothing unless it is practised – and virtuous practice is directed towards that which one loves and appreciates. However, if one is to develop the practice of love towards all of creation, it means that one needs to relate to it at all levels possible: not only by distanced on-looking but by allowing for experiences of nature's beauty and chaos, its power, its diversities and its impact on our emotions and sensations. We cannot love what we do not know in this way.[88] We cannot care for that about which we are ignorant. We cannot hope for another future unless we realize that the present conditions and our lifestyle jeopardize it.

---

88. A beautiful example of this is found in Edward O. Wilson, *Biophilia* (Cambridge, MA: Harvard University Press, 2019).

Chapter 9

AN INDUCTIVE, EXPERIENTIALLY ORIENTED THEOLOGY

The theological task of finding an adequate response to the climate crisis challenges us to consider the way we understand and practise theology. Against the backdrop of what has been presented about symbols and agency in this part of the book, I will summarize how we must imagine theological work in a contemporary context.

One prevailing notion of theology is that it starts with interpreting texts and employing these texts as a guide in organizing our reality and our experiences. This approach is rare in academic circles, but it is prevailing in pockets of lived religion worldwide. It runs the risk of developing a *deductive* theology in which one subjects reality to statements derived from doctrine – statements that were established with no reference to or not informed by the present empirical situation. We see one example of this approach in evangelical theology that subsumes experiences related to global warming to notions about God's sovereignty.

Several problematic consequences emerge from this approach. Firstly, it ignores some of its own suppositions. Theology never was a mere deductive enterprise. If we ask what has engendered theological reflection through the centuries, it is not the reading of texts in themselves that facilitate orientation and transformation, but the interaction between texts and the experiences that people have with the situation and the reality in which they find themselves. Secondly, it can only address topics that the text addresses, and it leaves everything else in the dark or ignores it as theologically irrelevant. Thirdly, it runs the risk of placing theology and religious engagement in a sphere isolated from believers and others' everyday experiences, since it, to no small extent, may be unable to address contemporary issues and topics adequately.

The alternative to this predominantly deductive approach is to use the reflective resources of theological symbols, narratives, doctrines, Bible and tradition, to interpret present experience to the extent that it is possible and to continue to develop imaginaries, notions and practices that open up different possibilities for doing theology when the resources of the past appear as insufficient. Although theology will always remain rooted in the resources that have their origin in the past, the contemporary situation must inform theological work. This fact places theology in a situation in which it is explorative and inductive rather than deductive. The explorative approach entails figuring out how symbols make new perspectives and experiences possible and how experiences may challenge established symbols and, at times, reveal their inadequacy or their shortcomings. Theology becomes creative when it develops responses to the present and suggests ways to respond to and relate to what we experience as present challenges. This indictive understanding of theological practice makes it experience-based and experience-related. Theology becomes an open enterprise informed and shaped by contemporary challenges. It is forward-looking in its uses of the past.

Hence, theology needs to engage the symbols of the past with the concern for how it allows us to address the contemporary situation – as Tillich also indicates when he speaks about the difference between living and dead symbols. Moreover, theology cannot merely aim at transforming the present situation and the practices of humans, but *theology must also be willing to undergo a transformation of its own* when it is not able to address the contemporary situation in an adequate manner.

Therefore, the main test for Christian theology under the present conditions will be to what extent it can be put to use in the way suggested earlier. Theology presumed to work in an isolated sphere with no reference to present experience and practice will soon be rendered obsolete. The growing awareness of the empirical context, and more specifically about the different pragmatic conditions at play in the actual use of theology, entails that we cannot consider theology as based merely on texts that need interpretation and understanding. The main question is how we can *use* such texts. Their use must be related to, informed by and developed with reference to empirical conditions studied from a scholarly and scientific perspective. Thereby, theological work's actual outcome proves relevant and not a mere statement of *a priori* claims. The empirical orientation implies that theology works in an interdisciplinary context, where social sciences contribute to understanding theology's role, function and contribution to human life. Theology does not any longer interact exclusively with philosophy and history but with other disciplines as well.

David G. Kirchhoffer writes about the challenges of theology and religion in light of the present situation. Against the backdrop of the aforementioned considerations, he helps us see their relevance concerning climate change. The insight that human beings can no longer be seen as separate from the dynamic ecological systems or processes of which we are part entails that we cannot see ourselves as 'external observers or even rational internal controllers of systems. Rather we are increasingly aware of our own place as part of these evolving interactions, changing and being changed by them'.[1] From this follows his assessment of the contemporary situation of religion and theology:

> While internal coherency is a necessary and worthy goal of any religion, where such a coherency is not in accord with what we know about the interconnectedness

---

1. David G. Kirchhoffer, 'How Ecology Can Save the Life of Theology: A Philosophical Contribution to the Engagement of Ecology and Theology', in *Theology and Ecology across the Disciplines: On Care for Our Common Home*, ed. Celia Deane-Drummond and Rebecca Artinian-Kaiser (London: Bloomsbury, 2018), 56.

of the world and the role of humans in it, the religion's truth claims can be called into question – especially where these claims may be contributing to harms of human beings, other organisms, and the environment. No matter how coherent a religious belief system may be, strongly egoistic-anthropocentric conceptions of existence are radically challenged by what we know from ecology, especially the understanding of existence as dynamic interconnections of which humans are an integral part, neither external nor in control.[2]

Kirchhoffer underscores, rightly, that theology must incorporate the knowledge about interconnectedness into its religious doctrine. From a critical point of view, it means that theology cannot 'accept outdated and inaccurate biologies and "ecologies" that have perpetuated the hegemony of egoistic anthropocentrism over other human beings and the natural world'.[3] If this transformative move is not made, 'theology is in danger of perpetuating the kind of thinking that has caused the harms highlighted by [Rachel] Carson and the IPCC, which are harms for everything and everyone'.[4]

The type of theology I argue for here has a pragmatic basis one cannot make generic theological statements without reference to the contexts in which these can or should be used. Kirchhoffer addresses this from his point of view (which is not explicitly pragmatist) by underscoring the interrelation between the focus on particulars, on the one hand, and more general contexts and practices, on the other hand. It is against this backdrop that the normative dimension in theology appears:

> While it is possible to make generalizable claims about human nature, this can distract theology from the unique histories and contexts of individual believers and nonbelievers, and their struggles to come to terms with the meaning and purpose of life, suffering, injustice, and the pursuit of truth, goodness, and beauty. Attending to these things is not to fall into relativism. Like the relationship between particular cases and generalizable principles in ecology, there is a dialectic between praxis and theory, between the particular and the universal, that tries to take both seriously. This approach also accepts that, while consensus may be possible at a generalizable level, consensus should not do so in a way that rides roughshod over the realities and uncertainties that arise from the complexities of particular cases and circumstances.[5]

The pragmatic turn in theology, which I develop further in this chapter, entails that theology is concerned with theological teaching's consequences in peoples' lives. The actual experiences that people interpret with the help of theology can

---

2. Ibid., 56–7.
3. Ibid., 57.
4. Ibid.
5. Ibid., 58–9.

give feedback to those who practise and use theological reasoning in various ways and contexts. Such openness to other disciplines and the cultural context that has changed theology over the last decades has contributed to seeing theology not only as ideology or doctrine but as practices. The theologian can no longer only be content with answering questions about what church doctrine is but has to take up responsibility with regard to how this doctrine affects peoples' lives and is used to orient or transform human life. The normative dimension in theology is expressed in how it can offer guidance for such use. Normative claims are always connected to and at least partly determined by the relationships in which they exist and the contexts they partake. Hence, normative claims cannot be based 'solely on some essentialist assertion about my existence, of the kind of being that I am (e.g., free and rational), and of principles deduced from that. The normative claim must also be based on the historical, contingent realities of my past, present, and future functions', Kirchhoffer claims.[6]

This pragmatist theology represents an alternative to 'essentialist assumptions' and 'contingent realities' as the basis for normative orientation aimed at transformation. This alternative, which I will develop more extensively in the next part of this book, we can identify in experiences and phenomena that are fundamental to all human life: the experience of being pregnant – or being borne. This fundamental feature can offer some fundamental guidance. Simultaneously, it can be applied in different ways in different practice contexts. The fundamental attitude shaped by imagining yourself as carrying the future under your heart entails that *you see all your actions as related to that which is to come*. This attitude can shape the virtue of ecological care and is opposite to attitudes that express laxism, indifference and relativism, a point that Kirchhoffer articulates as the consequence of the fact that an ecological view 'opens the possibility that different more general norms may develop over time in light of changed roles and relationships'. Thus, 'more formal norms, such as *epieikeia* – the norm dictating that one should be just, reasonable, and equitable in one's dealings with others – must be realized by taking cognizance of the truth of the historical relationships and roles present in each instance'.[7]

One consequence of the pragmatic turn in theology is that the subject of (academic) theology becomes wider. As indicated, it cannot only be text related or focus on articulating coherent and transparent doctrinal formulations and generic and/or essentialist principles. Theology needs to consider how it works in an actual social, historical and cultural context. Theological work cannot restrict itself to analyse and address religion primarily as propositions subject to arguments. Instead, the subject at hand is human experiences that may give rise to these propositions and experiences of how these propositions work and are used. Coherent theological arguments must also address its own implications: how theology can be used in good or bad ways for or against people who want to

---

6. Ibid., 62.
7. Ibid., 63.

change social, ecological, cultural or economic patterns they experience as unjust and oppressive. Various forms of contextual theology (as in liberation theology or feminist theology) provide good examples of how theology has become more empirically informed in ways that do indeed point to empirically informed reflection about its tasks and functions.

The aforementioned considerations also entail that there is a limit to what science can offer a pragmatic theology. Science offers a third-person-perspective on reality, and, thereby, it may contribute to the distanced approach to reality. However, when doing so, the first- and second-person perspective may fall under the table. There is a myriad of experiences of the world, in the world and with the world, and not all of them can be articulated in third-person perspectives. Some are deeply rooted in first-person sensitivities: experiences of beauty, loss, pregnancy, hope and expectation, or love. They count, and others may know that such experiences exist, but they are silenced and do not count in the context of science. We overcome these restrictions and allow experiences to count in the dialectic between knowledge, experience, evaluation and sensitivity. Why? Because we need to articulate experiences that open us up to the problems that face us and do so in ways that can generate consistent and persistent action for the better. We need symbols that can articulate such a comprehensive approach to experiences that humankind depends on and that can be recognized by all, although not all of us share them in the same way.

Theology and experience

The points just made indicate the necessity of taking the social context into account methodologically and systematically. Contrary to some theologians' delusions or self-perceptions, theology has always been empirically informed, in the sense that it has related to, made use of and built upon empirical elements in its context or environment. All theology must presuppose elements in the knowledge reservoir of its time and place. Even reference to divine revelation as the basis for theology does not eliminate this fact since revelation does not rule out experiential elements. Revelation occurs under historical and social circumstances requiring the hermeneutic resources to understand it by those who witness it. Personal experience cannot be ignored in the context of such theological work. Denis Edwards argues aptly:

> The ecological transformation needed by our world must be informed by the sciences and find expression in culture, politics, economics, and law. But none of this will be achieved unless there is also a transformation of human interiority – human feeling, knowing, and loving as well as long-term commitments. For those who are Christian believers, this interiority is at least in part shaped by their Christian faith. Ecological theology can function to educate such faith and to call believers to ecological conversion. It can thus provide meaning and motivation for joining with others in ecological commitment and practice. It

can help shape an ecological ethos and way of life and provide the foundation for ecological ethics.[8]

Although it can then be argued that theology has always been empirically informed in some way or another, we need to add a significant qualifier here and avoid simplifying the matter. One thing is to state, generically, that theology has always been empirically informed, but this does not imply that all empirical material that theology has engaged has been scientifically established and validated. A programmatic and methodological awareness of the empirical conditions for doing theology in the contemporary world enables us to identify four implications for contemporary theology understood as empirically informed.

First of all, it implies a criticism of any theology that perceives its own activity as self-contained and self-explanatory with no need for taking into account elements in its social context. The time is over when theology can operate without integrating elements from other disciplines or ignore critical elements and questions that other disciplines direct towards it.

Secondly, theology must recognize the methodological consequences of its own origin in experience: it builds on experience transmitted by sources, as well as experience of how traditioned experience works in the contemporary context. There is no access to theological topics unmediated by present experience. The theological tradition is always transmitted through social and historical contexts that shape the form, content emphasis, and outlook of what the community of believers holds true.

Furthermore, and thirdly, this means, as already suggested earlier, that the use of theology is first and foremost to contribute to the actual interpreting of experience by believers of past and present, as well as offering new chances for experiences by employing the resources for orientation and transformation of which religious traditions are stewards. Faced with the challenges of the climate crisis, religious people should be encouraged to confront and address the crisis informed by the resources provided by their religious tradition without trying to make this into something else than about the climate. The spiritual dimension inherent in the crisis is not the only thing that makes it necessary to address it. We need to look at the actual situation as more than a symptom for something else and more important. To address the situation with religious symbols and their concomitant practices cannot make our actual dealing with the catastrophe at hand less challenging. The climate crisis is about something in and of this world and not about something else that should take the attention away from it or make it less alarming.

---

8. Denis Edwards, 'Key Issues in Ecological Theology: Incarnation, Evolution, Communion', in *Theology and Ecology across the Disciplines: On Care for Our Common Home*, ed. Celia Deane-Drummond and Rebecca Artinian-Kaiser ((London: 2018: Bloomsbury, 2018), 65.

Finally, and fourthly, the implication of all the aforementioned is that theology only can benefit from closer contact with religious studies, cultural studies, sociology of religion and psychology of religion. The divide between theology and religious studies that remain in many academic contexts needs to be overcome, as a wider and interdisciplinary frame is necessary for theology to consider and address all its challenges regarding reflection about how religion is to be understood and practiced in concrete social contexts. The overcoming of this divide would most likely be beneficial for both disciplines. It may also benefit religious studies because it is essential for such studies to have a firm understanding of the religious convictions that shape religious agency and theology may contribute significantly to such understanding.

The pragmatic approach to theology suggested here entails that its doctrinal claims require a pragmatic justification in terms of how well it allows us to address our current predicament and inspire more just and sustainable practices. A mere doctrinal proposition cannot help us understand what its claim means for the interpretation, orientation, and transformation necessary. Theology is, to make a twist on Marx, not only about understanding the world but about changing it. Hence, it is not only an intellectual enterprise but also a social practice for specific purposes of orientation and transformation.[9]

A pragmatist theology

As has become obvious earlier, pragmatism informs the theological work in this book. Pragmatism underscores how human knowledge develops based on problematic situations in which we find ourselves and the practices we develop to handle these. Given this point of departure, one can ask the following critical question to the Christian tradition: To what extent, and in what way, do the resources in this tradition's symbols enable an adequate response to the climate crisis? If they do not, we may be faced with a deficit in relevant symbols and the theological tradition's lack of relevance. If we formulate in more positively, we can say that the pragmatic approach to religious knowledge means more than 'knowing that' – it means 'knowing how'. 'To have religious knowledge means to have the ability to handle existentially significant situations with the resources (myths, symbols, understandings of reality etc.) to which participation in religious practices offers access.'[10] And we are, indeed, in an existentially significant situation.

Among the pragmatist approach's fundamental advantages is that it sees humans as active and engaged with the world, not passive and detached observers. John Dewey refers to the latter position as 'the spectator theory' in which the

---

9. Cf. Henriksen, *Religion as Orientation and Transformation: A Maximalist Theory*; ibid.

10. These points are inspired by Mikael Sörhuus: *En känsla för det heliga*, (Diss, Uppsala 2020). The quote is from ibid., 177.

human is seen as independent of the world and assessed from a rather static perspective. However, the former position entails that humans exist in a dynamic and continuously interactive relationship with the world.[11] Thus, he develops a position in which it becomes impossible to separate humans from nature, and, thus, he sides with those I have already analysed in this part (Taylor, Chodorow, Jones).

Another advantage of a pragmatist approach to theology is that it does not see a principled conflict between science and religion/ethics. The focus is on practice. This focus allows for an assessment in which the implications of theology for human life in interrelation with other living beings are at the centre. Pragmatism works under the assumption that human beings must be considered 'in a double light, both as natural elements of the natural world and as free and autonomous agents – with agency arising from that very same nature'.[12] The focus on agency and practice addresses humans as 'normatively concerned creatures, beings habitually engaging in a continuous evaluation of our actions and practices. Our habits and actions are guided by values, goals, and ideals'.[13] Moreover, 'It does not deny values or normativity, because they are crucial to our self-understanding as agents'.[14] Accordingly, how symbols and imaginaries in the Christian tradition can shape and develop practices is among the potential achievements of adopting a pragmatist stance.

Furthermore, because human engagement with the world is conditioned by concepts that are rooted in practices, it is not fruitful to operate on the basis of 'the classical philosophical dualisms, such as mind and body, experience and nature, knowledge and action, science and technology, facts and values, or theory and practice [. . .]. Our human world is a mixture of these'.[15] Pragmatism thus enables a holistic approach. At the forefront is the 'practical testability' of religious ideas in how they result in practical action and ways of life. Religion is 'practically testable qua motives for action' and by the practical implications to which they lead. They may be accepted insofar as their practical results are defensible.[16]

The last point here, about a possible defense, is important. Although pragmatism explicitly denies the possibility for a 'God's eye view', it does not exclude normative judgements about what positions and ideas are good or not. However, the focus on the practical implications of ideas provides a basis for this assessment. The advantage of this approach is that we can avoid questions about the extent to which religious practice is 'true' generically – and ask instead to what extent it is justified

---

11. Cf. John Dewey, *The Quest for Certainty: A Study of the Relation of Knowledge and Action*, Gifford Lectures (London: Allen & Unwin, 1930), 26, 188.

12. Sami Pihlström, *The Bloomsbury Companion to Pragmatism*, Bloomsbury Companions (London: Bloomsbury Academic, 2015), 9.

13. Cf. ibid., 16.

14. Cf. ibid.

15. Ibid., 15.

16. Cf. ibid., 28–9.

under specific conditions, given its practical implications.[17] The main element in normative assessments is how practices enable and support the flourishing of all life on the planet.

A final element is that pragmatists acknowledge the finite character of any human position and judgement and all our positions' preliminary character. Concerning religion, this insight into the finite supports a crucial insight: 'If the ultimate is worth getting excited about, it would have to be bigger than what we can get our signs around', writes Robert Neville.[18] Because of this preliminary character, it always recommends itself to be open to other and new perspectives and resist the temptation to rely on or be content with the place in which one finds oneself already, and with the symbolic resources at hand.

---

17. The position that religion should be assessed with regard to how it can present justifications for its practices, instead of asking about to what extent it is true, is argued by Dirk-Martin Grube and Walter Van Herck, *Philosophical Perspectives on Religious Diversity Bivalent Truth, Tolerance and Personhood* (London: Routledge, 2018).

18. Robert C. Neville, *Defining Religion: Essays in Philosophy of Religion* (Albany, NY: State University of New York, 2018), 188.

Part III

SYMBOLS FOR PRACTICES

Wisdom only matters if it manifests itself in practices. This part will consider and discuss theological resources we can develop to counter the climate change catastrophe. How can they be resources for practical wisdom – knowledge that builds on the insight into how all that exists is connected and must be dealt with in ways that recognize how all our actions relate to the future of the planet? Taking our point of departure in the Jewish prophets' fundamental attitude who focused on events in history that manifested salvation or misfortune, we need to hold together scientific knowledge and the faith that God creates the world. We can then maintain a comprehensive approach to the contemporary situation in which we will not lose ourselves in either scientific details or other-worldly escapism and speculation.[1]

Parts I and II of this book demonstrated how religious symbols inspire, engage, preclude, impede and inform human activities, and widen or narrow the frameworks we have for understanding ourselves in the world. The task now is to ponder the potential constructive (and sometimes destructive) contributions of different imaginaries in the Christian tradition that can help us address the situation. Hence, focus on how to best *use* theology in the present situation is the task – not to discern the final truth about religious or secular matters. In this, I adopt the *pragmatic approach* to the theological work presented in the previous chapters. The underlying question is: *In what ways and to what extent can diverse religious imaginaries help us to develop the necessary resistance against the accelerating climate change catastrophe and make us better equipped to handle the situation?*

---

1. This is a continuous task of Christian theology, as described in critical detail by Habermas, *Auch Eine Geschichte Der Philosophie Band 1: Die Okzidentale Konstellation Von Glauben Und Wissen Band 2: Vernünftige Freiheit. Spuren Des Diskurses Über Glauben Und Wissen*.

Chapter 10

GOD AS CREATOR

A CRITICAL SYMBOL?

The common assumption is that the way Christians see God and God's relationship to the world orients their behaviour. However, a person's understanding of God also depends on her context, the available types of knowledge (e.g. scientific, traditional) about the world, and other imaginaries that allow a person to interpret and engage the world. In the Christian tradition, God is the creator and redeemer of the world. These designations are linked closely to how we understand the created world. It is crucial, however, to ask how an understanding of God may contribute to orientation and transformation in light of the climate crisis. Can the symbol 'God' help us engage the world and be of relevance for our practices? If we are to answer such questions affirmatively, we may have to let go of notions of God that depict God as transcendent, sovereign, distant and separated from the world. Other imaginaries, less resembling a distant father and more resembling a mother who is actively engaged in her offspring with mind and body, may prove more adequate and aligned with features in the biblical tradition when not read through a patriarchal lens.

God of life or God of death?

Symbols open up our imaginations and allow us to see new possibilities for seeing and experiencing the world. They question our taken-for-granted ways of understanding and may disorient them to open up our imagination to a new orientation.[1] Moreover, symbols can engender imaginations that provide opportunities for hope insofar as the imaginations express the power of the possible and open up a new world.[2] Against this backdrop, we must ask, what does it mean to see belief in God as a contribution to human *orientation*? It means that the

---

1. Cf. Paul Ricoeur, *Figuring the Sacred: Religion, Narrative, and Imagination*, trans. David Pellauer (Minneapolis: Augsburg Fortress, 1995), 281, and Christina M. Gschwandtner, 'Ricoeur's Hermeneutic of God: A Symbol That Gives Rise to Thought', *Philosophy and Theology* 13, no. 2 (2001): 301.

2. Cf. Gschwandtner, 'Ricoeur's Hermeneutic of God: A Symbol That Gives Rise to Thought', 304.

symbol God enables us to see where we come from, our origin, our possible futures, opportunities and prospects. Thus, it suggests basic features for understanding the situation in which we find ourselves. Moreover, orientation means considering things from the point of view of values and qualities. Thereby, the symbol 'God' makes possible an evaluation of the present situation and contributes to a deeper understanding of it. But 'God' does more. God points to the fundamental features and relationships that determine life: our interdependence with everything that is created, and the world's origin in God and how it is dependent upon God's continuous creativity. To orient yourself from God is, therefore, to orient yourself from that which matters most. But what matters most to us? That is not a given, and it is against the backdrop of the realization of that fact that we can start by revisiting Luther's definition of what a god is, in order to appropriate it for the critical task of assessing the contemporary situation. In the explanation of the first commandment in the *Large Catechism*, we saw that Luther wrote:

> What is to have a god? What is God? Answer: A god is that to which we look for all good and in which we find refuge in every time of need. To have a god is nothing else than to trust and believe him with our whole heart. As I have often said, the trust and faith of the heart alone make both God and an idol. If your faith and trust are right, then your God is the true God. On the other hand, if your trust is false and wrong, then you have not the true God. For these two belong together, faith and God. That to which your heart clings and entrusts itself is, I say, really your God.[3]

Luther's formal definition of what a god is serves as an important point of departure as we are confronted with the present catastrophe: What do we put our trust in? The answer to this question determines if we serve and worship God or an idol. In the present situation, this is not a mere theological question – it is a question of life and death. Let me illustrate.

If we expect the good to come from continued consumption and a 'business as usual economy', that expectation is doomed to fail and will lead to death because our planet cannot bear its consequences. As I write this, the world is still in the midst of the Covid-19 pandemic, and there is public discourse about when we can expect to turn back to normal, to business as usual. The assumption that this is possible and even will mean that we will be out of trouble is false. Any return to the normal will lead to more death in the long run – because of the planet's situation. The god of business as usual, the god who demands continued consumption of material goods and fossil fuel, is the idol of death. During the pandemic, we have seen this clearly in the urge of politicians for people to return to normal before the pandemic was under control: As I write these sentences, the US death toll

---

3. Martin Luther and F. Samuel Janzow, *Luther's Large Catechism: A Contemporary Translation with Study Questions* (St. Louis: Concordia Pub. House, 1988), I, 1. Cf. also the remarks I made on Luther's understanding of God in Chapter 3.

has passed 350,000 – and continues – only because having the consumption- and fossil-driven economy as the all-determining reality that can keep people in power was prioritized above anything else. To put your trust in and expect all that is good to come from the god of fossil-driven economy means death. Still, however, it is to this god that the hearts of many are clinging, and it is this god who promises its 'goods' to whom many feel attracted.

Luther's formal and universal definition of God opens up to several different layers of meaning. Even though he does not mention it explicitly, the understanding of God developed here makes it possible to articulate not only what it means to have a God but also why it is necessary to believe in a *true God*. Thus, the *existential* dimension or concern in Luther's theology becomes apparent. How a human being orients herself in the world by means of faith is the decisive element for him. To speak about God is to speak about the instance from which one governs and orients one's own life. Hence, it all hangs on believing in a true God, that is, a God who deserves to be called God, and who *can* be God.

Who is this God? It is the God of life, who creates and relates to the world by offering chances for faith, hope and love. It is the God who does not destroy what God has created.[4] This God works continuously to provide new chances for life, renewal, diversity and a flourishing future. This point may also be understood in light of Luther's explication of the basic definition of God as offered earlier. A human who puts her trust in herself and her own works or merits makes herself god – yet this god is an idol. Accordingly, Luther's understanding of God directs the human being away from a focus on herself and her achievements and towards the basis given in the gifts of God. By directing the human being outside herself, towards God's works instead of herself, Luther indicates that the only reliable God is *extra nos*, that is, one who is not ourselves.

Luther's 'definition' of what a god is in the *Large Catechism* can thus serve as a critical tool in the present situation because it engages the human being in a critical self-assessment: In who and what do you trust? This approach does not intend to bring about a fundamental lack of trust in oneself but aims at directing one's trust towards a God who offers life to all of creation and fights against its destruction.

A further element in Luther's explanation of the first commandment is that it *relates God and the good to each other,* as we already have indicated earlier. Thus, the human *expectation for goodness* is connected intimately with the notion of God. God is trustworthy because this God is the source of goodness, the one who provides human life with what humans need and for which they strive. For Luther, this is important because it allows humans to see the experienced goodness as not originating from themselves and their own work but from the abundance

---

4. It is important to state that this notion of God is one that contradicts imagery of God as violent, or as simply blessing 'our multiplying human populations and resource-expensive economic cycles of production, consumption and waste'. Cf. Primavesi, *Gaia and Climate Change: A Theology of Gift Events*, 32–3.

offered by the generous God. In turn, the goodness we experience in creation is not originating from our own works and merits, but neither is the justification God offers us by faith alone. In both cases, we are referred to God as the only reliable source of the qualities we need.[5] Accordingly, the meaning of the first commandment is that it directs the human being (outwards) towards the only reliable source from which he or she is to expect the good:

> we are to trust in God alone, and look to Him and expect from Him naught but good, as from one who gives us body, life, food, drink, nourishment, health, protection, peace, and all necessaries of both temporal and eternal things. He also preserves us from misfortune, and if any evil befalls us, delivers and rescues us, so that it is God alone (as has been sufficiently said) from whom we receive all good, and by whom we are delivered from all evil. Hence also, I think, we Germans from ancient times call God (more elegantly and appropriately than any other language) by that name from the word Good, as being an eternal fountain which gushes forth abundantly nothing but what is good, and from which flows forth all that is and is called good.

That God and goodness are linked so closely together furthermore means that Luther's understanding of God's gifts can be expressed in the understanding of God as *love*. It is because God loves the human being that he bestows his gifts on them. Thus, God's nature is love, a point that also comes to full expression in his how God gives humans the eternal goods in his Son – and thus Godself as well.[6] The fact that this loving God is the one and only *summum bonum* constitutes, in turn, the creature's obligation to let God, and nothing else, be God.

I will later return to how the aforementioned conception of God as the one you put your trust in is the adequate backdrop for understanding sin in the context of climate change. Here, however, two other questions need discussion.

Firstly, if it is from God that we are to expect all that is good – what does it mean for the understanding of human agency? Is there a risk of passivity here – leaving all to God and keep on as before? Given that humans face the task of countering climate change consequences, will the idea of trusting that all good comes from God impede necessary human activity? That may be the case as long as one sees

---

5. This point comes clearly to expression in the continuation of the text: 'Therefore it is the intent of this commandment to require true faith and trust of the heart which settles upon the only true God, and clings to Him alone. That is as much as to say: "See to it that you let Me alone be your God, and never seek another," i.e.: Whatever you lack of good things, expect it of Me, and look to Me for it, and whenever you suffer misfortune and distress, creep and cling to Me. I, yes, I, will give you enough and help you out of every need; only let not your heart cleave to or rest in any other'. Luther and Janzow, *Luther's Large Catechism: A Contemporary Translation with Study Questions*, I, 4.

6. Cf. Paul Althaus, *The Theology of Martin Luther* (Philadelphia: Fortress Press, 1996), 115–16.

God as the only agent behind the good. However, if we see humans as images of God, that is, as those who are called to mediate goodness by being God's stewards,[7] the impression of this notion leading to passivity may be overcome. Then it is the task of humans in their works to make manifest God's creative and redeeming love for all of creation – and to love the world as God does. The one who loves searches for the good for the beloved – not for its destruction. Hence, underscoring God's sovereignty as the fundamental source of goodness should not be taken as an opportunity to exclude the participation of humans in bringing forth goodness, growth and flourishing. Instead, God's action is mediated by means of the already pre-existing creation. God creates freely, but with the participation of that which is other than God. Thus, God manifests and mediates Godself through creation.

Secondly, given the close connection between God and goodness, we may ask what kind of notion of goodness is at work as we see 'God' as a symbol for orientation and transformation in the way Luther allows us to consider. This question can also be asked in another way: What kind of god is the one to whom we are attracted? There is a considerable difference between seeing goodness from an anthropocentric point of view – where the rest of creation is there for humans to use and exploit freely for their own good or seeing goodness as manifest in how all creation's flourishing is linked together. We learn from the Anthropocene situation that the first option is no longer viable: There cannot be any lasting goodness for humans unless all creation is considered. Hence, anthropocentrism presents the temptation of idolatry: to think that humans are the only ones who matter and that goodness is restricted to what is desirable for and serves only our gratification. Therefore, a shift from anthropocentrism to ecocentrism is not a shift in terms of priority but more a question about how we see the human relationship with the rest of creation or not. 'It is a move from assuming that all of life centers on the human, to recognizing that this is biologically not true.'[8] Accordingly, it means that the moral universe expands beyond the human and narrow and short-sighted human interests.

The experiential and practical use of the symbol 'God' is therefore linked to other conceptions and imaginaries that I will discuss in this chapter: the notion of creation and humans as created in God's image. Moreover, it is related to the notion of *sin*, which means misplaced trust and misplaced orientation. Luther's positive contribution to the critical use of the notion of God nevertheless remains: Do we put our trust in a god that means life or death, and who offers goodness to the few chosen or to all of creation? In what way the symbol 'God' is put to use is, therefore, not only a question about how it is employed as a critical concept, but it

---

7. The notion of humans as God's stewards is controversial in an ecological context and needs more specification if its deficits are to be overcome. This task will be taken up in the following text, pp. 142ff.

8. Cynthia D. Moe-Lobeda, 'Finding Common Ground on a Moral Vision for a Good Society', in *T&T Clark Handbook of Christian Theology and Climate Change*, ed. Ernst M. Conradie and Hilda P. Koster (London: New York: T&T Clark, 2020), 166f.

is also a question about the pragmatic context in which that takes place. However, on its own, it is not clear what the concept 'God' can contribute without supplying it with other symbols and concepts. The primary among these is the notion of creation.

When understood in the way Luther suggests, the conception of God is not relevant for believers or Christians only. It serves as a critical tool for asking what human orientation leads to in terms of practising the virtue of ecological care or in terms of destroying conditions for life for both humans and other species. Consequently, whom or what one believes in is not only a question of whom you worship in a religious service, but what you practise as your fundamental beliefs in all realms of life, whether you consider yourself religious or not. Is your fundamental orientation from the consumer god who lives on fossil fuel and claims destruction of habitats and species, or from a God of love, who creates in order to let all life flourish in abundance and calls us to protect the conditions for this flourishing?

Although the notion of God thus can serve as a symbol for a critical assessment of basic orientation and concomitant conduct, it does not mean that notions of God, or humans as created in the image of God, can contribute directly and immediately to practices of ecological care. They lack a direct experiential basis that can mediate this care, and, thus, they require further specification in terms of the agency to which they should lead. However, they can serve as elements in the context of understanding where such practices can take place. Hence, there is a pragmatic deficit in the symbol 'God' as it exists in the Christian tradition insofar as its ecological relevance is not spelled out. This deficit can only be overcome by specifying and developing elements beyond the conceptual and experiential context in which it traditionally has found its place.

Creation: Interconnectedness deep down entails responsibility

What does it entail for our actions and agency to think of the world as *created* by a loving God? Is that notion sufficient to motivate persistent action over time, even when it seems to be a few reasons for hope and not many signs of positive change?

In Part I, we saw that *nature* is a concept that has often been used in contrast to other realms of human life or in order to designate that which was less than human, less worthy of consideration, and with no inherent value. Accordingly, the concept of nature is tied up with several metaphysical problems that theology needs to be aware of.[9] Moreover, it has also been a concept that, when applied to humans, served to mark them as more emotional and less rational. Nature has been used to identify that which is other than history and culture – two concepts closely linked

---

9. Cf. Gordon D. Kaufman, 'A Problem for Theology: The Concept of Nature', *The Harvard Theological Review* 65, no. 3 (1972).

to human activity and creativity. Thus, humans have been conceptually set apart from nature – at least the male, presumably rational, version of humanity.

If we are to overcome some of the misconceptions connected to the notions of God and goodness, as I indicated earlier, we need to reappropriate the notion of creation – not as an opposite to God, but as the manifestation of, and a representation of, God's creative love. Only then can we see how the understanding of God as creator, redeemer and sustainer of all life can contribute to engendering human action vis-à-vis the present crisis. This reappropriation may also entail a broader role for experiences that allow for another approach to and engagement with the world than the one that favours the distant, spectator-like attitude, and that includes emotional, sensory and aesthetic components as well as rational ones.

The point here is not to promote an idealized approach to nature that sees it from the point of view of beauty and magnificence only. It is to allow for a loving approach to nature that sees it in its highly ambiguous character: as beauty and magnitude, as well as destruction, extinction and devastation. To overcome instrumentalist and exclusively resource-oriented attitudes to creation, we need to see it as loved by God and something we are called to love as well. What you love, you do not destroy. Hence, the deficit in the one-sided notion of creation-as-nature, which allowed for exploitation and attitudes like those Lynn White Jr's infamous accusations were based on, can only be overcome by an attitude that allows for a fuller experience of what creation is like in its present form – for good and for bad.[10]

The reappropriation of the notion of creation against this backdrop entails understanding our relationship with the rest of the world as manifest in connections that go deep down: the interrelationship that becomes manifest to the full extent in the notion of the Anthropocene shows itself in how humans and other living beings, and the non-living environment as well, partake in the same creative processes and are interconnected, interrelated and codependent. That God creates all that exists means that there is nothing outside the scope of God's creativity. This creativity manifests itself in the conditions for a flourishing life, in life itself, and in phenomena like birth, growth and development. The experiences of the

---

10. Accordingly, we can, with Cynthia D. Moe-Lobeda, summarize what is required when it comes to the perception of the world in the following four components: It entails

> seeing what is going on in whatever situation is at hand, especially unmasking systemic evil that masquerades as good; seeing what could be, that is, alternatives; seeing evermore fully the sacred Spirit of life coursing throughout creation and leading it, despite all evidence to the contrary, into abundant life for all; and seeing, in the midst of brutality, also the magnificent beauty that surrounds and imbues the ordinary everyday realities of life. Moral perception will hold these four together in one lens. Vision of this sort is subversive because it keeps the present provisional and refuses to absolutize it.

Moe-Lobeda, 'Finding Common Ground on a Moral Vision for a Good Society', 165.

diverse flows of creation and creativity give humans experiential opportunities to live, love, hope and have faith in the future. These experiences allow human beings to see God as the Creator of all, as well as the one who continually struggles to liberate creation from destruction and devastation.

Hence, when the Christian tradition assigns the notion 'creation' to reality, this designation immediately establishes an optic in which the world appears under a specific point of view: *creation is a relational term*.[11] The relationships the notion opens up are twofold. Firstly, and primarily, the creation is related to the Creator, the source and origin of all that is, and whose power sustains and renews it and manifests itself in its ability to develop further. Secondly, 'creation' relates all elements of creation to each other. Humans are not the only creation of God but are part of creation and, thereby, related to all other parts of the created world. Moreover, as evolutionary theory and genetics teach us, we would not be if there had not been conditions external to us that have provided the potential and opportunities for us to be. Hence, the created reality in which humans find themselves is *given* as a valuable fact – it is impossible to separate fact and value at the fundamental level of reality.[12]

The fundamentally relational character of creation is of vital importance for how we understand human responsibility. Responsibility presupposes relations. Because humans cannot untie themselves from their relationships with the rest of creation, responsibility is not an optional attitude. We are responsible whether we want to be or not because we are part of creation. This responsibility implies

---

11. Main elements in the following section are based on a reworking of my 'Religions and Responsibility', in *The Bloomsbury Companion to the Doctrine of Creation*, ed. J. Garoncy (London: Bloomsbury, 2021).

12. Accordingly, one can understand the given character of the natural environment as the wider and, to some extent, independent background of human practices.

> The independence and the resistance that this background poses to our interests and desires respond to a sense of fundamental importance and depth. . . . The independence and the distance established by animals and environments is a kind of fact which articulates our overall conceptual dimension: it is in fact the background which makes sense of the importance and of the depth of our inhabiting the world, of our encounters with others and of the many activities discussed in the text. It is a fact which *concerns us*: we can account for it only by deploying the overall scheme of human values. . . . The reality of the environment, of animals, and nature is not detached from the overall pattern of values, from the sense of importance and depth it expresses.

Piergiorgio Donatelli, 'The Environment and the Background of Human Life: Nature, Facts, and Values', in *Facts and Values: The Ethics and Metaphysics of Normativity*, ed. Giancarlo Marchetti and Sarin Marchetti (New York: Routledge, 2017), 261. Of course, the situation of the Anthropocene complicates this independence, insofar as it implies that humans are now shaping the total character of the Earth and its natural condition to an extent that hitherto was not the case.

that we cannot see the present and future state and condition of creation as independent of our actions. Presently, more than ever before, we learn that the future of the creation of which we are part depends on how we carry out our responsibilities. This point needs underscoring. Although we can say that we are more dependent on the rest of creation than the rest of creation is on us, that is not the full picture anymore. The Anthropocene situation[13] suggests otherwise; humans have a tremendous impact on the natural environment's shape and future, and the consequences of human activity on the rest of creation cannot be ignored. If there is to be any viable notion of human stewardship for creation, it must be rooted in recognition of this responsibility.[14]

To be responsible is to be response-able. It entails being able to orient oneself about what is happening, understand it, and respond adequately. Thus, responsibility requires both knowledge and the capacity to act according to knowledge and values. Responsibility also implies that one has more than one option about what to do: when you have no choice and are forced to act in a specific way, it is hard to speak about responsibility. Hence, to take up responsibility presupposes that one also is responsible for keeping the space open for different possible actions. Unless this space is open, there cannot be any responsible action.

Given these considerations, it is essential to see that responsibility cannot be ascribed exclusively to our past actions, those for which we had a choice between different options. We are also responsible for the future and for keeping the space open for different types of actions that can be chosen responsibly as a reaction to the challenges at hand.[15] This is presently an important challenge, as the windows of opportunity will narrow the more the catastrophic events develop.

---

13. See Celia Deane-Drummond, Sigurd Bergmann, and Markus Vogt, *Religion in the Anthropocene* (Eugene, OR: Cascade Books, 2017).

14. Hence, the complicated discussion of human stewardship over nature needs to take its point of departure in the responsibility that we have due to not only our interdependence but also our power and how much depends on us. To simply state that we are one agent among others (as Latour's flat ontology seems to suggest, see later in this chapter) or that 'we are just another species, neither the owners or the stewards of this planet', as Anne Primavesi argues, citing Lovelock (Primavesi, *Gaia and Climate Change: A Theology of Gift Events*, 34.) is insufficient for determining our responsibilities. For further discussion of this symbol (steward), see the next section.

15. The nuances in the notion of responsibility need not occupy us here. It is sufficient to note that responsibility entails that human agency is subjected to a normative assessment that constitutes the possibility for ascribing blame or praise to a person and their actions. It means that one can hold the person accountable for how she or he has acted or intends to act in view of a normative context for assessing behaviour and its motivation, its background desires or the reasons behind it. For more on the different nuances of responsibility, see Nicole A. Vincent, 'A Structured Taxonomy of Responsibility Concepts', in *Moral Responsibility: Beyond Free Will and Determinism*, ed. Nicole A. Vincent, Ibo van de Poel, and Jeroen van den Hove (New York: Springer, 2011); and Ibo van de Poe, 'The Relation

The relational element that constitutes responsibility suggests the ability to detect or perceive how what one does affects others. Actions are never only about myself and what I do. They impact others with whom I have a relationship. These others need not only be my immediate acquaintances. They may also be members of future generations. To respond to what my actions do to others and be susceptible to their reactions is part of the capacity to act responsibly and a capacity we are responsible for developing.

We become individuals because we are part of creation, and we are responsible for the same reason. Hence, a theological approach to human responsibility means that one cannot understand the human as placed over against nature and the rest of creation or see responsibility as independent of this participation. It means that we cannot choose to take on responsibility after we have become acting subjects. Responsibility is based on the relational character of being and constitutes us as acting subjects.

From the outset, our subjectivity (self-relation) is a morally charged phenomenon. Humans are constituted as responsible beings due to their relationship with the rest of creation. We are fundamentally and originally in a position that entails being-for-others and being-with-others. Whatever else we may say about human agency, its conditions, presuppositions and consequences, it comes after this fact. We do not become who we are as separated from others, and, therefore, our being for others and our responsibility is inseparable from the outset.[16] The other is the one who makes me, and by making me, she also makes me responsible. Who this other is may differ, but from a theological point of view, God creates me by using the persons and the natural and material conditions present to do so.

To be responsible entails being responsive to the values inherent in creation. These goods are experientially accessible in the flourishing of creation. Whenever there is freedom, justice, good conditions for environmental development and sustainability, richness and variation in species, and safeguarding of natural landscapes, goodness manifests itself in ways that allow for more freedom for all of creation. However, the internal relationship between responsibility and goodness does not imply that responsibility makes a person good. A person is responsible for the good, but he or she may also act contrary to goodness. A human being who is at a loss with regard to his or her responsibility thereby expresses how he or she has lost the fundamental orientation that renders humans responsible.

Responsible stewardship?

Responsibility and stewardship belong together. If humans develop a self-understanding as stewards of the goodness for which God has provided the

---

between Forward-Looking and Backward-Looking Responsibility', in Nicole A. Vincent, Ibo van de Poel and Jeroen van den Hoven (ed.), ibid.

16. Cf. Emmanuel Lévinas, 'Substitution', in *The Levinas Reader*, ed. Seán Hand (Oxford; Cambridge, MA, USA: B. Blackwell, 1989), 105.

possibilities by creating, this has several consequences, all of which are related to the traditional notion of human beings as stewards of creation. The symbol 'steward of creation', which links back to Genesis 1, has been criticized for different reasons.

Richard Bauckham analyses the notion of stewardship and its biblical background. He makes a strong case for rejecting it, although he is fully aware that would say that contemporary scholars often will interpret Genesis 1:28 not as a mandate to exploitation but as an appointment to relate to other creatures with care and service, exercised on behalf of God, and with accountability to God. Bauckham recognizes that the notion of stewardship, along with terms such as 'guardianship' or 'earthkeeping' have enabled 'Christians to reimagine the human relationship to the rest of creation and to begin to undertake the responsibilities that entails in our age of ecological catastrophe'.[17] Despite these positive intentions, he also identifies limitations with the symbol: it suggests that humans are needed for nature to become improved or ordered. Thus, the notion of stewardship proves to be ambiguous insofar as it may cover up the fact that nature is intricately ordered in ways that encompass change. Humans are nevertheless 'more prone to disrupt its order than to improve it'.[18] Moreover, 'we now urgently need to preserve wilderness, to let wild nature be itself without human interference, insofar as that is still possible. The notion of "stewardship" too easily implies that nature in some way needs us if it is to realize its full potential'.[19] His main reason for identifying deficits in this symbol for human self-interpretation is nevertheless the following:

> [M]uch modern Christian thinking about the human relationship to the rest of creation is deeply in error, in that it has been understood as a purely vertical relationship, a hierarchy in which humans are placed over the rest of creation in a position of power and authority. [...] But humans are also related horizontally to other creatures; we, like they, are creatures of God. To lift us out of creation and so out of our God-given embeddedness in creation has been the great ecological error of modernity. We urgently need to recover a biblical view of our solidarity with the rest of God's creatures on this planet, which is our common home. We need to locate ourselves once again where we belong – within creation.[20]

---

17. Richard Bauckham, 'Being Human in the Community of Creation', in *Ecotheology – a Christian Conversation*, ed. Kiara Jorgenson and Alan G. Padgett (Grand Rapids, MI: William B. Eerdmans Publishing Company, 2020), 19. Bauckham offers a more extensive, constructive interpretation of stewardship based on an analysis of biblical material in *Bible and Ecology: Rediscovering the Community of Creation* (2010): 1–36. The discussion of stewardship is also mapped in Steven Bouma-Prediger, 'The Character of Earthkeeping: A Christian Ecological Virtue Ethic', in *Ecotheology: A Christian Conversation*, ed. Kiara A. Jorgenson and Alan G. Padgett (Grand Rapids, MI: William B. Eerdmans Publishing Company, 2020), 122–5.

18. Cf. Bauckham, 'Being Human in the Community of Creation', 19f.

19. Ibid., 20.

20. Ibid. For a more extensive argument on Bauckham's part against the stewardship symbol as adequate, see his Bauckham, *Bible and Ecology: Rediscovering the Community of Creation*, 1–12.

Thus, Bauckham provides important arguments for rejecting an understanding of stewardship based on the following interconnected elements. Stewardship cannot entail (1) dominion as exploitation, (2) participation in God's rule over creation, (3) *imago Dei* as authorizing humans to serve as God's representative on Earth, (4) human distinctiveness authorizing humans to speak for other creatures or mediate God for them and (5) other claims that sever human beings' fundamental kinship with other creatures.[21]

If we proceed from these distinctions and move towards more constructive interpretations of what stewardship might entail, we can look at Christian Baumgartner's valuable contribution.[22] Baumgartner distinguishes between two types of stewardship, both of which represent options in the Anthropocene. Both understand stewardship as a mode of forward-looking responsibility, much along the lines of what has been elaborated earlier in the previous section, and with a distinct awareness of future generations' needs.[23] However, my aim is not to elaborate on the differences that Baumgartner teases out between Christian and planetary stewardship, as he calls them, but a vital element in his main conclusion: Under the present conditions of the Anthropocene, 'it is more plausible to understand stewardship as the shared forward-looking responsibility of all people; it is a responsibility that each person bears but does not bear alone'.[24] Hence, stewardship entails a common responsibility for the future of the planet, although we still need to distinguish among different groups as to their different responsibilities when it comes to what humans have caused in the past for allowing climate to change. Stewardship is not an individual task.

Furthermore, Baumgarten's approach thus seems to address some of the deficits in a traditional understanding of stewardship, as he opens up an understanding responsibility not only as shared, but also as *collective*. For him, planetary stewardship in the Anthropocene builds on humanity's shared and collective responsibility. This *collective* responsibility presupposes the formation of a group agent with its own point of view from which to deliberate and act. It entails an imperative for the 'global humanity to develop a cosmopolitan understanding as group agent and to establish just and robust international institutions'.[25] It is on the level of such institutions 'that one can take into account the differences in backward-looking responsibility for the causation of global environmental crises in the development of effective and fair instruments and strategies to achieve

---

21. Summarized thus in Cynthia D. Moe-Lobeda's response to Bauckham, in Kiara Jorgenson and Alan G. Padgett, *Ecotheology – a Christian Conversation* (Grand Rapids, MI: William B. Eerdmans Publishing Company, 2020), 48f.

22. Christoph Baumgartner, 'Transformations of Stewardship in the Anthropocene', in *Religion in the Anthropocene*, ed. Celia Deane-Drummond, et al. (Eugene, OR: Cascade, 2017).

23. Cf. ibid., 54f.

24. Ibid., 65.

25. Ibid., 66.

the central goal of [. . .]stewardship: [. . .] the protection of an environment that is hospitable both to the entirety of contemporary humanity and to future generations of humanity'.[26]

If we sum up what this discussion of responsible stewardship means, we need to underscore from the outset that responsibility and goodness do not have their origin in human agency, but humans become responsible agents through God's creative act. A contemporary understanding of humans as stewards of creation is, *pace* Lynn White, not a carte blanche for doing whatever one wants with nature and the environment but is shaped fundamentally by our collective responsibility for the web of relationships that creation manifests and for its flourishing. It is also not a warrant for an anthropocentric approach to creation but one that may contribute to underscoring the intimate, interdependent and profoundly relational character between all creatures. Human uniqueness consists of our ability to act responsibly – a capacity called for in the present more than ever. Greta Thunberg speaks of the Cathedral builder attitude[27] – the attitude in which we see our agency as contributing to a task that will be paramount for future generations. It entails that everyone is called to look beyond his or her short-term goals for the benefit of the long-term goal of a sustainable future for all of creation, including humanity.

Responsibility manifests itself in practices. A practice is a pattern of activity with a specific aim, an aim that is not external to the agent. It manifests the agent's quality and responsibility towards herself as well as towards the goal of the practice. A practice can be developed and performed in various ways. Practices have their origin in different human motivations and desires. Alasdair MacIntyre understands a practice as follows:

> By a 'practice' I . . . mean any coherent and complex form of socially established cooperative human activity through which goods internal to that form of activity are realized in the course of trying to achieve those standards of excellence which are appropriate to, and partially definitive of, that form of activity, with the result that human powers to achieve excellence, and human conceptions of the ends and goods involved, are systematically extended.[28]

This understanding of practices ties up well with the aforementioned understanding of humanity's collective responsibility. Responsibility as practised is linked to a wide variety of other human activities which humans learn through participation. Practices of ecological care, love and stewardship build on, presuppose and relate the practitioner, to other practitioners as well as to the rest of creation. Practices are

---

26. Ibid.
27. Greta Thunberg in a speech to the European Parliament 16 April 2019. See http://newstoryhub.com-/2019/04/it-will-take-cathedral-thinking-greta-thunbergs-climate-change-speech-to-european-parliament-16-april-2019/ (accessed 3 December 2019).
28. Alasdair C. MacIntyre, *After Virtue: A Study in Moral Theory*, 2nd edition (Notre Dame, IN: University of Notre Dame Press, 1984), 187.

a mode in which elements in creation interact with and affect one another. Ideally, religions would offer various patterns for practices that manifest ways to take on and acknowledge human responsibilities for creation. Some practices might be symbolic in character, whereas others have concrete and actual effects on how to take care of, sustain and improve the qualities given with creation. My thesis about the symbol deficit in the Christian tradition is an attempt to address this point.

Although all practices are related to human responsibility, their religious character is dependent on how it is rooted in, motivated by or expressed as a manifestation of the stories that religions build on and in which they have their origin.[29] The relationship to this origin is not (only) a matter of historical legitimation (although that can also be the case). More importantly, it is a way to recognize the link between the practices in question and the divine realities and powers that supersede the abilities present in human agency. When practices take on a religious character, it is because they allow practitioners 'to gain access to and communicate or align themselves with . . . superhuman powers. The hope involved in the cultural prescribing of these practices is to realize human goods and to avoid bads, especially (but not only) to avert misfortunes and receive blessings and deliverance from crises'.[30]

Responsibility for more than human nature: From Levinas via Latour to Vetlesen

Recent contributions to moral philosophy cannot build on the idea of human freedom from causations of nature, as in Kant, but needs to be rooted in the realm of necessity because our duty to care for the Earth must precede all others, claims Hans Jonas.[31] What does this claim entail? How may we understand the human responsibility for nature and avoid the pitfalls of past distinctions and separations that conceive nature as a mere object of human concern? This section will provide some reflections on that topic in order to address some of the deficits that may emerge from a relatively unspecified notion of human responsibility. This discussion may, in turn, inform the way theologians can think about human responsibility in a context that stresses human interrelations with nature and nature's impact on human agency.

In Emmanuel Lévinas's ethics, some elements seem to suggest the strong and internal moral relationship that constitutes the moral subject as a subject in the

---

29. On the principles for understanding practices in this way, see Henriksen, *Christianity as Distinct Practices: A Complicated Relationship.*

30. Christian Smith, *Religion: What It Is, How It Works, and Why It Is Still Important* (Princeton: Princeton University Press, 2017), 3.

31. Hans Jonas, *Das Prinzip Verantwortung: Versuch Einer Ethik Für Die Technologische Zivilisation*, (Frankfurt am Main: Suhrkamp, 1989). Further on Jonas in the next chapter.

first place. Levinas's work on this has inspired and deepened the understanding of the responsibility we have for other humans and contains valuable insights. However, his work also presents us with significant shortcomings that we need to address if we consider what it would entail for our relationship with *nature*. Hence, some of the deficits of his work need to be identified and adjusted. In this section, I will try to do that by discussing his work in the light of two other contributions, namely those of Bruno Latour and Arne Johan Vetlesen.

Levinas underscores the passivity and the vulnerability that characterize human existence and the impossibility of founding ethics in any kind of reciprocity. He sees the meaning of existence as emerging from the presence of the other – and this other, which for him is always a human, constitutes a moral subject. Accordingly, morality is not rooted in the activity and the decisions of an already-established subject but in facing the other – the one whom Levinas underscores must be understood in his alterity to not be integrated into the sphere of sameness shaped by intentionality. Furthermore, he underscores the fundamental asymmetry between the parties involved.[32]

It is easy to commend Levinas's insistence on passivity and vulnerability as initial elements that characterize human existence. It fits well with what we will develop further below in terms of how the infant challenges us to act responsibly. It represents an ethical demand by its very existence, with no chance of reciprocal exchange. However, these features characterize other living beings, as well. They are also vulnerable, dependent on us and on others, and call for care and concern.

While Levinas is correct when underscoring that we become moral subjects by being confronted with the other's face, which is the call or command to act responsibly, his account seems to reduce moral responsibility to the sphere of humans. As such, Levinas maintains the problematic dualism between humans and nature that is among the fundamental deficits in the concept of responsibility.[33] Moreover, while he is correct when warning against reducing the other (human) or that other (of nature) to the sameness expressed in our intentions, he is wrong when insisting that this difference between sameness and other is total. For when the other, as an infant, or that other, as an animal, a habitat or a river are something we are confronted with, they belong already to my existence and to that with which I am interrelated. So, although Levinas seems right in emphasizing the interrelational character of all existence and its fundamental significance for

---

32. For an introduction to Levinas, see Emmanuel Lévinas, *The Levinas Reader* (New York, NY: B. Blackwell, 1989), and Simon Critchley and Robert Bernasconi, *The Cambridge Companion to Levinas* (Cambridge: Cambridge University Press, 2002). A more extensive analysis of Levinas's on morality is presented in Jan-Olav Henriksen, *Grobunn for Moral: Om Å Være Moralsk Subjekt I En Postmoderne Kultur* (Cappelen Damm Høyskoleforlaget, 1997).

33. Cf. for this critique, spelled out more in detail, Vetlesen, *Cosmologies of the Anthropocene: Panpsychism, Animism, and the Limits of Posthumanism*, 147–9.

morality, his insistence on difference and alterity seems to preclude recognizing the interrelational bond rooted in shared and natural conditions for existence.

The impact nature can have on us is perhaps most consistently developed by Bruno Latour, who, in his recent work, sees agency as present in all of nature and not only in humans. Latour argues, as does Levinas, that 'Being a subject does not mean acting in an autonomous fashion in relation to an objective context; rather, it means sharing agency with other subjects that have also lost their autonomy'.[34] Hence, no one can claim autonomy in any absolute sense in a world of interrelations. Accordingly, the traditional subject-object relationship needs reconfiguration. We do not only have to give up any illusions about control: Nature also has some impact on us and our agency because nature itself has agency: 'As soon as we come close to nonhuman beings, we do not find in them the inertia that would allow us, by contrast, to take ourselves to be agents but, on the contrary, we find agencies that are no longer without connection to what we are and what we do.'[35] Hence, Latour suggests that nature should be understood as impacting human life based on nature's own agency. However, I would add, this is an agency without subjectivity, insofar as nature is not able to thematize itself symbolically in the ways humans can.

What this adds to Levinas's position is precisely the ability to speak of nature as performing agency. In this optic, nature is not appearing only as matter or substance. Latour's understanding of actants as performing actions and contributing to an unstable and changing condition seems more apt than traditional substance ontology that defined interrelations as secondary to objects or substances. Hence, he can expand the impact of what shapes humans' (responsible) agency beyond what Levinas can do. However, this also has consequences for how we see the interrelationship between humans and nature:

> Conversely, on its side (but there are no more 'sides'!), the Earth is no longer 'objective,' in the sense that it can no longer be kept at a distance, considered from the point of view of Sirius and as though it has been emptied of all its humans. Human action is visible everywhere in the construction of knowledge as well as in the generation of the phenomena to which the sciences are called upon to attest. It is impossible, from now on, to play at dialectically opposing subjects and objects.[36]

This approach to the human–nature relationship exhibits that human knowledge about nature can no longer consider it from the point of view of understanding it as mere objects. Therefore, dynamics that are always in play need to be considered from a perspective in which nature impacts our knowledge and our agency by

---

34. Bruno Latour and Catherine Porter, *Facing Gaia: Eight Lectures on the New Climatic Regime* (Cambridge: Polity Press, 2017), 62.
35. Ibid.
36. Ibid.

exhibiting its own agency, even if we do not consider nature as having a subjectivity of its own.

However, there are severe and complicating elements in this expansion that we need to consider, which also entail some necessary criticism of Latour. Arne Johan Vetlesen has pointed to how Latour and others avoid discussing in detail the severity of the present situation because of the 'flat ontology' that enables us to see everything as *actants* existing at the same level. Even though Latour opposes the Cartesian notion of matter as inert and insentient, this concept (*actants*), which points to entities exhibiting powers of agency that allows for seeing planet Earth as an organism, brings problems with it. Hence, although his ontology represents an alternative to the cartesian divide, Vetlesen argues that

> the new dialectic playing itself out: the result of humans' treating the Earth Cartesian-like as matter, and so as inanimate, inert, and – essentially – unchangeable, now turns out to have produced an effect for which the cosmology accompanying, and legitimizing, that thing-like, means-oriented treatment is eminently ill-prepared: the effect being the animation – or should we say reanimation? – of all sorts of forces denied agency. Having been denied, and thereupon mistreated, exploited, subjugated for so long, those nonhuman agencies now strike back at us, doing so with such vehemence as to prompt scholars (such as Lovelock and, though less decidedly and unequivocally, Latour) to speak of their 'revenge' and of the 'power of the Earth to kill' as the unforeseen result of how we have been 'abusing the Earth'. The dialectic takes the form of a literally deadly payback.[37]

Hence, the notion of actants allows us to see that the Earth is very much alive and very potent in responding to the planetary impact caused by human activities in the present era of unprecedented alteration within ecosystems everywhere. However, Latour's proliferation of all sorts of non-human actants/agencies is at odds with what the actuality of the Anthropocene is about: the decimation of the myriads of other-than-human creatures and life-forms that planet Earth historically has seen evolving and thriving. Hence, Vetlesen criticizes the excessive inflation of agency in Latour, in which his 'flat ontology' causes the responsibility exclusive to human actors to be lost. This inflation covers the fact that humans are responsible in a way that other agents are not.

Vetlesen points to how we need to recognize the specific character of human agency as responsible. This means that human agency (as stewardship, cf. aforementioned) requires further qualifications than those found in ontologies that put all living beings on the same level. He argues that the insights found in anthropologists who have been studying non-modern, non-anthropocentric cosmologies 'makes us recognize that what promised to be gained by exploding

---

37. Vetlesen, *Cosmologies of the Anthropocene: Panpsychism, Animism, and the Limits of Posthumanism*, 212–13.

anthropocentrism and its peculiar way of contrasting culture and nature, all too easily end up effacing the very distinctions, the real-life presences of "othernesses", that any valid cosmological alternative has to prove itself able to do justice to, conceptually and practically'.[38] Hence, 'the eagerness to remove humans from their (our) positing ourselves on a pedestal, as superior over all other beings in every important regard, ends up neglecting what *is* peculiar about us as one species among many. And failing to recognize our own peculiarities is no less serious a mistake than failing to acknowledge those of (our, many) others'.[39]

As I read him, Vetlesen's underscoring of interconnectedness with other living beings, together with his underscoring of the human responsibility for present destruction and degradation, demonstrates that not all actants are equal in every regard. Responsibility is a specific human feature. It becomes apparent, of course, in the very fact that 'all ecological injunctions [. . .] are clearly rooted in the idea of human distinctiveness; for "insofar as the appeal is to humanity to alter its ways, it presupposes our possession of capacities by which we are singled out from other living creatures and inorganic matter", responsibility being of course one crucial such capacity', he writes, quoting Karen Soper.[40] Hence, there is still reason to insist that differences and asymmetries matter because some have more power and responsibilities than others.[41]

Responsibility belongs to the distinctively human mode of being in the world. This does not exclude that we can, to some extent, detect its presence in how other species take care of their kin, as well. Hence, it is rooted not only in subjectivities' awareness of interconnectedness and vulnerability but also in natural dispositions. However, in humans, it can also be rooted in theological virtues such as faith, hope and love. These are components that the following chapters will elaborate on in detail.

---

38. Ibid., 250.
39. Ibid.
40. Ibid., 251.
41. Cf. ibid., 148–9.

Chapter 11

FROM ANTHROPOS TO ALL OF CREATION

The experiential basis for a metaphor that mediates actions

God creates through birth, growth, and development. These are all interactive phenomena. Hence, unlike God's creating in the beginning (*creatio originalis*), God's continued creation (*creatio continua*) depends on creation – even when God creates something novel.

Against the backdrop of the aforementioned claim, the present chapter represents the present book's core suggestion: to delineate the main elements in a virtuous attitude that guides, informs and shapes cooperative human action in light of the present climate catastrophe. This attitude is rooted in elements that surround procreation and birth, as these are the fundamental conditions for future life and, as we shall see, for understanding human responsibility for the future. The chapter aims to ground the virtue of ecological care in phenomena deeply situated in human embodiment, specifically in the human experience of pregnancy and birth. Despite being limited to half of the human population, this experience is not without implications for the other half: it is usually not only the woman herself that invests interests, hope, aspirations and expectations in the future she bears under her heart. Pregnancy and birth are phenomena that all of humankind can relate to.

In the following, I will start by discussing authors that have elaborated on different aspects concerning the coming or future generations. From then on, I will extract some fundamental implications that can serve as analogies for an attitude that can metaphorically inform all human actions. Against the backdrop of these analyses, the following chapters will have a basis on which we can discuss the relevance of other, pre-existing symbols in the Christian tradition.

Hans Jonas: Responsibility for future generations

In his groundbreaking work *The Imperative of Responsibility*, Hans Jonas points to the incompleteness (or deficit) of previous notions of ethics when dealing with nature.¹ Among the new conditions for human morality is the realization of nature's fundamental vulnerability.² He claims that the current situation entails that we need to seek the good for all that exists, and not only for humans. To do so, one must recognize the inherent value of all that exists and how it has a goal in itself. This, in turn, expands the notion of the human good and is something all previous ethics has not prepared us for – except for the religious – and the scientific understanding of nature even less.³

Jonas articulates his moral imperatives for our age in confrontation with Kant's moral imperatives. Against Kant's programmatic neglect of the actual consequences of human actions in defining what is right, Jonas sees the moral task as one in which one needs to take into consideration the actual effects or consequences of human agency concerning the continued existence of humans on Earth, and also consider the time span of these actions – unlike Kant.⁴ Despite this seemingly anthropocentric approach concerning the basis for action, we need to keep in mind Jonas's fundamental realization of humans' interconnectedness with other living beings. He formulates his imperative in different ways, and the following is the one that articulates most clearly the approach on which the following analysis is built:

> Act in such a way that you do not threaten the conditions for the indefinite continuity of human existence on Earth.⁵

Jonas's imperative builds on the assumption that we can act so that we, given the circumstances, can sacrifice our own life, but we have no right to sacrifice the life of future generations. He holds this imperative is nevertheless not easy to uphold unless it is given a religious warrant.⁶ Another way to formulate this is that *the present is here for the sake of the future*. One of the consequences of this approach is that the ethical good cannot be defined in terms of our own well-being only – the well-being of future generations is just as important.

Thus, Jonas develops an ethics oriented by future prospects. In its context, scientific knowledge has the task of providing us with information about elements that threaten human freedom in the future. Such knowledge contributes to the *heuristics of fear*.⁷ By identifying fear related to the future as the basis for action,

---

1. In the following, I use the original German edition of this work. Jonas, *Das Prinzip Verantwortung: Versuch Einer Ethik Für Die Technologische Zivilisation*, 22ff. Translations are mine.
2. Ibid., 26ff.
3. Ibid., 29.
4. Ibid., 37.
5. Ibid., 36. Jonas can therefore also claim that there is an unconditional duty to continue contributing to the existence of humanity, although that duty should not be confused with the one the individual has to exist. Cf. ibid., 80.
6. Ibid., 36, cf. 57f.
7. Cf. ibid., 63, 65.

Jonas admits that he takes his point of departure in the fact that the bad (*malum*) is infinitely more easy to grasp than the good (*bonum*) – it is immediately present and not something we need to search for.[8] There is no reason to argue with him on this fact, although some of the *malum* in the present situation can remain hidden from our eyes. My objection to this approach is nevertheless the same as I will develop against elements in the Christian tradition later: that such *negative* instances cannot mediate positive and persistent action. For that task, we need to turn to other elements in Jonas's ethics.

Jonas sees all life as demanding to live. However, in the part of his ethics that I will concentrate on hereafter, he focuses on how this demand articulates itself in the immediate, undisputed and non-reciprocal claim that the (unborn) child constitutes. From conception and later on, this demand guides our actions towards the child in need of care and support.[9] It is unconditional and given with nature itself. Without it, there would be no future for humanity.[10] Moreover, this duty precedes all emotion and cannot be based on compassion, empathy or love – it is given with the child's ontic facticity.[11] 'Thus, the "thou shall" manifests itself in the infant with unquestioned evidence, concreteness, and insistence.'[12] Jonas sees taking care of the child as one of the elements that the Creator God has handed over as a task that will continue God's work.[13] He elaborates far more on this than what we need to do in the present context. However, he also makes a claim that he most likely has from Hannah Arendt: with every child who is born, humanity starts anew in the face of mortality.[14]

However, Jonas is not focusing on future generations' rights. He holds that our duty is to make sure that future generations can realize *their* duties towards future generations when it comes to securing their existence. To deprive future generations of this ability is to deprive them of their humanity.[15] Hence, he sees responsibility as intergenerational. According to Jonas, there cannot be any strict separation between is and ought or between the factual and the normative.[16]

This foundation of humanity in the duty towards future generations is, in one sense, unavoidably anthropocentric. It focuses on the duty we have to secure that future humans can have duties to future generations. However, we need to remind ourselves of two things here: the non-reciprocal relationship to future generations and the fact that in order to secure their duties, we need to have all the conditions for future human life in mind. Thus, the interrelation and deep interdependence

---

8. Ibid., 63.
9. Ibid., 85.
10. Ibid.
11. Cf. ibid., 235.
12. Ibid., 242.
13. Ibid., 86.
14. Ibid., 241.
15. Cf. Ibid., 89.
16. Ibid., 92f.

manifested in the Anthropocene suggests that it is impossible to uphold these duties unless one also recognizes the demand that more-than-human world have on life. In this respect, Jonas sees an ontological value given with the existence of every living being, insofar as this claim is not dependent on human decision or recognition.[17]

Hannah Arendt on natality

I briefly mentioned an element in Jonas that reminds us of a central feature in Hannah Arendt's thinking: the notion of a newborn infant as a manifestation of the chance for something new. Arendt elaborates on this phenomenon in her analysis of different aspects of what she calls *natality*. In her thinking, this phenomenon is visible in different dimensions of human life, and I will concentrate here on aspects that are fundamental for human agency.[18] Thus, we can expand the notion of responsibility for the future as testified to in Jonas's analysis of the responsible relationship we have with the infant by looking at another fundamental element that also concentrates on the fundamental relational and vulnerable features in human life.

For Arendt, human natality testifies to our deeply relational character as humans. We are born into a community of others. Natality entails the *referential* character of our being, which is disclosed by three qualitative experiences, all of which relates us to the world: 'Firstly, natality is the product of love; secondly, natality appears in a communal context in which the question of one's unique identity as a natal is posed by others; and lastly, natality's ultimate and most profound witness in terms of the world is the attitude of *amor mundi*: a love for the world.'[19]

Arendt sees the birth of the child as the product of love. Of course, this is not always the case. Nevertheless, her point is that the birth makes it possible and necessary for the lovers, who are occupied with themselves and not with the world, to transgress their isolation and 'unworldly', a-political preoccupation with

---

17. Cf. ibid., 246, where Jonas speaks of the 'recently discovered community of fate between humans and nature and the independent dignity of nature, that goes beyond the mere utilitarian approach, and whose integrity needs safeguarding'. Cf. also Troster, 'Caretaker or Citizen', 392, who admits that even though Jonas speaks in a language of anthropocentric stewardship, his fundamental metaphysics can be understood as one that 'undercuts the distinction between anthropocentrism and biocentrism. For Jonas, living nature is a good in-itself which therefore commands our concern and even our reverence. Since all organisms are vulnerable ends-in-themselves and they all express concern for their own existence, humans have a particular responsibility as moral agents to protect them'.

18. Cf. Patricia Bowen-Moore, *Hannah Arendt's Philosophy of Natality* (Basingstoke: Macmillan, 1989), 1. The following presentation of Arendt is based mainly on Bowen-Moore's work.

19. Ibid., 16.

themselves. They are, so to say, 'under a spell'.[20] This is changed with the advent of the child:

> As long as the spell lasts, the only in-between which can insert itself between two lovers is the child, love's own product. The child, this in-between to which the lovers are now related and which they hold in common, is representative of the world in that it also separates them; it is an indication that they will insert a new world into the existing world.[21]

The important element in this context is that when the lovers are 'interrupted' by the child's advent, they have to take care of it in a way that also entails that they must be attentive to the world in which they all (child and parents alike) live. An isolated and self-occupied situation is no longer possible. The child has created a new situation and thus represents something indisputably new. The self-interested love of the lovers becomes substituted by the loving care for the child.

One cannot be born outside of a communal context. Almost stating the obvious, Arendt holds that natality is the precondition for all communal relationships; without the constant appearance of new human beings into the world, the world itself would cease to exist as a shared world:

> The miracle that saves the world, the realm of human affairs, from its normal, 'natural' ruin is ultimately the fact of natality, in which the faculty of action is ontologically rooted. It is, in other words, the birth of new men and the new beginning, the action they are capable of by virtue of being born.[22]

I read Arendt here as pointing to two different dimensions connected to the phenomenon of natality. On the one hand, she indicates that by entering the world the loving couple will need to address and approach the world in terms of their agency, that is, what it is required for them to do for the sake of safeguarding the infant. On the other hand, by virtue of being born, the child is given a chance to develop as an agent.

However, behind both these dimensions of agency is another element that Arendt does not elaborate. In both these instances, the capacity for agency is something given – it is constituted by some other than the lovers themselves or the infant herself. This point is tacitly present in her emphasis on the role of communal relationships but seems to be somewhat underdeveloped. The reason why I point it out here is that in both these instances it is the *other* that opens up to a new perspective on the world and what is required of my agency. Thus, individualism is *per definitionem* not possible for the one who loves in such a way that new life is

---

20. Cf. ibid., 17.
21. Hannah Arendt, *The Human Condition*, 2nd edition (Chicago: University of Chicago Press, 1998), 242.
22. Ibid., 247.

made possible. Arendt is thereby posing a severe blow to a culture that cherishes individualism, social atomism and free choice over concern and care for others – all traits that we see manifest in the consumer society. Care for others is given with the fact of natality in human life itself, and to ignore it is to ignore that which makes human life possible and responsible.

We can now see why Arendt moves from natality to its expression in love for the world, *amor mundi*. This love for the world is intrinsically connected to two other virtues that we have already encountered in a more theological context: faith and hope. We cannot love the infant and care for its future unless we also have hope and love. Bowen-Moore summarizes this in the following, extensive quote:

> The attitude of *amor mundi* views both the world and one's natality from the perspective of faith and hope. Arendt's conception of *amor mundi*, while based on the model of the three theological virtues, faith, hope and charity, assumes existential import in the appropriation of these experiences in the realm of human affairs. For faith in the world is an entirely human faith: it requires that the natal be faithful to the conditions of birth and the power to begin as well as entrusting this capacity to the world thereby ensuring its futurity. Espousing the attitude of *amor mundi*, the natal remains faithful to the promises inherent in birth: the promise to preserve and the promise to act. Hope in the world is an entirely human hope: it anticipates a world within which to act and it fully expects that the world, as a place for action, will endure. The attitude of *amor mundi* entails the hope that the world of human plurality will not only continue in time but will also continue to anticipate and to welcome newcomers into its communal experiences.[23]

Here, we see how the theological virtues faith, hope and love are redirected and reshaped in a way that entails care for the world in which humans live. We should not see this as an opposition to how these notions are used in a religious context. Instead, we should see the actualization of the virtues here as manifested in a context that cares for the world in which God works as creator.

There are two fundamental problems with Arendt's position on natality. First, her insistence on the newness and capacity for new beginnings in the world as that which gives meaning to human agency is developed by contrasting humans with other animals.[24] By emphasizing this contrast, she seems to ignore what humans have in common with animals regarding dependence on and interaction with their natural development. The one-sidedness in this approach is summarized well by Bowen-Moore:

> The natal's ability to exercise action is preceded by an innate principle for beginning. Conceptually, primary natality refers to man's unique capacity to initiate as something which inheres in the fact of birth. This principle for

---

23. Bowen-Moore, *Hannah Arendt's Philosophy of Natality*, 19.
24. Cf. ibid., 23.

beginning, coeval with his birth, identifies man's novel capacity as constitutive of his essential structure of being; it is the condition by which and through which human beings can commence action at all.[25]

Arendt's construction of the phenomenon of natality overlooks the impact of material and natural conditions and how traditions, concepts, imaginaries and learning shape and condition life from the very outset. There is no absolute beginning, and we are, even in our beginnings and our fundamental natality, dependent on more than our immediate peers. That she also emphasizes the difference between humans and animals by pointing to the political and historical reality that shapes the distinctively human reality points in the same direction.[26]

The second problem with Arendt's analysis of natality is related to the aforementioned. She understands the category of *world* 'as an entirely human construction conceived not only as the necessary pre-condition for the possibility of beginning but also as the concrete embodiment of the novelty which already has been inserted into it over the duration of time'.[27]

> Arendt's understanding of world includes a conception of it as that reality which houses human experiences; a human artifice made by human initiative; a common meeting ground of all for the display of action and speech in the enactment of human affairs. As distinguished from natural recurring processes (that is, nature), the man-made world and the reality of its experience are ultimately dependent upon the condition of natality.[28]

There is no reason to argue with Arendt about the ability to create and make something new that is implicit in the phenomenon of natality. Nor should we overlook her well-taken point that the advent of the infant breaks open the

---

25. Ibid., 24.
26. Arendt, *The Human Condition*, 19. Cf. Bowen-Moore, *Hannah Arendt's Philosophy of Natality*, 53.
27. *Hannah Arendt's Philosophy of Natality*, 102.
28. Ibid. Bowen-Moore backs up her analysis here with a quote from Margaret Canovan, *The Political Thought of Hannah Arendt* (1974), 81.

> When Hannah Arendt talks about the world she does not mean the physical world: indeed the world in her view is precisely what separates and shields man from nature. It is the human artifice of man-made objects and institutions that provides human beings with a permanent home. Civilisation, which has made man something more than an animal, has consisted precisely in the building of this world, a world of ploughed fields, roads and hedges instead of wild landscape, of buildings instead of the open air, of language and culture, communities and traditions, of art, law, religion and all the rest of the man-made things that nevertheless outlive the men who made them and form the inheritance of the human race.

Hereafter Bowen-Moore, ibid., 102f.

preoccupation of lovers and redirects them towards the world. It is also important to maintain that faith, hope and love are given with natality and that these are essential conditions for shaping human agency that cares for others and for the future of the planet. However, we need to reject her insistence on the *absolute* newness inherent in natality and the exclusive focus on its impact on human agency. This insistence ignores the dependence and the commonalities that humans share with other parts of nature, to which we are related.

At this point, comparing Arendt's account of natality to Hans Jonas's position is instructive. Whereas Arendt develops a notion of natality based on a concept of the world that separates humans from nature, Jonas's notion of responsibility for the future is not based primarily on human agency, but in the mere existence of the call from the infant. Jonas opens us up to the biological as relevant in a way that Arendt does not. Thus, he overcomes the limitations of a non-ecological approach to the world and human agency conditions.

Both Arendt and Jonas ground their conceptions in the most fundamental human experience: that of being born. Thereby, they both reject individualism or social atomism as an adequate approach to human life and agency. 'Natality primarily means that we are closely related corporeal beings' involved in processes of creativity.[29] They display fundamental modes in which the infant opens the world up to us in new ways.[30] As we shall see in the subsequent sections of this chapter, this is a promising approach to symbols for human action. It is also a fundamental feature of creation, in which we can see God at work in creating chances for faith, hope and love. As we shall see in this chapter, this is revealed in how Godself was borne and born as the incarnated Jesus Christ. Thus, natality understood in a broader sense than Arendt can help overcome some of the deficits that the Christian symbol tradition displays in the present situation.

Creation's future under your heart: Elaborating the fundamental metaphor

We can expand on the important intuitions found in Jonas and Arendt to identify an adequate attitude that governs and informs human action. The fundamental position in which all humans have to understand themselves if they are to develop practices that can impede the rapid development of climate change is *to see*

---

29. Cristina Grenholm, *Motherhood and Love: Beyond the Gendered Stereotypes of Theology* (Grand Rapids, MI: William B. Eerdmans Publishing Company, 2011), 57, 53. Grenholm builds part of her analysis of natality on Graze Jantzen. Jantzen, who notably expanded her notion of natality with that of flourishing, which opens up to dynamic and creative processes within creation. See Grenhom, ibid., 58.

30. A beautiful example of how this can happen is Martin Lee Mueller, 'Cascades of Giving: A More-Than-Human Ontology of the Gift-Giving Principle', in *Between Closeness and Evil: A Festschrift for Arne Johan Vetlesen*, ed. Odin Lysaker (Oslo: Scandinavian Academic Press, 2020).

themselves as pregnant with the future. It is possible for humans of all genders, young and old. In the following, I will discuss what such a self-understanding means and why we can and should develop practices based on understanding ourselves metaphorically in this way.[31]

Paul Ricoeur's famous dictum about the dynamic relationship between symbol and thought should be recalled here: symbols give rise to thought but thought has to return to the symbol to further develop our understanding.[32] Hence, symbols (including metaphors) must have a certain openness in order to overcome the dynamics. This is so also for symbols that engender human action and emotional response, including, for example, the symbol 'God'.[33] I mention this because we, as noted in the previous chapter, may be faced with understandings of God that lock God up in a totalitarian and non-dynamic context, in which it becomes impossible to employ it for creative practices that secure human flourishing. That is, for example, the case when a material growth economy is given preference instead of a preference for creation behind which the God of love stands.

God is the source of the *amor mundi* on which Hannah Arendt focuses. As the origin of love and thereby also of a creation that claims life and flourishing for itself, 'This sacred love is liberating and healing this good creation, and calls all of creation to receive this love – to relish it, revel in it and trust it. But that is not all. *We human creatures are called to embody this life-giving and life-transforming love; we are called to give it social form*'.[34] Thus, the deep and inner connection between God's creativity and human creativity is manifested.

The separation of God and the world in traditional Christian theology mirrors the separation of the (male) human from nature. Hence, we need to overcome this by pointing to yet another life-sustaining symbol, namely, seeing humans as intimately linked to God in a similar way to how an unborn infant is carried by her mother. This metaphor expresses that which is prior to human agency, and which carries us and the rest of nature. God is the one on whom we are dependent,

---

31. For a theoretical backdrop to the following, cf. the insights reported by Robert Wuthnow about how metaphorical references to bodily parts and functions occur through structuring practices – metaphorization – that thematizes what a person does and how he or she should feel: Furthermore, '[t]he important feature of bodies as symbols is that their applicability and potential versatility increase. The obdurate physical limitations of bodies as corporeal realities become less important because the ideas they symbolize can be more easily challenged, translated, interpreted, and misinterpreted'. See Robert Wuthnow, *What Happens When We Practice Religion?: Textures of Devotion in Everyday Life* (2020), 182–3.

32. Paul Ricoeur, *The Symbolism of Evil*, Religious Perspectives (New York: Harper & Row, 1967), 247ff.

33. Cf. Gschwandtner, 'Ricoeur's Hermeneutic of God: A Symbol That Gives Rise to Thought'.

34. Moe-Lobeda, 'Finding Common Ground on a Moral Vision for a Good Society', 158. My italics.

within whom we live, and nevertheless are also distinct from – but from whom we are nevertheless not separate.

Instead of construing the universal conditions with roots in male imagery of separation and distance, we need to find other human experiences in which to root basic metaphors that express our relationship to the future. At this point, the self of the maternal body again presents itself as a viable metaphor. As suggested earlier, a mother is one who includes another in oneself. To be pregnant is 'to include another on oneself in a relationship that constantly changes, so that what can be said to be the self, to be "mine", also changes'.[35] Thus, the planet's future is not separated from who you are, and how you deal with and relate to that of which you are part, and which is part of you. In such a relationship, there are no firm or fixed boundaries.

Accordingly, a dynamic symbol of God who creates through human activity and passivity metaphorically understood as pregnancy allows for a dynamic understanding of the conditions of human life – expressed in life, love and hope (as these phenomena may provide both the symbol of God and human life with concrete content). This perspective employs the symbol of God not primarily about *another* world but about being in this world in a specific way – by providing further chances for creation by engaging all that lives in a creative agency. It is a way of engaging with the world that may provide opportunities for nature's flourishing, concomitantly for personal growth, social and cultural development, and charging human experience with multiple layers of significance.

Combining the symbol of God understood through the metaphor pregnancy, and, especially, of bearing the future under your heart, provides chances for an alternative universal imagery than the one based on the male experience of separation. Catherine Keller argues that 'as the universal has served overwhelmingly as a male construct, the dominant anthropocentrism is almost inevitable androcentrism'.[36] This, in turn, entails that 'it has become rather evident that anthropocentrism at the global scale now spells "anthropocide."'[37] Hence, developing alternative, less-deficient symbols is not an academic enterprise carried out to secure politically correct interpretations of Christianity. On the contrary, it is of vital importance that we identify adequate symbolic resources that can manifest the close and embodied bonds between humans and the rest of creation. Understanding all humans as mothers of the future allows for the following considerations:

There is a dynamic element in these metaphors. Simultaneously, the open-ended character in metaphors helps us consider human action from the point of view of what we need to do. No systematic inferences can be made from metaphors.

---

35. Rachel Muers, *Living for the Future: Theological Ethics for Coming Generations* (London; New York: T&T Clark, 2008), 132.

36. Catherine Keller, *Intercarnations: Exercises in Theological Possibility*, First edition (New York: Fordham University Press, 2017), 170; 71.

37. Ibid., 170, 71.

Metaphors are open and invite response, but this response is not specified or pregiven but due to context and imagination. Metaphors are not components in a system, but we can see them as exploratory ways of articulating elements in reality.[38] I argue that the present situation entails that we see the future as the result of the dynamics that can be expressed as follows: God is the loving and creative source that encompasses everything, including our own lives. God is the source or womb from whom all emerge and in whom we have our being. Expanding on this metaphor, we can also consider *ourselves* as being pregnant with the future, no matter with which gender we identify. By seeing the future as the result of the interaction between God and humans, it is possible to articulate the chances for newness and hope articulated in Arendt's analysis of natality.

Consider yourself, then, from the point of view of the metaphor of being a mother to the future: *You are pregnant with what will be part of the world's future.* This means that there is an intrinsic and bodily mediated relationship between you and the future. The future is already part of your body and will be affected by what you do with it. Hence, when you consider yourself in relation to your environment, you are attentive to yourself and the future you bear. All your actions will have an impact on the future of your child. Hence, you are responsible for it, are related to it and need to be aware of its vulnerability and its susceptibility.

Moreover, this is not 'only in your head' – as an idea you can forget or ignore. It is a condition that your embodied existence manifests, even if you do not conceptualize this condition cognitively. And it is not a part-time occupation: being pregnant means that you are always pregnant with the future. You cannot excuse yourself from it. You may be inspired and hopeful or marked by exhaustion and fatigue, but no matter how you feel about yourself, this is your state. Pregnancy means pain, troubles, worry, inconvenience, hope, joy and anticipation. It may entail sacrifice and abstention but also a responsibility for finding the best possible nourishment for the child to be born. And it is not a mere individual condition or task: others are involved, to a greater or lesser degree, at different stages.

The situation given with the Anthropocene entails that we are all pregnant with the world's future, albeit we acknowledge it or not, and no matter how we understand it. To consider oneself as pregnant with the world's future entails that all actions you perform and what you abstain from doing will impact the future you carry within you. Moreover, it means that the future is affected by the environments in which you find yourself, and by the environments you develop. Hence, this is not an exclusively anthropocentric metaphor insofar as it also addresses the environment as valuable in its own right and affected by the outcomes of our agency.

Hence, as indicated, to be pregnant is not a mere state of passivity – you have to develop practices that ensure that everything is taken care of well. It is not sufficient to understand or to have knowledge about what is happening. Perception,

---

38. Cf. Sallie McFague, *A New Climate for Theology: God, the World, and Global Warming* (Minneapolis, MN: Fortress Press, 2008), 109.

attunement, recognizing the intimate relationship, consider the future, knowledge, emotions and practices are all involved. Pregnancy directs you towards the future – and how you handle it may also have significant consequences for your own life. You cannot be pregnant without taking the future into consideration.

Moreover, as Arendt underscores in her analysis of natality, the infant to be born opens those who expect her up to the world. Thus, to be expecting is to become political and try to find ways and practices that address structures and circumstances, conditions and powers that work contrary to the well-being of future life. To address these constructively means that one is pressed to develop a vision of how things could or should be otherwise.[39]

The strength of the metaphor of pregnancy is that it is all-encompassing and that it is based on an experience to which all human beings can relate, no matter your sexual orientation or gender. Although men obviously are not (yet) able to be physically pregnant, they too are invested in the future of the child and in its well-being during pregnancy. Thus, this metaphor serves as a point of departure for the diverse practices that address the future of the planet. The future of the planet is dependent on us because what we all do shape it.

The metaphor of pregnancy further presents the caring mother who takes her child into consideration and does all in order to secure its well-being as a person we find admirable, we may want to emulate or with whom may we would identify. Thus, we would identify with the condition and the gender that God has created as the primary bearer of the future for humans on Earth: women.

To see the fundamental disposition for agency as merely modelled in motherhood and pregnancy as a metaphor for guiding action is insufficient. From a theological point of view, there is more to this suggestion than a metaphor that points at similarities between two conditions or positions for action. At this point, the notion of *symbol*, as developed by Tillich, suggests itself. In Part II, we saw how Tillich claimed that religious symbols that point to the divine could be a true symbol only if it participates in the power of the divine to which it points.[40] The life or death of a symbol is dependent on its use by those who receive it as such. We can see mothering the future of creation as a symbol that engenders practices that not only point towards but participate in the reality of God, insofar as they relate to the world as God's creation and are manifesting the reality of God as it comes to expression in faith, hope and love. Thus, as a symbolic practice, it manifests a reality where goodness, compassion, hope for the future and love for all of creation

---

39. Cf. Cynthia D. Moe-Lobeda's remark about moral visions need to be reflected in social structures and institutions if they are not to become dreams deferred. Such visions also entail removing the blindfolds that distract people from what is going on. 'Therefore articulating a moral vision must include articulating some sense of its embodiment in social structures, institutions and policies, and of what changes – especially in distribution of power and vital resources – would be entailed in realizing this moral vision.' Moe-Lobeda, 'Finding Common Ground on a Moral Vision for a Good Society', 169.

40. Tillich, *Systematic Theology (Volume 1)*, 239.

are present. It is our intrinsic relationship and participation in the divine reality that makes this possible.

We see now how the theoretical elaborations about metaphors and symbols in Part II come to fruition in the present context. The pragmatic dimension of symbols entails that religious symbols offer *guiding principles for behaviour that are nevertheless not prescriptive rules*. The symbols of pregnancy and motherhood mediate personal and communal orientation and transformation and can engender enduring motivation for practices that counter the climate crisis. As such, it is a *positive* symbol. It does not criticize human behaviour and practices but guides them positively. Because symbols guide behaviour that engages us in/with the world, they refer us beyond ourselves and to God's reality as manifest in creation. By relating to 'the exterior' in this way, symbols are actually shaping us and the world simultaneously. Nowhere is this more visible than in the symbol of a mother who bears a child under her heart. By expanding the application of this symbolic metaphor to all humans, we can see that our responsibility is to bear the future in a similar way.[41] Thus, we can establish a context for understanding God, God's creation and ourselves that contributes to overcoming the symbolic deficit that may manifest itself in theologies and practices where a similar awareness is absent.

I do not develop this point to compensate for the often-unacknowledged role women have in the continued creation. The aim is to point to the fundamental guidance that we can identify in women's caretaking for the future when they bear or raise children. The practices this caretaking entails can be described based on the virtues we have encountered already.

Virtues of motherhood for all of creation

Previously, elements related to virtue ethics have been presented.[42] Here, I want to return to the virtues discussed briefly to specify some of the implications that the virtues may have for the care practices rooted in taking responsibility for the future of the planet. Thus, the following section attempts to tease out the implications of this chapter's previous sections utilizing a distinct ethical theory.[43]

---

41. Thus, the metaphors related to motherhood have a wider application and can be appropriated by all humans irrespective of gender and developed into a wide variety of practices. Other metaphors can contribute some of the same, although with less scope, I argue. For the latter, see, e.g. G. L. Schaab, 'A Procreative Paradigm of the Creative Suffering of the Triune God: Implications of Arthur Peacocke's Evolutionary Theology', *Theological Studies* 67, no. 3 (2006): 557ff., who suggests *midwifery* for similar purposes.

42. See pp. 109–20.

43. In the following, I build, in addition to the elements already suggested in Part II, on the elaborations in Steven Bouma-Prediger, 'Finding Common Ground on Ecological Virtues', in *T&T Clark Handbook of Christian Theology and Climate Change*, ed. Ernst M. Conradie and Hilda P. Koster (London; New York: T&T Clark, 2020). His contribution

Like the metaphorical symbol about being pregnant with, and thus intimately linked to the future, the advantage of the virtue ethics tradition is that it is reasonably open and flexible regarding relevant actions that follow from a given virtue. Accordingly, it can be adapted to different contexts and conditions.

Common to all virtues is that they belong in a context and require wisdom to be practised and active engagement on the part of the one who has them. This engagement entails a vision about what it is necessary to do and hope for what the virtuous action may accomplish.

Steven Bouma-Prediger suggests that climate change asks that, in addition to the virtues presented earlier, we attend to *humility, wisdom and ecological justice*. In his elaboration of humility, he focuses on its importance for accurately estimating our abilities or capacities. It entails both self-knowledge and knowing the limits of our knowledge. It means recognizing human finitude. Moreover, we are prone to failures and need to be aware of them. Our lack of perfection makes humility as a virtue necessary.[44]

According to Bouma-Prediger, two pitfalls are related to the virtue of humility: When we lack it, the vice is hubris or overweening pride. It entails 'the failure to acknowledge our limits and/or brokenness. When full of pride, we overestimate our abilities and are vain and boastful. Thinking ourselves in control, we make foolish decisions that wreak havoc for ourselves and for others', he claims.[45] On the other hand, too much humility may end up in self-deprecation, which entails that we become 'unable to acknowledge our actual gifts and abilities' or 'refuse to properly accept our genuine strengths.'[46]

Against this backdrop, *ecological humility* entails 'the disposition to act in such way that we know our place and fit harmoniously into it – whether our local community, our bioregion or our home planet'.[47] We need to realize our finite knowledge about the future and its consequences. Thus, we need to access as much knowledge as possible and 'explore alternatives, seek out blind spots and consider worst-case scenarios'.[48] In effect, this means to act cautiously.

The vices corresponding to this virtue are ecological arrogance and ecological self-deprecation. Bouma-Prediger describes them this way:

> Ecological arrogance puts us, cocky and confident, at the centre of the universe. And so, despite the manifest evidence of both unforeseen and unintended consequences, we go too fast and cut corners. Thinking we know everything, we ignore opposing points of view. Always in a hurry, we do not exercise caution or

there builds on his book *Earthkeeping and Character: Exploring a Christian Ecological Virtue Ethic* (2020).
44. 'Finding Common Ground on Ecological Virtues', 184.
45. Ibid.
46. Ibid.
47. Ibid.
48. Ibid.

go slow. And the natural world, of which we humans are an integral part, suffers. Ecological self-deprecation diminishes the role of humans as earthkeepers. If captured by this vice, we undervalue the important place we humans have as caretakers of creation and responsible agents of change for the good.[49]

Hence, we see here how the vices opposite to humility entail ignorance of knowledge and consequences, not looking beyond ourselves. In the virtue of ecological care that can be expressed in humility, the opposite is the case: there, all actions are performed with the care for the future life in mind. The future life and life conditions for all that exists are in focus. Thus, the virtues are not related to individual gains and outcomes, a point that becomes visible if we look at the ecological impact of the other virtues.

Ecological *wisdom* is the virtue that enables us 'to make insightful and discerning judgements about our common home, the earth.'[50] Ecological wisdom means to plan ahead and long-term, exercise restraint and take time. It recognizes the crucial importance of the worldwide web of biodiversity.[51] The opposite of this virtue is the foolishness that acts 'as if the earth is endlessly exploitable and expendable', and as if the future does not matter.[52]

The understanding of *ecological justice* can be expanded beyond what has already been suggested by pointing to how Bouma-Prediger uses an insight that Hans Jonas articulated previously: the demand of all living beings to live. This claim entails recognizing the legitimate claims of creatures, both human and non-human, for life, as well as showing 'respect for the value of domestic animals and wild plants, endangered species and damaged ecosystems. We render with equity to human and non-human alike what their worth requires. One timely example of this eco-virtue is climate justice or the disposition to treat fairly those affected by climate change.'[53]

Bouma-Prediger defines ecological injustice as a vice. It not only violates the rights of other humans but fails to exercise our duties to 'non-human creatures without rights but whose intrinsic value generates duties for us.'[54] He uses as examples how humans violate domestic animals' rights and fail to value wild landscapes properly. Moreover, 'In the case of climate change, injustice names the fact that those who contribute the least to carbon emissions are very often those who suffer the most from the negative consequences of climate change.'[55]

The present context suggests that a vital virtue for being pregnant with the future is the virtue of hope. It is a virtue that connects faith in God and God's

---

49. Ibid., 184f.
50. Ibid., 185.
51. Ibid.
52. Ibid.
53. Ibid., 186.
54. Ibid.
55. Ibid.

creating and loving work with the concrete actions and dispositions of humans.[56] As practised, this virtue means that humans 'yearn for and act to bring about God's good future of shalom for all the earth, rooted in confidence that such a future ultimately lies in God's good hands'.[57] Thus, acting on this virtue, God's reality and our action become connected in a way that corresponds to Tillich's notion of a symbol: our acts become symbols that point to and participate in God's future.

An obvious threat to this virtue is ecological despair when facing the present catastrophe. Hence, to act with hope also means an attempt to balance the impact of the continuous flow of information about climate change and degradation, species extinction, and the collapse of ecosystems. Furthermore, it is a problem when optimism replaces hope. That might entail what Bouma-Prediger calls 'ecological presumptuousness', which is 'a disposition of overconfidence that presumes something – perhaps some new-fangled technology – will save us'.[58] The danger of this vice is that it underestimates gravely the tasks with which we are faced and allows us to defer from immediate action. However, the point of the virtues is that they are not operative and worth anything in the present context unless we act from them and allow our practices to be shaped by them.

Ecological virtues in the context of exemplarist moral theory

In her moral theory, Linda Zagzebski points to the role of people she calls *exemplars*. These are people 'who show us the upper reaches of human capability, and in doing so, inspire us to expect more from ourselves'.[59] Although they may not be exemplary in every respect, as we have seen in Part II, they may be so in respect of things that matter to us in such a way that makes us admire them.

Zagzebski sees the exemplars in heroes, saints and sages. They are truly extraordinary, as her examples of Holocaust rescuers and L'Arche caregivers show. However, I argue that this extraordinary character is not exhaustive in terms of what may call for admiration. We recognize a good mother and admire her ability and how she cares for her child. She may not be perfect, but the devotion and care she gives to the child can nevertheless engender admiration and make us want to do something similar. We can look at a good mother and say, 'I want to be a person like that' – and no theory is needed to provide sufficient motivation for emulating her behaviour. Mothers are not saints, but we can recognize their qualities or their lack of qualities: 'It is not necessary for ordinary people engaged in moral practice to know the nature of good persons – what makes them good.

---

56. For an extensive theological treatise of hope, which also separates it from mere optimism, see Werner Jeanrond, *Reasons to Hope* (Bloomsbury T&T Clark, 2019).
57. Bouma-Prediger, 'Finding Common Ground on Ecological Virtues', 187.
58. Ibid.
59. Zagzebski, *Exemplarist Moral Theory*, 1.

In fact, it is not necessary that anybody knows what makes a good person good in order to successfully refer to good persons.'[60]

Hence, we must acknowledge that not only extraordinary achievements and virtuous behaviour are inspiring and motivating. Given the virtue of ecological care and concerns, I argue that the same applies to what we have come to consider more mundane, everyday duties. Everyday heroes are just as important for moral inspiration as exceptional people who get public attention. We can admire Greta Thunberg or Metropolitan Bartholomew for their public efforts in different contexts. However, that does not exclude that we can also be inspired by everyday individuals who refuse to fly, opt for a vegan or vegetarian diet, or dedicate their time and effort to providing others with information about what happens with the environment. The courage of the public climate change protesters around the world is just as admirable as that of Thunberg, and I argue that this is so even when they may not appear to be morally excellent in every other respect.

Hence, we need exemplars that inspire by their consistent commitment – just like a mother who cannot shy away from her task as mothering. Consistent commitment is exemplary. But in order to detect that, three conditions must be fulfilled:

a) There must be exemplars who show a consistent commitment to the task of countering climate change.
b) These exemplars cannot be so remote from our ordinary life that their distance to us makes it impossible for us to identify with them and want to emulate their virtuous agency.
c) We need knowledge about why exemplars do what they do – hence they (or others) need to clarify the context of their concerns and their behaviour to us.

Contrary to Zagzebski, I, therefore, argue in favour of *the role of everyday excellence*. We cannot detect this excellence unless we have access to knowledge and communication that can help us to identify and understand it. Hence, education is needed: not only to identify excellence in general and in others but also to identify and figure out what we can do on a concrete level ourselves. Here, exemplars of virtuous motherhood can provide inspiration, admiration, motivation and trajectories for action.

Of course, the critical task is how one can create an awareness of what is needed to do so that everyone understands the challenge to act as if they are pregnant with the future. Unlike a real pregnancy, where your body is affected and changing due to the condition, some of the signs of our relationship with the planet's future life are more hidden – although not absent. Hence, not only intellectually based knowledge is needed about what is happening, but also concrete experiences of nature in sensation and emotions.

60. Cf. Ibid., 15.

By proposing motherhood as the symbol for developing behavioural patterns, we have identified a point of departure in a phenomenon to which everyone can relate. It is part of the experiences almost every human being will face at some stage of their lives, in one way or another. It also connects well with Arendt's notion of natality and Jonas's notion about responsibility as expanded to future generations. Moreover, it is a phenomenon that can be interpreted within the context of different religious traditions. It is not exclusively Christian.

A foundation in Christian narrative elements

How is it possible to connect the aforementioned suggestions to elements in the Christian tradition? Christianity is not manifest as a myth beyond history but is first and foremost based on an interpretation of events and experiences in history and nature. Thus, it relates to phenomena that are common to humanity and familiar in different ways. If we ask for motherhood care models in their context, it is not surprising that we find them. We can see care for the future in the care of Moses's nameless mother and sister. They saved his life, and their action had consequences for the liberation of the people of Israel. The newness of the Exodus would not have been possible unless someone had cared for the child that God, in turn, could use as a servant. The cooperation of these women with God made it possible for God to raise a leader that liberated Israel from oppression.

Similar cooperation is visible in Mary's response to the annunciation and the way she, as an unmarried young woman, takes on her task as the mother of Jesus. It is through her motherhood that the saviour for all of the world is being revealed. Here, I only want to point to how a new epoch in God's history with creation was made possible through a woman.[61] Christians believe in a God who has been borne and born by a woman. By being born, God became one of us and joined with God's creation. Moreover, against the backdrop of the metaphor and the elements I developed earlier in the analysis of Arendt and Jonas, we see in the biblical material plenty of images about the newness that Arendt addresses with her notion of natality. To be reborn is to start over, and when this designation is applied to believers, it suggests that they take on the role of living in the creating and saving community with God that entails love for the neighbour and the world.

We can even see Christ's significance for the present context in how he manifests the deep and intimate relationship between God and humanity. Hence, what we find in Christ may also inform humans: Christ's universal significance may be articulated along the following lines, and against the backdrop of the earlier presentation: Christ is the firstborn of the new creation. As the one who sums up all of God's work in creation and reconciles it, he summons and encompasses

---

61. My intention with these remarks is not to continue the tradition of depicting Mary as an unattainable ideal for women, but to make this single point about the potential impact of motherhood.

all that is. As the manifestation of the divine *logos* that displays the beauty of the Creator and gives witness to it in faith, hope and love, he is also the true image of God (Cf. Col 1, 15–20). The focus of the creation and salvation process is Jesus Christ: in Him, everything is summed up; all that exists is participating and coming to expression in him in a way that also testifies to God's intrinsic relation to the world and to humanity.

In Christ, God and humans are united. They are united in a human being who serves God and the world with love and creates hope. This Christological approach allows for two consequences. First of all, it allows us to see all living beings as encompassed by God's creative and saving work. There is no need to draw any 'lines' that exclude any part of creation from this work. Primates, animals, humans, plants and rivers are all included in God's care, as we are called to manifest it. This follows from the insight found already in the Hebrew Scriptures, 'Let everything that breathes praise the Lord!' (Ps. 150.6). This praise can become realized as a consequence of God's work when all creation displays the will God has for justice, community and life. Thus, 'all of creation is embraced by a Love that 'will not cease in all the endless ages to come.' . . . Our primary calling in life is to receive and trust this justice-making and compassionate Love, and to live it into the world'.[62]

Furthermore, and secondly, the distinctive or unique character of humanity will, according to these suggestions, be a question about to what extent human beings can be witnesses to God's works for other creatures and perform the tasks they are called to perform in other ways and on another basis than do other living beings. As created in the image of God, human beings can understand themselves as precisely that – and they can do so because they have their unique symbolic capacities. Human beings are the species with the symbolic capacities to represent God in creation and represent creation before God in worship that includes practices and prayers for human and non-human reality.

This proposal's advantage is that we do not have to see salvation as exclusive in a way that makes it relevant only to those living beings who have our specific symbolic capacities, as they become expressed in a specific version of Christian faith. Whereas there are no reasons to downplay the importance of Christian faith for the interpretation of human experience in all its richness, the interpretation of reality that emerges from an understanding of the universal significance of the work of Christ will suggest that all life is in some way or another included in the salvific process. This point may also make sense in more ways than already indicated: Given that we see salvation as overcoming estrangement from God (Sin), which in humans comes to a concrete expression in their lack of trust and faith in God, salvation is as a process that God instantiates and fulfils on many levels and in different realms of reality. On the level of other species, it will mean that God eventually will restore their lives in a way that brings unambiguous witness to God's goodness and power, whereas in humans, it will mean that God provides the opportunities for healing and restoration that lead

---

62. Moe-Lobeda, *Resisting Structural Evil: Love as Ecological and Economic Vocation*, 6.

to the same consequence. Salvation then includes the promise that creation will continue to evolve, that there will be psychological, social and spiritual growth and development also in the future. Salvation thus has to do with all of life and includes elements of growth, maturation and reorientation in terms of values and understanding and how nature will be when consummated in the presence of God, when God is all in all.

Chapter 12

SYMBOLIC DEFICITS IN APOCALYPTICISM

TOWARDS A PRESENTIST ESCHATOLOGY

Among the challenges to a theological approach to the climate crisis is the temptation to employ language with roots in apocalyptic traditions. Such language engenders imaginaries related to the end of the world. Hence, the climate crisis and ecological problems generally are treated as illustrations of a trope that shapes the perceptions of what takes place as reflecting a predominantly pre-ordered pattern of events. As a result, apocalypticism contributes to a deductive mode of theology – the type of theology that was addressed critically at the end of Part II. It creates a spiritualized optic that decreases motivation for engaging in the necessary practices for change. Thus, severe deficits in the symbolic repertoire of apocalypticism become apparent. This chapter will point to some of its main components.

Catherine Keller's warnings

Catherine Keller is among those who have been criticizing the apocalyptic language's effect on active engagement.[1] Her emphasis on the profoundly relational character of everything leads her to consider what it means for the relationship between the present, past and future.[2] Rick Benjamins summarizes her position

---

1. This fact notwithstanding, Keller nevertheless seems to have an ambiguous attitude to apocalyptic language. She employs it extensively in one of her early publications on the topic of global warming. See Catherine Keller, 'The Heat Is On: Apocalyptic Rhetoric and Climate Change', *Journal for the Study of Religion, Nature and Culture* 7 (1999). Notable changes are also detectable in her recent book, *Facing Apocalypse: Climate, Democracy, and Other Last Chances* (Maryknoll, NY: Orbis Books, 2021).

2. The following section on Keller is a reworking of my analysis of elements in her work previously published in Jan-Olav Henriksen, 'Hope – a Theological Exploration', *Studia theologica* 73, no. 2 (2019). I build on the thorough analysis of her work in Rick Benjamins, 'Apophatic Panentheism: Catherine Keller's Constructive Theology', *Neue Zeitschrift fur Systematische Theologie und Religionsphilosophie* 60, no. 1 (2018).

thus: 'In our global world, we can only prevent the worst or strive for the better if we recognize that humans are intimately intertwined with their surroundings and the world, with each other and God, which is precisely ignored if either a modern autonomy of the subject or a postmodern radical alterity of the other is emphasized'.[3] The alternative to these pitfalls is that those future possibilities that we hope for, and which we may even consider impossible, 'do not come from the outside, like the advent of an event, but come forth, or become, from the incalculable and inscrutable relationships that make up the being of our world'.[4] Hence, Keller points to an alternative to a pre-established, almost determinist mode of thought: hope is rooted in that which is partly outside our control – because we cannot control everything in the web of relations of which we are part. Hope for change cannot be rooted merely in calculations of our own agency's effects, although it does not exclude such agency, either. Hope is for more than what we can control, but it is not unrelated to the conditions in which we live.

Accordingly, Keller's notion of hope is not constituted by a refuge to apocalyptic imaginaries that represent a full break with the present. 'Instead of a radical alterity, Keller adheres to an unsurveyable relatedness, for if being is in relation [. . .], an unrelated alterity makes no sense.'[5] Thus, Christian hope is not so much the manifestation or the supersession of a supernatural reality as the graceful realization of what the created world can be.

Against this backdrop, it becomes more understandable why Keller offers critical *and* self-critical reflections about the self-righteous convictions of leftist, feminist liberationist groups, or affiliated groups and parties who strive for a better world and reject apocalyptic doom scenarios. These groups may tacitly reproduce patterns of thought that are similar to those they reject. Hope for a better world in the future, different from the present, may easily have the consequence that opponents of this hope are demonized for obstructing the new world's realization. 'These features contribute to an anti-apocalyptic way of thought that is still apocalyptic under the surface and can, therefore, be labeled as retro-apocalyptic or crypto-apocalyptic.'[6] The problem with (more or less) disguised apocalyptic patterns of thought is that they 'close down history by pressing it into the schemes of a fixed ideological worldview. Within these schemes resides the tacit presupposition of an ultimate triumph over the old world and its adherents'.[7] In contrast, Keller wants to 'sustain

---

3. Rick Benjamins, 'Apophatic Panentheism: Catherine Keller's Constructive Theology', *Neue Zeitschrift für Systematische Theologie und Religionsphilosophie* 60, no. 1 (2018): 105f. Referring to Catherine Keller, *On the Mystery: Discerning Divinity in Process* (Minneapolis, MN: Fortress Press, 2008).

4. Benjamins, 'Apophatic Panentheism: Catherine Keller's Constructive Theology', 105.

5. Keller, *On the Mystery*, 4, 10,11, referenced by Benjamins, ibid.

6. Benjamins, 'Apohatic Panentheism', 112, with reference to Catherine Keller, *Apocalypse Now and Then: A Feminist Guide to the End of the World* (Boston: Beacon Press, 1996), 7, 8.

7. Benjamins, 'Apophatic Panentheism: Catherine Keller's Constructive Theology', 112.

resistance to destruction without expecting to triumph'. The idea of triumph might turn humans into destructive and self-righteous martyrs or victors who block the road to the better world that they strive for, ignorant of the opportunities for improvement given at the moment.[8]

In his analysis of her work. Benjamins shows that Keller develops her reflections on the apocalyptic mindset in 'a postmodern critique of the modernist attempt to achieve ideals on the basis of some *arche* and *telos* of history'.[9] Her critique builds on a process-theological approach that prioritizes *creativity in an open process*. This important point links together creation and the future in a way that allows for an open future and not for conformity to an already-established pattern or ideal design. It also allows for acknowledging the fully relational character of the already-mentioned relational character of all beings. 'A better world will not appear by the enforcement of our ideals, but requires that we stay in touch with the relations that make up our world as it is now since these relations provide us with the opportunities for the better.'[10] Against this backdrop, it is possible to argue that apocalypticism serves to exclude the combination of ecology and eschatology and the commitment to practices that can promote a better future.

One more element follows from the deeply relational approach in Keller's theology that she does not develop. This is spelled out clearly by Robert C. Neville. He has pointed to how past, present and future must be seen as *internally related*, albeit different, in the creative act on which hope rests. Whereas the essential components of the past have to do with fixed and finished actuality, the present has to do with spontaneous creativity. Neville writes on the interrelation between the three *tempora* in a quite dense quote, which points to how both divine and human agency with regard to the future rests on conditions of the past and the present. Both past and present inescapably contribute to the content of the hope for the future:

> Each mode [of time] also receives conditional components from both of the others. From the past, the future receives a plurality of actual things that have to be unified; hence, the future is not pure indeterminate unity but rather patterns of determinate possibilities, often containing alternatives. From the present, the future receives constantly shifting demands of relevance, requiring that the future provide possibilities for decisive actualization relative to each present. Thus the future is an ever-changing kaleidoscope of possibilities relevant to every moment as it is present.[11]

---

8. Ibid.
9. Ibid., 113.
10. Ibid.
11. Neville, *Defining Religion: Essays in Philosophy of Religion*, 252–3. He elaborates these considerations further, thus: 'From the past the present receives conditioning components in the form of potentialities to integrate in its creative selections, and from the future the present receives as conditioning components the possibilities for present

Neville is pointing here to what most believers are aware of but which is not always made explicit: the contents of this world and its former and present state is what makes hope in the future relevant, actual and constantly changing, due to the always-existing transformations, changes, disruptions, terrors and creative potentials that emerge in history. Thus, hope is never only about the present; it also provides us with assessments and optics for the present's potentials and an assessment of the past. The flipside of this insight is that apocalypticism, which implies disruption, breaks and shifts, cannot account for a similar type of this-worldly hope.

Further criticism: Hermann Timm

The aforementioned critique of apocalypticism has severe consequences for its potential when it comes to addressing the climate crisis. Philosopher of religion Hermann Timm contributes further to this critique by pointing to how apocalypticism also presupposes the image of the end of the world as we know it. To the extent that ecological concerns employ such imagery, it becomes impossible to imagine any alternative mode in which the present world can exist. Everything must become totally different if anything more can happen at all. How this 'different' world should be, nevertheless, remains mainly unimaginable, he holds.[12]

Timm finds other problems with apocalyptic imagery, as well. One is that apocalypticism suggests that all will be well in the end because God will intervene. This idea has an immediate effect on how humans will perceive their conditions for agency. In the precarious situation in which we now find ourselves, with no easy or apparent pathways out, apocalypticism offers false consolation: it may look bad, but God will make it good at the end.

Moreover, Timm finds that the 'apocalyptization' of the contemporary tendencies in nature allows it to become incorporated into a metaphysics of history[13] – a point that supports my claim about the deductive character of this theology. Hence, passivity in the face of the challenges of the present catastrophe seems like an acceptable and possible response. The effect is, of course, that the

creativity; the dynamism of the present is the creative novelty of deciding which of the alternate possibilities will be actualized in the integration of the potentialities acquired from the past. From the future the past receives as conditioning components the formal structures that are actualized, including the value in those structures; from the present the past receives ever-growing new actualizations so that the structure of the past, including its value and meaning, are constantly changing.'

12. Hermann Timm, ‚Evangelische Weltweisheit: Zur Kritik Der Ökotheologischen Apokalyptik', *zeittheokirc Zeitschrift für Theologie und Kirche* 84, no. 3 (1987): 347. I am here referring only to two of the main points in Timm's critique, which also contains elements with which I cannot identify, or which are obviously dated.

13. Ibid., 352.

situation only becomes more severe. Thus, the deficits of this type of imagery become even more apparent.

Eschatology reconfigured to address the present: Hope and healing (Barbara Rossing)

What about elements in traditional Christian eschatology that are not shaped by the context of apocalypticism? Are they still helpful for addressing the present situation – not as a deductive tool for spiritualizing the perception of the present, but as contributing to enduring and sustained practices of ecological care? A recent contribution by Barbara Rossing, which directly addresses climate change, points towards a positive answer to this question.[14]

Rossing interprets *eschaton,* which can mean both being at the end and being at the edge, with the biblical notion of healing. From this, she explores a possible trajectory that she claims has been largely overlooked in eschatological thinking: the trajectory of healing for our world: 'In our context of planetary crisis, when climate change represents the largest public health crisis humans have ever faced, the trajectory of healing becomes urgent', she holds.[15] Recent examples of people who have been forced to relocate and have lost their means for livelihood due to the crisis underscores her point. These are the people living on the edge of the climate crisis, and they are among the poorest and most vulnerable. They have done almost nothing to cause the crisis, but still they suffer the consequences of it.[16]

What to do, then? Rossing claims that 'What we need is a "bridge" that will safely help us cross over from crisis to sustainability' and that 'eschatology, reimagined, can help us find that bridge. It can help us cross over to healing for ourselves and our world'.[17] The stakes for this claim are high because it presupposes that we need to develop imagery that represents an alternative to other eschatologies, such as those of escapist rupture, the economic eschatology of endless growth and dystopic eschatological storylines frequently presented in movies and popular culture. The alternative should, accordingly, sustain a reasonable hope that connects the present and the future.[18]

In her constructive approach to these challenges, Rossing points to elements in the biblical imagery that are in line with the overall suggestion in this book:

---

14. See Barbara R. Rossing, 'Reimagining Eschatology: Toward Healing and Hope for a World at the Eschatos', in *Planetary Solidarity: Global Women's Voices on Christian Doctrine and Climate Justice,* ed. Grace Ji-Sun Kim and Hilda P. Koster (Minneapolis: Fortress Press, 2017).
15. Ibid., 324.
16. Ibid., 325.
17. Ibid.
18. Cf. ibid., 326f.

The eschatological imagery of birthing and labour pains, which is the imagery of vulnerability and hope in combination. It suggests that 'the world is about to turn. We and the whole creation participate in this birth together'.[19] Among the advantages of this image is that it also entails 'the agony of labor pains to frame our own painful experiences of crossing over from crisis to sustainability', even in the face of the risk of death.[20] Hence, it is a realistic and not a utopian image.

Rossing discusses critically several strands in the biblical eschatological material and its reception that I will not go into here. One element that she notes, though, is that 'Nowhere do we find the idea that the purpose of life is to go to heaven after death. That idea of leaving Earth to go to heaven after death, which has become so prevalent in the popular mind-set, is rather a Platonist eschatology'.[21] Instead, she argues that we need to see *eschatology as resistance*.[22] 'Eschatology recognizes that things are not how they are meant to be. The current situation is one in which unjust structures of power have temporarily taken over the world and its life—but this system will not last forever.'[23]

Accordingly, it is the combination of resistance and healing that shapes the content of Rossing's proposal for eschatology, and which forms the basis for the possibility of hope. The strength of the proposal is that it actively involves us in various ways: by framing the issues of climate in terms of sickness and healing, it both affects us and calls for our response: 'The world is ill; we are making ourselves sick. We need healing', she writes.[24] Thus, we are not only responsible for the condition in which we find ourselves – we are also called to make a remedy. Perhaps this has not ever been better illustrated than during the times I am writing this book: during the Covid-19 pandemic, which shows in which entanglement our health is situated.

To address eschatology from the perspective of health and healing allows for seeing how it comprises multiple dimensions. It allows for focusing on a variety of illnesses (literal and metaphorical), as well as on activities that foster healing and wholeness for not only humans but the whole biosphere.[25] This, Rossing connects to the biblical stories about healing, but also to research in evolutionary anthropology and neuroscience that show how 'Compassion, cooperation, and altruism are attested in the human fossil record dating back at least 300,000 years, and perhaps much longer'.[26] This material testifies to how 'Early humans cared

---

19. Ibid., 328.
20. Ibid.
21. Ibid., 331.
22. Ibid., 338.
23. Ibid., 339.
24. Ibid.
25. Ibid., 340.
26. Ibid. Cf. also how altruism is discussed further in relation to Sarah Coakley's work in Chapter 15, pp. 227ff., and the relationship between grace, hope and healing in relation to Jay B. McDaniel's work below, pp. 238ff.

for those who were disabled' and for 'extensive care of injured or incapacitated individuals'.[27]

Hence, the past points to how human communities have focused on care and healing since their beginnings. Can this serve as a basis for expanding this care to the biosphere and generate actions for the future's benefit? Here Rossing develops another crucial biblical concept for understanding healing, namely *salvation*. In Greek, the word 'save' means 'heal' or 'make whole', and, thus, it includes healing. The Latin word for salvation also encompassed safety, welfare and health. Hence, salvation is intrinsically bound up with healing, she argues.[28]

Christianity has always also been a tradition that emphasizes the healing of body and soul.[29] Rossing argues that today 'Eschatological reimagining seeks to bring together the multiple dimensions of *sōzō* to encompass healing beyond physical healing'. It entails 'to take this biblical trajectory of salvation as healing in more eschatological, ecological, and social directions'.[30] The social dimension implies that justice becomes a central part of an ecological eschatology:

> Eschatology must include justice, God's vindication for innocent sufferers [. . .] In formulating an eschatology of healing that can help us in a time of climate injustice and planetary solidarity, we need to broaden our images of justice and judgment to foreground scenes of judgment that can address structural sin.[31]

Rossing also points to how Revelation's imagery presents a funeral that performatively enacts the end of the Roman economic system. We can emulate this funeral, she suggests, as a way to 'announce the "end of the system of this world" today, the fossil-fuel economy that devours lands and peoples'.[32]

Rossing does not present many concrete suggestions for action, but her eschatology does suggest an optic in which healing practices of different kinds become central for practising hope. Among practices that suggest such hope is also one that points to trees as signs of life – an image that runs through the Bible from its first pages to the last ones.[33] Trees that live can mediate both life, healing and wisdom or be signs of these. Therefore, eschatological imagery of trees can suggest what will be lacking where there are no trees anymore. Trees need water, and, thus, both trees and water become signs of life. Where there are no trees and no life, hope is lost.

---

27. Ibid.
28. Ibid., 342.
29. See Amanda Porterfield, *Healing in the History of Christianity* (Oxford; New York: Oxford University Press, 2005).
30. Rossing, 'Reimagining Eschatology: Toward Healing and Hope for a World at the Eschatos', 342.
31. Ibid., 344.
32. Ibid.
33. Cf. Ibid., 342ff.

Rossing uses Wangari Maathai as a contemporary example of how trees are part of a practised eschatology. Maathai 'describes the power of trees to reveal both the eschatological wounds of our world and also the power of healing'.[34] She continues by quoting Maathai, who speaks about who the prophets of today are and what they do. According to her, they depict

> an alternative to the degradation of the environment that has turned waters of life here and earth that were 'bright as crystal' into mud and silt, and the 'tree of life with its twelve kinds of fruit' into stumps and charcoal, and has led to nations not being healed but rather fighting one another for access to the remaining clean water and food supplies.... These prophets are asking why we do this to the earth, and they are commanding us to heal and replenish it now.[35]

One is reminded here of the story ascribed to Martin Luther, when asked about what he would do if he learned that the world would end tomorrow: He answered that he would enter his garden and plant an apple tree. Hence, for him, eschatological consciousness would not preclude long-term-oriented action.

---

34. Ibid., 344.
35. Wangari Maathai, *Replenishing the Earth: Spiritual Values for Healing Ourselves and the World*, 1st edition (New York; London: Doubleday, 2010), 125, here quoted after Rossing, 'Reimagining Eschatology: Toward Healing and Hope for a World at the Eschatos', 344.

Chapter 13

SIN

Let me start this chapter with a quote from a lecture Hans Jonas gave:

> It was once religion which told us that we are all sinners, because of original sin. It is now the ecology of our planet which pronounces us all to be sinners because of the excessive exploits of human inventiveness. It was once religion which threatened us with a last judgment at the end of days. It is now our tortured planet which predicts the arrival of such a day without any heavenly intervention. The latest revelation – from no Mount Sinai, from no Mount of the Sermon, from no Bo (tree of Buddha) – is the outcry of mute things themselves that we must heed by curbing our powers over creation, lest we perish together on a wasteland of what was creation.[1]

Although the aforementioned quote starts with speaking about sin, we should, first of all, note that Hans Jonas also does two other things in it. Firstly, he points to how we can read the present situation as a sign. There is a semiotic dimension in the situation that opens up to the theological notions of sin and judgement. Secondly, he suggests that whatever theological notions we use, we need not refer to a divine intervention to warrant them: they are mediated through the signs of the times. In other words: the divine manifests itself negatively in reality. I write 'manifests negatively' because reality appears as the opposite of how Christians believe that God has revealed Godself through cooperation and community, beauty, health, flourishing and diversity.

Presently, a growing number of people realize that it is impossible to continue with 'business as usual', based on material growth in the Western world that leads to the exploitation of humans elsewhere and to increasingly more ecological degradation. Nevertheless, we seem to be captured in an economic system and in

---

1. Hans Jonas and Lawrence Vogel, *Mortality and Morality: A Search for the Good after Auschwitz*, Northwestern University Studies in Phenomenology and Existential Philosophy (Evanston, IL: Northwestern University Press, 1996), 201., quoted from Lawrence Troster, 'Caretaker or Citizen: Hans Jonas, Aldo Leopold, and the Development of Jewish Environmental Ethics', in *The Legacy of Hans Jonas: Judaism and the Phenomenon of Life*, ed. Hava Tirosh-Samuelson and Christian Wiese (Leiden; Boston: Brill, 2010), 373.

behaviour patterns that repeatedly deflect us from following these insights. People and governments in the Western hemisphere seem to be addicted to consumerism and its concomitant partner, economic growth. The long-term consequences of this addiction to consumption as a central part of life are covered up or mostly ignored. The situation reminds us of Paul's analysis in his letter to the Romans: 'For I do not do the good I want to do, but the evil I do not want to do – this I keep on doing' (Romans 7, 19). Paul connects this analysis to the impact of sin in our lives.

For some, the current environmental predicament may prove the relevance of sin as a theological notion. This chapter is nevertheless no apology for this much used and abused notion. Instead, I want to address the symbolic deficit the notion of sin manifests insofar as it is not specified further with attention to the climate crisis or other predicaments. This deficit can only be addressed against the backdrop of an analysis of how the notion is employed as a symbol for interpreting human behaviour. Hence, we need to ask to what extent it contributes to orientation and transformation in light of the current crisis.

The notion of sin should not be read as an empirical explanation of the present ecological conditions. We should not use it as a generic reference to the causes of climate change. It needs more specification in terms of which actions and attitudes that appear as a result of human sin. In itself, a reference to sin is not providing us with any helpful insights or explanations. Instead, it may remove us from some of the challenging tasks we need to address. At best, then, we can use 'sin' as an entry point for critical self-scrutiny and as part of a theological interpretation of the predicament we face – but not as an explanatory tool.[2] There can be no competition between theology and science when it comes to understanding the causes for climate change; sin is a notion that places us in a specific condition (orientation) and invites change (transformation). The reasons for criticizing it as an explanation will be discussed in the next section.

Nevertheless, the concept of sin can be helpful for interpreting the present situation in a theological context. When seen as a theological, and not merely as a moral concept, sin entails that the human relationship with God is broken: We lack trust in God and in God's call for us to be representing God in faith, love, hope and care for all of creation. The flip side of this trust is to be enclosed in oneself – a point I will return to in the following text when I discuss some of the psychological dimensions of sin. Thus, the symbol 'sin' can help us understand some of the mechanisms we need to be aware of when we address what has gone wrong and what we need to be aware of to establish better competencies for an environmentally responsible agency.

I have repeatedly underscored how religious resources serve the tasks of orientation and transformation. As a symbol of self-interpretation, sin might

---

2. Note that I here make a deliberate distinction between explanation and interpretation: Theology is, in general, not about explaining the world in terms of causality, but about interpreting the world in terms that clarify what our experiences entail with regard to the tasks of orientation and transformation.

contribute to these tasks in ways that are relevant to the problems discussed in this book. Biblical faith holds a far more complex and far-reaching notion of sin than one which focuses on it as individual wrongdoings (thoughts, words, feelings, acts, etc.). 'Sin in its fullest sense refers to disorientation from right relationships with God, which then leads to disorientation from right relationship with self, others, and all of creation. That disorientation results in wrongdoings. Sin is dislocating God from the center of reality.'[3] Thus, it entails that we see reality from our own, self-centred perspective instead of from the perspective of the Creator.

Uses of sin 1: To defer and deflect political action and environmental concern

In Part I, I referred to Robin G. Veldman's study of evangelical climate change deniers. Her informants use the notion of sin to address environmental degradation. Their use is generic and not specified with regard to what is caused by human action and what is due to non-human causes. Some of them see both earthquakes and pollution as a result of sin having entered the world. Thus, for them, 'sin' is a category with which they can explain all that is wrong in the world – without relating all of it to shortcomings or failures in their personal agency. This unspecified use also means that any distinction between generic and anthropogenetic climate change falls under the table.[4] However, sin does not operate primarily as a causal explanation of the environmental situation. They see sin in exclusively spiritual terms as rebellion against God.[5]

When Veldman analyses this position in detail, her results are intriguing. She notices that her informants reframe environmental problems in religious terms when they use the notion of sin. Thus, environmental problems become religious problems instead of problems in their own right. This use has profound consequences because the solution to a religious problem is not human agency but religious means provided by God (salvation). It entails a refocus in which it is not environmental degradation that is the primary problem, but its cause in sin. 'Environmental degradation as a problem in and of itself did not connect meaningfully to the group's understanding of the way the world worked. But environmental degradation made sense in the light of sin', Veldman argues.[6]

---

3. Moe-Lobeda, *Resisting Structural Evil: Love as Ecological and Economic Vocation*, 58.

4. This distinction is utilized in a helpful way in Ernst M Conradie, 'The Emergence of Human Sin', in *T&T Handbook of Christianity & Climate Change*, ed. Ernst M. Conradie and Hilda P. Koster (London; New York: Bloomsbury T&T Clark, 2020), 392.

5. Veldman, *The Gospel of Climate Skepticism: Why Evangelical Christians Oppose Action on Climate Change*, 63. Cf. ibid., 117.

6. Ibid., 64.

In this context, sin is the causal force between the negativities of the world.[7] Thus, it serves as a tool by which one can interpret all imperfections in the world generically and without discrimination. Moreover, because these imperfections are seen a result of *original* sin, that is, the fundamental corruption of human society by way of the sin of 'the first humans', sin is conceived as an empirical reality independently of human individual agency. Accordingly, social and environmental problems are relegated to another sphere than the one that calls for political and social action. The focus on sin and salvation therefore reduces the urgency of addressing the situation and reframes the concerns in a predominantly spiritual context – it makes it unnecessary and even spiritually unwise to care about climate change as such.[8] Moreover, in the context where her informants are placed, sin manifests itself as an individual, not a structural problem.[9]

This use of the notion of theological symbol 'sin' exhibits its deficit in the context of climate change. The use gives those who think of sin in this way the opportunity to defer necessary actions and commitment or deflect from it altogether. Accordingly, the interpretation of the present situation utilizing this concept does not help engender a responsible agency or providing people with a sense of commitment or urgency in light of the present crisis.

Uses of sin 2: An entry point for self-criticism and repentance

Icelandic theologian Arnfridur Gudmundsdottir provides an alternative approach to the aforementioned use of sin. She argues that key theological terms, such as sin, repentance and salvation, can prove relevant when addressing the severe consequences of irresponsible treatment of nature and natural resources, particularly global climate change.[10] We note here right away that she specifies her use of the notion. It is about the serious consequences of irresponsible treatment of nature. Hence, she uses the notion to *evaluate* specific actions and does not see it as a causal factor isolated from empirical consequences that everyone can detect. This use is in striking contrast to the previous position I analysed.

Moreover, Gudmundsdottir manages to hold together theological concerns that allow sin to be understood as more than a moral concept, with an outlook to the challenges to action. She writes:

7. Ibid.
8. Cf. Ibid., 101.
9. Cf. Ibid., 250, n. 27.
10. Arnfridur Gudmundsdottir, 'The Fire Alarm Is Off: A Feminist Theological Reflection on Sin, Climate Change, Energy, and the Protection of Wilderness in Iceland', in *Planetary Solidarity: Global Women's Voices on Christian Doctrine and Climate Justice*, ed. Grace Ji-Sun Kim and Hilda P. Koster (Minneapolis: Fortress, 2017), 136.

When we forget who we are as stewards of God's creation, when we forget about others and we ourselves become the center of our universe, then we bend in toward ourselves and become twisted and ingrown. To be fully bent in on ourselves is what it means to be *caught in sin*. Sin is a relational concept. It signifies a broken relationship to God, our Creator, as well as to our neighbor, nature, and ourselves. From an ecological perspective, it is crucial that we understand sin as pertaining not exclusively to the individual but also to 'the social structural relationships that shape our societies and their impact on eco-systems'.[11]

Thus, Gudmundsdottir's analysis points to both the collective dimension in stewardship and its failing, and the structural dimension in sin. Accordingly, it becomes apparent that the pragmatic context for using the notion of sin is related to the human calling to be in partnership with nature. Whereas she continues to use the notion of stewardship to denote the human responsibility for nature, she employs this notion in a way that overcomes the human separation from the rest of nature. Moreover, she contrasts the notion of stewardship with the notion of sin and holds that 'sustainable living and fair distribution of material goods are in accordance with good stewardship'.[12] Thereby, she expands the discussion of stewardship in Chapter 10 by relating the symbols 'stewardship' and 'sin' to each other. Consequently, she argues that

> the notion of stewardship is a clear antithesis to any form of hubris, including the exploitation of the environment, which is inducing the severe threat of global warming. If someone has transformed her call to stewardship into sheer domination and selfishness, use has turned into abuse. Pollution, greed, and exploitation are all consequences of a shortsighted and selfish perspective, which goes against prioritization of the benefit of human and nonhuman others.[13]

Gudmundsdottir's circumscription of sin with notions like *hubris* and selfishness can also be seen in relation to our previous analysis of hubris as a vice in relation to the virtue of humility. It means putting oneself above anything else. Selfishness and hubris belong together insofar as a selfish orientation entails that one primarily cares for oneself – and excludes the concern for others, the environment and the future life on the planet. Hence, other consequences become apparent as well, connected to selfishness and greed: pollution and exploitation of resources.

An obvious consequence of this approach is that sin cannot be individualized, privatized or limited to the personal sphere. Hence, Gudmundsdottir stresses the collective and structural manifestation of sin. Referring to Cynthia D. Moe-Lobeda,

---

11. Ibid. The quote in the quote is from Moe-Lobeda, *Resisting Structural Evil: Love as Ecological and Economic Vocation*, 59.
12. Gudmundsdottir, 'The Fire Alarm Is Off: A Feminist Theological Reflection on Sin, Climate Change, Energy, and the Protection of Wilderness in Iceland', 136.
13. Ibid.

she argues that in the present situation, 'social structural sin makes monumental demands on the practice of faith and of morality, and many of those demands remain largely unacknowledged.'[14] This lack of acknowledgement we saw demonstrated in Veldman's analysis, as referred to in the previous section.

In her analysis of structural sin, Moe-Lobeda points to these four features:

a) It is relatively invisible to those who do not suffer directly from it,
b) It continues regardless of the virtue or vice of people involved,
c) It transmits from generation to generation unless exposed and confronted,
d) It expands as a result of concentrated power.[15]

Against the backdrop of her constructive analysis of the sin symbol, we also need to address one potential shortcoming in Gudmundsdottir's contribution. She makes an inference that is not sufficiently warranted when she claims that 'Sin-talk, then, allows us to describe our human situation, recognize what is wrong, and identify what needs to be done in order to make things right.'[16] That is not the case. Although a specified notion of sin and its consequences can help us to identify what is wrong, this identification will not by and for itself help us understand what must be done. It requires another perspective and a broader context of interpretation for that to happen. The notion of sin can provide insight into what we should not do, at best. Herein lies one of the deficits of the notion of sin.

Nevertheless, this deficit does not exclude that recognition of sin can contribute to orientation and transformation. Gudmundsdottir quotes Moe-Lobeda, writing, 'the recognition that something is wrong is the first step toward setting it right again. There is no help for those who admit no need of help. There is no repair for those who insist that nothing is broken, and there is no hope of transformation for a world whose inhabitants accept that it is sadly but irreversibly wrecked.'[17] Thus, the notion may serve as gateway to change and transformation that also has consequences for how people act to counter climate change.

Gudmundsdottir finds the broader context for a positive and informed agency in the biblical notion of salvation, understood as more than a spiritual gift to the individual. 'If the gospel of God's forgiving grace really means good news about the renewal of broken relationships between us and God, between us and our neighbor, and between us and the rest of the creation, then the social significance of the gospel is unmistakable.' This Gospel is about all of our existence, and it 'calls

---

14. Ibid., 140.
15. Moe-Lobeda, *Resisting Structural Evil: Love as Ecological and Economic Vocation*, 60.
16. Gudmundsdottir, 'The Fire Alarm Is Off: A Feminist Theological Reflection on Sin, Climate Change, Energy, and the Protection of Wilderness in Iceland', 139.
17. Ibid., 140. Moe-Lobeda, *Resisting Structural Evil: Love as Ecological and Economic Vocation*, 59.

us to a social responsibility and solidarity with the rest of creation'.[18] Hence, she recontextualizes traditional theological notions like sin, gospel and repentance. Sin can become a sign of hope 'when it symbolizes a new beginning through repentance toward salvation'.[19]

At this point, it is tempting to point to how salvation is described as being born again in the New Testament. In light of Arendt's notion of natality, it means that salvation entails chances for something new and hopeful to happen. Salvation means that God offers us a new beginning. The gift of salvation has consequences for all our relationships and entails another way of experiencing the world. It is against this backdrop that some of Gudmundsdottir's final remarks become especially relevant:

> God calls us out of our sinful state and into the new beginning: the renewal of our relationships with God, our neighbor, the whole creation, and ourselves. Such transformation takes place when we, as individuals and as communities, recognize where things have gone wrong and decide to turn around, to change the way we think and act, and open up for God's gift of salvation.[20]

Recognition of sin is a condition for repentance and a new start with regard to how we relate to the rest of creation. Therefore, Christian theology's task is to spell out more clearly what salvation means for all of creation and what our calling is in making it happen without compromising salvation as a fundamental gift of God.

Uses of sin 3: Sinful actions in specific contexts

Ernst Conradie has published a further contribution to investigating options for overcoming the sin symbol's deficit when addressing climate change in an article with the title 'The Emergence of Human Sin'.[21] He warns against pointing towards sin as its primary or only cause. 'This is obviously facile given the painstaking work done by scientists, economic analysts, political observers, sociologists, activists, and the like.'[22] As we have seen, references to sin may not only lead Christians to dismiss the work of others, but it may also lead others to see a Christian contribution as unconnected to the important work done by others. Consequently, the reference to sin may create a hiatus between theology and other types of knowledge.[23]

---

18. Gudmundsdottir, 'The Fire Alarm Is Off: A Feminist Theological Reflection on Sin, Climate Change, Energy, and the Protection of Wilderness in Iceland', 141.
19. Ibid., 154.
20. Ibid.
21. See Conradie, 'The Emergence of Human Sin'.
22. Ibid., 385.
23. Ibid.

Like Gudmundsdottir, Conradie is also open to the contemporary relevance of the Christian vocabulary for addressing climate change. For him, sin is not a mere inner-theological notion. It can identify elements that are visible outside the religious context. He lists six examples:

- *Anthropocentrism* sees the world from the perspective of humans' interests without recognizing our continuity with other species.[24]
- *Consumerist greed* entails the 'escalation of needs, wants and desires that have become infectious'. It appears in different contexts. In the wealthy part of the world in 'conspicuous consumption', and the desire to demonstrate superiority over others, or in the consumerist desires of the global poor who struggle for things that are paraded by others. This greed ignores that 'it would not be sufficient to replace carbon-based energy sources with more sustainable alternatives if the underlying problem of expanding resource consumption is not addressed'[25].
- *Sloth*. 'We sin not only in what we do but in what we have left undone.' This goes for all of humankind. However, Conradie claims that the 'emphasis on responsibility is easily corrupted by a capitalist emphasis on the virtues of productivity, entrepreneurship, efficiency, education, training and development. The argument is that climate mitigation and adaptation do not call for restraint but for innovation and transformation.'[26]
- *Domination* is based on differences of gender, class, race, sexual orientation, education and especially species and 'reinforced by a set of interlocking binary oppositions, hierarchies and ideologies'. In response, there is a need for solidarity with the victims of climate change, including concerns over marginalized land and its biodiversity.
- *Alienation* from the Earth as the only home that humans have is expressed in the disenchantment of nature, and loss of a sense of the sacred.[27]
- *Folly* is expressed in climate denial, deception (misinformation), falsity, callousness, hypocrisy, ignorance and senselessness would be typical expressions of this type of sin.[28]

Conradie's contribution helps us address specific vices directly related to climate change. It allows for a contextual specification of sin language that is important to employ to overcome the deficits connected with this symbol for self-interpretation. Among his contextual considerations is his claim that the 'North Atlantic Christian discourse on sin' hardly can contribute to a collaborative diagnosis on climate change if others suspect that the outcome of this diagnostic process may be that

---

24. Ibid., 385f.
25. Ibid., 386.
26. Ibid.
27. Ibid., 386f.
28. Ibid., 387.

the problem is caused mainly by the sins of North Atlantic Christians. That is a point well taken.

Another advantage of his analysis is that the contextual conditions of common claims about sin may cause this notion to operate differently in different contexts. The claim about sin's *universality* may cover up that some bear more of the burden of climate change than others, whereas others are more to blame for the present situation.[29]

Furthermore, sin can be fundamentally *misunderstood* in some contexts if it is personalized or reduced to a list of dos and don'ts. Accordingly, it must be expanded to include what humans do to themselves, others, and nature and incorporate more than acts: it is about dispositions, attitudes and attachments, about the failure to accept responsibility, lack of character and broken relationships.

Conradie also is among the scholars who argue that sin is most adequately from a structural perspective, as inflicting structural violence.[30] This more in-depth understanding of sin as structural leads Conradie to make some important remarks about how to understand sin as a combination of guilt and power. To only focus on individual guilt or the guilt of groups or organizations is one-sided, but so is the focus on sin as (external) power, as this will place sinners in an inescapable situation beyond control. 'To focus on individual actions is to trivialize sin, to look for particular instantiations of sin as if there are other actions, attitudes, dispositions, and thoughts that are not contaminated by sin.'[31] Moreover, the exclusive focus on sin as power 'portray individuals and groups as victims of forces beyond their control for which they therefore ultimately do not need to accept responsibility'.[32] Conradie is right in pointing out that this only undermines human agency, including the agency of victims. Hence, it is necessary to 'combine an understanding of sin as power and as guilt in order to avoid such excesses'.[33] All humans are subject to both dimensions of sin.

A final element in Conradie's analysis deals with the theological understanding of sin as linked to a 'fall' and 'original sin'. He argues against a historical understanding of the fall. Both 'fall' and 'original sin' can, at best, point to the inescapability of sin. They indicate a situation we cannot overcome on our own. However, we know from the history of evolution that much of what traditionally was understood as sin's consequences were there long before humans appeared on the earth.[34] Hence, to interpret all that is wrong from the perspective of the human relationship with the Earth, as the before-mentioned evangelicals do, is not adequate. From an empirical point of view, human sin cannot be identified as the sole cause of wrongness.

29. Ibid., 388.
30. Ibid., 389.
31. Ibid., 390.
32. Ibid.
33. Ibid., 390.
34. Ibid., 391.

Although important elements in Conradie's analysis suggest a connection between sin and climate crisis, this analysis' layout contributes to an understanding that emphasizes sin primarily as a moral problem. This impression is not overcome by the fact that he also sees it as an expression of a misunderstanding of God. He argues that 'the specifically religious dimension of sin becomes manifest in quasi-soteriologies – putting one's trust, in life and death, in false saviours'. Hence, sin is expressed in different idolatries, where one 'put one's trust in education, the market, pension funds, military defense structures, democracy, or the power of positive thinking'.[35] It is easy to agree on this from the point of view of Luther's definition of God as I have referred to it earlier, but the problem is that sin here again has to do with what humans do wrong – and that we admire the false gods. It does not identify sin as a fundamentally theological notion that addresses the broken relationship between humans and God. However, the benefit of pointing to sin as idolatry is that it can open up to a constructive discourse about what it entails for ecological care to believe in the Christian God instead of believing in these idols. Thereby, sin-talk could still have relevance in the public sphere.

Narcissism: A metaphor for a sinful relationship between humans and nature

The consumer society feeds on our insecurities and discontent when we compare ourselves with others. It requires such insecurity to maintain consumption patterns, but this insecurity also places people in a situation where the mechanisms that cause narcissism can find thriving conditions. Narcissism is the psychological condition in which you relate to the world as the means for compensating for lack of self-esteem and self-confidence. It is the condition of the insecure self on an eternal quest for self-affirmation. The narcissist is circling around herself. She pulls the world into this circle to the extent that it provides relief from the insecurity and offers means for mirroring herself positively, experiencing herself as in charge and having power over others, or receiving recognition from them. She distrusts the world insofar as it does not offer her any chances for self-affirmation. However, a narcissistic approach to the world entails using the world to secure the self in vain.

It is tempting to connect the Lutheran view on sin with narcissism and see narcissism as one of the psychological expressions of sin. The circling around oneself and the lack of fundamental trust in the world that results from the lack of fundamental personal security is an obvious candidate for making this connection. Not every sinner is a narcissist. However, some empirical elements in narcissism may shed light on humans' negative relationship with nature and the environment. In this section, I will try to spell out how that may be the case.[36]

---

35. Ibid., 394.

36. I have previously developed more extensive analyses of narcissism and sin in Jan-Olav Henriksen, *Imago Dei. Den Teologiske Konstruksjonen Av Menneskets Identitet*

Narcissism is a negative form of self-love insofar as it only seeks confirmation of itself and emerges from a desire to see oneself as the centre of the universe. This self-love is destructive in terms of the opportunities it provides for deep and mature relationships with others. It also precludes the self from seeing herself as vulnerable and dependent. Because the narcissist lives with a fundamental wound in the self, caused by neglect and lack of care and affirmation, it must protect itself and cover all signs of vulnerability and dependence of others that remind of this wound. To compensate for the lacking care during her upbringing, the narcissistic person remains with a grandiose self.

Narcissism is not a mode of being in the world one chooses. It is usually a pre-subjectively conditioned mode of selfhood shaped by early childhood experiences of lack of care, empathy, positive affirmation and realistic mirroring. It is the result of how the (m)other is responding insufficiently to the infant's desire for recognition. The consequence is a self that is always self-seeking in her relationship with the other because the other has not allowed him or her to experience himself or herself as being *relatively independent*. I write here 'relatively independent' because it is not a question of dissolving the relationship with the world. It is about being able to experience oneself as part of a mature relationship shaped not only by needs. This is a condition for a mature partnership with the world that is not based on one's needy exploitation of it. An infant whose need for affirmation has not been met will not experience the world independently of her needs. The permanent need for affirmation shapes her relationship with the world – and presumably also with nature.

An attitude towards nature that sees nature simply as a resource for yourself, for your use and needs, and not as having a relative standing in itself that should be recognized and respected, provides us with a clear case of narcissistic attitudes. Nature becomes pulled into a circle of self-needs and desires for control, safety and security. Thus, narcissism and the subjection of nature exist in tandem. Control over nature is a defense against the anxiety caused by the lack of a solid and secure self. To experience loss of control and powerlessness is covered up by pretending to be all-knowing and almighty.[37] Dominion over others, and over one's own body, and neglect or avoidance of suffering (which suggests or reminds of vulnerability) shape the behavioural pattern.[38] Insofar as it does not allow for the unrestricted unfolding of the grandiose and 'powerful' subject, nature in all its

---

(Oslo: Gyldendal akademisk, 2003), 207ff. and in detail in *Relating God and the Self: Dynamic Interplay* (Ashgate, 2013), passim. However, in those works I did not discuss what narcissism may entail with regard to the relationship with the environment.

37. Cf. Horst-Eberhard Richter, *Der Gotteskomplex: Die Geburt Und Die Krise Des Glaubens an Die Allmacht Des Menschen* (Hamburg: Rowohlt, 1979), 21.

38. Ibid., 129f.

forms must be repressed and subjected.[39] Feelings of suffering and vulnerability can be compensated by consumerism and an extensive focus on health.[40]

How can the development of narcissism be prevented? By good mothering and adequate parenting. By mirroring and responding to the child's needs and emotions, the parent allows the child to develop a sense of self that is not dependent only on living up to others' expectations and developing an emotional repertoire that includes empathy and awareness of one's feelings. Here, again, we can see a metaphorical connection between adequate caretaking of a child and the development of capacities for ecological care. In both cases, it is a question of learning to know yourself adequately and develop an understanding of who you are in relationship with others. It means that the child is enabled to positively affirm both the relationship with others and others' relative independence.

Moreover, psychologists use the notion 'optimal frustration' to make sure that there is also an acknowledgement of the limits of the self's unfolding. Such frustration represents a vital element in the constitution of a solid self that can rely on herself while still maintaining a positive and affirming relationship with others. It entails non-traumatic experiences of whom one may potentially be, thus, becoming increasingly able to differentiate oneself from the idealized object and achieve a more nuanced understanding of the limits of one's grandiosity. The outcome is a mature and integrated self with a solidified psychic structure with a sense of cohesion and continuity and need not look outside itself to achieve this sense.

These elements in narcissism allow us to see that exploitation of nature and the ignorance of the environmental conditions may also be resulting from psychological conditions. Lack of care, love and responsive affirmation in a child leads to a lack of care, love and affirmation in the child's relationship with others – which might include nature. To put it theologically, sin leads to sin. On the other hand, parenting that allows children to develop emotional awareness and capacities, including empathy and appreciation for others in their own right, might contribute to some of the capacities we need to counter climate crisis – because it allows us to *feel* its impact.[41] Thus, we may also have to admit our vulnerability insofar as we are dependent on the environment. The opposite would entail a grandiose and self-centred attitude to nature in which denial of the catastrophe would be in tandem with continuous and reckless exploitation.[42]

39. Cf. ibid., 98f.
40. Ibid., 166ff.
41. This point is also underscoring the conditions for experiencing ecological grief, due to the loss of species or habitats that express the multitude and diversity of creation. It may also be the condition for eco-love. For a recent development of these emotional capacities, see Lysaker, 'Ecological Love: Reflections on Morality's Existential Preconditions', 79–82.
42. Cf. the aforementioned considerations about hubris as an ecological vice.

Sin as interpretative category: Summary of findings

Sin can serve as an interpretative category for orientation if it is specified in terms of the empirical consequences that help us understand more of the reality of which we are part. To speak of sin is a first step towards identifying human disorientation in our relationships and institutions. Sin may also be a gateway to more transformative symbols such as repentance and renewal, but then it needs a broader framework of interpretation than one which focuses on the negative consequences of individual human agency only. It is not a well-functioning interpretative category; it is used generically as a 'spiritual explanation' that prevents us from facing these realities. If we ignore the empirical, that is, the structural and psychological dimensions of sin, we will not counter its consequences.

Sin as disorientation entails serving one's uncensored desires and perceived interests regardless of the cost to self-relations, the Earth and others. However, it is essential to underscore that sin can also result from a disorientation in which self-centredness is not the primary feature. Cynthia D. Moe-Lobeda points to how sin may also be manifest in people for whom 'full self and center have been denied them. For those who have been socialized or coerced into self-sacrifice, self-denial, or self-hatred, sin may take the form of not attending to one's own well-being'. Thus, sin 'counters the call to love God with 'heart, soul, mind, and strength,' and to love neighbor as self'[43] – the neighbour here including other species and living beings on the Earth.

The deficits related to the sin symbol call for the supplement from other symbols to engender constructive practices. Given a more comprehensive symbolic framework, sin can be considered an essential element for critical self-assessment – when seen as something that specifies itself and expresses itself in sinful deeds, actions and attitudes. We cannot do without it insofar as it also may shape our understanding of what needs remedy. 'What the human predicament identifies that sin *is* determines what constitutes salvation, freedom, or liberation from it, and the path toward that freedom. A reduced understanding of sin means a truncated vision of salvation', claims Moe-Lobeda, rightly.[44] Furthermore, she also argues that attempts to solve problems connected to structural sin by individual means and individualized responses 'not only fails to solve the problem, but also reinforces its invisibility'.[45]

Sin entails a structural element and cannot be reduced to individual failures. It is embedded deeply in unjust and exploitative structures and practices, including psychological ones. In and of itself it is therefore not a good symbol for providing us with enduring and long-lasting practices to counter climate change. Perhaps this lack of positive impact can be expressed best in the fact that there is nothing to

---

43. Moe-Lobeda, *Resisting Structural Evil: Love as Ecological and Economic Vocation*, 58.
44. Ibid., 60.
45. Ibid., 77.

admire or desire in people who appear as sinners, and, hence, nothing to emulate. However, there are things to emulate in those who act in ways that prevent sin from happening and take care of their children in ways that do not lead to narcissistic attitudes and practices towards nature and the environment. Hence, the deficit of sin as a symbol for countering climate change can only be overcome by turning to more constructive sources and symbols.

Symbols for the ecological consequences of sin, and their implications for practice

The following subsections briefly consider some narratives or symbols in the biblical material that can contribute to a theological understanding of the ecological disaster that we find ourselves in at present. These can be used creatively to shed light on it, although they have their origin in a different time and situation. The main aim with the following is to explore potential biblical narratives, parables, or symbols, with reference to how they may inform the present situation and guide believers and others) in their actions. The following is restricted to what I call *negative symbols*, that is,, symbols that identify and shed light on what is wrong and why it is so, more than on what is possible to do. As such, they may nevertheless have a positive function in suggesting what one should *not* do.

Lost in the desert

The book of Exodus is about how the people of Israel were liberated from slave labour and given a new start. We can interpret the liberation as initiating a new identity. After the exodus, they were no longer defined by and exploited by others but allowed to develop as a people of God and serving God by upholding the commandments that should protect them from injustice, violence and envy. They were called to be responsible in front of the God of love who liberated them. The Exodus story has inspired people suffering from oppression ever since. It points to a God who wants to secure humans and provide for them – although what they get to eat on their way to the promised land is not from the cauldrons full of meat.

On their way to the promised land, people soon lose their patience. They lose sight of that which is not ready at hand and make their own idol to worship in the present. This symbol of wealth can give them neither food nor any other means to live by; it is a golden calf.

Apart from the obvious theme of idolatry, which has already been touched on several times in the previous chapters, other elements are at stake here. First of all, there is the prioritizing of the present over the future. Secondly, there is the apparent element of desire being directed towards elements that cannot provide or sustain life. Thirdly, we can see a lack of trust in those who promised a better future when one had passed the trials of travelling through the desert.

The fundamental disorientations led to the people remaining in the desert for forty years. The narrative suggests that those who turned to the golden calf were not admitted to the promised land. They had to live in the desert for the rest of their lives. We can read this as a parable about what happens when we prioritize present over future and material goods over the qualities that make a good and sustainable community in the long term.

Moreover, the desert itself is a symbol: when one remains in the desert, one lives in a site where not much life is possible and where life-sustaining elements are scarce. A mere focus on material goods leaves us in the desert and gets us lost in finding the way to something better.

Focus on material wealth and material growth will not get us out of the desert. Only a life in which we live on the promise of something better, on a hope for a world in which love for others and the environment shapes our actions and guides our concern for the future, will. Ignoring those elements that keep us in the desert will only lead to more death. (As I write this, the demand is made for opening up schools, restaurants and businesses to return to 'the normal' and boost the economy, while one ignores the fact that millions of people have already died from Covid-19 worldwide. In the United States, the economy still seems prioritized over safety in some areas.)

Thus, the exodus story provides us with a warning against trusting in material growth as the means that will save us from ecological disaster. It says that the opposite will be the result: that more focus on material growth will lead to more disorientation and no chance of coming to the promised land, that is, a land where ecological balance and partnership between species are safeguarded. It identifies elements from which one needs to orient oneself away to act in more morally and ecologically sustainable ways.

Judged by our actions

In Matthew 25, we find the parable about the last judgment.[46] The parable's existential meaning is primarily to underscore that God takes seriously the suffering of those who are not met by their neighbours' mercy and compassion. The judgement point is that humans are called to recognize those who are suffering and give them their due. Without such judgement, there is no real recognition of the one who suffers or suffering and injustice. The judgement makes it possible for humans to verbalize both injustice and justice.

Under the conditions of the climate crisis, increasingly more people will be suffering – and the parable tells us that we will be judged by our actions – or our lack of such. But not only fellow human beings suffer – also other species are suffering from our exploitation of the environment and our emission of

---

46. I have analysed this parable more in detail in Jan-Olav Henriksen, *Desire, Gift, and Recognition: Christology and Postmodern Philosophy* (Grand Rapids, MI: William B. Eerdmans Publishing Company, 2009), 188ff.

greenhouse gases. Hence, the answer to the question 'who is my neighbor?' must be expanded to include also other living beings than humans, with whom we are in partnership and with whom we share this planet. This approach allows us to read the parable about the last judgement with significant contemporary relevance for assessing our practices. The following explorative interpretation builds on the following premise, formulated by Cynthia D. Moe-Lobeda:

> Neighbor-love as an interpersonal and economic norm has two faces: compassion and justice. Neighbor-love as an ecological norm adds a third: Earth's well-being. We have only begun to uncover the conundrums inherent this third face of love in love. The challenge of re-theorizing love as an ecological vocation is a weighty and morally compelling challenge for religion of the early twenty-first century.[47]

We will be judged according to how we can identify and recognize the neighbours' needs and the injustice they suffered. However, those who are positively recognized by the judge in the parable have not acted to achieve some good for themselves. Their intention has not been to secure some kind of advantage for themselves, in terms of fitness or otherwise. They acted solely for the sake of the other and for the sake of sharing goods, and have recognized others as belonging to their own sphere of consideration. They have adopted the mode of being in the world that is shaped by love, and, as such, they have not given their own merit any thought.

The lack of personal motives for doing good to others need not preclude the existence of an internal relationship between the one doing good and the recipient of that deed. Moreover, it is possible to see how the good deed is marked by, or even constituted by, a perceived relationship on the side of the agent. This relationship, in turn, also reveals a relationship with the judge (Christ). The judge says that 'what you did to the least of these that are members of my family, you did to me'. Anyone who keeps these gifts for herself or uses them for her own purposes contradicts and violates the open and positive community that all these gifts are meant to serve.

When you address one in need or trouble in the manner described earlier (unconditionally, without personal interest, even without the interest in relieving your uncomfortable status when confronted with someone in an unjust situation), you are addressing them as someone who belongs to your world, and who is justified in breaking into your world with their call. What you do is not only determined by you but by their calling to you. You recognize yourself as the other's neighbour and the other as yours. Hence, here is implied recognition of how you belong together, and this self-perception means that you are in no way justified in excluding other living beings from your world.

The parable seems to suggest that what ends up as most important is the ability to recognize others in need as part of my world and with a valid and justified call

---

47. Moe-Lobeda, *Resisting Structural Evil: Love as Ecological and Economic Vocation*, 199.

to justice and care. In the situation of the climate crisis, it means that other living beings not only belong to my world as such. They belong to my world as a gift from God, which I am called to share with them in a partnership that extends beyond stewardship.

Thus, this expanded interpretation of the parable identifies a basic and underlying presupposition for the whole outcome of the judgement: the ability to recognize oneself and all other living beings as rooted in the creative act of a giving God. The theological expression for this recognition is usually faith. By living out of faith in these gifts, one is set free from self-concern and can care for all of creation. Thus, faith opens up to salvation in the broad sense of the word. In this sense, salvation is based on faith, not works, but it is nevertheless also internally related to good works and expresses itself in restoring justice in a world that expresses God's will for the flourishing life.

Furthermore, the parable seems to imply that those who are judged negatively lack the ability to recognize others as related to them. They are unable to see the call of other living beings as an expression of Christ's call to love and service. Accordingly, a double problem is implied in the answer they give to the judge when he confronts them with what they did not do. Firstly, they ask when they have met situations of suffering, hunger, and so on, thereby indicating that if they had done so, they would have done what needed. Secondly, the same answer also reveals an attempt to be self-righteous. They justify their lack of care for others and for justice by saying that they did not recognize the call in any of the situations they found themselves. Put bluntly, they try to justify themselves by saying that they had no opportunity to do good works. They ignore the structure of God's gifting (to which I shall return later), which implies that their world is given to all by a loving God. Their response reveals that they view their own works as just another means for gaining merit. This justification does not work because it implies that they can establish their righteousness apart from how they relate to the rest of creation. The conclusion to this way of life, in which one basically is oriented only towards oneself, is that life in community with the rest of creation is ruled out. In other words, one excludes oneself from community and fellowship by not recognizing all of creation as part of the world for which one is being called to care. The one who is judged as not righteous is thus the one who, by excluding the other, excludes herself. She is the one who lets her own concerns determine the world, instead of letting the other be one who opens up the world to more than the self.

The conclusion to this interpretation of the parable is that its pragmatic effects are not merely negative: it points to elements for a constructive and caring agency as well as towards the consequences of the lack of such. Hence, it can serve as a symbolic resource for both orientation and transformation in the face of the present situation of climate change.

The ecological hell: Created by humans

The Bible contains no full-fledged description of hell. It remains an image of a place or situation in which God is absent and where people suffer from the consequences of their lack of concern for others, as exemplified in Jesus's parable about the rich man who did not care for his servant Lazarus (Luke 16, 19ff).

The pragmatic effect of the imagery of hell is to warn people about the consequences of their lack of concern for others. Hell is the consequence of human action or inaction. Most theology today seems to conclude that it is impossible to reconcile the notion of a loving God with the notion that *God* wants or prepares hell – no matter how it is conceived. Those who want to maintain the relevance of that imagery can therefore say that 'Those in hell are there because of their determination to avoid the company of the redeemed and the God who redeems'.[48] Then it is understood as the result of peoples' own determination and not as an expression of God's retribution. Hell is both made by and for those who make hell for others – and thereby also make the world into hell. The main agents behind all hellish conditions are humans who do not care for others. Hell may thus be another image for the announced suicide towards which humanity rapidly is heading.

Given that most of the people in the Western world are complicit in maintaining a world order and an economic system that leads to vast ecological degradation, the extinction of species, and continued emission of greenhouse gases with catastrophic consequences, one could ask if any of us can avoid the hell we are ourselves in the midst of creating.

How then, to understand the relationship between a creative and loving God and the hell we make? In order to reflect on this, we can use Marilyn McCord Adams' reflection on hell in *Christ and Horrors*, where she criticizes conceptions of hell on the basis of a specific understanding of God.[49] She writes:

> Traditional doctrines of hell err again by supposing either that God does not get what God wants with every human being ('God wills all humans to be saved' by God's antecedent will) or that God deliberately creates some for ruin. To be sure, many human beings have conducted their *ante-mortem* lives in such a way as to become anti-social persons. Almost none of us dies with all the virtues needed to be fit for heaven. Traditional doctrines of hell suppose that God lacks the will or the patience or the resourcefulness to civilize each and all of us, to rear each and all of us up into the household of God. They conclude that God is left with the option of merely human penal systems – viz., liquidation or quarantine![50]

The notion of God behind these imaginaries needs criticism. McCord Adams, therefore, claims that 'Traditional doctrines of hell go beyond failure to hatred and cruelty by imagining a God who not only acquiesces in creaturely rebellion

---

48. Jonathan L. Kvanvig, *The Problem of Hell* (New York; Oxford: Oxford University Press, 1993), 158.
49. For the following, see Marilyn McCord Adams, *Christ and Horrors: The Coherence of Christology* (Cambridge: Cambridge University Press, 2006), 229–30.
50. Ibid.

and dysfunction but either directly organizes or intentionally "outsources" a concentration camp (of which Auschwitz and Soviet gulags are pale imitations) to make sure some creatures' lives are permanently deprived of positive meaning'.[51]

Against this notion of a post-mortem idea of hell, she reconstructs the conception with reference to present conditions, in line with what I suggested earlier, although not with a specific outlook on nature and the environment. Her conception builds on the idea that 'ante-mortem horror-participation is hell enough'. Humans experience how horrors 'constitute the prima facie destruction of the positive meaning of our lives', and 'for God to succeed, God has to defeat horrors for everyone'. However, 'To be good to us, God will have to establish and fit us for wholesome society, not establish institutions to guarantee that horrors last forever in the world to come!'[52]

In other words, the notion of hell serves here as an interpretation of contemporary human experiences. Therefore, McCord Adams's approach is favourable because it roots the Christian hope where it should be rooted: in God and what we hope for God to do. It is God who enables the Christian community to hold 'the conviction that there is a common hope and a common vocation for human beings'.[53] However, this hope is not restricted to the human community. Hope is hardly meaningful in an ecological sense if it does not include every living being. To believe in a loving God entails believing that there is hope for all of creation to avoid an ecological hell.

These considerations indicate that it makes sense to talk about hope for the future exactly because God is consistently both love and empathic personal power, struggling to realize love in God's creation. This love orients humans in their agency and opens us to the gifts of life through hope. In such a conception of God, the notion of hell has no place except for being a counterpart to images in which love and care for all of creation are manifest.

Hell can serve as a symbol that places us in the midst of the consequences of our actions. It is an orientational symbol that only can promote transformation if it provides a counter-image to the reality that God struggles to create by calling us to responsible action. To face, engage and structure reality from the perspective of faith, love and hope is to counter hell. To concentrate on hell and its conditions is not. The Christian hope concerning hell is that the actual hells that humans make will no longer be a possibility in the future.

Moreover, it is by understanding the creative and sustaining loving power that is present in all of reality, and which is struggling to come to the fore, that we can uphold a vision of the world and life that continually manifests itself in new forms of community, creativity and renewal. With the perspective of love as a basis for

---

51. Ibid., 230.
52. Ibid., 230.
53. Thus Rowan Williams, *On Christian Theology*, Challenges in Contemporary Theology (Oxford; Malden, MA: Blackwell, 2000). 20.

living, it makes sense to keep on the quest for justice, goodness and the integrity of creation, without giving in to the powers that create hell and threaten efforts to achieve these aims. In other words, the hell we create is the opposite of the paradise God wants to realize by our participation. The paradise imagery I will return to in Chapter 15.

Chapter 14

CARING RELATIONSHIPS

FUNDAMENTAL MOTIFS REVISITED

We all need to understand ourselves as carrying the future of creation under our hearts – some of us in a real way, others more metaphorically. No matter which of these groups we find ourselves in, the facts this situation entails are present whether we acknowledge it or not. Furthermore, if we see our situation as one analogue to being pregnant (with future life), this fact is not constituted by any prior knowledge; it is there no matter what we think. To be pregnant does not make you search for alternative facts that allow you to ignore the situation. The condition will not change if you ignore it. Hence, it means that you have responsibility for that which is dependent on you.[1] In the Anthropocene, we are responsible for everything because we, as humans, have come to be those who determine the future of the planet. Like a pregnant mother, all our practices and actions need to consider our relationship with this future.

To practice Christian religion in today's work and under the present contextual circumstances is to act in ways that affect creation's future – and not only for humanity's future (which would be impossible, anyway). Christian practices of orientation and transformation can take their point of departure in the metaphor of being pregnant, and be informed and made transparent by relating these practices to central elements in the Christian tradition's narratives and values. Practices of care for creation are not optional expressions of Christian faith – it is *the way* to practise Christianity in light of the challenges we face.

The metaphor of being pregnant, that is, deeply, internally, and unavoidably related to future life in an embodied way, can be developed into various care practices, most of which are contextually shaped. However, prior to identifying such practices, we need to elaborate on how our experience of being embodied beings may open us to a diversity of situations and responsibilities.

---

1. This notion of responsibility, which specifies further Jonas's notion of responsibility as developed earlier in Chapter 11, draws on a Ingerid S. Straume, 'That Which Depends on Us: Responsibility, Democratic Courage and Shame', in *L'autonomie En Pratique(S)*, ed. Caumières Philippe and Klimis Sophie (Saint-Louis: Presses de l'Université Saint-Louis., 2019).

Introduction: That which is closest to us: The caring body

Our most immediate experiences are not only mediated by our bodies, but our immediate experience is that *of* our own bodies. The body is closest to us; it is what carries us and makes us what we are. Our history becomes inscribed in our bodies, and they have themselves an interaction with our history and the conditions and circumstances that make up our lives. The immediate body awareness is pretheoretical. It means that as experiencing beings, we *are* a body; we not only have it or experience it as an object.[2]

The body conditions our experiences and shapes them, as well. It gives us access to the proximate and sensual experiences of ourselves and our world, including the natural world. The body's life would not be possible unless there were exchanges with the environment, including metabolism, that make possible further life on different levels.[3] Every human being's interwovenness with the rest of nature is given with our embodied condition. What we eat can expose us to harm. What we breathe can infect us. How warm or cold it is may affect our health. Through the body, we experience ourselves as vulnerable and dependent on elements that are not established by our own actions and as desiring the necessary means for life and nourishment and for sex and recreation. The body is a gateway to contingency experiences caused by incidents, illnesses and accidents that we cannot control. It manifests our finitude insofar as it restricts our capacities and range of action. Moreover, we share this embodied entanglement with nature with every other living being.

In the Anthropocene, contingency, vulnerability and finitude go both ways: nature's contingent existence is mirrored in ours, as are its vulnerability and finitude. It is not a given that neither nature nor humans will persist in its present form in the future – most likely, they will not. Humans are an endangered species because we endanger other species. Thus, we are deeply contingent and vulnerable beings, along with the rest of nature. Contingency refers to that which is dependent on something else. Thus, the body exposes us to our vulnerabilities:

> The recognition that my being depends on – is contingent upon – other beings brings demands, struggles, and limits to freedom. It does not wipe out agency, and yet it does circumscribe personal agency in some ways. At the same time, being that is situated around its individual, collective, and species contingency also brings possibilities of a different kind of relationship between persons and the larger environment.[4]

---

2. This is not the place for a full-fledged phenomenology of the body. For that, see Maurice Merleau-Ponty, *Phenomenology of Perception* (New York: Humanities Press, 1962).

3. Cf. the analyses in Hans Jonas, *The Phenomenon of Life: Toward a Philosophical Biology; Essays*, 1st edition (New York: Harper & Row, 1966).

4. Cf. Mercer, 'Environmental Activism in the Philippines: A Practical Theological Perspective', 303.

Admission of contingency and vulnerability entails the possibility of empathy that includes non-human creation as well as fellow humans who suffer. As Joyce Mercer suggests, because humans can be empathic, 'an acknowledgment of human contingency in relation to the non-human environment can invite persons to "feel with and for" plants, rivers, land, birds, mangroves, and animals whose existence and wellbeing is often at risk and also obviously contingent—often upon human decision-making and concern for what is clearly "other"'.[5] Accordingly, 'the cultivation of empathy a primary characteristic of contingent human existence has vast implications for everything from how Christians nurture the young to the ways we observe and honor with gratitude other creatures' contributions to our living'.[6]

This sketch of some elements in the embodied condition implies a rejection of any fundamental distinction between mind and body, ontology and epistemology. The Cartesian separation of mind and body has led to the exclusion of a vital resource for care: that of embodied experience as the point of departure for experiencing oneself and the rest of nature. Suppose we accept that embodied existence and emotional competence are linked together. In that case, this acceptance means that the emotional competence required for developing empathy and care for others is nourished insufficiently within a rationalist paradigm that prioritizes the cognitive over the emotional and abstract reasoning over concrete experience. Again, mothering suggests itself as an alternative model, in which all these dimensions are held together, and practical wisdom results from balancing them adequately.[7]

Care for the environment should be a natural extension of how all our embodied practices are directed towards the future, in one sense or another. Some of our actions and practices are short-term-directed, whereas others are based on long-term goals. No matter which, we do what we do with reference to our future. At this point, Heidegger seems to be right when he points to *care* (German: *Sorge*) as a fundamental (existential) element in human existence.[8] Although some of his analyses require that we go beyond the world of humans, we can nevertheless utilize his insights into care as an *existential* constructively as follows.

The fundamental human mode of being, which Heidegger calls 'Being-in-the-world' (German: *Dasein*), is care, concern. However, in his analysis, it involves more than caring for someone or caring about somebody. As the fundamental-ontological, intentional way of being by which all our actions are directed, it manifests itself ontically in that about which we care. I will argue that care

---

5. Ibid.
6. Ibid.
7. This line of reasoning is also why I have presented some sections that include more psychological elements in the previous discussions: to ignore the psychological and emotional dimension in dealing with the problems at hand would entail a severe restriction of what we need to be aware of.
8. Cf. Martin Heidegger, *Being and Time* (Oxford: Basil Blackwell, 1962), 83, 227.

understood thus is relevant for interpreting the fundamental orientation in human life.

Moreover, Heidegger also underscores that we are never alone and cannot understand ourselves as isolated 'I's', but that our existence is *alongside* – and I would say, not only alongside other humans but nature as well. Or, to put it more specific than Heidegger does: we participate in a broader context in which our concern or care expresses itself and which conditions our care. As Heidegger says, 'Being-alongside something is concern, because it is defined as a way of Being-in by its basic structure – care.'[9]

Two more elements in Heidegger's analysis prove relevant for understanding the fundamental orientation of care for the future. He argues that '"Care" cannot stand for some special attitude towards the Self; for the Self has already been characterized ontologically by "Being-ahead-of-itself", a characteristic in which the other two items in the structure of care – Being-already-in . . . and Being-alongside . . . – have been jointly posited [*mitgesetzt*]'.[10] The 'Being-ahead-of itself' points to the fundamental future-oriented mode of human life, whereas the care structure itself would not be if we were not already part of the world as being in it alongside others. Thus, Heidegger explicates the fundamental elements that condition all human experience, although he does not elaborate on how nature and the environment, in general, are part of that experience. Accordingly, it becomes a fundamental task to manifest the ontological structure of care in ontic expressions that take into consideration the wholeness of our existence in and with nature. Against the backdrop of that aim, the relevance of the fundamental character of care, as summarized in the following quote, can attain a more profound and ecologically relevant meaning:

> Care, as a primordial structural totality, lies 'before' ['vor'] every factual 'attitude' and 'situation' of Dasein, and it does so existentially a priori; this means that it always lies in them. So this phenomenon by no means expresses a priority of the 'practical' attitude over the theoretical. When we ascertain something present-at-hand by merely beholding it, this activity has the character of care just as much as does a 'political action' or taking a rest and enjoying oneself. 'Theory' and 'practice' are possibilities of Being for an entity whose Being must be defined as 'care'. The phenomenon of care in its totality is essentially something that cannot be torn asunder, so any attempts to trace it back to special acts or drives like willing and wishing or urge and addiction, or to construct it out of these, will be unsuccessful.[11]

My intention in underscoring the phenomenon of care here is that Heidegger's analysis shows how humans are not only fundamentally and structurally constituted as caring (although their care may be misguided, misoriented or directed towards

---

9. Ibid., 237.
10. Ibid.
11. Ibid., 238.

the wrong things). Embodied practices express care that directs us toward the future. If humans structure care in analogy with what a good mother who carries a child does, then these practices, which presuppose and include the world in which we are placed and the other species with which we shape this world, can find an enduring and positive expression.

Care is manifest in different modes and not with any fixed or pre-given scope, though. Hence, the challenge with reference to Heidegger's analysis of care as a fundamental characteristic of human conduct is to overcome an anthropocentric understanding of embodied care. To achieve such a goal, we need more than thinking about our actions and practices in analogy with motherhood. To shape a caring character requires experience, knowledge, rehearsal and active participation in practices that allow for experiencing nature with body and mind, reason, knowledge, senses and emotion. Care about me and mine cannot be only about me and mine because we are interwoven with the rest of creation. Full access to embodied experience, which includes concrete and sensual experiences of nature, may help us realize that. Hence, to understand our responsibility for the future is not only based on a metaphor. It is 'a material fact that needs to be taken more carefully into account'.[12]

Although I have some reservations with regard to Sallie McFague's proposal for seeing the world metaphorically as God's body (as discussed in the following), some insights in her proposal might help underscore what I try to develop here with regard to embodied existence. McFague underscores that humans are able to relate to God as another Thou. 'The presence of God to us in and through God's body is the experience of encounter, not of submersion. For the saving love of God to be present to human beings it would have to be so in a way different from how it is present to other aspects of the body of the world – in a way in keeping with the peculiar kind of creatures we are, namely, creatures with a special kind of freedom, able to participate self-consciously (as well as be influenced unconsciously) in the evolutionary process.'[13] Against this backdrop, which emphasizes our embodied existence, she articulates humans' special status and responsibility:

> We are the ones like God; we are selves that possess bodies, and that is our glory. It is also our responsibility, for we alone can choose to become partners with God in the care of the world; we alone can – like God – mother, love, and befriend the world, the body that God has made available to us as both the divine presence and our home.[14]

McFague expands our responsibility beyond that which is limited to the consciousness of our own personal bodies or even of the human world. She sees it as extending to 'all embodied reality, for we are that part of the cosmos where the cosmos itself comes to consciousness. If we become extinct, then the cosmos will

---

12. Cf. Muers, *Living for the Future: Theological Ethics for Coming Generations*, 128.
13. McFague, *Models of God: Theology for an Ecological Nuclear Age*, 76.
14. Ibid.

lose its human, although presumably not its divine, consciousness.'[15] Against this backdrop, we can see the theological symbol of incarnation as the fundamental religious symbol for expressing our caring relationship with all of reality. It provides a context in which humans see God's activity as involving the cosmos through humanity. This perspective is perhaps most profoundly developed in recent contributions to the notion of *deep incarnation*.

The born and embodied God of Cosmos: Deep incarnation

Theologian Niels Henrik Gregersen has developed the much-discussed and profoundly inspiring notion of *deep incarnation*. His contribution to Christology expands this complex symbol in Christianity in a way that might overcome the deficits inherent in its traditional form concerning climate change. These deficits are mostly identified as expressing an anthropocentric position.[16] In this section, I will develop the elements of the concept of deep incarnation that Gregersen relates to climate change.[17]

Gregersen starts by pointing to the embodied features we take for granted, like breathing: we breathe without giving it a second thought, and most of our metabolic processes go without us paying any attention to them. We can only control these up to a point. Moreover, most of the time we do not experience the processes that keep us alive – only when these automated processes are interrupted or disturbed, we become aware of them.[18]

Not only do the processes internal to our body and its well-being point to our interconnectedness with the rest of creation. 'We are also atmospheric beings', claims Gregersen. He points to how our moods may vary due to sun, rain and atmospheric pressure. However, these natural processes that we are involved in and connected to manifest themselves in pre-reflexive silence. Most of them, including global warming, cannot be experienced directly through our senses, but only indirectly, by their consequences.[19]

When Gregersen moves from our entanglement with nature as embodied beings towards the present challenges of global warming, he points to how this differs from other challenges in three respects: (a) It is planetary. (b) It is silent,

---

15. Ibid.
16. A critique of Gregersen in this respect has been launched in Matthew Eaton, 'Beyond Human Exceptionalism: Christology in the Anthropocene', in *Religion in the Anthropocene*, ed. Celia Deane-Drummond, et al. (Eugene, OR: Cascade 2018). As will become apparent in the present section, I hold this critique to be misplaced.
17. The following builds on Niels Henrik Gregersen, 'Christology', in *Systematic Theology and Climate Change: Ecumenical Perspectives*, ed. Michael S. Northcott and Peter M. Scott (London; New York: Routledge, 2014).
18. Ibid., 33.
19. Cf. ibid.

that is, the routes from causes to effects are dispersed, work over long distances and are accumulated over time. (c) The exchange between carbon dioxide and oxygen is 'natural' insofar as it is 'basic to all life and has been a natural ingredient in the metabolism of living creatures since the dawn of life on our planet'. However, the balance is disturbed and has become toxic.[20]

How is it possible to move on from these initial remarks about the human and natural condition towards an approach that can employ the Christian tradition and mine its sources for interpretation and motivation for agency? One can argue that this is not a likely enterprise without further qualifications. Gregersen argues that 'it would be anachronistic to expect that we could, today, derive specific ethical directives or political solutions from the Jesus tradition'.[21] The problems we face today were not known at the time of Jesus. It is nevertheless possible to find some resources in this tradition. The fact that Jesus sees the world as God's own creation

> required a mental reorientation that has immediate, practical consequences for his followers' relation to God, other people and the environment. [. . .] The relevance of the synoptic Jesus tradition (Mark, Matthew, and Luke) for ecological issues is thus mediated by the theology of creation implied in Jesus' teaching, as well as in his preaching of the kingdom of God to come. He preached this coming kingdom in analogy to the eschatological vision that the Spirit shall be 'poured out on all flesh' (Joel 2. 28, quoted Acts 2. 17-21). In this sense, Jesus' preaching was earth-bound from beginning to end – without ever separating God and world.[22]

The lack of separation of God and the world is what becomes profoundly apparent in the incarnation. Accordingly, Gregersen formulates his main claim as follows: 'Christology is carried by the conviction that God's eternal Logos has revealed and re-identified itself – once and for all – *as* Jesus Christ *within* the matrix of materiality that we share with other living beings.'[23] Thus, in Christ, immanence and transcendence, God and the world, are held together in a union that came to the world as being born by a woman. As Gregersen claims, 'that God has a human face can only be maintained if God assumes a real human body, situating him in continuity with the rest of the material world'.[24]

In his further development of this conception, Gregersen argues against any backward-oriented approach to Jesus Christ. Instead, he argues for the present and future relevance of addressing the world from the perspective of Christology. The understanding of God's unity with the world as manifest (or revealed) in Christ is only possible if God is the encompassing reality – the loving source of *all* reality,

---

20. Ibid., 34f.
21. Ibid., 36.
22. Ibid.
23. Ibid.
24. Ibid., 44.

including the created conditions that made incarnation possible in the first place. It is at this point that we encounter the core of the notion of deep incarnation.

Gregersen describes Jesus in a way that mirrors the analyses of being-with and being-alongside that I presented earlier via Heidegger. He points to how a 'human body is a metabolic organism and each body is a centre of experience that has an "internal" experiential side even as it interacts with "external" circumstances'.[25] This relation is a whole and 'cannot be broken down into something primary and something secondary'. Body and mind belong together, and accordingly, 'human consciousness is always co-determined by natural environments and cultural artefacts'.[26] If we read the report of Jesus's life in light of these insights, we see that

> the body and mind of Jesus appear to be agitated by the life contexts in which he finds himself - in various ecological spaces (deserts, lakes, rivers, hills) as well as in diverse social and cultural contexts (town and country, friends and enemies, Jews and Romans). In this sense, we might refer to Jesus as an *extended body* as well. Jesus' body is described as comprising the three overlapping life-circles – of nature, sociality and personhood. Who Jesus is as a person is shown by his relation to other people; he himself is touched both bodily and spiritually by others, just as he touches others and affects his surroundings. The kingdom of God is the extension of the body of Jesus, just as his body is a crystallization point of the divine reign.[27]

Jesus's life is interwoven with the life of others in another way, as well. The New Testament inscribes him in an intergenerational context. Thus, he is recognized as part of the history of the Jews and all of humankind, and thereby also as a partaker in God's history.[28] However, in the New Testament, this participation is not expanded beyond humanity's history. At this point, Gregersen suggests that although God's blessing of Adam and Eve in Genesis takes place within the context of the blessings of animals, the NT authors 'do not refer to the ancestral bonds of Jesus with other animals. This is their shortcoming', he argues.[29] Together with the later doctrinal severing of the ties between human and non-human nature, it complicates the Christian tradition's chances to focus beyond that of humanity when it comes to salvation and participation in God's gifts.

The incarnation entails that God is at home in the world and continues to love God's work even under conditions of sin and disorder.[30] God dwells in the actual living flesh of Jesus. God does not hide behind the flesh (which would make the material an outward and insignificant factor in pointing towards 'the real thing'),

25. Ibid., 39.
26. Ibid.
27. Ibid., 39.
28. Cf. ibid.
29. Ibid.
30. Cf. ibid., 38.

but God *became* flesh, and 'was present in Jesus *as* flesh, *with* the flesh, and *for* all flesh'.³¹ Thus, Jesus shares the conditions of biological and social existence with human beings in general. His body and mind 'share the same conditions of metabolism and climate-dependence as any other living organism, human or not'.³² Gregersen summarizes the main points in thinking 'deep' about incarnation thus:

> The dwelling of God's Word in the world was not confined to his skin and skull. In Jesus Christ, the divine Logos assumed the entire realm of humanity, biological existence, earth, and soil. God's Logos/Word/Wisdom shares the conditions of material existence with all the flesh that comes into being in order later to disintegrate. Here we see the basic contours of the meaning of deep incarnation. Deep incarnation speaks of a divine embodiment, which reaches into the roots of material and biological existence as well as into the darker sides of creation.³³

The strength of this Christology is that it explicates the close and internal bonds between God and humanity, and between humanity and the rest of the planet. Not only does God have a concrete human face, but this face is depicted in such a way that it also sheds light on the conditions of other humans. It anchors human and divine existence in interrelation and interdependence with the rest of creation. Thus, it provides chances for considering practices of care based on the emulation of Jesus and his practices of love and care towards others. However, the deficit of Jesus as a symbol can only be overcome if we expand the object of this love and care beyond humanity. Gregersen points us in that direction, when he argues that the extensive scope of human existence as articulated in *deep incarnation* 'has immediate repercussions for a contemporary interpretation of what it means to be a *neighbour* to one another'.³⁴ Unlike in the world of antiquity, where neighbour care was about helping the poor who had an urgent need of assistance, today's global interdependencies entail that our webs of neighbouring are both widening and tightening. What we do and how we live 'have consequences for the life-conditions of people around the equator just as the diminishing of the rainforests has global effects on our shared climate conditions'.³⁵

> Moreover, our generation's human life-styles will unilaterally constrain or facilitate the conditions under which our own grandchildren and other future offspring can thrive, or not. In a sense, non-human creatures have also become

---

31. Ibid., 45.
32. Ibid. From this, Gregersen also infers that 'even on anthropocentric premises (that is, in the soteriological interest of humanity) there *must* be a healing also of non-human existence, *if* the whole of humanity is to be healed' (ibid.).
33. Ibid.
34. Ibid., 46.
35. Ibid.

our neighbours since we are breathing the same air and using the same resources as they do. We are deeply intertwined with nature through our dependence on fresh air and sunlight for our existence, and also by being doomed to boredom without the existence of bees and bears, dogs and dolphins in the world around us. Their lives depend on us and ours on them.[36]

I will return to Gregersen's point about the way we unilaterally constrain or facilitate the life conditions of future generations in the next chapter when I discuss sacrifice as a symbol. However, one constructive element in his elaborations connects our responsibility for future generations with the future-oriented aspects of Jesus's teachings. Here, he discusses the parable about the final judgement I analysed in Chapter 13.[37] He points to how the parable identifies the poor and needy as present in non-visible ways and argues that due to our 'contemporary awareness of our co-dependence on all life, our neighbours might indeed live far away from us'.[38] They might also include non-human species, as well as future generations of human beings and other beings.

Thus, Gregersen's Christology makes it possible to identify and emphasize the whole biosphere as God's wider dwelling place. On this planet, he argues, all are co-dependent neighbours of each other. We all share a common atmosphere – and a common vulnerability.[39] His Christology thus provides us with a symbol that serves as a concrete reference and context for human practices that concern the future of this planet. It can inform and orient human practices, and these practices can serve as models for emulation. The constructive expansion of Christology we find in his work is a good example of how a symbol works according to Ricoeur: it gives rise to thought and allows thought to return to – and employ – the symbol as a motivation for further practice. Although we are not Christ, we are part of the world and the humanity with which God united in Christ. Hence, we can admire and emulate his unity with and love for the world in our own caring practices.

The world as God's body?

For decades, Sallie McFague stood out among the constructive contributors to ecological theology. Her metaphorical theology resulted in different models of God. The one I will consider briefly here is of *God as mother*. The reason for this consideration should be apparent. I have pointed to motherhood as a fundamental metaphor for how one should engage with nature and develop sustainable practices for the future. However, as we shall see, there are also some limitations inherent in considering the Earth as God's body, despite the positive imaginary options that

---

36. Ibid.
37. Cf. above, 193ff.
38. Gregersen, 'Christology', 46.
39. Ibid., 46–7.

result from thinking of God as mother. The following presentation is divided in two. Firstly, I consider her proposal of thinking of the world as God's body, and then I address her proposal for seeing God as mother. The two lines of thought are closely related.

To understand the world as God's body entails the awareness that we, as worldly, bodily beings, live in God's presence.[40] Thus, McFague formulates the same concerns about God as present in our world as Gregersen does, but without the Christological underpinning. Instead, she develops a *sacramentalism* that underscores

> the world's vulnerability, its preciousness, its uniqueness. The beauty of the world and its ability to sustain the vast multitude of species it supports is not there for the taking. The world is a body that must be carefully tended, that must be nurtured, protected, guided, loved, and befriended both as valuable in itself – for like us, it is an expression of God – and as necessary to the continuation of life.[41]

It is important here to see that the world is valuable in itself, and that this motivates concern for it. However, there are also some problems with this way of understanding the world. Firstly, if the world is an *expression* of God, does that mean that 'the real thing' is something else? Furthermore, does everything that happens in the world as God's body express God? McFague would probably admit that this is not the case since sinful humans are also part of God's body, but her determinations nevertheless make such questions possible.

A more serious objection from a *pragmatic* point of view, though, is what understanding the world as God's body entails for human practices. We will always have to remodel and intervene with natural processes in order to secure our survival. Hence, it is not wise to imagine that we can live in full harmony with nature – that is, without altering, adjusting and changing it for our purposes. Accordingly, to say that we are called to tend to, nurture, protect and befriend nature appears as one-sided and covers over the interventions that humans, by necessity, must do to shape their lives. If the metaphor about the world as God's body means that humans violate God whenever they make a road or cut down a tree, this imagery places humans in a situation of unavoidable violence. That we must do such things is our condition as part of creation, and not only because we are sinners. Hence, this image is insufficient and manifests a deficit in spite of all good intentions. No one who believes in God wants to violate God – but that seems to be the outcome of this metaphor.

On the other hand, the metaphor opens up to understanding sin as the rejection of community with God in a deeper sense than usually articulated in theology. McFague sees sin as the refusal to be part of this body. Hence, sin has earthly consequences: it entails that we

---

40. McFague, *Models of God: Theology for an Ecological Nuclear Age*, 77.
41. Ibid.

refuse to take responsibility for nurturing, loving, and befriending the body and all its parts. Sin is the refusal to realize one's radical interdependence with all that lives: it is the desire to set oneself apart from all others as not needing them or being needed by them. Sin is the refusal to be the eyes, the consciousness, of the cosmos.[42]

What is entailed in this dimension of the metaphor is that humans, due to their special capacities, are responsible for the rest of creation and can see things from the point of view that goes beyond what is determined by concerns and interests that focus only on themselves. To be the eyes of the cosmos means that we are partaking in God's continuous creation insofar as we see, care for and love creation like God does. We articulate the personal dimension in God's love in our love for the world God has created and continues to create.

God imagery opens up this personal dimension if it is connected to and developed by personal metaphors. In her work, McFague developed these with the metaphors of mother, lover and friend. She offers several strong arguments for the employment of such imagery, but the most important, she claims, is that such metaphors can connect personal agency with 'a view of God's activity in the world as radically relational, immanental, interdependent, and noninterventionist'.[43] Hence, she can build on the widespread agreement that the self exists in relation to its own body (as embodied self) and in relation to others (as profoundly embedded in and constituted by those others): 'The evolutionary, organic complex is widely considered the context in which to interpret personal agency—with the agent as part of an intricate causal network that both influences it and is influenced by it—and this allows for an understanding of personal presence credible within the new sensibility'.[44]

Understanding God's activity in the world epitomizes personhood, that is, intrinsic relations with all else that exists. When we define a person in terms of relationships, 'the Thou with the greatest conceivable degree of real relatedness to others – namely, relatedness to all others – is for that very reason the most truly absolute Thou any mind can conceive'.[45] Personhood defined in terms of intrinsic relations with others means that 'to think of God as personal in no sense implies a being separate from other beings who relates externally and distantly to them'.[46]

It is against the backdrop of her analysis of personal metaphors that McFague develops her understanding of God as mother. Motherhood links to the mystery of new life and is how creation expresses itself in bringing new life into existence. Humans share motherhood with other living beings: we pass life along. Thus, it also allows us to experience the awe of existence. Moreover, it is a physical act, and

42. Ibid.
43. Ibid., 83.
44. Ibid.
45. Ibid.
46. Ibid.

this is where McFague sees the power of the symbol deriving from: To give birth is connected to the great symbols of life and life's continuity: blood, water, breath, sex and food.[47] Thus, to speak of God as mother and involved in processes that entail these elements is to overcome the spiritualization of God's relationship with creation. It also links God closer to the experiences of many women.

Combining the model of God as mother with the world as God's body allows for a deeper understanding of creation: It allows for seeing 'creation as bodied forth from the divine being, for it is the imagery of gestation, giving birth, and lactation that creates an imaginative picture of creation as profoundly dependent on and cared for by divine life'.[48] This imagery suggests a profound interdependence and interrelatedness of all life with its ground. Moreover, 'All of us, female and male, have the womb as our first home, all of us are born from the bodies of our mothers, all of us are fed by our What better imagery could there be for expressing the most basic reality of existence: that we live and move and have our being in God?'[49]

Among the advantages of the combined metaphor of God as mother and the world as God's body is that although it suggests a close and intimate, including physical, relationship between God and the world, it does not necessarily lead to the identification of God with the world. Good mothers 'encourage the independence of their offspring, and even though children are products of their parents' bodies, they are often radically different from them'.[50]

God creates a home for humans in the world, marked by love and nurture. Simultaneously, humans are challenged to partake in creation in ways that secure inclusive justice shaped by love, McFague argues.[51] She develops her understanding of this in a way that portrays God as the one who feeds creation. Thus, God is understood in analogy with a parent who feeds the young and, by extension, the weak and the vulnerable. Thus, God cares about the most basic needs of life in its struggle to continue.[52] Against this backdrop, it becomes profoundly relevant to understand human care for the future of creation as emulating God.

McFague develops these insights further and much richer than I can do here. What we need to do now is to ask, again, what are the implications of this imagery for human practices? Perhaps the most important consequence of her rich theology is that it allows us to see that we are dealing with God when we are dealing with creation. We are embedded in the creation that expresses God. Thus, combined with how God receives a human face in the life and practices of Jesus Christ, we have a comprehensive context for understanding and developing human

---

47. Cf. Ibid., 104–5.
48. Ibid., 106.
49. Ibid.
50. Ibid. The same relative independence is also apparent in Jesus's parable of the prodigal son. I have developed this more systematically in Henriksen, *Imago Dei. Den Teologiske Konstruksjonen Av Menneskets Identitet*, 159f.
51. McFague, *Models of God: Theology for an Ecological Nuclear Age*, 106.
52. Ibid., 107–8.

behaviour and in which to ground responsible human agency. To describe God as a mother validates concrete and good mothering practices concerning humans as well as for other species. Thus, McFague's contribution overcomes some of the symbolic deficits connected to the understanding of God as sovereign, detached, transcendent or a king or a ruler.

Creation as gift? On gift and responsibility

In the previous parts of this book, I have referred to creation as God's gift. In a similar vein, we also talk about *life* as a gift. The symbol gift points to both a giver and a receiver. However, even this symbol may imply some deficits, which call for a further specification of its content. In this section, I will discuss what the symbol of creation or life as a gift entails and what we should not take it to mean. A primary line of reasoning here is that we need a theologically based understanding of gifts that can link it to an understanding of human responsibility.[53] All responsibility is constituted by and relates to God's gifts. There is always an element of gifting in all human responsibility because it relies on God's gifts and implies passing these gifts on or enabling them for their further flourishing.

The fundamental gift-charter of creation implies that neither gift-exchange nor charitable giving can provide us with good models for an economy of grace that presupposes God as offering us the gifts of creation to steward.[54] These forms of giving fail to establish what we might consider being the most crucial horizon for providing a gift, namely *relationship*. The gift of creation and the goodness implied therein is not external to creation or an instrument that can be arbitrarily exchanged. The responsibility of giving transcends duty: it is a manifestation of the realization of human interconnectedness as it expresses itself in relation to other humans as well as towards the rest of creation. Thus, the gifts we offer to others might be understood as good in themselves and not only good with regard to what they offer to others to meet their needs or provide them with benefits. The theological warrant for such understanding is underscored by how God's unconditional gifting is the precondition for how to exercise responsible stewardship in creation: God's unconditional giving is 'not obligated by the prior performance of the recipients and . . . not conditional upon a return being made by them. This principle marks all these relations off from *do ut des* giving, or "I give so that you will give", the alternative principle of conditional giving that covers

---

53. For another approach to a theology of gift in light of climate change than the one I present here, see Primavesi, *Gaia and Climate Change: A Theology of Gift Events*.

54. Cf. Kathryn Tanner, *Economy of Grace* (Minneapolis: Fortress Press, 2005), 56. I underscore that the notion of stewardship employed here and in the following builds on the discussion in Chapter 10.

barter, commodity exchange, and debtor-creditor relations of all sorts'.[55] This point is most evident in how God creates the world. Creation cannot be a response to anything creatures have done. Kathryn Tanner calls this fact God's 'total gift'. Nothing obligates God in any way in creation or in God's setting up covenant relations. It is done out of 'sheer free beneficence'.[56]

The gracing fellowship with the rest of creation based on God's gifts provides another chance for a community than one based on economic exchange or merit. It is *inclusive in the sense that everyone who sees himself or herself as a possible participant is allowed to enter and be recognized as a participant on equal terms.* It also means that humans can see themselves as related to and participating in a fellowship that includes non-human living beings and even landscapes, oceans and forests. Everyone and everything is entitled to participate in the sharing of God's gifts.

We can elaborate on this point further with the help of Marilyn McCord Adams's almost poetic reflections on hospitality and sharing of a table.[57] In her reflections on hospitality as expressed in meals, she points to how a banquet signalizes a community where many things are happening at once: such meals are events in which 'we meet *embodied* person to *embodied* person, make shared food the material medium with which to eat and drink, bite and chew our way into social identities and shared lives'.[58] She develops this further in reflections that make visible how our embodied vulnerabilities are also implied in our sharing of meals with others:

> Table fellowship is a risky business, for eating betrays our vulnerability. By opening our mouths, taking something from outside in, we prove that we are *not self-contained*. To be sure, our human bodies have a natural shape, boundaries giving definition. Paradoxically, these cannot be sustained unless they are regularly compromised -food, water, oxygen, enter to become part of us; carbon dioxide, useless leftovers expelled, in and out according to natural rhythms, necessary for life. The body's doors couldn't serve if they didn't open on passages that reach deep within us. Yet, precisely because they do, they put us at risk, allow the wrong things to penetrate too deeply, lock them inside for too long. Little wonder if the distinction between clean and unclean foods becomes sacred. What happens around the table is literally a matter of life and death! [59]

---

55. Ibid., 63. Cf. Kathryn Tanner, *Jesus, Humanity and the Trinity: A Brief Systematic Theology*, Scottish Journal of Theology. Current Issues in Theology (Edinburgh: T&T Clark, 2001), 2–3.

56. *Economy of Grace*, 63.

57. For the full context of the following, see Adams, *Christ and Horrors: The Coherence of Christology*, 292–5.

58. Ibid., 292.

59. Ibid.

This description of what happens in a meal shared by humans recounts how all that happens there is nevertheless also dependent on, and interacts with, natural elements that condition the event and that are *given*. Hence, despite its anthropocentric outlook, there is more to it than humans in isolation. However, other species are absent in McCord Adams's description. But many human meals, as well as what other species eat, presuppose the existence of other species again, and thereby, interdependence.

God invites us to a meal in the Eucharist – and this meal may signify more than a meal between humans because it also manifests the interconnectedness of all of creation, in bread, wine and communal interdependence. The Eucharist is a sign of God's persistent giving. Although God's giving is not dependent upon human reception, humans cannot simply fail to receive some of God's gifts as part of the created world.[60] Moreover, 'the unconditionality of God's giving is saved despite all our failures of reception and response because anything that might look like a condition for the reception and good use of God's gifts is really itself the gift of God. There is nothing good about us that is not also the gift of God, and this includes the acts by which we receive those gifts and put them to good use'.[61] We cannot make an adequate return to God's giving.[62] Accordingly, the responsibility for stewarding creation as a gift is not constituted by human agency alone but by God's continuous work in creation.

The gift notion is discussed widely in contemporary scholarship.[63] The discussion originated from the work of French anthropologist Michel Mauss.[64] His contribution analysed the dynamics of gifts and gift-giving. These dynamics were focusing on gift-giving as interwoven with social acts of reciprocity and expressing calculating intentions of motives. This anthropologically based understanding of gift seems insufficient for a theological conception of creation and life as gifts. However, a fruitful element in Mauss is that a gift manifests a special relationship and that gifts also lay some obligations on the donée.

Recent contributions have identified problems with the understanding of gift as found in Mauss. For instance, Jacques Derrida separates a gift from the exchange economy Mauss saw as fundamental.[65] Derrida also discloses several aporias

---

60. Cf. Tanner, *Economy of Grace*, 66.
61. Ibid., 67.
62. Ibid., 68.
63. For some of this discussion, see my elaboration in Henriksen, *Desire, Gift, and Recognition: Christology and Postmodern Philosophy*. Some of the following paragraphs in this section are a reworking of that work.
64. See, Marcel Mauss, *The Gift: The Form and Reason for Exchange in Archaic Societies* (London: Routledge, 1990).
65. The following is, if not otherwise indicated, based on Jacques Derrida, *Given Time: 1. Counterfeit Money* (Chicago: University of Chicago Press, 1992).

related to gift and gift-giving[66] and emphasizes the unconditional character of a gift by showing how we continuously turn it into something else than gift when we understand it from the point of view of economic exchange.[67] Derrida thereby discloses a possible understanding of gift that seems close to a theological understanding of *grace*. Grace is what cannot be determined by humans and cannot be fully grasped, but we can see its traces.

The *economically* constituted exchange of gifts does not allow for anything new to happen; there is no opening for radical transformation of relationships. All remains within the sphere of what can be constituted by human action. Says Derrida: 'This motif of economy is the – circular – return to the point of departure, to the origin, also to the home.'[68] However, the true gift disrupts and disturbs human action as the fundamental condition for relationships and engenders new possibilities. Hence, we can read the following quote bearing in mind what it can say about God's gift of life in creation:

> But is not the gift, if there is any, also that which interrupts economy? That which, in suspending economic calculation, no longer gives rise to exchange? That which opens the circle so as to defy reciprocity or symmetry, the common measure, and so as to turn aside the return in view of the no-return? If there is gift, the *given* of the gift (*that which* one gives, that which is given, the gift as given thing or as act of donation) must not come back to the giving (let us not already say to the subject, to the donor). It must not circulate, it must not be exchanged, it must not in any case be exhausted, as a gift, by the process of exchange, by the movement of circulation of the circle in the form of return to the point of departure. If the figure of the circle is essential to economics, the gift must remain *aneconomic*.[69]

To develop an understanding of the gift outside the circle of economy seems to indicate an attempt at the impossible. That a gift is given unconditionally means, in practice, that it has no clearly defined place in history. It emerges from no condition that we can identify or determine as part of a previous sequence of incidents:

> For there to be a gift, there must be no reciprocity, return, exchange, countergift, or debt. If the other gives me back or owes me or has to give me back what I give him or her, there will not have been a gift, whether this restitution is immediate

---

66. A remark typical for the way Derrida deals with Mauss is the following: 'On the one hand, Mauss reminds us that there is no gift without bond, without bind, without obligation or ligature; but on the other hand, there is no gift that does not have to untie itself from obligation, from debt, contract, exchange, and thus from the bind.' Ibid., 27.

67. Cf. Risto Saarinen, *God and the Gift: An Ecumenical Theology of Giving*, Unitas Books (Collegeville, Minn.: Liturgical Press, 2005), 25.

68. Derrida, *Given Time: 1. Counterfeit Money*, 7.

69. Ibid.

or whether it is programmed by a complex calculation of a long-term deferral or difference.[70]

Derrida suggests that a gift given transforms the situation into what previously was not the case. This represents an *interruption* of the same, an *event* of something new and more radical than what happens in the event of a birth as Arendt describes it. It is more than what can be determined from the present and breaks the circle of determination. Thereby it suggests that reality contains more than what we can determine within a framework of previous conditions in space and time.

Hence, Derrida helps us formulate the basic conditions for understanding creation and life as a gift: it does not depend on anything being done in order to be received. On the contrary, the gift of life or the gift of creation constitutes that or those that are gifted. The fundamental unconditional element in the gift makes it a profound theological notion.

Creation, understood as a gift in the sense here suggested, *inserts itself between human activity and passivity*. So far, I have described the passive element with the help of Derrida. On the other hand, some expectations and obligations follow from the gift. These are not conditions for it to be received, but for it to work well for the donée. Creation and life can be used and abused, enjoyed or destroyed. Nevertheless, it is given as that we are involved with and to which we need to relate. I argue that our response to life and creation as gifts make it possible to see how God's activity in the world comes to expression in human practices and agency.

God's continuous acts of giving in and through creation are also connected to humans continue to give: not in order to receive something back, but out of love and care for the other. In her work on *charitable giving*, Kathryn Tanner claims that giving from such motivations differs from gift exchange. Charitable giving meets the needs of the recipient. It is not intended to keep gifts circulating or to bind the donée to the giver, but to allow the gift to settle with the one who needs it. Tanner writes about this type of gifting:

> The point of the giving is not to keep the relationship up. To the contrary, charitable giving often justifies the donor's not having anything further to do with the recipient. The giving of gifts now means that the recipient can be excluded in good conscience from all the usual social or exchange relations that make up the donor's life. The fact of charitable giving might help to legitimate, in for example, the fact that one is not empowering the recipient for the sort of participation in capitalist exchange that might make him or her less needy. Unlike gift exchange, in which circulation seems almost to become an end in itself, the important thing about charitable giving is the gift and the benefits it

---

70. Ibid., 12.

brings to others, not the act of giving and receiving or the sort of relationship it sets up.[71]

Tanner offers a formulation for the 'pure' gift that might be easier to make operational than the one we found in Derrida. 'A real gift has to have the spontaneous expression of good will behind it, over and above the call of duty. Something is really a gift only when it is not being used to put pressure on you, when the gift is given simply for your benefit and is not serving any ulterior motive.'[72] Thus, the gift transcends duty and expresses the spontaneous will that operates outside of an economic circle. When the only thing in focus is the *benefit* of the recipient, this is a good *in itself*, not something one attempts to achieve for the sake of something else. I deliberately phrase it like this because that allows us to say that such *a gift is a good in itself*. Thus, this type of gifting also overcomes an instrumental approach to the gift, which sees creation and its goods only connected with some other, external purpose.

No matter what the human response is, God continues to give. The non-conditional character of God's giving also expresses itself in the fact that God continues to give despite our misuse of God's gifts. Had God then stopped giving, it would have placed God's giving within the economy of exchange again, where our failures prompted a response forfeiting these gifts. But that is not what happens. When we experience the loss of these gifts, says Tanner, it is not because of God stopping to give, but rather because of our sin. This point allows us the read the following in light of what we have previously developed as an ecologically relevant understanding of sin:

> It may seem to us as if God takes away gifts in response to our sin. But it is our sin itself that interrupts the reception and distribution of God's gifts, bringing suffering and death in its train. The loss of what we might have enjoyed is not God's punishment of us, but the natural consequence of our turning away from and refusing what God is offering us for our good. God's gifts continue to stream forth to us in the way they always have; we are simply failing to avail ourselves of them, to our own destruction and harm.[73]

Tanner's angle allows for three insights that are valuable in the present context: *Firstly*, she underscores how God's giving is not dependent upon our reception, but on the other hand, there are some of God's gifts that humans cannot simply fail to receive as part of the created world.[74] *Secondly*, 'the unconditional character of God's giving is saved despite all our failures of reception and response because anything that might look like a condition for the reception and good use of God's

---

71. Tanner, *Economy of Grace*, 55.
72. Ibid., 58.
73. Ibid., 64–5.
74. Cf. Ibid., 66.

gifts is itself the gift of God. There is nothing good about us that is not also the gift of God, and this includes the acts by which we receive those gifts and put them to good use'.[75] Thirdly, Tanner affirms that we cannot make an adequate return to God's giving.[76] This final point underscores that humans cannot integrate the gifting of God within an economy under our control.[77] We cannot put ourselves in God's place when we deal with creation.

The aforementioned analysis' theological and pragmatic implications suggest the following for understanding creation and life as a gift: it constitutes a relationship with both God and other creatures. This relationship is nevertheless not based on merit. It places humans in the tension between passivity (in reception) and activity (in safeguarding the gift as gift). Concomitant with the latter point is that the gift is not to be understood as handed over to the donée for her possession. The gift is maintained and engaged only by making sure that we can pass it on to others in practices that ensure that life continues and flourishes. The abuse of the gift is to keep it to yourself.

We can develop these considerations further by referring to Anne Primavesi's analysis of the gift phenomenon in light of climate change. She makes the following reflection:

> [T]he current climate change crisis signals a systemic failure on our part to see ourselves as products of past, present and (potentially) future gift events, and therefore to realize that we provide the initial conditions that make life-giving and receiving possible for future generations. The life-enhancing threads that attach us to all those who came before and should attach their gifts, through us, to all those who come after are being broken and disconnected. Contemporary accounts of the potential 'tipping points' in the loss of biodiversity, the accelerating destruction of rainforests and the exhaustion and polluting of underground freshwater aquifers indicate that we shall not have to wait until the end of the world to imagine the effects of this failure. We shall see them in our lifetime.[78]

To keep the gifts of creation to ourselves with no regard for future generations will lead to future generations not being able to experience life and creation as gifts but as a curse. A planet with deteriorated conditions for life will make the future hard and challenging, and humans will be dependent on intense work for compensating for the failures and sins of previous generations. Again, the mothering care metaphor suggests itself as the alternative: A good mother wants to give her child the best. She sees her child as a gift, and she also wants to give the child a good future. If we understand creation in analogy with this, it means that

---

75. Ibid., 67.
76. Ibid., 68.
77. Cf. ibid., 65–7.
78. Primavesi, *Gaia and Climate Change: A Theology of Gift Events*, 84.

we not only received it as a gift but that we also care for its future. The child and creation are not there for our sake and interest – but we are there for them and their benefit. Only in this way can we make sure that both creation and the future can be understood and experienced as gifts.

The biblical reference to what I have developed here is the parable about using the talents (Matthew 25,14ff.[79]): God entrusts humans with the gifts of creation, and only when we use these gifts in such a way that the gifts develop and flourish, we fulfil the giver's intentions. If we do not use the gifts in this way or see them as something we should make sure that we can continue to possess, they serve no purpose. Then the obligation that follows from the gift is dissolved – with severe consequences for the future.

Nature as sacred?

Can declaring nature as sacred prevent humans from destroying the environment? In that case, the notion of sacred nature would indeed serve to guide and shape human action. Hence, it might be rewarding to consider that option. This section aims at that purpose.

What does it mean that something is sacred? A standard definition of 'sacred' is that which is 'considered to be holy and deserving respect, especially because of a connection with a god'.[80] Other definitions highlight how the sacred is 'dedicated or set apart for the service or worship of a deity' and worthy of veneration, reverence and respect.[81] The 'set apart' dimension also entails that the sacred denotes the holy in contrast to the secular or profane.[82] In everyday use, it can also hold meanings connected to what we do not want to change or that which should be unaffected by our intervention and remain with integrity. Moreover, the sacred is that which should be protected from defilement. In her seminal study on *Purity and Danger*, Mary Douglas points to how this protection nevertheless seems to become compromised in ways that result in transgressing the divide between the sacred and the profane.[83]

Douglas's observation might provide us with a relevant point of departure for identifying the problems connected to declaring nature as sacred. Even life-related elements that religions sometimes declare as sacred, such as semen (Hinduism)

---

79. It is worth noting that this parable comes just before the parable about the last judgement, which both Gregersen and I have been using in previous parts. This suggests that there is a close connection between how we use the talents and how we take care of those in need.

80. https://dictionary.cambridge.org/dictionary/english/sacred

81. Cf. https://www.merriam-webster.com/dictionary/sacred

82. Cf. ibid.

83. Cf. Mary Douglas, *Purity and Danger: An Analysis of the Concept of Pollution and Taboo; with a New Preface by the Author*, Routledge Classics (London: Routledge, 2002).

or blood (Hebrew religion), are occasionally spilled. As already pointed to, humans also have to intervene to some extent in existing ecosystems to secure their living by hunting, agricultural practices, or work to provide means for shelter and security. If these natural elements were sacred, it would nevertheless mean that their sacred status regularly is compromised by human actions and practices. Thus, the intention of calling something sacred will not automatically protect it from human intervention.

What then about the other features connected to the sacred? If the sacred is worthy of veneration, reverence or respect, what would that mean? Indirectly, if the world and nature are what God uses to sustain us, it might be possible to see it as an object of veneration. Still, from a Christian point of view, the one who should be the sole receiver of human veneration and worship is God. To venerate nature would entail that we worship the created instead of the Creator. Moreover, given the human tendency to single out particular objects for veneration, to worship nature or parts of creation would shift focus or attention from the whole creation to parts of it, with the potential risk of ignoring its wholeness and integrity or prioritizing some parts at the cost of others.

These considerations need not imply that we should not approach the created world with some sense of awe or respect. That is a natural response to how we may experience the richness, diversity, magnificence and interaction of creation in all its forms. The respect we have for it and its integrity may also inform us about the need to restrict our interventions as much as possible. Many indigenous people who live or lived in closer contact with nature than we do shape their practices in accordance with such responses and their concomitant insights.[84]

According to the aforementioned, to declare or designate something as sacred to protect it from human touch or other forms of intervention may not be an adequate strategy. Protection is better served by other means, including practices emerging from a thorough knowledge of that which is subject to protection. The aforementioned elements of awe and respect could secure the protection of

---

84. Cf. The examples in Vetlesen, *Cosmologies of the Anthropocene: Panpsychism, Animism, and the Limits of Posthumanism*. Vetlesen also points to how this opens up to a specific human relationship due to our ability to narrate and thereby integrate within a symbolic order the understanding of our actions. Referring to Tim Ingold, he points to how humans are unique in their capacity to *narrate* encounters with nature. They can

> tell stories about them, sometimes based on factual encounters, sometimes being pure fiction that only humans have the required imaginative powers to concoct (we humans tend to believe; and we may or may not be right). However, his point is that 'no-one can construct a narrative . . . who is not already situated in the world and thus already caught up in a nexus of relations with both human and non-human constituents of the environment' (ibid., 169).

His line of reasoning (including the quote) is based on Tim Ingold, *Perception of the Environment: Essays on Livelihood, Dwelling and Skill* (London: Routledge, 2011), 52.

creation just as well without the support of such a declaration, especially because interventions will happen.

My main objection against declaring nature as sacred is related to how it leads to the sacred (whatever it is) as set apart from the everyday. However, there is nothing in the natural world that 'sacred' in and for itself – because everything belongs together in the fullness and wholeness of creation. To see something as 'set apart' suggests that elements that have religious significance are not part of our everyday life conditions. However, the notion of creation suggests that all parts of life and everything in creation have religious significance. Everything created is an expression of God's creative and loving activity. The notion of the sacred as 'set apart' covers up the interdependence and intertwinement of God and the world, the human and the non-human.

Moreover, from a psychological point of view, the designation of something as sacred may appear as empty words, or the qualification may lose some of its impact if we experience that it is disrespected continuously, subjected to transgression or ignored. Consequently, it may lead to a certain numbing of our attention because what it was meant to protect no longer appears as sufficiently important, due to it continually becoming compromised as sacred. As all numbing, it is easier to avoid such numbing if we engage more intimately with that which is in need of protection and try to see it in a wider context that allows us to experience it as valuable in itself. Perhaps the best example of such numbing due to violence against the sacred is Christians's attitude towards the cross of Christ: this torture instrument is rarely taken in as such in their everyday religious observance. It is overused as a symbol for salvation, and, hence, often has lost its ability to shock and engender disgust, sorrow or pity.

Given these reservations, I conclude that employing the symbolic designation 'sacred' for nature exhibits considerable deficits. Although it may initially serve to develop some restrictions in our dealings with nature, it is too ambiguous and has too many problematic connotations to guide action.

Is there an alternative in Christian theology to declare creation as sacred? I think there is. In the previous discussions about the incarnation, and the world as God's mothering body, we found ways to express the close intertwinement between the holy God and God's creation that does not compromise God as *the* sacred, whereas simultaneously recognizing the world as valuable in itself as the expression of God's active love. The incarnation entails that the world and God belong intimately together and that the world, therefore, requires our care and love as God's gift to us.

Chapter 15

SACRIFICE, HOPE AND GRACE

Sacrifice is at the centre of Christian theology. Christ is the one who sacrifices his life or is sacrificed by others, depending on the perspective. Recent discussion has centred around whom he is sacrificed by (God or the Romans?), and what resulted from this sacrifice in terms of salvation. Moreover, part of the discussion on sacrifice has focused on the general dynamics of sacrifice, especially due to René Girard's contribution.[1] Abuse of the sacrifice motif has also been part of the contemporary discussion, problematizing ideals about its gain – mostly to keep women in their (unjust) place.[2]

Hence, sacrifice is a highly controversial theme in theology. Its symbolic content is disputed, contested or seen as only of theoretical relevance insofar as the discussion represents attempts to come to terms with the death of Jesus. The symbol's deficit is that it is either backward-looking in its interpretation of past events or is used to justify the suffering of those who have to bear the burdens of injustice. In the present chapter, however, I will ask to what extent the death of Jesus, understood as a sacrifice, can shed light on present circumstances. The argument for this approach goes along the following lines:

This generation, and especially those of us who live in the affluent West, will have to make sacrifices to save the planet from the most devastating consequences of our lifestyle. We are not called to sacrifice our own life but will nevertheless have to renounce our carbon-based lifestyle's main components.[3]

---

1. Cf. René Girard, *The Scapegoat* (London: Athlone Press, 1986); *Violence and the Sacred* (London New York: Continuum 2005).

2. See S. Mark Heim, *Saved from Sacrifice: A Theology of the Cross* (Grand Rapids, MI: William B. Eerdmans Publishing Company, 2006); Marit Trelstad, *Cross Examinations: Readings on the Meaning of the Cross* (Minneapolis, MN: Fortress Press, 2006); J. Denny Weaver, *The Nonviolent Atonement* (Grand Rapids, MI: William B. Eerdmans Publishing Company, 2001); Henriksen, *Desire, Gift, and Recognition: Christology and Postmodern Philosophy*.

3. It is crucial to read this claim as a backdrop to all the discussions of sacrifice in the present chapter. I am not advocating for a generic ideal of sacrifice, and the specifications I develop are intended to overcome some of the deficits and abuses of such ideals. Accordingly, the following discussions are intended to argue in favour of the necessity for our generations' sacrifice of components of our consumerist, carbon-based mode of life,

The flip side of this claim is that if we do not make these sacrifices, we will sacrifice not only the environment in which future generations were to live their flourishing lives but also the lives of many of the future generations who will die from hunger, drought, flooding, hurricanes, pollution and more. They will be the victims of our lack of willingness to sacrifice what is needed. On the other hand, this is not only about the future: we should not ignore those already suffering and dying due to the present catastrophe.

Hence, there is a severe asymmetry in terms of sacrifice. If we make the necessary sacrifice, others will not be victims of our way of life to the same extent. But if we do not, we will end up sacrificing the lives of others. The only way to avoid a large amount of sacrifice of life is to sacrifice and dramatically adjust our own way of life. Sacrifice you perform for the sake of others is for the purpose of giving further life a chance. Sacrifice that you force others to make may lead to their death. They become the victims of our lack of willingness to sacrifice something ourselves.

Accordingly, a certain dialectics is involved if we see sacrifice from the aforementioned perspective. Jay B. McDaniel adds a consideration that ties up with this dialectics and which points to the experiential complexities of sacrifice and victimization:

> If we are victimizers, we hide from the fact that we are harming others. We pretend that we are not hurting anyone. On the other hand, if we are victims, we may hide from the fact that, even as others may harm us, we have freedom in how we respond to what they do, either inwardly or outwardly, apart from which we harm ourselves. And if we are ordinary people, we hide from the fact that most of us are hybrids: both victimizers and victims.[4]

Hence, any discussion of sacrifice needs to be about more than who did what. It is also about acknowledging the vulnerability of being human and what must be done to avoid making further victims while still acknowledging that sacrifice is called for to improve the planetary conditions for future generations.

The sacrifice of Jesus as informative?

If we refer to the circumstances around Jesus's death as potentially shedding light on using the symbol of sacrifice for what is required in the present circumstances, we have to be selective. Not every element can be identified as relevant and recommendable, or can be easily imitated. Hence, I am not suggesting that we emulate Jesus or act like him in every respect, but suggest that the symbol of sacrifice, as shaped by his fate and actions, may shed some light on how we

---

and should not in any way be read as an argument in favour of unspecified ideals of self-sacrifice. Such ideals have all too often been connected to motherhood, and that is not my intention here.

4. McDaniel, 'The Passion of Christ: Grace Both Red and Green', 204–5.

are to understand the sacrifices that may be implied in the present situation of climate change. By identifying different components inherent in this symbol, we may overcome the deficit that superficial approaches to the sacrifice symbol may otherwise entail.[5]

- Jesus was willing to let his life become a sacrifice because of his love for those to whom he was sent to proclaim the kingdom of God
- As a result, Jesus cared more for others and for the future community than for himself, and prioritized others over himself.
- Sacrifice, in this sense, was the result of his commitment to what he was convinced was the best for humanity.
- Jesus sacrifices his body, that is, his biological well-being.
- From a theological point of view, Jesus's death as a sacrifice created new chances for life for all of creation.
- A theological approach to Jesus's death as sacrifice underscores that it provided hope for humankind's future and offered chances to become liberated from sin and its consequences.

If we consider these elements in Jesus's voluntary sacrifice,[6] it should be evident that the intentions or motivations here should be possible to emulate and adopt as part of the present motivation for action. We cannot avoid sacrificing some of our well-being in terms of what is agreeable or comfortable for us if we prioritize future generations' well-being. By making such sacrifices, we can provide future generations with opportunities to avoid some of the consequences of the present generation's sins against God and the globe. Thus, our actions may also provide chances for a better life for future generations.

If we turn to sacrifice from another, passive angle, Jesus died because others were willing to sacrifice him for their own gain and benefit. This perspective might

---

5. The contemporary discussion of to what extent Jesus's death can be understood as a sacrifice is complex and varied. For womanist perspectives that problematizes the notion of sacrifice from different angles, but also offer constructive proposals to traditional notions, see e.g. JoAnne Marie Terrell, *Power in the Blood?: The Cross in the African American Experience* (Eugene, OR: Wipf & Stock Publishers, 2005). Delores S. Williams, *Sisters in the Wilderness: The Challenge of Womanist God-Talk* (Maryknoll, New York: Orbis Books, 2013); 'Black Women's Surrogacy Experience and the Christian Notion of Redemption', in *Cross Examinations: Readings on the Meaning of the Cross*, ed. Marit Trelstad (Minneapolis, MN: Fortress Press, 2006). Important for the following analysis are the womanist insistence on the difference between voluntary and involuntary sacrifice, as well as the question about who has power to decide when a sacrifice changes history or not – and for whom.

6. I underscore that these are just some of the elements inherent in understanding Jesus's death as *his* sacrifice; here developed for the purpose of considering the potential relevance of that symbol for understanding what may be entailed in our necessary sacrifices for the future of humanity.

shed some light on what happens if one generation prioritizes itself at the expense of someone else's. Accordingly, we see several negative motifs in the sacrifice of Jesus by others:

- To fulfil the desire for calm and avoiding unrest – a desire held by Romans and Jewish leaders alike (cf. John 11, 50)
- To have an outlet for their anger and frustration with Jesus as not being the person they had anticipated.
- It was the result of rivalry and envious desire, manifest as evil will (cf. Girard)[7]
- Jesus's death is a manifestation of profound injustice and infliction of evil by others.

In a previous work, I developed a more elaborated approach to the death of Jesus as the result of collective evildoing, building on the work of Arne Johan Vetlesen.[8] Here, I want to point to some elements in that interpretation that suggest the connection between the individual and the institutional, thus suggesting that individualizing approaches are insufficient to explain what takes place. The contemporary relevance of understanding the willingness to sacrifice others for our own benefit comes to the fore in the following quote:

> Rather than collective evil resting on an uncoupling between the single individual's beliefs and desires and the goals pursued on a macro-level by the large institutions in which individuals perform the actions required of them, such organized evil will often occur in a situation where these individual and institutional factors meet halfway; when they are allowed to merge, to work in tandem in the same direction.[9]

I argue that this merging of individual, collective and institutional interests, all focused on short-term benefits, leads to the lack of willingness to prioritize future generations over our well-being. From the point of view enabled by the symbol sacrifice as inherent in the Jesus story, it means that one prioritizes evil over good. We can see the Jesus story as a revelation of the struggle between good and evil. A similar struggle is implicit in our present lack of engagement as bystanders to the catastrophe that already hits people in many places in the world and will hit even more in the future. Here, we can define evil in a more precise manner as the very rejection of the conditions for created life – as this is apparent both in the sacrifice of Jesus and in our sacrifice of future generations.[10]

---

7. Cf. Henriksen, *Desire, Gift, and Recognition: Christology and Postmodern Philosophy*.
8. See, ibid.
9. Arne Johan Vetlesen, *Evil and Human Agency: Understanding Collective Evildoing*, Cambridge Cultural Social Studies (Cambridge: Cambridge University Press, 2005), 50–1.
10. For an important study of the intergenerational dimension in the sacrifice of our own children, although not with reference to the specific situation of global warming, but

However, we need not stop here. Vetlesen holds that our vulnerability and dependence *qua* human beings play an equally fundamental part in our wishing to do evil to others and in our own susceptibility to suffering evil as victims. When we inflict evil upon others, it is because we thereby get relief from our vulnerability and gain a sense of mastery over it.[11] In other words, we do evil to others so that we do not have to face it as part of our own possibilities. Hence, evil appears as the opposite of good in a way that structurally is the exact opposite of what is expressed in the norm 'In everything do to others as you would have them do to you; for this is the law and the prophets' (Matt 7:12). Evil is to do to others what you will not and cannot perceive as being done to yourself. By inflicting it on others, you attempt to avoid facing your own vulnerability. Thus, to do evil by sacrificing others is the utmost version of hubris, and it creates and sustains an illusion about who you are yourself. This illusion is possible to express metaphorically as the conception that you are similar to God – that is, outside the limits that mortality, vulnerability and fragility impose on you.

Translating the situation of Jesus suffering evil to our own situation, we can now understand our deferral of the costs of our fossil fuel-intensive lives to later generations as an attempt to ignore our vulnerability. I have repeatedly argued that one way to improve our sensibility to the Earth's precarious situation is to accept and recognize our own vulnerability. That includes an awareness of our relationship with the conditions for life and with nature. We need to acknowledge that our actions may also have implications for our ability to live well together with other living beings in the long run. Instead of securing our life and protecting us from vulnerability, sacrificing others may lead to more death, also in contexts where we are ourselves involved.

Moreover, the death of Jesus resulted from violating the physical and spiritual integrity of a person who belonged to the community. In that respect, we can interpret the death of Jesus in light of Girard's notion of scapegoating. This approach is not directly transferrable to how we might be creating victims in future generations. Nevertheless, we can see our lack of care for future generations in the way we live our lives as a possible way to maintain some – short-sighted – stability in the present society. But where Girard sees the scapegoat as subversive in relation to the present society, we can see the future generations as those who would jeopardize and challenge our current lifestyle. Although this interpretation goes beyond the intentions of Girard's analysis, it concurs with his notion that the sacrifice of the scapegoat leads to presumed social stability. Future generations

---

with much potential for developing the negative dimensions of that symbol, see Rachel Muers, 'Idolatry and Future Generations: The Persistence of Molech', *Modern Theology* 19, no. 4 (2003). See also for further development of this motif Willis Jenkins' development of Muers' and others' work in Jenkins, *The Future of Ethics – Sustainability, Social Justice, and Religious Creativity*, 308.

11. Cf. Vetlesen, *Evil and Human Agency: Understanding Collective Evildoing*, 10.

become our scapegoat insofar as they are sacrificed for the consumer society's calm and stability.

The main elements in the aforementioned analysis do not require Christian faith to be understood and recognized. Nevertheless, it is informed by how the symbol 'sacrifice' can be understood in the Christian tradition and still shed light on the present situation. Christians see Jesus's death on the cross as revelatory. It reveals who God is – God is the one who gives life so that others should live. On the other hand, it also reveals who we are as humans: we are those who are willing to sacrifice others for our benefit. In the present situation, this might be more revelatory than what we could have foreseen a few decades ago. This double perspective allows us to see Jesus's death as a sacrifice in a way that can illuminate the conditions in which we live in the present world. To some extent, the motifs he displays himself behind his sacrifice can be emulated by us when we consider our role and actions in relation to future life and future generations. In the following, I develop other elements that can serve a similar purpose.

Sacrifice as life-condition: Sarah Coakley

The sacrifice symbol draws on a wide variety of resources, of which some are not immediately religious. In her recent work on sacrifice, theologian Sarah Coakley develops an understanding that is rooted in the biological conditions for human existence, and from there on, moves towards its existential and theological potential. In this section, I analyse selected components of her work on this topic before I move on to see the connection between sacrifice and motherhood in the next section. Thus, I hope to show that sacrifice is part of the biological conditions for life in general, as well as connected to the practices entailed in motherhood. In sum, it will provide the basis for one of the main arguments in this chapter, namely the already-mentioned claim that sacrifice can be considered a symbol that informs future practices in response to climate change.

The initial context for Coakley's work on sacrifice is linked to research about conditions for human cooperation. Such cooperation entails that the individual must renounce some benefits for the sake of the larger community. Thus, her analysis also has bearings on understanding the biological conditions for morality. As such, it supplements the elaborations in Part II of this book,[12] and does so with specific relevance for understanding sacrifice. It allows us to address the relationship between cooperation and morality in a way that can lead us out of the impasse of a reductive biological explanation of morality as (covert) self-interest.

Coakley defines cooperation as 'a form of working together in an evolutionary population, in which one individual pays a cost (in terms of fitness, whether genetic

---

12. See Chapter 8, especially pp. 101ff.

or cultural) and another gains a benefit'.[13] Such cost is hard to see as possible for someone to be willing to pay unless there is some attachment between the parties involved. Moreover, in order to have cooperation, *motivation* is required. The most obvious candidate for cooperation shaped as altruism would be love. However, love for future generations remains abstract in many cases, except when one considers one's (potential) grandchildren. Hence, one also needs to promote motivation by other means. It can be mediated culturally via knowledge – by learning to see the world and others from a specific perspective. Without this cultural dimension, there is probably no possibility of seeing that morality may add to, or transcend, the realm of naturally constituted self-interest for oneself and kin.[14]

The problem inherent in altruism beyond that related to the immediate kin is that it requires more than an attachment relationship to others where self-interest is involved. Coakley defines altruism as 'a subset of cooperation, reserved for conditions of additional affective intentionality' that involves *good will or love*. 'Altruism is a form of (costly) cooperation in which an individual is motivated by good will or love for another (or others).'[15] Accordingly, in altruism, constitutive elements appear that are operating not only on the biological level. It does not represent a level of cooperation based on aims and goals that necessarily are shared by all parties involved.

A crucial argument in Coakley's development of the topic is that sacrifice is primarily providing conditions for further life – and, therefore, should not be seen as inherently violent. This claim is the main reason for including her in the present treatise. To argue thus, she must, however, take issue with some of the moral concerns that have been expressed concerning the problematic sides of the notion of a sacrifice for others. She sees the enlightenment critique of sacrifice as one that opposes sacrifice and rationality. Coakley writes about the heritage from the Enlightenment:

> We inherit a paradox, and a deep problem. If we have a new universal project of moral rationality which must suppress, hide, or sideline sacrifice, and eviscerate it of its specifically ritual power, then this may actually create and sustain an

---

13. See Sarah Coakley, 'Sacrifice Regained: Evolution, Cooperation and God', in *The Gifford Lectures* (University of Aberdeen, 2012), Lecture 2, 6–7.

14. This point can be sustained by an understanding of the moral stance as not intrinsic to human (biological) nature, but as reliant on our capacities for symbolic representation. Thus, morality in humans is not necessarily rooted *directly* only in 'simpler' social behaviours that we find in other species, as these are not in the same manner dependent on symbolic representation. Hence, the ethical stance of humans can be distinguished qualitatively from the fitness-seeking behaviour that characterizes cooperation in other species, without denying that such behaviour *as well* may be part of human life. For this argument, see Deacon, *The Symbolic Species: The Co-Evolution of Language and the Brain*, 431.

15. Coakley, 'Sacrifice Regained: Evolution, Cooperation and God', Lecture 2, 6f.

opposite – in which sacrifice becomes the more irrational and violent. The rationality of the moral law, we might say, is covertly predicated on its reverse.[16]

Thus, sacrifice appears to be a problem for a modern, universal form of morality. However, that is not necessarily the case, Coakley argues. There is a rational element in sacrifice, linked to its inherent place in human life-conditions. Current biology identifies *sacrifice as a feature in evolution*. This approach makes it possible to argue that instead of ruthless competition and exploitation as the basic orientation of human practices, evolution has made it possible to substitute these self-centred elements with sacrifice and altruism as fundamental elements in the evolutionary process.[17] 'We now know why "sacrifice" in Darwin's sense (technically termed "cooperation", and signifying the forgoing of a fitness advantage, whether physical or cultural, so that another may have it instead) can not only become evolutionarily stable under certain particular conditions but also, and crucially, provide the creative matrix for further evolutionary advances', she writes.[18] Selfish behaviour is not the only modus operandi of evolution.[19] Given that evolution works on rational premises, this approach suggests that sacrifice can be considered rational already at the evolutionary level, not only as a result of cultural development.

We might intuitively be inclined to predict that selfish strategies work to a fitness advantage. However, given that others are simultaneously cooperating, this is not always the case. Therefore, 'if more and more individuals in a population adopt defective (or "selfish") strategies, there will inevitably be an overall declining average fitness'.[20] This point has apparent applications for our behaviour in an ecological context, as well – although Coakley does not develop these. Although selfishness may pay off initially and only work at the cost of others, once all adopt the same strategy, the whole species suffers.[21] Furthermore, we can add: not only the species but the whole ecology to which it is connected. The important conclusion for our context is that selfishness is not to the benefit of long-term evolution, not even at a biological level.

It is here that cooperation presents itself as a viable option. Coakley sees it as the 'thin purple line' in evolution – 'the patterning of the plenitude and productivity of sacrifice'. Evolutionarily stable cooperation 'could have brought about the

---

16. Ibid., Lecture 2, 9.
17. Ibid., Lecture 2, 17.
18. Ibid.
19. Ibid., Lecture 2, 18. Coakley refers to her colleague Martin Nowak, who has been working on mathematical evolutionary dynamics and who has clarified that the conditions of the so-called 'social dilemma' are such that cooperation can indeed emerge as evolutionarily stable. See M. A. Nowak and Sarah Coakley, *Evolution, Games, and God: The Principle of Cooperation* (Cambridge, MA: Harvard University Press, 2013).
20. Coakley, 'Sacrifice Regained: Evolution, Cooperation and God', Lecture 2, 18.
21. Ibid.

breakthrough events in the whole upward thrust of evolutionary development'. At key moments in evolution, cooperation has been vital at all levels.[22]

However, cooperation is not identical to sacrifice. Hence, we need to follow Coakley's argument further to determine to what extent *sacrifice* may also be seen as rational on a mere biological basis. Because cooperation represents a higher principle in evolution than selfishness, this point may even vindicate the reintroduction of 'teleological language' within evolution.[23] From a theological perspective, it would entail that nature and grace are not separated; grace is at work within nature, even somehow part of it (i.e. by introducing more than what is present at a previous level of biological evolution).

Further clarification of the relationship between sacrifice, cooperation and altruism seems called for.[24] To see a further movement from selfishness via cooperation and towards altruism will allow us to recognize how these notions may, in turn, be necessary for the notion of sacrifice. Coakley clarifies as follows:

- *Cooperation* denotes a form of working together in which one individual pays a cost (in terms of fitness, whether genetic or cultural) and another gains a benefit.
- *Altruism* is a subset of cooperation, reserved for conditions of additional affective intentionality: 'Altruism is a form of (costly) cooperation in which an individual is motivated by good will or love for another (or others).'[25]

Nevertheless, the argument for this notion of sacrifice requires more than what has hitherto been presented. We need to trace the necessary steps towards it. Against the backdrop of admitting that it is possible to see sacrificially creative actions as a result of the evolutionary process, the following reflections present themselves.

Firstly, human cooperation is *ambiguous* in terms of how well it works to benefit humankind and the rest of the Earth. Cooperation is at work in great atrocities and destructive actions, and not only in heroic deeds for others. Human cooperation has been and still is instrumental to much ecological damage. Accordingly, the distinction between cooperation and altruism proves relevant. Ants and Nazis are examples of cooperation, but they do not act according to *altruistic* behaviour principles. This distinction makes it possible to evaluate some types of cooperation among humans as positive and 'considered alongside any specifically altruistic religious motivations and movements of the will and affect that sustain them', Coakley writes, and continues:

> Are there indeed evidences of supreme manifestations of altruism that far exceed what could be accounted for even in terms of cultural fitness? If so,

---

22. Ibid., Lecture 2, 18f.
23. Ibid, Lecture 2, 19.
24. Cf. ibid., 6f.
25. Ibid.

would they be best be accounted for, as part of an argument to the 'best explanation', in terms of a hypothesized participation in the life of a loving and sacrificial God? Can the lives of the saints, in other words, manifestators of Christian altruism well beyond the calculations of 'fitness', provide the best argument for God?[26]

We find ourselves here at a point where several motifs in the previous parts of this treatise run together. One is the existence of the actual presence of sacrificial altruism in creation as a sign of a benevolent, loving and graceful God. This love would not be possible to experience unless we could detect it in representations of it – that is, in God's representatives, the saints. These are then the ones we might emulate to realize God's loving intentions for the creation and thereby fulfil our calling to be images of God.

Again, *love* surfaces as the central theme for introducing God as related to human experience. Knowledge shaped by love makes humans unique among the animals in how we possess unique powers of choice and are responsible: it is due to our knowledge, calculations and insights that we may affect the planet for good or bad. Coakley suggests that love must enter into the equation because 'our human sacrificial choices – . . . our capacities for consciousness, language and communication – have enormously powerful implications, just as our defective choices have equally devastating potential force.'[27]

However, the rational insights into the need for changing human practices and behaviours are not sufficient to change our *will*. Coakley, therefore, sides with E.O. Wilson in suggesting that 'only the power of a sacrificial, *religious* motivation can sufficiently redirect human will to undertake the changes we need to save us from ecological disaster.'[28] In other words: we are called to make sacrifices for the sake of future generations and to give up our privileges. The change cannot be accommodated unless there is also a change in *heart* (or will). Here, religion becomes important, as 'the "rationality" of religious belief that may emerge from reflection on the mathematical patternings of evolution can never safely be divorced from the affective transformations of religious rituals and practices.'[29]

Coakley develops these points further by claiming that 'it would probably take the positive and affective commitment and hope of *religious* people internationally,

---

26. Sarah Coakley, *Sacrifice Regained: Reconsidering the Rationality of Religious Belief: An Inaugural Lecture by the Norris-Hulse Professor of Divinity Given in the University of Cambridge, 13 October 2009* (Cambridge, UK: Cambridge University Press, 2012), 27.

27. Ibid.

28. Ibid. Cf. Coakley, 'Sacrifice Regained: Evolution, Cooperation and God', Lecture 1, 18.

29. *Sacrifice Regained: Reconsidering the Rationality of Religious Belief: An Inaugural Lecture by the Norris-Hulse Professor of Divinity Given in the University of Cambridge, 13 October 2009*, 28.

to mobilize such a new level of cooperation, a prospect that may be being held to us as perhaps the "next evolutionary transition" without which humankind itself will be increasingly under stress'.[30] This might entail a new type of asceticism, as well as excessive manifestations of altruism that can 'inspire a new generation of commitment to goals other than and beyond the individual or even the national'. Moreover, she asks if 'this possibility can even be theorized without the theological language of grace and participation?'[31]

As we see, Coakley presents a strong argument for engaging religious symbols for the sake of the planet, even when we speak of a symbol like sacrifice, although this is not her main aim in dealing with the symbol. Moreover, by addressing the emotional component, she foregrounds that sacrifice involves more than calculation. It engages the whole person, similar to many other religious symbols. As a symbol of orientation, it suggests that there is more at stake than increasing fitness when we perceive it from a rational point of view.

Humans, with our capacities and power, can employ the sacrifice symbol in a wide variety of ways. It is therefore of utmost importance to specify it adequately in order to overcome its potential deficiencies. It can be manipulated into acts of war and violence in the name of religion, as well as 'theorized qua violence as foundational to the very possibility of culture and religion'.[32] However, sacrifice can also have crucial importance for human life at a fundamental level. Coakley points to how 'sacrifice is being done all the time physiologically in the tiring and painful human business of pregnancy, birthgiving and lactation'.[33] From such a perspective, sacrifice as providing life opportunities is primary and rooted in common human experiences. Hence, we need to highlight how it can be generative and transformative.[34] From what she writes, it also emerges as a tacit argument for seeing sacrifice as a condition for providing chances for a flourishing future Earth, in which not only privileged humans live well.[35]

Coakley refers to Jesus's sacrifice in the continuation of her remarks about women's sacrifice, but not in a way that identifies them. In him, she claims, we face a 'supernormality' that involves 'an altruism beyond calculation'.[36] His sacrifice is nevertheless excessive in its rationality, and it only needed to be done once. From her overall argument, it makes sense to underscore that no one should see a sacrifice like that of Jesus's life as necessary to repeat – also not the present generation in its relation to the next.

---

30. 'Sacrifice Regained: Evolution, Cooperation and God', Lecture 6, 19.
31. Ibid.
32. Ibid., Lecture 6, 17f.
33. Ibid., 17.
34. Ibid., Lecture 4, 20.
35. Cf. ibid.
36. Ibid., Lecture 6, 17.

Motherhood and sacrifice

Sarah Coakley has provided a context for seeing sacrifice as a rational act of love and an act that we can see manifested in motherhood practices. I have already suggested that this means that acts of sacrifice can provide a relevant symbol for interpreting necessary practices related to climate change. We have also seen that although Jesus's sacrifice illuminates some essential elements in how sacrifice may still be a valid symbol for interpreting practice, it cannot be understood as something to be repeated. However, it seems to be more related to sacrificial elements in human life than what appears on the surface. Hence, it is possible to link it to the main phenomenon in human life that unavoidably calls for sacrifice, although seldom referred to or recognized as such: the sacrifices related to motherhood.[37] In line with what I have developed so far in this book, it is also possible to further develop the connection between motherhood and sacrifice in the Anthropocene context.

Mary Streufert develops her understanding of Jesus's sacrifice from the basis of maternal sacrifice, but I will argue that her considerations on maternal sacrifice have bearings for understanding sacrifice beyond that specific task. She sees maternal sacrifice by both body and energy. Against those who would see sacrifice primarily in relation to Jesus's redemptive death, Streufert refocuses on the life-giving and non-violent aspects of sacrifice.[38] Because the 'maternal life of birthing and rearing children lies at the heart of reality for us: without these feats, we would not be', she claims.[39] Consequently, these life-promoting practices should be seen as normative and even serve as admirable, similar to how heroes are. Thus, she points to an element that links to the exemplary ethic discussed in Part II.[40]

Maternal sacrifice consists of two elements: the maternal body and the actual maternal life that entails raising children. It requires 'the courage necessary to endure the physical demands of motherhood'.[41] However, such sacrifice also implies generativity and creativity, both emerging from the demands and joys of raising children.[42] Thus, the understanding of sacrifice expands beyond sacrifice as linked to death. Thereby, some of the deficits for employing this symbol in the context of climate change are overcome.

---

37. A notable exception to this absence is the womanist reflections in JoAnne Marie Terrell, 'Our Mother's Gardens', in *Cross-Examinations: Readings on the Meaning of the Cross Today*, ed. Marit Trelstad (Minneapolis, MN: Fortress Press, 2006). There, she also offers an overview of other womanist approaches to sacrifice.

38. Mary J. Streufert, 'Maternal Sacrifice as a Hermeneutics of the Cross', in *Cross Examinations: Readings on the Meaning of the Cross*, ed. Marit Trelstad (Minneapolis, MN: Fortress Press, 2006), 71.

39. Ibid.

40. See the discussion of Zagzebski in Chapter 8.

41. Streufert, 'Maternal Sacrifice as a Hermeneutics of the Cross', 71.

42. Ibid.

The physical elements in maternal sacrifice are several, both during pregnancy and after birth. In addition to how pregnancy alters a woman's body, Streufert lists many of the challenges: nausea, vomiting, shortness of breath; stretch marks; haemorrhoids; varicose veins; and high blood pressure, to name a few. These uncomfortable, sometimes painful elements in bearing someone under your heart are nevertheless 'the beginning of sacrifice for life to come from life'.[43]

After birth, sacrifices for the sake of life continue in various ways as the body changes. However, the physical alterations are for Streufert not reported 'in an attempt to receive pity for women who give birth, nor to glorify biological mothers over others', but for the purpose of pointing to the *courage* that pregnancy and childrearing requires. Sacrifice requires courage – the courage to give life for life.[44]

Stepping back from this concrete and physical description of what is required to secure future life, we must ask to what extent taking on this task can also be informative for others than actual, physical mothers. To what extent can people in the Western world, and beyond, be willing to bear the uncomfortable consequences of reducing their energy consumption, change their eating habits, reduce their holiday travels, and so on, and give up the physically comfortable life of the few for the sake of future generations? The more or less heroic sacrifices of motherhood, which are implied in how we already live, are challenges to ponder concerning our present planetary condition.

Maternal sacrifices are the result of active choices and not mere passively accepted tasks. It requires active participation all the way, as does the different tasks we need to engage in to improve this planet's conditions. Such active participation is required for everyone who sacrifices something for the sake of the other: it was so for Jesus's sacrifice, it is like this for mothers, and it is, in the end, like this for all of us. We are called to an active and creative participation in sacrificial practices.[45]

As we see, Steufert's analysis contributes to the symbol of sacrifice undergoing a significant transformation that can make it relevant for addressing climate change: Instead of appearing as a manifestation of Christian religious necrophilia, sacrifice must be understood from the vantage point of *zoophilia*, the love of life.[46] In this way, it is linked internally to the conditions for life. Moreover, sacrifice in a positive sense becomes possible to distinguish clearly from the sacrifices we inflict on others, leading to (their) death. Streufert sees this in light of the *imitatio Christi* motif, which we can link to the exemplary ethic already mentioned. Emulation of Christ's sacrifice entails 'a genuine return to each other, indicative of parental generativity' manifest in the 'embodiment of the risk to love'.[47] Consequently, what she calls the 'life-for-life model of sacrifice inherent to motherhood' entails

---

43. Ibid.
44. Ibid., 71f.
45. Ibid., 72.
46. Ibid.
47. Cf. ibid.

a transformation that makes thriving and flourishing possible. In Christian terms, this is an expression of the restorative salvation we find in God through Jesus Christ. 'The restorative wholeness of relationship, both with God and with neighbor, redeems. Relationship, as the heart of life, indeed, as the heart of the gospel itself, saves', Steufert claims.[48] Hence, she links sacrifice for life to the centre of the Christian message.

Hope and grace reconsidered

An obvious question in light of the previous section is to what extent there are resources in the Christian tradition that can help us identify resources for hope in the present situation of planetary predicament. Hope is a central element in the Christian reservoir of symbols, but how can we understand it in the Anthropocene context, where everything seems to be determined by human action?

One way of thinking about hope is to see it as a result of the fact that we cannot determine and control everything, including the final outcomes of our actions. We need to hope for this outcome to be good. However, hope may also entail things to happen or emerge due to something not caused by our actions. That is also the case in terms of the actions, practices and events that can impede the destructive trajectory we are currently on in the climate catastrophe. Hope contains a component of what is beyond our action and control.[49]

Everything that humans do is directed towards future-oriented aims and purposes that entail some element of hope for their realization. The conditions and the content of hope need to be specified further unless the symbol 'hope' will remain a generic one that does not aid and guide human action but instead becomes an excuse for inactivity in the face of the present catastrophe.

Werner Jeanrond approaches hope from the point of view of humans as relational beings – a point that has immediate connections to the topic of this book.[50] He defines hope as

> neither a principle nor a general expression of the conviction that in the end all will be well. Rather, hope results from the intimate and dynamic connection between God and human beings, or, more concretely, between divine and

---

48. Ibid.
49. Perhaps this point about hope being about something outside our control is most profoundly expressed in the Christian belief in the *resurrection*. An observant reader will note that I do not develop that motif in the present context. The reason is that resurrection, as understood in the Christian tradition, is about a new heaven and a new earth, whereas I am concerned with symbols that can be directed towards the interpretation of presently existing conditions for life.
50. Cf. Jeanrond, *Reasons to Hope*, 2ff.

human love. Hope dies when this love relationship dies. Then hopelessness and despair reign.[51]

To believe in God is to believe in someone good not yet arrived, something good still to come, in something new and different.[52] The fundamental expression of this good is love. Against this backdrop, hope is always for a change for the good, of for something better than what is present at hand. Hope and the good are linked internally and intimately. Hope transforms us, and hope is about transformation. As intimately connected to our desires, hope opens us up to a world that is not determined by violence, destruction, evil and injustice. If love and goodness disappear, hope may diminish. With new chances for goodness, hope may increase.

Presently, many forces challenge our ability to hope and threaten to take hope away. Things do not look good. The ties between hope and goodness are under siege. However, we are even worse off without hope because the content shapes our fundamental orientations. As the aforementioned quote from Jeanrond suggests, love – for nature and the flourishing world – may be a central element in change for the better for which we hope.

To hope means to make a distinction between what is present and what is hoped for. Thus, hope is a manifestation of difference and of absence. That which one hopes for is absent, or it is only present in hope, as something not yet there. This manifestation of the absence of the hoped-for in the present shapes the perception of the present as a situation of lack: not all is what is hoped for. Something may be missing. Without hope, this difference between what is and what one hopes for is not possible to manifest. However, in hope, both the present and the future are perceived in light of the difference between present and future, what is and what is to come. If the difference is suspended, we are caught in the present, determined by the past and not provided with a view for what is still possible but not yet the case.

From a pragmatic point of view, this means that hope, similar to other symbols, shapes the perception of reality in which we find ourselves. However, this is not a mere theoretical perception of what is. Hope provides means for orientation in the present, for passing judgement on it, assessing it and criticizing it by making, marking and manifesting a difference. Hope is judgement of the present. Even when what we hope for is that the future shall be a continuum of the present, such judgement is made – because this hope is then expressing a positive affirmation of the present and the hope that it will continue.

Hope's manifestation of difference is involved in the tension between activity and passivity: Hope can instigate activity, make the one who hopes active, and

---

51. Ibid., 3.
52. Further on the logic (or rather, the phenomenology) of hope, see the brief but lucid analysis in Markus Mühling, *T&T Clark Handbook of Christian Eschatology* (London: Bloomsbury T&T Clark, 2015), 32–7.

simultaneously shape the way she orients herself in the world and perceives opportunities for transformation. This *active hope* is the hope that opens up to responsibility and action. Hence, hope instigates action. However, hope is also connected to what humans experience as passive receivers of the gifts of creation. However, before we proceed to speak about how hope is connected to human activity, we need to make a detour and reflect on another central theological symbol: the symbol *grace*.

Grace is about the gifts unconditioned by our actions. It is about that which does not depend on myself but on God's generosity. Grace provides new chances for creation's redemption from sin and its consequences. Grace is life-changing and interrupts the familiar and points towards the goodness we are given through others and life's different manifestations and conditions. Grace manifests the possibility of becoming liberated from the negative past. It expands conditions for life and agency by manifesting itself in events and powers that originate beyond our control. To become aware of how and where grace appears changes our notion of agency and thus our mode of being in the world. Accordingly, grace is connected to elements that may sustain hope. Hence, grace and hope are intimately linked together.

If we look at traditional notions of grace, the interconnection between grace and hope is nevertheless not without problems. Terra Schwerin Rowe has pointed to how knowledge about ecology and conditions for climate change challenges theologians to rethink grace in light of human activity and passivity. She argues against seeing 'God's primary redemptive activity in terms of external relations (*extra nos*) aimed primarily at isolated individuals abstracted from the rest of creation (*pro me*)'.[53] The awareness of the dynamics and complexities of internally related systems makes it impossible to uphold a Cartesian-Newtonian world view as a framework for articulating the theological notion of grace. Hence, 'the detrimental effects of idealized divine relations as external, unilateral, uncooperative, nonreciprocal, and lacking participation'[54] must be overcome, as they point to deficits in how the traditional symbol of grace has been articulated. She asks:

> What would grace look like if we could no longer assume we were isolated individuals or that an individual could essentially be extracted from the web of relations that not only supports them but also constitutes them? What does *extra nos* mean in an ecological universe where no thing can be said to be absolutely separate or outside relation with others? Or what does *pro me* mean when there is no 'me' apart from a community of others?[55]

---

53. Rowe, *Toward a Better Worldliness: Ecology, Economy, and the Protestant Tradition*, xiv.
54. Ibid., xix.
55. Ibid., xxvii.

Schwerin-Rowe suggests that we need to see grace as more than aligned with 'an interruption or even annihilation of the economic exchanges that sustain the world' and avoid seeing it as 'the continual recurrence and idealization of the original unilateral divine gift'.[56] She proposes an understanding of grace that overcomes the mere passive element that has shaped the notion in much Protestant thought and sees 'the gift of grace as unconditioned and multilateral in the sense that it may refuse a capitalizing return to its origin and, instead, continue to disperse, sparking a wider exchange of gifts rather than an opposition to exchange'.[57]

> Grace, here, is not some gift object passed between discrete parties, nor does it depend on preconditions. It does, however, presume relationship, a connection that counts. Where the gift might not return to its origin, grace is the occasion – no state suggesting simple location – that allows for a different kind of encounter, a kind of love given with the understanding that it may not be a good, capitalizing investment for the giver. Even as one always hopes for the return of relationship, grace is not given with the condition of a return to its origin.[58]

Hence, 'Grace emerges as a possibility within an entangled relationality'[59] – the very reality that faces climate change. Entanglement and vulnerability are connected and may leave us 'incredibly vulnerable to shortsighted and self-interested acts – vulnerable, that is, to the consequences of a maintained illusion of separative individualism'.[60] Grace provides opportunities for overcoming individualist notions of the self and the realization of interconnectedness. It is 'the experience of being opened by gratitude to the multitude of others (divine, human, and other-than-human alike) who are gifts to us'.[61] As a consequence, grace builds extensive communities among all living beings.

We can develop further how grace works at different levels of creation by engaging Jay B. McDaniel's distinction between *red and green grace*.[62] He connects red grace to positive responses to suffering, whereas green grace expresses itself in the diverse gifts of creation. He defines red grace thus:

> Red grace is available to everybody. It is the healing that occurs when we become aware of unwanted suffering in others and ourselves; when we assume responsibility for whatever harm we have done to ourselves and others, some of which originates in unhealthy attachments to finite things as if they were

56. Ibid., 171.
57. Ibid.
58. Ibid., 172.
59. Ibid.
60. Ibid.
61. Ibid., 174.
62. McDaniel, 'The Passion of Christ: Grace Both Red and Green'.

infinite; and when we allow our own sins and sufferings to be transformed into creativity and love. From a Christian perspective, this transformation occurs through the healing power of God's indwelling Spirit, thus named or not.[63]

This understanding of red grace is directly relevant to the present situation: This grace relates us to the tragic side of life, which is an unavoidable part of life in its fullness. This grace is not merely about the spiritual forgiveness of sins but about being able to address the world's sufferings and contribute to its healing. Moreover, as becomes clear, the presence of this grace depends on taking up the responsibility for healing and letting go of unhealthy attachments, of which the consumer society is full. McDaniel contributes to overcoming the deficit in the symbol grace by directing it towards our responsibility to address sin in ways that contribute to healing. He connects this ability to become liberated from the past to the life-giving Spirit of God, which is the power that creates hope.[64]

Green grace points to the sheer goodness of life, despite the tragedy addressed by red grace. It is not related to suffering and healing but appears in the continuous creativity in creation, independent of human powers and control. Here, God's life-giving Spirit in creation creates the conditions for life at a fundamental level and in a way that is primary to that in red grace.

> Green refers to the lilies of the field, to which Jesus referred when he enjoined his disciples to live simply and gratefully; and more generally to the beauty of the earth and its many living beings, all of whom God declared very good on the sixth day of creation (Luke 12:27; Gen. 1:31). Green grace occurs when we enjoy rich bonds with people, plants and animals, and the earth. In moments when we taste green grace, we experience the Spirit, not as a reality within us or beyond us, but rather between us. It is holy communion itself.[65]

The two forms of grace constitute complementary modes of experiencing the world. Red grace has an immediate ethical side, whereas green grace is responsive to beauty. Both are necessary. 'Red grace without green grace is morbid, lapsing into a rigid control of others in the name of being holy and pure; and green grace without red grace is naive, easily lapsing into a self-absorbed narcissism.'[66]

McDaniel sees Christian religion as rooted in both forms of grace, even though some traditions overemphasize the red and subordinate the green. The effect of a lack of balance between them is that our chances for experiencing beauty,

---

63. Ibid., 197.
64. Cf. ibid. Cf. also how grace is described here, and how hope and healing are connected in Barbara Rossing's work, as discussed earlier, pp. 175ff.
65. Ibid.
66. Ibid.

enjoyment and relationship qualities are reduced.[67] Then the sensitivity to loss and damage of nature decreases, as well. However, to experience green grace is, in fact, a precondition for red grace. Accordingly, the two elements seem to be connected. He elaborates on this interaction in the following way:

> Red grace, when it takes the form of sensitivity to the sufferings of others, is a form of green grace. This means that green grace need not be happy in order to be fulfilling. There is a harmony in shared suffering that is beautiful but painful. This beauty is part of green grace: the sharing of pain so that it does not have to be born alone.

It is important to note here that McDaniel is not idealizing or promoting the suffering side of red grace. Instead, he sees it as preparing 'the way for the enjoyment of the happier sides of green grace'.[68] Thus, 'green grace, then, is not simply the grace of an originally good creation'.[69] It points us to the relational mode of being in the world, where we are dependent on the goods mediated to us by others; 'reminding us that we are not the center of the universe'.[70]

The experience of grace is a crucial element in taking up the responsibility for the whole of creation. Its relational character entails that grace also makes us experience our failures and our vulnerability. Thus, we need to overcome the restricted and sometimes superficial understanding of grace as the forgiveness of sins. McDaniel points to three different elements involved in red grace that, I argue, are of utmost importance for our relationship with creation, red grace, he holds, occurs

(1) when we are mindfully present to the suffering that lies within us and in others;
(2) when we acknowledge the ways in which, in some circumstances, we are responsible for some of this suffering that we experience in ourselves and others;
(3) when we allow both of these realities – the suffering and the sin – to help us grow in our capacities for wise and compassionate living, as precipitated by a 'letting go' of attachment to finite things as if they were infinite.[71]

The relevance of highlighting these components of grace for ecological care should be obvious: the first element impedes the 'emotional anesthesia' that blocks out suffering, as well as the 'debilitating numbness, in which case we hurt so deeply

---

67. Ibid.
68. Ibid., 198.
69. Ibid.
70. Ibid.
71. Ibid., 204.

that we cannot feel the pain anymore'.[72] However, the second element McDaniel mentions, acknowledgement of our complicity in suffering, needs further specification. We are not only complicit in the suffering of other humans, but also in the destruction of habitats and the extinction of other species, as well as in upholding social and economic structures that contribute to the continuous degradation of the environment and to climate change. Nevertheless, McDaniel is right in pointing out that this acknowledgement entails that we cannot see all these elements as the result of others' actions and doing.

In the third element on the list McDaniel presents, two elements are especially worthy of consideration: the fact that grace leads to transformation, and that this transformation is dependent on more that we can expect to master by ourselves only, although it does not exclude our participation in the transformative process. To let sin become transformed into creativity and love is only possible 'when we let go of the illusion that we are masters of our destiny and thus open ourselves to a healing Spirit at work in the world, within us yet beyond us, whose very nature is to bring new life into the world, moment by moment'.[73]

One reading of McDaniel makes it open to the justified accusation that Christians place themselves in a state of passivity when responding to the injustices and sins under which the world suffers. To acknowledge that we are not the masters of our own destiny seems to place everything in the hands of God. However, a close reading of him counters this objection. Transformation is not left to God alone but depends on God doing God's work in humans through the Spirit. Hence, the Protestant Christian emphasis on humans as saved by grace through faith rather than good works cannot be used to bolster a passive state that does not respond actively to suffering and destruction.[74]

McDaniel elaborates on the distinction between green and red grace by underscoring what I have pointed to as an important element for motivation earlier: the ability to experience nature in its richness and variety. Thus, he precludes moralist activism that almost inevitably ends up in exhaustion. Moreover, he affirms a fundamental feature in the theological notion of grace: it is a gift and not the result of human activity. Hence, he writes:

> In our time there is a profound need to remember our bonds with the more-than-human world. Red grace can only take us so far in this remembrance. It helps us understand that we are connected with all creatures of the flesh who suffer and that we share a common plight. Green grace, however, helps us revel in beauty. The enjoyment of green grace includes a sense of sacred awe in the presence of the heavens; a sense of kinship with other living beings; a sense of belonging to a particular portion of land; a healthy relation to our own body; the enjoyment of companionship with other animals. If the calling of our time

72. Ibid.
73. Ibid., 205.
74. Cf. ibid.

is to help build communities that are socially just, ecologically sustainable, and spiritually satisfying for all, then the all must include the other living beings. We find our home in this more inclusive consciousness by opening ourselves to green grace. The world cannot be saved by moral earnestness alone. It must also be saved by delight in beauty.[75]

As I now return to the discussion of hope, I want to point out what the present discussion of red and green grace implies: it means that we have to trust in more than what we can accomplish by ourselves. However, it does not mean that we are outside the picture. The hope that things might change for the better is rooted in the expectations inherent in both red and green grace. Thus, hope expands beyond what is under our control and calculations. Hope, just as grace, entails both an active and a passive dimension.

Similar to what I have suggested earlier, Ingolf U. Dalferth describes hope as our human sense for the possibility of the good and sees it as a fundamental human resource of life. Werner Jeanrond addresses Dalferth's position critically, primarily because Dalferth underscores that we should not understand hope in terms of human activity. The receptive or passive nature of hope entails that, by hoping, one is open to the gift of the possibility of the good. Hence, Dalferth makes the valid point that the good to be hoped for cannot be identified with possible human achievements. Instead, the way we are hoping discloses our principal orientation in life.

Jeanrond wants to avoid the one-sidedness in Dalferth's position and argues that hope also entails responsible human activity. This claim is due to the relational character of hope that we have already considered. Accordingly, he proposes to see that 'hope is always already linked to concrete personal relationships and ensuing journeys. Hence, hope is about the divinely initiated personal and communal relationship of love that brings about the good in the first place. In this love relationship the human subject can develop into becoming a genuine agent and subject of hope'.[76]

Jeanrond explicates this point of activity further by pointing to how 'Christian discipleship has always been characterized by more or less adequate responses to the challenges of faith, hope and love'.[77] The elements faith, hope and love are, as we have seen, the three theological virtues. They are gifts of God, and to respond to God's call in an adequate way entails that these virtues shape our way of life. Hence, although the reception of the gifts manifests a passive element, all three virtues are essential for instigating enduring human action in response to God's call concerning the world's suffering. Thus, to have faith in the future, to hope and to love is to enable further chances for the creation to flourish.

---

75. Ibid., 206.
76. Jeanrond, *Reasons to Hope*, 10.
77. Ibid., 11.

Overcoming ambiguities of orientational symbols: Exodus and Paradise

Among the functions of orientational symbols in religion are those that point to where the world has its origin and towards the aim it is headed for. Two of the most powerful symbols in the Christian tradition that serve this function are *Exodus* and *Paradise*. However, in the light of the climate crisis, they need to be critically assessed with regard to how, or to what extent, they can contribute to practices that sustain individual and shared efforts in a long-term perspective. The Paradise symbol raises significant concerns about its potential escapist effects and its possible focus on other-worldly conditions instead of enabling people to focus on the present and the problems at hand. The Exodus symbol seems to point to instances in the past with no immediate relevance for the present. Can both of these symbols be reinterpreted in ways that overcome such deficits and demonstrate their possible relevance for the present climate change crisis?[78]

The Exodus motif has proved so crucial for the civil rights movements and liberationist theologies because it points to the possibility of becoming liberated from injustices and oppression. The liberation shapes the identity of a community in search of a better place to live. Thus, the symbol points backward in time, as well as towards a possible future. However, what this future holds is not specified much, apart from its ability to nourish well those who live in it.

A contemporary Exodus will involve a move away from a society that builds on the death and suffering of others, humans as well as other species and habitats. But it also means a move away from practices of excessive consumption and exploitation of resources. Unlike the original Exodus, most of the destruction, suffering and injustice from which we need to depart are hidden from the sight of those who need to break up. The comprehensiveness of that which we have to leave behind can hardly be overestimated. On the other hand, it is crucial to be aware that we cannot simply leave this situation behind: the Exodus from the carbon-emitting consumer society does not imply that we can leave it and close the door: we have to remain in the midst of it and all its problems, simply because we have only this planet.

One element that complicates employing the Exodus symbol in the present is the fact that for many of us, we are not only suffering oppression, injustice and oppression together with other species: We are oppressors, as well, willingly or not, as long as we are part of a system that presupposes material and financial growth as its fundament. Hence, we cannot externalize oppression and injustice to what others do – we are part of it.

---

78. For a recent attempt to develop an interpretation of the Exodus text for ecological concerns, but in a way that does not take up what the critical aspects of climate crisis and what I develop as the contemporary relevance of the Exodus event, see Yonathan Neril; Leo Dee, *Eco Bible: An Ecological Commentary on Genesis and Exodus* (The Interfaith Center for Sustainable Development, 2020).

Another motif in the Exodus symbol is that it entails a departure from a specific way of ordering society that builds on slavery and exploitation, but not from nature. It is impossible to depart from nature, as it is the precondition for every society. Hence, Exodus cannot mean that we depart from that which is our fundamental origin. From a theological point of view, this allows us to see that our origin in God's creative work is not mediated through society only (which can take on different shapes, more or less shaped by injustice or destruction, or justice and flourishing), but also on natural conditions. The original Exodus visualizes the dependence on natural conditions in how Israel left Egypt behind and entered the wilderness – but continued to remain a community in need of natural resources. The relationship with nature cannot be severed, even when it is not manifest in the optimal conditions for flourishing. The Exodus event originally meant that one had to rely on a more vegetarian diet instead of the meat that people had received from the fleshpots in Egypt (Exodus 16, 3ff.).

Christian imagery allows for seeing the human condition as constituted by two main symbols: on the one hand, they result from the creative work of a loving and caring God who wants creation to flourish. On the other hand, this God is the one who calls humans out of oppressive and destructive conditions and back to a life shaped by care, love and justice. Hence, the Exodus has a backdrop in God's original intentions for creation, and this should not be overlooked as a motivational force for completing the Exodus. The Paradise symbol that I discuss in the following text also visualizes this positive context.

Concerning a contemporary interpretation of the Exodus event as inspiring practices of environmental concern, we have to ask, pointing to our times: Who is the new community that is established by this Exodus? Where is it headed? The original Exodus created a nation that grounded their identity in their distinctiveness from the others surrounding them. That cannot be the task today. Tribalism and nationalism will not solve the problems, and the Exodus to which all humans are called cannot exclude anyone. Instead, the recognition that we all carry the future under our hearts entails that every human being today has a share in the call to depart and shape new and better conditions for future generations. Not everyone may identify with this community and recognize the task, but no one can be excused from it in principle.

It is more difficult to answer the other question: Where are we headed? To a large extent, the future ecological world remains unspecified because many different variables are at play, and they change all the time. The lack of a clear vision for alternative societal structures and the encompassing and deeply entrenched behavioural patterns that contribute to global warming and destruction of the environment nevertheless make it all the more pressing to consider and scrutinize all our actions in terms of what they entail for the prospects of future generations and their life-conditions.

The biblical narrative places the origin of humans in the Garden of Eden, often also identified as Paradise. Hence, we have our origin in a better state than the one in which we now find ourselves. I am not here arguing for a literal reading of the Genesis text, but for attention to its pragmatic relevance. When we interpret their existence in the light of that symbol, the original ecological state of humans appears as different from the one present at hand. Thus, Paradise imagery represents a counter-image against which one can assess the present conditions. If it is used in this way, it can serve other purposes than engendering escapist delusions.

The Paradise imagery is historically varied, and theologians have developed it in different ways. The following identifies some aspects in an analysis of this history that aims at pointing to the this-worldly relevance it may have.[79]

In their study of the Paradise motif in the history of Christianity, Rita Nakashima Brock and Rebecca Ann Parker discovered that in early Christianity paradise was something other than 'heaven' or related to life after death. Among the crucial things to note here is that paradise and death remain mutually exclusive in the Paradise symbol. Paradise was depicted in various expressions of Christian art. Brock and Parker describe it as follows, with apparent references to nature's role in the constitution of Paradise:

> In the early church, paradise – first and foremost – was this world, permeated and blessed by the Spirit of God. It was on the earth. Images of it in Rome and Ravenna captured the craggy, scruffy pastoral landscape, the orchards, the clear night skies, and teeming waters of the Mediterranean world, as if they were lit by a power from within. Sparkling mosaics in vivid colors captured the world's luminosity. The images filled the walls of spaces in which liturgies fostered aesthetic, emotional, spiritual, and intellectual experiences of life in the present, in a world created as good and delightful.[80]

Images show that God blessed the earth with the breath of Spirit 'that permeated the entire cosmos and made paradise the salvation that baptism in the Spirit offered'. Paradise became 'the most blessed place imaginable' and 'even heaven was a dimension of this life; it was the mysterious abode of God from which blessings flowed upon the earth'.[81]

By placing Paradise on Earth, the early church situated it within the experiential realm of human existence. It became 'an experience and a place, as well as work yet to be completed'.[82] It was not seen as a mere future state and

---

79. Others have previously developed the resources of Paradise imagery, so what I am doing here, is simply to develop a selection of elements that can be related to climate change. For an example of how the imagery can inform ecological concerns in general, see Norman Wirzba, *The Paradise of God: Renewing Religion in an Ecological Age* (Oxford: Oxford University Press, 2003).

80. Rita Nakashima Brock and Rebecca Ann Parker, *Saving Paradise: How Christianity Traded Love of This World for Crucifixion and Empire* (Boston: Beacon Press, 2008), xv.

81. Ibid.

82. Ibid., 88.

encompassed various dimensions material and spiritual, awaited and fulfilled. Perception and knowledge connected these dimensions, and Christians gained them through their lifelong training of perception and spiritual practices in worship that developed ethical discernment about good and evil. To know how to distinguish good and evil required acute attunement to the present and reflection about ethical behavior. Through such wisdom, Christians sought to live joyfully and enact justice, nonviolence, and love.[83]

It is hard to assess how comprehensive the practices were that the Paradise symbol engendered. It is nevertheless important to point out that Brock and Parker's analysis identifies an explicit ethical component in its imagery. This component speaks against those who see Paradise imagery as a reason for escapism and against those that use it for that purpose to avoid addressing the challenges of the present.

Paradise was, and is, associated with beauty. This point is also well exhibited in Brock and Parker's study. We need to underscore that point in relation to what has been developed earlier: the need to involve sensual experience and other, more participatory ways of experiencing nature as a condition for building up the virtues of ecological care and love. To depict Paradise in images of beauty 'engage the more holistic, emotional, and sensory-laden dimensions of experience and memory. They capture multilayered experiences of imagination, feeling, perceiving, and thinking'. Thus, 'the aesthetic, emotional, sensory, and intellectual dimensions of life can come together and be mixed in fresh ways'.[84]

Beauty is manifest in how it elicits love. This love entails a desire for the beautiful and the good – expressed in the symbol God as well as for developing virtues such as justice, courage, prudence and charity.[85] However, this love/desire is different from that which presently 'trivialize beauty as a vain preoccupation with physical appearance' or confirming to dehumanizing advertised ideals about what it is to be human.[86] The love in question emerges from beauty as different from materialist idols. It is contrary to 'the indulgence of the wealthy, who buy luxurious objects for display',[87] and orients itself towards a sense of wholeness and well-being not dependent on material goods. It focuses on the qualities of the present relation to others and the environment.

Brock and Parker show that Paradise imagery may promote a sense of beauty and care. However, they also see the problems and dangers related to such imagery. One of the places where they find it is in the book of Revelation. It is important to note this critical attitude towards images of Paradise because such criticism provides assessments of what matters and what should not. Thus, it can

83. Ibid.
84. Ibid., xvi.
85. Ibid., 149.
86. Ibid.
87. Ibid.

identify better means for both orientation and transformation. In their criticism of Revelation, they hold that

> *Revelation's* paradise is too thin and meager to carry the weight of its fury. In being obsessed with the dualism of good and evil and galvanizing its attention on empire, it closes the door, finally, on any possibility of forgiveness, and it envisions a denatured new Jerusalem that is out of this world. It loses its grounding in the world as a gift of God. Once its volcanic heat is blown, it can only offer a crystalline, cold comfort. It promises a glittering antiworld, a place absent meadows, night, dreams, animals, companionship, and pleasure.[88]

However, Brock and Parker criticize not only selected strata in the biblical imagery of Paradise. They also address the segregation of nature and civilization inherent in American romanticism. This move divides life into different spheres and has severe consequences: '[A]s such efforts imagine paradise as purification and salvation as the ultimate and final separation of the pristine from the corrupt and the wild from the civilized, visions of paradise will foster disassociation from the present in all its complex demands.'[89] Instead of seeing Paradise as a place and an event of purification and elimination, they hold that 'Life is actually sustained, however, by integration, interaction, and exchange in the present– it is ecological, not eschatological'.[90]

Thus, an argument for the relevance of the Paradise symbol entails that we relocate it from an eschatological to an ecological context. This relocation overcomes some of the deficits usually connected to this symbol and makes it possible to activate Paradise as a symbol that critically addresses the present and precarious situation, whereas simultaneously engenders a vision of its alternative. Moreover, by avoiding imagery of purification, the symbol cannot be used for totalitarian purposes that seek to create heaven on earth at the expense of those who do not commit to the vision. To avoid a totalitarian and violence-enforced eschatological vision of paradise is contrary to the ecological vision of integrity, interdependence, natural growth, compassion, love and flourishing for all species. As Brock and Parker writes:

> Paradise is human life restored to its divinely infused dignity and capacity, and it is a place of struggle with evil and injustice, requiring the development of wisdom, love, nonviolence, and responsible uses of power. Paradise can be experienced as spiritual illumination of the heart, mind, and senses felt in moments of religious ecstasy, and it can be known in ordinary life lived with

---

88. Ibid., 79.
89. Ibid., 388.
90. Ibid. It is worth noting here how their interpretation offers an alternative to the apocalyptic versions of eschatology discussed in Chapter 12.

reverence and responsibility. Paradise is not a place free from suffering or conflict, but it is a place in which Spirit is present and love is possible.[91]

In this perspective, Paradise is not a future endpoint in a transcendent realm.[92] However, their argument for this interpretation also implies what they suggested in the aforementioned quote, namely that it cannot be understood thus without also having to entail suffering and conflict: 'Paradise is not withheld, closed, or removed from us. Realizing this requires us to let go of the notion that paradise is life without struggle, life free from wrestling with legacies of injustice and current forces of evil. Assuredly, we are in a world in which the struggle continues.'[93] Hence, Paradise understood thus suggests active participation in the practices required in order to improve the present situation and escape from the consequences of the climate catastrophe. This understanding of Paradise is relevant for the present predicament and overcomes the deficits under which the symbol has often suffered. They end their book with the following words:

> We reenter this world as sacred space when we love life fiercely and, in the name of love, protect the goodness of earth's intricate web of life in all its manifold forms. We feast in paradise when we open our hearts to lamentation, to amplitudes of grief for all that has been lost and cannot be repaired. [. . .] We recommit ourselves to this world as holy ground when we remember the fullness of life that is possible through our communities, our life-affirming rituals, and our love of beauty. Thus immersed, we are more responsive to and responsible for life in this world. We give thanks for gifts of love that have been ours all along, an ever-widening circle of beauty, the Spirit in life. We enter fully – heart, mind, soul and strength – into savoring and saving paradise.[94]

91. Ibid., 409.

92. Of course, they are not alone in this in the present situation. For example, Catherine Keller also argues as follows:

> In the light of the slow-fast velocity of the crisis and the maddening multiplicity of our issues, we might insist that both political motions, the coming down of sovereignty to earthly responsibility and the becoming of new popular alliances, movements, strikes, cosmopolites, must work in simultaneity. And in the earth, which – as its own cry is heard – becomes audible within all of our agencies. A political theology of the earth will attend with plasticity to the possibilities. If they may come increasingly beclouded by the impossible, what excuse is that for paralysis? Theologically we may translate the eschatological hope for the new heaven and earth, *hashamayitn y haeretz*, quite literally, into the new atmosphere and earth.

Keller, *Intercarnations: Exercises in Theological Possibility*, 192.

93. Brock and Parker, *Saving Paradise: How Christianity Traded Love of This World for Crucifixion and Empire*, 417.

94. Ibid., 420.

Hence, the answer to the question, Where are we going? is answered. We are called to engage the present, practising an Exodus, with a vision of Paradise that calls us to action to benefit the future of this planet. Paradise is not mere futurity. It is the social and the natural together in integrity. This vision shapes our assessment of the present as more than a counter-picture because nature can still engender our response to beauty and wonder, variety, diversity and the awesome. Moreover, no action would be possible unless there was hope for the future. Such hope is inherent in the call for care and justice.

Paradise and Exodus both imply dimensions of salvation. Contemporary employment of the symbols in the Christian tradition cannot locate salvation only in the future, although it also implies a promise for the future. Without such promise, we cannot sustain any hope or any reason to care for creation's future life under our hearts.

CONCLUSION

Christianity represents an enormously large and dynamic symbolic tradition. Its symbols and imaginaries can be applied in a wide variety of contexts. Nevertheless, Christianity originated in contexts with no knowledge or experience that match the present catastrophe we face due to global warming. Accordingly, it is an important task to reconsider the resources of that tradition in order to overcome the deficits, shortcomings and problems that it may manifest if it is to have any lasting impact on believers' orientation in the situation and their motivation for practices that can lead to long-term transformations of the present destructive conditions. The previous chapters have tried to show how such reconsiderations can be done to overcome deficits, but it is a permanent task for the stewards of the tradition to continue to do so. Uncritical repetition of past uses of the symbols is not a viable option. The task is to engage symbols and develop them for the future instead of continuing the deference to past interpretations only.

Part of the deficit in symbols can also be identified in the fact that Christianity has not been a strong advocate of women's experiences. These experiences have not been employed comprehensively in the development of the symbolic reservoir. Although not totally absent, experiences of relationality, embodiment and vulnerability have not been foregrounded. Today we can realize that such experiences and phenomena, as they come to expression in pregnancy, birth and childrearing, may provide a fundamental metaphorical symbol or model for developing virtues and attitudes that allow for a more profound engagement with nature. These experiences allow for a better articulation of the cognitive, emotional and sensual dimensions that can foster the care and concern we need to avoid making future generations the victims of our lifestyle. Although I will not argue that a stronger emphasis on women's experiences previously would have precluded the current situation, it is likely to assume that more attention to these experiences could have provided alternative modes of experiencing the predicament we create in our relationship with nature. Stronger emphasis on such experiences could have provided a more comprehensive range of practices based on love, care, insight, emotion and long-term considerations – in close communication with our and our children's living conditions. Mothers have the direct experience of being responsible for the infant that depends on them. Closeness to experiences of nature's beauty and diversity and the losses and destructions presently taking place are essential elements for motivation and for developing enduring commitment and practices for change.

By pointing to pregnancy, birth and childrearing experiences as a model for our relationship with nature, we can root the care needed in what all humans are involved in, irrespective of their religious traditions. I have tried to show how such experiences are framed and can appear as a meaningful entry to the Christian tradition and how this tradition can interpret such experiences with reference to the present predicament. However, the fact that such experiences are open to interpretation in different religious traditions makes it possible to see them as a fruitful entry point for developing these traditions in a similar manner. Hence, the relevance of what I have done in the previous chapters would, at least methodologically, suggest a potential model for what other religious traditions than Christianity can do, as well.

I have suggested that the person who can serve as a model for responsible conduct and virtuous response to climate change would be the good mother. However, this is not to single out one specific group of humans and idealize them. Many human beings are not, and cannot be, mothers. Neither do I intend to suggest that only actual mothers can serve as models or that women are closer to nature than men are because of their reproductive functions. Such ideas would imply a continuation of patriarchal imagery that has legitimized women's submission under men's interests and control. Instead, seeing good mothers as models for agency that is expressed in responsible conduct and virtuous response is possible because their experiences can help us see the deeper connection that we all have to nature and emulate the responsibility that they take us as one that applies to everyone. We can all be like a good mother by engaging in practices that others can emulate and find inspiration and motivation in – others whom we admire for their consistency, integrity and creativity in finding practices for change. Everyday heroes are not necessarily saints, and they may not be admirable in every respect – given that all humans have flaws and limitations – but such heroes are those who take up the necessary tasks, inspire others and command support for their efforts.

Caring for children and caring for the wider environment and the consequences of climate change are tied closely together. Presently, women struggle with these challenges all over the world. In a recent book, Mary Robinson tells the stories of the diversities of their struggles. It contains examples from Uganda, Mississippi, Alaska, a Sami hometown, Vietnam, Kiribati and Australia. All the women have in common that they consider it as their duty to respond to the impending problems and contribute to helping people adapt to changing circumstances. Robinson wants the testimony of these women and their practices to encourage other people in similar situations to work with hope instead of becoming overwhelmed by hopelessness.[1] Thus, her book also points to how children direct us towards a future for which we need to maintain hope for them and the world at large – together. The benefit of this approach is that it roots what has been said earlier about good mothering in stories about women whose lives have been uprooted

---

1. Mary Robinson and Caitríona Palmer, *Climate Justice: Hope, Resilience, and the Fight for a Sustainable Future* (New York: Bloomsbury, 2019).

by climate change, and who are fighting for the survival not just of their family and communities, but the planet. They have turned their personal struggle for survival into care for the planet and its future. By pointing to their survival and resilience, these stories avoid speaking in the abstract about good mothering: good mothering happens in the midst of structural injustice and violence and takes courage. Thus, these women represent models all humans can emulate.

Some say that humanity heads for a suicide announced a long time ago. This claim represents a worst-case scenario and one that can only be countered by consistent action for another world order, in which we act in faith, hope and love for the Earth and all who live on it. To develop an alternative to the present entails a rejection of the present order and a consistent commitment to change. This commitment cannot be derailed by questions about what we should prioritize: humans or other species and life-forms. It is a false dilemma. We must find ways to care for both. Caring for one is to care for the other and for all. Hence, to overcome traditional anthropocentrism, in religion and otherwise, is the flip side of concentrating on long-term interests for humanity and the rest of our planet. These long-term interests cannot be named 'business as usual' or continue to promote our addiction to consumerism with further material growth as the leading star.

Global warming has made us the victims of our own malpractices. It is up to us to make sure that those who live under our hearts and who represent our hope for the future become less the victims of our conduct than the present prospects tell us. God help us – and them!

* * *

At the site where Ok, the first Icelandic glacier to disappear because of climate change, once was, there is a plaque with a letter written by the poet Andri Snær Magnason. The plaque tells about the glacier's disappearance and the expectation that all the main glaciers in Iceland will follow the same path in the next 200 years. Then the *Letter to the future* reads:

> This monument is to acknowledge that
> We know what is happening
> and what needs to be done.
> Only you know if we did it.[2]

---

2. Cf. Andri Snær Magnason, *On Time and Water* (London, UK: Serpent's Tail, 2020).

BIBLIOGRAPHY

Adams, Marilyn McCord. *Christ and Horrors: The Coherence of Christology*. Cambridge: Cambridge University Press, 2006.
Adorno, Theodor W., and Max Horkheimer. *Dialectic of Enlightenment*. Verso Classics. London: Verso, 1997.
Alison, Stone. 'Adorno and the Disenchantment of Nature'. *Philosophy & Social Criticism* 32, no. 2 (2006): 231–53.
Althaus, Paul. *The Theology of Martin Luther*. Philadelphia: Fortress Press, 1996.
Arendt, Hannah. *The Human Condition*. 2nd edition. Chicago: University of Chicago Press, 1998.
Attanasi, K., and A. Yong. *Pentecostalism and Prosperity: The Socio-Economics of the Global Charismatic Movement*. 1st edition. New York: Palgrave Macmillan, 2012.
Barad, Karen. 'What Flashes Up: Theological-Political-Scientific Fragments'. In *Entangled Worlds: Religion, Science, and New Materialism*, edited by Catherine Keller and May-Jane Rubenstein, 21–88. New York: University of Fordham Press, 2017.
Bauckham, Richard. 'Being Human in the Community of Creation'. In *Ecotheology – a Christian Conversation*, edited by Kiara Jorgenson and Alan G. Padgett, 15–47. Grand Rapids, MI: William B. Eerdmans Publishing Company, 2020.
Bauckham, Richard. *Bible and Ecology: Rediscovering the Community of Creation*. London: Darton, Longman & Todd, 2010.
Baumgartner, Christoph. 'Transformations of Stewardship in the Anthropocene'. In *Religion in the Anthropocene*, edited by Celia Deane-Drummond, Sigurd Bergmann, Markus Vogt and Heinrich Bedford-Strohm, 53–66. Eugene, OR: Cascade, 2017.
Bedford-Strohm, Heinrich. 'Foreword'. In *Religion in the Anthropocene*, edited by Celia Deane-Drummond, Sigurd Bergmann and Markus Vogt. Eugene, OR: Cascade Books, 2017.
Benjamins, Rick. 'Apophatic Panentheism: Catherine Keller's Constructive Theology'. *Neue Zeitschrift für Systematische Theologie und Religionsphilosophie* 60, no. 1 (2018): 103–21.
Bernstein, Richard J. *The Pragmatic Turn*. Cambridge; Malden, MA: Polity, 2010.
Bonneuil, Christophe, and Jean-Baptiste Fressoz. *The Shock of the Anthropocene: The Earth, History, and Us*. London: Verso, 2017.
Bouma-Prediger, Steven. 'The Character of Earthkeeping: A Christian Ecological Virtue Ethic'. In *Ecotheology: A Christian Conversation*, edited by Kiara A. Jorgenson and Alan G. Padgett, 119–52. Grand Rapids, MI: William B. Eerdmans Publishing Company, 2020.
Bouma-Prediger, Steven. *Earthkeeping and Character: Exploring a Christian Ecological Virtue Ethic*. 2020.
Bouma-Prediger, Steven. 'Finding Common Ground on Ecological Virtues'. In *T&T Clark Handbook of Christian Theology and Climate Change*, edited by Ernst M. Conradie and Hilda P. Koster, 178–88. London; New York: T&T Clark, 2020.
Bowen-Moore, Patricia. *Hannah Arendt's Philosophy of Natality*. Basingstoke: Macmillan, 1989.

Brock, Rita Nakashima, and Rebecca Ann Parker. *Saving Paradise: How Christianity Traded Love of This World for Crucifixion and Empire*. Boston: Beacon Press, 2008.

Canovan, Margaret. *The Political Thought of Hannah Arendt*. Albany: State University of New York, 1974.

Carbine, Rosemary P. 'Imagining and Incarnating an Integral Ecology: A Critical Ecofeminist Public Theology'. In *Planetary Solidarity: Global Women's Voices on Christian Doctrine and Climate Justice*, edited by Grace Ji-Sun Kim and Hilda P. Koster, 47–66. Minneapolis: Fortress Pres, 2017.

'The Cathecism of the Catholic Church: Chapter One: The Dignity of the Human Person. Article 7: The Virtues'. https://www.vatican.va/archive/ccc_css/archive/catechism/p3s 1c1a7.htm.

Chaves, Mark. *American Religion: Contemporary Trends*. 2nd edition. Princeton, NJ: Princeton University Press, 2017.

Chodorow, Nancy. *Feminism and Psychoanalytic Theory*. New Haven, CT: Yale University Press, 1989.

Clingerman, Forrest. 'Geoengineering, Theology, and the Meaning of Being Human'. *Zygon* 49, no. 1 (2014): 6–21.

Clingerman, Forrest. 'Theologies of the Climate'. *Religious Studies Review* 42, no. 2 (2016): 71–6.

Coakley, Sarah. *Sacrifice Regained: Reconsidering the Rationality of Religious Belief: An Inaugural Lecture by the Norris-Hulse Professor of Divinity Given in the University of Cambridge, 13 October 2009*. Cambridge, UK: Cambridge University Press, 2012.

Coakley, Sarah. 'Sacrifice Regained: Evolution, Cooperation and God'. In *The Gifford Lectures*: University of Aberdeen, 2012. https://www.giffordlectures.org/lectures/sacr ifice-regained-evolution-cooperation-and-god

Conradie, E. M., and Hilda P. Koster. *T&T Clark Handbook of Christian Theology and Climate Change*. T&T Clark Handbooks Series. London: T&T Clark, 2019.

Conradie, Ernst M. 'The Emergence of Human Sin'. In *T&T Handbook of Christianity & Climate Change*, edited by Ernst M. Conradie and Hilda P. Koster, 384–94. London; New York: Bloomsbury T&T Clark, 2020.

Critchley, Simon, and Robert Bernasconi. *The Cambridge Companion to Levinas*. Cambridge: Cambridge University Press, 2002.

Crutzen, Paul J. 'Geology of Mankind'. *Nature* 415, no. 6867 (2002): 23.

Crutzen, P. J. 'The "Anthropocene"'. In *Earth System Science in the Anthropocene*, edited by Krafft T. Ehlers E. Berlin, 13–18. Heidelberg: Springer, 2006.

Davies, Douglas James. *Emotion, Identity, and Religion: Hope, Reciprocity, and Otherness*. Oxford: Oxford University Press, 2011.

Deacon, Terrence William. *The Symbolic Species: The Co-Evolution of Language and the Brain*. 1st edition. New York: W.W. Norton, 1997.

Deane-Drummond, Celia, Sigurd Bergmann, and Markus Vogt. *Religion in the Anthropocene*. Eugene, OR: Cascade Books, 2017.

Derrida, Jacques. *Given Time: 1. Counterfeit Money*. Chicago: University of Chicago Press, 1992.

Dewey, John. *The Quest for Certainty: A Study of the Relation of Knowledge and Action*. Gifford Lectures. London: Allen & Unwin, 1930.

Donatelli, Piergiorgio. 'The Environment and the Background of Human Life: Nature, Facts, and Values'. In *Facts and Values: The Ethics and Metaphysics of Normativity*, edited by Giancarlo Marchetti and Sarin Marchetti, 246–63. New York: Routledge, 2017.

Douglas, Mary. *Purity and Danger: An Analysis of the Concept of Pollution and Taboo; with a New Preface by the Author*. Routledge Classics. London: Routledge, 2002.

Eaton, Heather. 'An Earth-Centric Theological Framing for Planetary Solidarity'. In *Planetary Solidarity: Global Women's Voices on Christian Doctrine and Climate Justice*, edited by Grace Ji-Sun Kim and Hilda P. Koster, 19–44. Minneapolis: Fortress Press, 2017.

Eaton, Matthew. 'Beyond Human Exceptionalism: Christology in the Anthropocene'. In *Religion in the Anthropocene*, edited by Celia Deane-Drummond, Sigurd Bergmann, Markus Vogt and Heinrich Bedford-Strohm, 202–17. Eugene, OR: Cascade 2018

Edwards, Denis. 'Key Issues in Ecological Theology: Incarnation, Evolution, Communion'. In *Theology and Ecology across the Disciplines: On Care for Our Common Home*, edited by Celia Deane-Drummond and Rebecca Artinian-Kaiser, 65–76. London: Bloomsbury, 2018.

Francis, Pope. *Laudato Si': On Care for Our Common Home*. Frederick, Maryland: The Word Among Us Press, 2015.

Fuentes, Agustín. 'Becoming Human in the Anthropocene'. In *Religion in the Anthropocene*, edited by Celia Deane-Drummond, Sigurd Bergmann and Markus Vogt, 103–18. Eugene, OR: Cascade, 2017.

Gardner, Gary. 'Engaging Religions to Shape Worldviews'. In *2010 State of the World: Transforming Cultures: From Consumerism to Sustainability* edited by Erik Assadourian, Linda Starke and Lisa Mastny, 244. New York; London: W. W. Norton & Company, 2010.

Gebara, Ivone. 'Women's Suffering, Climate Injustice, God, and Pope Francis' Theology: Some Insights from Brazil'. In: *Planetary Solidarity: Global Women's Voices on Christian Doctrine and Climate Justice*, edited by Grace Ji-Sun Kim and Hilda P. Koster, 67–80. Minneapolis: Fortress Press, 2017.

Gilkey, Langdon. *Nature, Reality, and the Sacred: The Nexus of Science and Religion*. Minneapolis: Fortress Press, 1993.

Girard, René. *The Scapegoat*. London: Athlone Press, 1986.

Girard, René. *Violence and the Sacred*. London New York: Continuum 2005.

Gregersen, Niels Henrik. 'Christology'. In *Systematic Theology and Climate Change: Ecumenical Perspectives*, edited by Michael S. Northcott and Peter M. Scott, 33–50. London; New York: Routledge, 2014.

Grenholm, Cristina. *Motherhood and Love: Beyond the Gendered Stereotypes of Theology*. Grand Rapids, MI: William B. Eerdmans Publishing Company, 2011.

Grube, Dirk-Martin, and Walter Van Herck. *Philosophical Perspectives on Religious Diversity Bivalent Truth, Tolerance and Personhood*. London: Routledge, 2018.

Gschwandtner, Christina M. 'Ricoeur's Hermeneutic of God: A Symbol That Gives Rise to Thought'. *Philosophy and Theology* 13, no. 2 (2001): 287–309.

Gudmundsdottir, Arnfridur. 'The Fire Alarm Is Off: A Feminist Theological Reflection on Sin, Climate Change, Energy, and the Protection of Wilderness in Iceland'. In *Planetary Solidarity: Global Women's Voices on Christian Doctrine and Climate Justice*, edited by Grace Ji-Sun Kim and Hilda P. Koster, 135–54. Minneapolis: Fortress Press, 2017.

Habermas, Jürgen. *Auch Eine Geschichte Der Philosophie Band 1: Die Okzidentale Konstellation Von Glauben Und Wissen Band 2: Vernünftige Freiheit. Spuren Des Diskurses Über Glauben Und Wissen*. Frankfurt: Suhrkamp, 2019.

Habermas, Jürgen. *Knowledge and Human Interests*. 2nd edition. London: Heinemann, 1978.

Haraway, Donna. 'Anthropocene, Capitalocene, Plantationocene, Chthulucene: Making Kin'. *Environmental Humanities* 6, no. 1 (2015): 159–65.
Hartman, Laura M. 'Consumption'. In *Routledge Handbook of Religion and Ecology*, edited by Willis Jenkins, Mary Evelyn Tucker and John Grim, 316–25. London: Routledge, 2017.
Harvey, David. 'The "New" Imperialism: Accumulation by Dispossession'. In *The New Imperial Challenge*, edited by Colin Leys and Leo Panitch, 63–87. London: Merlin, 2004.
Hasler, Ueli. *Beherrschte Natur: Die Anpassung Der Theologie an Die Bürgerliche Naturauffassung Im 19. Jahrhundert (Schleiermacher, Ritschl, Hermann)*. Basler Und Berner Studien Zur Historischen Und Systematischen Theologie. Bern: P. Lang, 1982.
Hayhoe, Katharine. 'Foreword'. In *Ecotheology: A Christian Conversation*, edited by Kiara A. Jorgenson and Alan G. Padgett, xiii–xviii. Grand Rapids, MI: William B. Eerdmans Publishing Company, 2020.
Heidegger, Martin. *Being and Time*. Oxford: Basil Blackwell, 1962.
Heim, S. Mark. *Saved from Sacrifice: A Theology of the Cross*. Grand Rapids, MI: William B. Eerdmans Publishing Company, 2006.
Henriksen, Jan-Olav. 'Body, Nature and Norm'. *Irish Theological Quarterly* 55, no. 4 (1989): 308–23.
Henriksen, Jan-Olav. *Christianity as Distinct Practices: A Complicated Relationship*. London: Bloomsbury T&T Clark, 2019.
Henriksen, Jan-Olav. *Desire, Gift, and Recognition: Christology and Postmodern Philosophy*. Grand Rapids, MI: William B. Eerdmans Publishing Company, 2009.
Henriksen, Jan-Olav. 'God in Martin Luther'. *Oxford Research Encyclopedia of Religion*. 5 Aug. 2016; Accessed 26 Aug. 2021. https://oxfordre.com/religion/view/10.1093/acrefore/9780199340378.001.0001/acrefore-9780199340378-e-325.
Henriksen, Jan-Olav. 'God Revealed through Human Agency – Divine Agency and Embodied Practices of Faith, Hope, and Love'. *Neue Zeitschrift für systematische Theologie und Religionsphilosophie* 58, no. 4 (2016): 453–72.
Henriksen, Jan-Olav. *Grobunn for Moral: Om Å Være Moralsk Subjekt I En Postmoderne Kultur*. Oslo: Cappelen Damm Høyskoleforlaget, 1997.
Henriksen, Jan-Olav. 'Hope – a Theological Exploration'. *Studia theologica* 73, no. 2 (2019): 117–33.
Henriksen, Jan-Olav. *Imago Dei. Den Teologiske Konstruksjonen Av Menneskets Identitet*. Oslo: Gyldendal akademisk, 2003.
Henriksen, Jan-Olav. *Life, Love, and Hope: God and Human Experience*. Grand Rapids, MI: William B. Eerdmans Publishing Company, 2014.
Henriksen, Jan-Olav. Mennesket Som Natur: *En Systematisk-Teologisk Analyse Av Forholdet Mellom Antropologi Og Naturforståelse I Wolfhart Pannenbergs Teologi*. Oslo: Det teologiske Menighetsfakultet, 1989.
Henriksen, Jan-Olav. *Relating God and the Self: Dynamic Interplay*. Farnham: Ashgate, 2013.
Henriksen, Jan-Olav. *Religion as Orientation and Transformation: A Maximalist Theory*. Religion in Philosophy and Theology. Tübingen: Mohr Siebeck, 2017.
Henriksen, Jan-Olav, and Bispemøtet. *The Consumer Society as an Ethical Challenge: Report for the Norwegian Bishop's Conference 1992*. 2nd edition. Oslo: Church of Norway Information Service, 1995.
Herman, S. W. 'On Primal Fear and Confidence: Reinterpreting the Myth of the Flood as the Climate Changes'. *Word & World* 29, no. 1 (2009): 63–74.

Hewitt, Andrew. 'A Feminine Dialectic of Enlightenment? Horkheimer and Adorno Revisited'. *New German Critique* 56 (1992): 143–70.

Hursthouse, Rosalind, and Glen Pettigrove. 'Virtue Ethics'. In *The Stanford Encyclopedia of Philosophy*, edited by Edward N. Zalta. Stanford, 2018.

Ingold, Tim. *Perception of the Environment: Essays on Livelihood, Dwelling and Skill*. London: Routledge, 2011.

Jeanrond, Werner. *Reasons to Hope*. London: Bloomsbury T&T Clark, 2019.

Jenkins, Willis. *The Future of Ethics – Sustainability, Social Justice, and Religious Creativity*. Georgetown: Georgetown University Press, 2013.

Jenkins, Willis. 'After Lynn White: Religious Ethics and Environmental Problems'. *The Journal of Religious Ethics* 37, no. 2 (2009): 283–309.

Jonas, Hans. *Das Prinzip Verantwortung: Versuch Einer Ethik Für Die Technologische Zivilisation*. Bibliothek Suhrkamp. 1. Aufl. Frankfurt am Main: Suhrkamp, 1989.

Jonas, Hans. *The Phenomenon of Life: Toward a Philosophical Biology; Essays*. 1st edition. New York: Harper & Row, 1966.

Jonas, Hans, and Lawrence Vogel. *Mortality and Morality: A Search for the Good after Auschwitz*. Northwestern University Studies in Phenomenology and Existential Philosophy. Evanston, IL: Northwestern University Press, 1996.

Jones, James William. *Religion and Psychology in Transition: Psychoanalysis, Feminism, and Theology*. New Haven, CT: Yale University Press, 1996.

Jones, Serene. *Feminist Theory and Christian Theology: Cartographies of Grace*. Guides to Theological Inquiry. Minneapolis: Fortress Press, 2000.

Jorgenson, Kiara, and Alan G. Padgett. *Ecotheology – a Christian Conversation*. Grand Rapids, MI: William B. Eerdmans Publishing Company, 2020.

Kaufman, Gordon D. 'A Problem for Theology: The Concept of Nature'. *The Harvard Theological Review* 65, no. 3 (1972): 337–66.

Keller, Catherine. *Apocalypse Now and Then: A Feminist Guide to the End of the World*. Boston: Beacon Press, 1996.

Keller, Catherine. *Facing Apocalypse: Climate, Democracy, and Other Last Chances*. Maryknoll, NY: Orbis Books, 2021.

Keller, Catherine. 'The Heat Is On: Apocalyptic Rhetoric and Climate Change'. *Journal for the Study of Religion, Nature and Culture* 7 (1999): 40–58.

Keller, Catherine. '"I Can't Breathe": The Whole Earth Echoes the Cry for Justice'. *ABC Net*, https://www.abc.net.au/religion/catherine-keller-i-cant-breathe-the-cry-for-justice/12332954.

Keller, Catherine. *Intercarnations: Exercises in Theological Possibility*. 1st edition. New York: Fordham University Press, 2017.

Keller, Catherine. *On the Mystery: Discerning Divinity in Process*. Minneapolis, MN: Fortress Press, 2008.

Keller, Evelyn Fox, and Jane Flax. 'Missing Relations in Psychoanalysis: A Feminist Critique of Traditional and Contemporary Accounts of Analytic Theory and Practice'. In *Hermeneutics and Psychological Theory: Interpretative Perspectives on Personality, Psychotherapy and Psychopathology*, edited by S. B. Messer, L. A. Sass, and R. L., Woolfolk, 334–69. New Brunswick: Rutgers University Press, 1988.

Kirchhoffer, David G. 'How Ecology Can Save the Life of Theology: A Philosophical Contribution to the Engagement of Ecology and Theology'. In *Theology and Ecology across the Disciplines: On Care for Our Common Home*, edited by Celia Deane-Drummond and Rebecca Artinian-Kaiser, 53–64. London: Bloomsbury, 2018.

Kloster, Sven Thore, Gina Lende, Ole Jakob Løland, and Vebjørn L. Horsfjord. *Global Kristendom: En Samtidshistorie*. Oslo: Universitetsforl, 2018.

Konisky, David M. 'The Greening of Christianity? A Study of Environmental Attitudes over Time'. *Environmental Politics* 27, no. 2 (2018): 267–91.

Kvanvig, Jonathan L. *The Problem of Hell*. New York; Oxford: Oxford University Press, 1993.

Lakoff, George, and Mark Johnson. *Metaphors We Live By*. Chicago: University of Chicago Press, 2003.

Latour, Bruno, and Catherine Porter. *Facing Gaia: Eight Lectures on the New Climatic Regime*. Cambridge: Polity Press, 2017.

Lenfesty, Hillary L., and Thomas J. H. Morgan. 'By Reverence, Not Fear: Prestige, Religion, and Autonomic Regulation in the Evolution of Cooperation'. *Frontiers in Psychology* 10 (2019): 1–13.

Lévinas, Emmanuel. *The Levinas Reader*. New York, NY: B. Blackwell, 1989.

Lévinas, Emmanuel. 'Substitution'. In *The Levinas Reader*, edited by Seán Hand, 88–126. Oxford; Cambridge, MA, USA: B. Blackwell, 1989.

Lewis, S. L., and M. A. Maslin. 'Defining the Anthropocene'. *Nature* 519, no. 7542 (2015): 171–80.

Luther, Martin, and F. Samuel Janzow. *Luther's Large Catechism: A Contemporary Translation with Study Questions*. St. Louis: Concordia Pub. House, 1988.

Lysaker, Odin. 'Ecological Love: Reflections on Morality's Existential Preconditions'. In *Between Closeness and Evil: A Festschrift for Arne Johan Vetlesen*, edited by Odin Lysaker, 55–88. Oslo: Scandinavian Academic Press, 2020.

MacIntyre, Alasdair C. *After Virtue: A Study in Moral Theory*. 2nd edition. London: Duckworth, 1985.

Magnason, Andri Snær. *On Time and Water*. London, UK: Serpent's Tail, 2020.

Mauss, Marcel. *The Gift: The Form and Reason for Exchange in Archaic Societies*. London: Routledge, 1990.

McDaniel, Jay B. 'The Passion of Christ: Grace Both Red and Green'. In *Cross Examinations: Readings on the Meaning of the Cross*, edited by Marit Trelstad, 196–207. Minneapolis, MN: Fortress Press, 2006.

McFague, Sallie. *Blessed Are the Consumers: Climate Change and the Practice of Restraint*. Minneapolis, Minnesota: Fortress Press, 2013.

McFague, Sallie. *The Body of God: An Ecological Theology*. London: SCM, 1993.

McFague, Sallie. *Models of God: Theology for an Ecological Nuclear Age*. London: SCM, 1987.

McFague, Sallie. *A New Climate for Theology: God, the World, and Global Warming*. Minneapolis, MN: Fortress Press, 2008.

Mercer, Joyce Ann. 'Environmental Activism in the Philippines: A Practical Theological Perspective'. In *Planetary Solidarity: Global Women's Voices on Christian Doctrine and Climate Justice*, edited by Grace Ji-Sun Kim and Hilda P. Koster, 287–308. Minneapolis: Fortress Press, 2017.

Merleau-Ponty, Maurice. *Phenomenology of Perception*. New York: Humanities Press, 1962.

Moe-Lobeda, Cynthia D. 'Finding Common Ground on a Moral Vision for a Good Society'. In *T&T Clark Handbook of Christian Theology and Climate Change*, edited by Ernst M. Conradie and Hilda P. Koster, 157–73. London: New York: T&T Clark, 2020.

Moe-Lobeda, Cynthia D. 'Response to Steven Bouma-Prediger'. In *Ecotheology: A Christian Conversation*, edited by Kiara A. Jorgenson and Alan G. Padgett, 156–60. Grand Rapids, MI: William B. Eerdmans Publishing Company, 2020.

Moe-Lobeda, Cynthia D. 'Climate Change as Climate Debt: Forging a Just Future'. *Journal of the Society of Christian Ethics* 36, no. 1 (2016): 27–49.

Moe-Lobeda, Cynthia D. *Resisting Structural Evil: Love as Ecological and Economic Vocation*. Minneapolis, MN: Fortress Press, 2013.

Moe-Lobeda, Cynthia D. *Living for the Future: Theological Ethics for Coming Generations*. London; New York: T&T Clark, 2008.

Mueller, Martin Lee. 'Cascades of Giving: A More-Than-Human Ontology of the Gift-Giving Principle'. In *Between Closeness and Evil: A Festschrift for Arne Johan Vetlesen*, edited by Odin Lysaker, 125–52. Oslo: Scandinavian Academic Press, 2020.

Muers, Rachel. 'Idolatry and Future Generations: The Persistence of Molech'. *Modern Theology* 19, no. 4 (2003): 547–61.

Mundey, Peter. 'The Prosperity Gospel and the Spirit of Consumerism According to Joel Osteen'. *PNEUMA* 39, no. 3 (2017): 318–41.

Maathai, Wangari. *Replenishing the Earth: Spiritual Values for Healing Ourselves and the World*. 1st edition. New York; London: Doubleday, 2010.

Nelson, Eric S. 'Revisiting the Dialectic of Environment: Nature as Ideology and Ethics in Adorno and the Frankfurt School'. *Telos* 155 (2011): 105–27.

Neril, Yonathan, Dee, Leo Mark. *Eco Bible: An Ecological Commentary on Genesis and Exodus*. The Interfaith Center for Sustainable Development, 2020.

Neville, Robert C. *Defining Religion: Essays in Philosophy of Religion*. Albany, NY: State University of New York, 2018.

Neville, Robert C. *The Truth of Broken Symbols*. Suny Series in Religious Studies. Albany: State University of New York Press, 1996.

Northcott, Michael S. 'Do Dolphins Carry the Cross? Biological Moral Realism and Theological Ethics'. *New Blackfriars* 84, no. 994 (2003): 540–53.

Northcott, Michael S. *A Political Theology of Climate Change*. Grand Rapids, MI: William B. Eerdmans Publishing Company, 2013.

Northcott, Michael S. *Systematic Theology and Climate Change: Ecumenical Perspectives*. London; New York: Routledge, Taylor & Francis Group, 2014.

Nowak, M. A., and Sarah Coakley. *Evolution, Games, and God: The Principle of Cooperation*. Cambridge, MA: Harvard University Press, 2013.

Pannenberg, Wolfhart, and Niels Henrik Gregersen. *The Historicity of Nature: Essays on Science and Theology*. West Conshohocken, PA: Templeton Foundation Press, 2008.

Pihlström, Sami. *The Bloomsbury Companion to Pragmatism*. Bloomsbury Companions. London: Bloomsbury Academic, 2015.

Pineda-Madrid, Nancy. '¡Somos Criaturas De Dios! Seeing and Beholding the Garden of God'. In *Planetary Solidarity: Global Women's Voices on Christian Doctrine and Climate Justice*, edited by Grace Ji-Sun Kim and Hilda P. Koster, 311–24. Minneapolis: Fortress Press, 2017.

Poe, Ibo van de. 'The Relation between Forward-Looking and Backward-Looking Responsibility'. In *Moral Responsibility: Beyond Free Will and Determinism*, edited by Nicole A. Vincent, Ibo van de Poel and Jeroen van den Hoven, 37–52. New York: Springer, 2011.

Porterfield, Amanda. *Healing in the History of Christianity*. Oxford; New York: Oxford University Press, 2005.

Portin, Fredrik. 'Consumerism as a Moral Attitude: Defining Consumerism Through the Works of Pope Francis, Cornel West, and William T. Cavanaugh'. *Studia theologica* 74, no. 1 (2020): 4–24.

Primavesi, Anne. *Gaia and Climate Change: A Theology of Gift Events*. London; New York: Routledge, 2009.

Rasmussen, Larry, and Paul Santmire et al. *God's Earth Is Sacred: Essays on Eco-Justice*. National Council of Churches Eco-Justice Program, 2011.

Rasmussen, Larry L. *Earth-Honoring Faith: Religious Ethics in a New Key*. New York: Oxford University Press, 2013.

Richter, Horst-Eberhard. *Der Gotteskomplex: Die Geburt Und Die Krise Des Glaubens an Die Allmacht Des Menschen*. Hamburg: Rowohlt, 1979.

Ricoeur, Paul. *Figuring the Sacred: Religion, Narrative, and Imagination*. Translated by David Pellauer. Minneapolis: Augsburg Fortress, 1995.

Ricoeur, Paul. *The Symbolism of Evil*. Religious Perspectives. New York: Harper & Row, 1967.

Ricoeur, Paul, Robert Czerny, Kathleen McLaughlin, and John Costello. *The Rule of Metaphor: Multi-Disciplinary Studies of the Creation of Meaning in Language*. London: Routledge & Kegan Paul, 1978.

Robinson, Andrew. *God and the World of Signs: Trinity, Evolution, and the Metaphysical Semiotics of C. S. Peirce*. Philosophical Studies in Science and Religion. Leiden; Boston: Brill, 2010.

Robinson, Andrew. *Traces of the Trinity: Signs, Sacraments and Sharing God's Life*. London: James Clarke & Co, 2014.

Robinson, Mary, and Caitríona Palmer. *Climate Justice: Hope, Resilience, and the Fight for a Sustainable Future*. New York: Bloomsbury, 2019.

Rossing, Barbara R. 'Reimagining Eschatology: Toward Healing and Hope for a World at the Eschatos'. In *Planetary Solidarity: Global Women's Voices on Christian Doctrine and Climate Justice*, edited by Grace Ji-Sun Kim and Hilda P. Koster, 323–45. Minneapolis: Fortress Press, 2017.

Rowe, Terra Schwerin. *Toward a Better Worldliness: Ecology, Economy, and the Protestant Tradition*. Minneapolis, MN: Fortress Press, 2017.

Rutherford, Paul. *The Problem of Nature in Contemporary Social Theory*. Canberra: Australian National University, 2000.

Schloss, Jeffrey P., and Michael J. Murray. 'Evolutionary Accounts of Belief in Supernatural Punishment: A Critical Review'. *Religion, Brain & Behavior* 1, no. 1 (2011): 46–99.

Schloss, Jeffrey P., and Michael J. Murray. 'How Might Evolution Lead to Hell?'. *Religion, Brain & Behavior* 1, no. 1 (2011/02/01 2011): 93–99.

Schneider, Laurel C. et al. *Awake to the Moment: An Introduction to Theology*. 1st edition. Louisville, KY: Westminster John Knox Press, 2016.

Schwöbel, Christoph. 'Divine Agency and Providence'. *Modern Theology* 3, no. 3 (1987): 225–44.

Schaab, G. L. 'A Procreative Paradigm of the Creative Suffering of the Triune God: Implications of Arthur Peacocke's Evolutionary Theology'. *Theological Studies* 67, no. 3 (2006): 542–66.

Smith, Christian. *Religion: What It Is, How It Works, and Why It Is Still Important*. Princeton: Princeton University Press, 2017.

Stout, Jeffrey. *Blessed Are the Organized: Grassroots Democracy in America*. Princeton, N.J.: Princeton University Press, 2010.

Straume, Ingerid S. 'That Which Depends on Us: Responsibility, Democratic Courage and Shame'. In *L'autonomie En Pratique(S)*, edited by Caumières Philippe and Klimis Sophie, 157–78. Saint-Louis: Presses de l'Université Saint-Louis, 2019.

Streufert, Mary J. 'Maternal Sacrifice as a Hermeneutics of the Cross'. In *Cross Examinations: Readings on the Meaning of the Cross*, edited by Marit Trelstad, 63–75. Minneapolis, MN: Fortress Press, 2006.

Saarinen, Risto. *God and the Gift: An Ecumenical Theology of Giving*. Unitas Books. Collegeville, MN: Liturgical Press, 2005.

Tanner, Kathryn. *Christianity and the New Spirit of Capitalism*. New Haven: Yale University Press, 2019.

Tanner, Kathryn. *Economy of Grace*. Minneapolis: Fortress Press, 2005.

Tanner, Kathryn. *Jesus, Humanity and the Trinity: A Brief Systematic Theology*. Scottish Journal of Theology. Current Issues in Theology. Edinburgh: T&T Clark, 2001.

Taylor, Charles. 'Buffered and Porous Selves'. In *The Immanent Frame*, 2008. https://tif.ssrc.org/2008/09/02/buffered-and-porous-selves/

Taylor, Charles. *Human Agency and Language*. Cambridge, UK; New York: Cambridge University Press, 1985.

Terrell, JoAnne Marie. 'Our Mother's Gardens'. In *Cross-Examinations: Readings on the Meaning of the Cross Today*, edited by Marit Trelstad, 33–49. Minneapolis, MN: Fortress Press, 2006.

Terrell, JoAnne Marie. *Power in the Blood?: The Cross in the African American Experience*. Eugene, OR: Wipf & Stock Publishers, 2005.

Tillich, Paul. *Systematic Theology (Volume 1)*. London: SCM Press, 1978.

Timm, Hermann. 'Evangelische Weltweisheit: Zur Kritik Der Ökotheologischen Apokalyptik'. *Zeitschrift für Theologie und Kirche* 84, no. 3 (1987): 345–70.

Trelstad, Marit. *Cross Examinations: Readings on the Meaning of the Cross*. Minneapolis, MN: Fortress Press, 2006.

Troster, Lawrence. 'Caretaker or Citizen: Hans Jonas, Aldo Leopold, and the Development of Jewish Environmental Ethics'. In *The Legacy of Hans Jonas: Judaism and the Phenomenon of Life*, edited by Hava Tirosh-Samuelson and Christian Wiese, 373–96. Leiden; Boston: Brill, 2010.

Veldman, Robin Globus. *The Gospel of Climate Skepticism: Why Evangelical Christians Oppose Action on Climate Change*. Oakland, CA: University of California Press, 2019.

Veldman, Robin Globus, Andrew Szasz, and Randolph Haluza-DeLay. 'Social Science, Religions, and Climate Change'. In *How the World's Religions Are Responding to Climate Change: Social Scientific Investigations*, edited by Robin Globus Veldman, Andrew Szasz and Randolph Haluza-DeLay, 3–20. London: Routledge, 2016.

Vetlesen, Arne Johan. *Cosmologies of the Anthropocene: Panpsychism, Animism, and the Limits of Posthumanism*. 1 edition. New York: Routledge, 2019.

Vetlesen, Arne Johan. *The Denial of Nature: Environmental Philosophy in the Era of Global Capitalism*. Ontological Explorations. London: Routledge, 2015.

Vetlesen, Arne Johan. *Evil and Human Agency: Understanding Collective Evildoing*. Cambridge Cultural Social Studies. Cambridge: Cambridge University Press, 2005.

Vetlesen, Arne Johan. *Perception, Empathy, and Judgement: An Inquiry into the Preconditions of Moral Performance*. University Park, PA: Pennsylvania State University Press, 1994.

Vetlesen, Arne Johan, and Rasmus Willig. *Hva Skal Vi Svare Våre Barn?* Oslo: Dreyer, 2018.

Vincent, Nicole A. 'A Structured Taxonomy of Responsibility Concepts'. In *Moral Responsibility: Beyond Free Will and Determinism*, edited by Nicole A. Vincent, Ibo van de Poel and Jeroen van den Hove, 15–35. New York: Springer, 2011.

Weaver, J. Denny. *The Nonviolent Atonement*. Grand Rapids, MI: William B. Eerdmans Publishing Company, 2001.

Wenzel, Knut. *Negativistic Affirmation – Doing Theology in a Secular World*. University of Oslo Guest Lecture, 2019.

Wenzel, Knut. 'The Other Language: Religion in Modernity'. In *Dynamics of Difference: Christianity and Alterity: A Festschrift for Werner G. Jeanrond*, edited by James Matarazzo Ulrich Schmiedel, 153–60. London: Bloomsbury, 2015.

West, Cornel. *Democracy Matters: Winning the Fight against Imperialism*. New York: The Penguin Press, 2004.

Whitebook, J. 'The Problem of Nature in Habermas'. *Telos* 1979, no. 40 (1979): 41–69.

Whitney, Elspeth. 'Lynn White Jr.'s "The Historical Roots of Our Ecologic Crisis" after 50 Years'. *History Compass* 13, no. 8 (2015): 396–410.

Williams, Delores S. 'Black Women's Surrogacy Experience and the Christian Notion of Redemption'. In *Cross Examinations: Readings on the Meaning of the Cross*, edited by Marit Trelstad, 19–32. Minneapolis, MN: Fortress Press, 2006.

Williams, Delores S. *Sisters in the Wilderness: The Challenge of Womanist God-Talk*. Maryknoll, New York: Orbis Books, 2013.

Williams, Rowan. *On Christian Theology*. Challenges in Contemporary Theology. Oxford; Malden, MA: Blackwell, 2000.

Wilson, Edward O. *Biophilia*. Cambridge, MA: Harvard University Press, 2019.

Wirzba, Norman. *The Paradise of God: Renewing Religion in an Ecological Age*. Oxford: Oxford University Press, 2003.

Wuthnow, Robert. *What Happens When We Practice Religion?: Textures of Devotion in Everyday Life*. Princeton: Princeton University Press, 2020.

Zackariasson, Ulf. 'Religious Agency as Vehicle and Source of Critique'. In *The Reformation of Philosophy*, edited by Marius Timmann Mjaaland, 209–20. Tübingen: Mohr Siebeck, 2020.

Zagzebski, Linda. 'Admiration and the Admirable'. *Supplement to the Proceedings of The Aristotelian Society* 89, no. 1 (2015): 205–21.

Zagzebski, Linda. 'Moral Exemplars in Theory and Practice'. *Theory and Research in Education* 11, no. 2 (2013): 193–206.

Zagzebski, Linda Trinkaus. *Exemplarist Moral Theory*. New York: Oxford University Press, 2019.

Zaleha, Daniel Bernard. *A Tale of Two Christianities: The Religiopolitical Clash over Climate Change within America's Dominant Religion*, University of California Santa Cruz Dissertation, 2018.

Zerubavel, Eviatar. *Social Mindscapes: An Invitation to Cognitive Sociology*. Cambridge, MA: Harvard University Press, 1997.

NAMES INDEX

Adorno, Theodor W.   9, 18–25, 31, 47, 55, 79, 80, 90
Arendt, Hannah   153–9, 161, 162, 168, 185, 216
Aristotle   91, 96, 114

Bartholomew, Metropolitan   167
Bauckham, Richard   143–4
Benjamins, Rick   171, 173
Bouma-Prediger, Steven   164–6
Bowen-Moore, Patricia   156
Brock, Rita Nakashima   245–7
Buber, Martin   25

Carbine, Rosemary   51–2
Carson, Rachel   123
Chodorow, Nancy   78–80, 128
Coakley, Sarah   227–33
Conradie, Ernst   185–7
Crutzen, Paul   12

Dalferth, Ingolf U.   242
Deacon, Terrence W.   71–3
Derrida, Jacques   214–17
Dewey, John   127
Douglas, Mary   219

Eaton, Heather   38
Edwards, Denis   125

Flax, Jane   79
Francis, Pope   35, 36
Francis of Assisi   17, 18

Gardner, Gary   32
Girard, René   222, 225, 226
Gregersen, Niels Henrik   204–9
Gudmundsdottir, Arnfridur   182–5

Habermas, Jürgen   22, 24, 55, 88–90, 92, 94, 96
Haraway, Donna   53

Harvey, David   28
Heidegger, Martin   201–2, 206
Hewitt, Andrew   23
Horkheimer, Max   9, 18–24, 31, 47, 79, 80, 90

Jeanrond, Werner   235, 236, 242
Jenkins, Willis   109
Johnson, Mark   73, 75–7
Jonas, Hans   146, 151–4, 158, 168, 179
Jones, James W.   79–82, 128
Jones, Serene   50

Kant, Immanuel   21, 22, 55, 84, 87, 146, 152
Keller, Catherine   24, 80, 171–3
Keller, Evelyn Fox   79
Kirchhoffer, David G.   122–4
Koster, Hilda   47–8

Lakoff, George   73, 75–7
Latour, Bruno   146–9
Lenfesty, Hilary   101–2, 104
Lévinas, Emmanuel   146–8
Lewis, Simon L.   12
Luther, Martin   30, 134–8, 178, 188
Lysaker, Odin   93–4

Maathai, Wangari   178
McCord Adams, Marilyn   196–7, 213, 214
McDaniel, Jay B.   223, 238–41
McFague, Sallie   11, 203, 208–12
MacIntyre, Alasdair   115, 145
Magnason, Andri Snær   252
Marx, Karl   1, 127
Mary (Mother of Jesus)   168
Maslin, Mark   12
Mauss, Michel   214
Moe-Lobeda, Cynthia D.   183–4, 191, 194
Morgan, Tom   101–2, 104
Moses   168
Murray, Michel, P.   100–1

Næss, Arne 1
Narvarez, Darcia 116
Nelson, Eric A. 19, 21, 22, 24, 59, 86
Neville, Robert C. 62–7, 73, 76, 129, 173–4
Northcott, Michael 114–17

Parker, Rebecca Ann 245–7
Peirce, Charles S. 59, 61–2
Peterson, Anna 109
Pineda-Madrid, Nancy 5
Portin, Fredrik 29, 35–6
Primavesi, Anna 218

Ricoeur, Paul 73, 159, 208
Robinson, Mary 251
Rossing, Barbara 175–8

Schloss, Jeffrey P. 100–1
Schwerin-Rowe, Terra 56, 237–8
Streufert, Mary 234, 235

Tanner, Kathryn 213, 216–18

Taylor, Charles 84–6, 88, 128
Thunberg, Greta 108, 145, 167
Tillich, Paul 61–2, 70, 122, 162, 166
Timm, Hermann 174
Trump, Donald J. 100

Veldman, Robin G. 38–43, 77, 78, 181
Vetlesen, Arne Johan 13, 22, 44, 88–91, 93–5, 113, 146, 149, 150, 225–6

Wenzel, Knut 20, 87
West, Cornel 36
Whitebook, Joel 89, 92
White Jr., Lynn 9, 16–19, 21, 25, 42, 54, 71, 139, 145
Wilson, Edward O. 231
Wittgenstein, Ludwig 59

Zackariasson, Ulf 67–8
Zagzebski, Linda T. 104–8, 111, 113, 114, 166, 167
Zerubavel, Eviatar 77

SUBJECTS INDEX

act(s) of God 11–12, 14–15, 53, 216
admiration 103, 105–8, 110, 166, 167
agency, human 5, 6, 8, 11, 15, 21–3, 25, 26, 31, 53–7, 61, 66, 68, 70, 75, 83–8, 91–9, 103, 109–11, 127, 128, 136, 138, 142, 145, 146, 148–9, 151, 152, 154–6, 158–62, 167, 172–4, 180–2, 184, 187, 191, 195, 197, 200, 205, 210, 212, 216, 237, 251
aggression/aggressive 78, 80, 101, 104
alienation 186
altruism 110, 176, 228–32
Amor mundi (in H. Arendt) 154, 156, 159
androcentric 50, 160
Anthropocene 9, 11–13, 15, 18, 53–5, 137, 139, 144, 149, 154, 161, 199, 200, 233, 235
anthropocentrism/anthropocentric 17, 25, 43–6, 48, 50, 88, 90, 93, 98, 117, 123, 137, 149, 152–3, 160, 161, 186, 203, 204, 214, 252
apocalyptism/apocalyptic 171–5

birth 115, 139, 151, 154–7, 176, 211, 216, 232–4, 250, 251
body/bodies 91, 93, 94, 128, 133, 136, 160, 161, 167, 177, 189, 200–1, 203–11, 213, 221, 224, 233, 234, 241, *see also* embodiment/embodied
broken symbols 62
business as usual 4, 134, 179, 252

care, environmental 109, 146, 156, 165, 168, 201, 202, 211, 252
caregiver 48, 78, 109, 166
carrot (type of moral motivation) 98–9
Catastrophism 13
Cathedral builder attitude 145
child/children 45, 67, 86, 108, 109, 111, 112, 115, 117, 153–5, 161–3, 166, 168, 189, 190, 192, 207, 211, 218, 219, 228, 233, 234, 250–1
Christian Right 41–2

climate scepticism 39–42
consumerism 9, 19, 29, 32, 34–7, 45, 47, 180, 190, 252
consumer society 119, 156, 188, 227, 239, 243
control (over nature) 1, 11, 13, 15, 20, 21, 23, 31, 69, 80–1, 83, 84, 88, 94, 101, 112, 123, 128, 164, 172, 187, 189, 204, 218, 235, 237, 239, 242, 251
courage/courageous 105, 114, 167, 233, 234, 246, 252
Covid-19 (pandemic) 27, 134, 176, 193

death 24, 29, 33, 37, 39, 54, 68, 94, 95, 133–5, 137, 162, 176, 193, 213, 217, 222–7, 233, 234, 243, 245
deductive theology 121, 171, 174
deep incarnation 204, 206–7
defection 98, 100–2, 229, 231
dependence/interdependence 14, 20, 24, 29, 47, 48, 53, 55, 68–70, 78, 86, 91, 94, 96, 115–17, 134, 140, 153, 156, 158, 189, 190, 207, 208, 210–11, 214, 221, 226, 244, 247
desert 192–3, 206
desire(s) 29, 33–6, 70, 81, 84, 85, 98, 103–5, 107, 110, 112, 119, 145, 186, 189, 192, 210, 225, 236, 246
detachment/detached 55, 57, 67, 75, 81, 83, 90, 99, 105, 111, 127, 212
dispossession 28–9
domination 16, 19, 21, 24, 79–81, 85, 86, 92, 183, 186
dominion, human 18, 19, 21, 23, 144, 189
dualism 147, 247

embodiment/embodied 23–6, 55, 57, 70, 74, 77, 81, 82, 84, 91–3, 115, 117, 151, 157, 160, 161, 199–201, 203, 204, 207, 210, 213, 234, 250
emotion/emotional 4, 47, 65, 66, 70, 79–84, 86, 94, 103, 104, 106–8, 111,

112, 115, 117, 120, 138, 139, 153, 159, 162, 167, 190, 201, 203, 232, 240, 245, 246, 250
empathy/empathic   51, 55, 78, 94, 116, 117, 153, 189, 190, 201
emulation of behaviour   17, 54, 55, 63, 102, 103, 105, 109, 162, 166, 167, 177, 192, 207, 208, 211, 223, 231, 251
eschatology/eschatological   40, 171, 173, 175–8, 205, 247
evangelical/evangelicals   32, 38–43, 78, 121, 187
evolution   15, 45, 57, 71, 72, 99–101, 103, 140, 187, 210, 227, 229
excellence (moral)   100–11, 113–15, 145, 167
Exodus   168, 192–3, 243–4, 249
exploitation   1, 16–18, 21, 31, 47, 48, 89, 137, 139, 143, 144, 149, 165, 179, 183, 190–3, 243, 244
extinction   45–7, 83, 139, 166, 203, 241

fall, the   187
feminist theology   50, 55, 125
flat ontology   149
flood/flooding   6, 36, 48, 223
flourishing   14, 15, 20, 33, 35, 55, 65, 68, 70, 73, 86, 95, 98, 110, 111, 117–19, 129, 135, 137–9, 142, 145, 159, 160, 179, 195, 212, 218, 219, 223, 232, 235, 236, 242, 244, 247
fracking   47–8

gift/gifts   14, 15, 29–31, 33, 95, 135, 136, 164, 184, 185, 194–5, 197, 212–19, 221, 237, 238, 241, 242, 248
grace   50, 172, 184, 212, 215, 230–2, 237–42
greed   32, 53, 183, 186
grief, ecological   47, 248

healing   159, 169, 175–8, 238, 239, 241
health   32, 34, 45, 48, 93, 94, 136, 175–7, 179, 190, 200, 238, 239, 241
hell   74, 101, 195–8
heresy   32, 33, 35–7

heuristics of fear (in H. Jonas)   152
hope   3, 28, 34, 35, 50, 62, 70, 72, 101, 118–20, 125, 133, 135, 138, 140, 146, 150, 156, 158, 160–2, 164–6, 169, 172–7, 180, 184, 185, 193, 197, 224, 231, 235–9, 242, 249, 251, 252

idolatry/idol   25, 27, 29–31, 35, 47, 55, 134, 135, 137, 188, 192, 246
image of God   49, 138, 144, 169
imagery (religious)   27, 38, 40, 49, 52, 99, 160, 174–7, 196, 198, 209–11, 244–7, 251
imago Dei, *see* image of God
imitation, *see* emulation of behaviour

judgment, the last   179, 193–5, 208

metaphor/metaphors   47, 73–7, 80, 82, 98, 109, 111, 158–64, 168, 188, 190, 199, 203, 208–11, 218, 226, 250
moral agent/agency, *see* agency, human
mother/mothering   78, 79, 86, 94, 108, 109, 133, 159–63, 166–8, 190, 199, 201, 203, 208–12, 218, 221, 227, 233–4, 250–2
motivation   6, 81, 85, 89, 91, 98–9, 101, 103, 107, 125, 145, 166, 167, 171, 208, 216, 224, 228, 230, 231, 241, 244, 250–1

narcissism   188–90, 192, 239
natality   154–8, 161, 162, 168, 185
naturalist/naturalism   84, 85
normotic personality   82

paradise   198, 243–9
Paris Agreement   1, 100
passivity   55, 70, 95, 136, 137, 147, 160, 161, 174, 216, 218, 236, 237, 241
patriarchal/patriarchy   49, 50, 80, 81, 133, 251
pragmatic/pragmatism   3, 30, 57, 62–3, 67, 68, 76, 77, 106, 122–5, 127–9, 131, 138, 163, 183, 195, 196, 209, 218, 236, 244
pregnant/pregnancy   74, 75, 77, 86, 111, 116, 124, 125, 151, 159–65, 167, 199, 232, 234, 250, 251

prestige psychology   101–2, 104
prophetic practice   36, 51, 131, 178
prosperity gospel   33–7
prudence, *see* wisdom
punishment, divine   99, 101–4, 106, 217

repentance   182, 185, 191
responsibility   11, 12, 15, 32, 43, 51, 54, 56, 87, 93, 96, 109, 119, 124, 138, 140–51, 153, 154, 156, 158, 161, 163, 165, 168, 176, 180, 182, 183, 185–7, 192, 197, 199, 203, 208, 210, 212, 214, 231, 237–40, 242, 247–8, 250–1

sacrifice   28, 30, 32, 152, 161, 191, 208, 222–35
selfishness/selfish   183, 229–30
self-preservation   19, 89
semiotic   59, 61, 63, 179
senses/sensibility   34, 36, 68–70, 80, 84, 89–92, 96, 97, 203, 204, 210, 226, 247
sensual experience   23, 25, 81, 92, 200, 203, 246, 250
sin   120, 136, 137, 179–92, 206, 209–10, 217, 218, 224, 237, 239–41
sloth   186
social mindscapes   84, 110, 113
stewardship/steward   15, 71, 126, 137, 141–5, 149, 183, 195, 212, 214, 250

stick (type of moral motivation)   98–9
suicide   196, 252
susceptibility   93, 95, 142, 161, 226
symbolic practices   51, 61–2, 64, 67–71, 74, 82, 84, 97, 118, 162
symbols, dead   122
symbols, negative   63, 99, 101, 192
symbols, positive   99, 118, 163

temperance   114, 117, 119
trust   30, 108, 119, 134–7, 169, 180, 188, 192, 193, 242

vice(s)   164–6, 183, 184, 186
violence/violent   20, 47, 117, 187, 192, 209, 221, 228, 229, 232, 236, 247, 252
virtue(s)/virtuous   17, 19, 36, 57, 67, 95, 98, 102, 107–20, 124, 138, 150, 151, 156, 163–7, 183, 184, 194, 196, 242, 246, 250–1
vulnerable/vulnerability   20, 33, 45, 48, 69, 92–4, 117, 147, 150, 152, 154, 161, 175, 176, 189–90, 200–1, 208, 209, 211, 213, 223, 226, 238, 240, 250

wisdom   12, 14, 53, 91, 97, 114, 117–19, 131, 164, 165, 177, 201, 207, 246, 247
womb, God as   161

www.ingramcontent.com/pod-product-compliance
Lightning Source LLC
Chambersburg PA
CBHW052220300426
44115CB00011B/1762